The Geography of American Poverty

D1028411

The Geography of American Poverty

Is There a Need for Place-Based Policies?

Mark D. Partridge
Dan S. Rickman

2006

W.E. Upjohn Institute for Employment Research
Kalamazoo, Michigan

Library of Congress Cataloging-in-Publication Data

Partridge, Mark D.
   The geography of American poverty : is there a need for place-based policies? /
Mark D. Partridge, Dan S. Rickman.
      p. cm.
   Includes bibliographical references and index.
   ISBN-13: 978-0-88099-286-2 (pbk. : alk. paper)
   ISBN-10: 0-88099-286-7 (pbk. : alk. paper)
   ISBN-13: 978-0-88099-287-9 (hardcover : alk. paper)
   ISBN-10: 0-88099-287-5 (hardcover : alk. paper)
1. Poverty—United States. 2. Poverty—United States—Prevention. 3. Urban poor—
United States. 4. Rural poor—United States. 5. United States—Social conditions. I.
Rickman, Dan S. II. Title.
   HC110.P6P37 2006
   339.4'60973—dc22

2006017557

Cover design by Alcorn Publication Design.
Index prepared by Diane Worden.
Printed in the United States of America.
Printed on recycled paper.

Contents

Figures

Tables

Boxes

Acknowledgments

We wish to thank many people for this project, including Josefin Kihlberg, Rose Olfert, Jamie Partridge, Steven Miller, and Stephen Schultz. We appreciate the help of two anonymous reviewers, and we are grateful to Tim Bartik and Kevin Hollenbeck of the W.E. Upjohn Institute for Employment Research for their help as well. We also greatly appreciate the help of Benjamin Jones for his tireless editing assistance, and of Erika Jackson for her painstaking typesetting of the tables. In addition, we thank session participants at the 2003 and 2004 Southern Regional Science Association Meetings and the 2003 North American Regional Science Association Meetings. Finally, we acknowledge the financial support provided by the Upjohn Institute.

1

Spatial Concentration of American Poverty

Should We Care, and What Are the Options?

An expanding economy no longer seems a panacea, allowing us to reduce poverty while we all become richer.
 —Rebecca Blank, a member of the Clinton administration's Council of Economic Advisers, speaking about how poverty rose in the 1980s

The best antipoverty program is still a job.
 —President Bill Clinton at a 1996 news conference on welfare legislation

The intergenerational poverty that troubles us so much today is predominantly a poverty of values.
 —Vice President Dan Quayle in his famous 1992 "Murphy Brown" speech, arguing that a lack of personal values is the primary cause of poverty

Concern about the well-being of the least fortunate Americans has ebbed and flowed over the last century. The New Deal initiatives of the 1930s stimulated interest in helping those hit hardest by the Great Depression. During the war years and the prosperous 1950s, the presence of the poor faded from the consciousness of many Americans, but concern for their plight again intensified during Lyndon Johnson's War on Poverty in the 1960s. Since then, interest in reducing poverty has continued to experience ups and downs: poverty rates are no lower today than when the War on Poverty ended in the late 1960s; on the contrary, high poverty exists in many regions of the country. To be sure, the aftermath of Hurricane Katrina once again reminded Americans that concentrations of high poverty remain within our borders.

Much of the current popular discourse is driven by the view that public efforts to reduce poverty are not worthwhile, let alone effective (Moore 1997). One result of this skepticism was the landmark 1996 reform of federal welfare policy, which greatly increased the personal responsibility of the disadvantaged for their own well-being. In fact,

1

reducing overall poverty was not even an explicit goal of the 1996 welfare reform legislation (Ellwood and Blank 2001). Policies designed to eliminate regional pockets of poverty have been criticized on the grounds that it would be more effective to direct policies at individuals and not at places (Peters and Fisher 2002).

Even as interest in antipoverty efforts waned and skepticism grew, the U.S. poverty rate fell to 11.3 percent in 2000 (the lowest it had been since 1974), including a record low average rate of 13.4 percent in nonmetropolitan areas (ERS 2004). This could be interpreted as being the result of a favorable link between growth and poverty-rate reduction that had seemingly been nonexistent from the 1970s through the early 1990s but that had reestablished itself since then (Blank and Card 1993; Freeman 2001). The Council of Economic Advisers (1999) and O'Neill and Hill (2001) argue that welfare reform was the impetus behind the reduced number of welfare caseloads, which may then have contributed to lower poverty. Yet others note the potential interaction between a strong economy and the success of welfare reform (e.g., Moffitt 1999).

Despite the nationwide antipoverty gains of the 1990s, poverty rates remained high in many metropolitan central cities and inner suburbs (Jargowsky 2003) and in remote nonmetropolitan areas (Miller and Weber 2004). This raises the question of whether these areas experienced subpar economic performance compared to the nation or whether there was less of a connection between local economic growth and poverty in these areas. The answer to this question would relate to whether there is a need for place-based policies and would help inform their design.

In the remainder of this chapter, we first provide a rationale for society to become more engaged in reducing poverty, including at the regional level. We then briefly review the evidence on the connection between employment growth, welfare reform, and poverty at the national level. The implications of the national trends for regional poverty follow; we particularly consider the relative merits of place-based and person-based policies for evening out spatial concentrations of poverty. This includes a discussion of the role space plays in poverty outcomes, because national growth policies alone may do little to ameliorate persistent regional pockets of poverty. We introduce the possibility that local economic growth, using place-based employment supports, may be a needed tool for reducing poverty. The chapter concludes with an overview of the remainder of the book, whose primary emphasis is the spatial dimension of the relationship between economic performance and poverty, including an examination of competing explanations such as federal and state welfare reform.

WHY SOCIETY SHOULD CARE ABOUT POVERTY

There are both philosophical and practical reasons why the American public should be concerned with the well-being of its poorest members. For one, according to the Rawlsian view, if individuals in a group selected a distribution of income for the members of the group before they knew how each of them would fare—i.e., if they had a "veil of ignorance" concerning the outcome—risk-averse individuals would pick the distribution that maximized the well-being of the least-well-off member of the group (Rawls 1971). In our wealthy society, application of Rawlsian logic would eliminate poverty. Nevertheless, while the notion that individuals are risk-averse and interested in justice *before* the fact is thought-provoking, public policy does not work in the realm of the "veil of ignorance." Rather, it is affected by politicians reliant on voters who are fully aware of their actual or most probable place in the income distribution.

Beyond the abstractions of philosophical arguments, Americans are well grounded in notions of justice, equity, and a sense of fair play. Madden (2000) presents evidence showing that a strong majority of the U.S. public prefers a more equal distribution of income. However, the catch is that the public tends to be very skeptical of whether government intervention is the proper vehicle to satisfy its desire for equity. Indeed, the issue reflects a fundamental tenet of neoclassical economics, which is that there is an equity-efficiency tradeoff (Okun 1975): societies can achieve more equity and less poverty through redistribution of income, but by blunting economic incentives, attaining this goal comes at the expense of economic efficiency and growth. Yet other economists argue against the existence of an inverse relationship between equity and efficiency, instead contending that greater inequality reduces growth by producing societal upheaval, inefficient government redistribution, and suboptimal investment in human and physical capital.[1]

Besides notions of equity and fairness, there are practical reasons for society to be concerned about the well-being of its lowest-income members. For example, lower poverty may encourage disadvantaged segments of the population to become more civilly engaged in their communities because they feel they are legitimate stakeholders. Higher poverty, on the other hand, adversely affects the physical health of the workforce, which, besides reducing poor people's quality of life, reduces their workplace productivity and ultimately increases public health care expenditures and their reliance on other government programs (Scott 2005). If poverty is reduced through improved labor market participation, then benefactors will enjoy long-term gains through enhanced labor market experience, increased skills upgrading, and, in turn, higher future earnings (Bartik 2001).

Perhaps the largest societal gains from poverty reduction occur through intergenerational linkages. The environment created by families facing severe financial stress is not optimal for raising children, particularly for developing their cognitive and noncognitive skills. There are significant ramifications in adulthood when children from difficult circumstances fall behind early. There is growing consensus in the literature that the income of a child's family has long-term impacts on that child's health, education, nutrition, and future income and welfare as an adult (Carneiro and Heckman 2003; Case, Fertig, and Paxson 2003; Karoly et al. 1998). These intergenerational effects suggest the potential benefits from poverty reduction can be large simply in terms of future earnings and health care savings from the children of disadvantaged families. In contrast, Carneiro and Heckman (2003) note that later interventions, such as tuition policies for underprivileged college students, likely have smaller marginal effects on improving future earnings.

Another indirect benefit of poverty reduction relates to the link between labor market conditions and crime (Freeman 2001; Freeman and Rodgers 1999; Raphael and Winter-Ember 2001). These studies suggest that 33–40 percent of the large decrease in crime during the 1990s can be attributed to the strong economy of those years.[2] This effect implies large antipoverty benefits in terms of savings from reduced victimization, lower expenditures on protective measures, and lower incarceration costs associated with reduced recidivism.

In summary, reducing poverty can provide substantial benefits in many ways: improved social engagement, higher economic potential, greater long-term earnings for positively affected individuals, lower crime, and significant long-term gains for affected children in terms of health, education, and income in adulthood. Associated gains include eventual reductions in government expenditures for public assistance, health care, and the criminal justice system. Along with even modest concerns for equity and fairness, these advantages provide continued justification for aggressively fighting poverty. And the potential gains are likely greatest where poverty is geographically most concentrated.

NATIONAL POVERTY AND ECONOMIC GROWTH

Numerous measures of poverty exist, each with relative advantages and disadvantages. We use the official federal poverty rate (see Box 1.1), which is not perfect but is well known and has been consistently measured over time. Also to its advantage, the official federal rate is used both in assessing and in setting government policy. As an example of the federal definition of poverty, a household with one adult (under 65 years of age) and two children had to have earned more than $14,824 to be above the poverty line in 2003, while a household containing two adults (under 65) and two children had to have earned more than $18,660.

As shown in Figures 1.1 and 1.2, there were remarkable reductions in poverty during the 1960s and early 1970s. This was true regardless of whether one considered person or family poverty rates (Figure 1.1), or even female-headed-family poverty rates (Figure 1.2). With that progress, an observer in the early 1970s had reason to be optimistic that the War on Poverty would ultimately be won. Nevertheless, subsequent trends show that poverty has remained a persistent element of American society.

Even though the 1980s and 1990s had two of the three longest economic expansions on record, the person and family poverty rates in 2002 were little changed from what they were when the War on Poverty ended more than 30 years ago (Figure 1.1). In fact, U.S. Census Bureau (2004a) data suggest that while real median-family income rose by 7 percent between 1973 and 1993, the person poverty rate increased from 11.1 percent to 15.1 percent (the second highest rate since 1965). Figure

Box 1.1 Official Federal Poverty Thresholds

Social Security Administration economist Mollie Orshansky originally developed the official federal poverty criteria in 1963–1964 (U.S. Census Bureau 2004h; Fisher 1997). Orshansky calculated the economy food budgetary requirements of 58 family types based on age and family size (currently 48 family types are used). For each family type, she simply multiplied this figure by three to obtain what is now called the poverty threshold. For the most part, Orshansky's definition has remained unchanged except that it is adjusted upward for inflation every year.

In determining poverty status, before-tax income is used, including public assistance but not capital gains. The official poverty rate is not adjusted for several factors such as the Earned Income Tax Credit or in-kind public welfare programs like Medicaid. Nor is it adjusted for regional cost-of-living differences. To give a feel for the resulting thresholds, we present the following examples: a three-person household with one adult (under 65 years of age) and two children needed to earn more than $15,219 to be above the poverty line in 2004, while a two-adult (under 65) and two-child household needed to earn more than $19,157. Comparable three- and four-person households needed to earn $13,423 and $16,895 in 1999 and $9,990 and $12,575 in 1989—the increase reflects inflation (U.S. Census Bureau 2005e).

The official definition can be criticized for not adjusting for taxes and in-kind contributions. It also does not account for the notion that poverty is often viewed as a relative concept: what is considered economic deprivation changes over time with rising living standards.[a] For example, an upper-middle-class standard of living a century ago would now be one devoid of modern conveniences. Nonetheless, developing alternative measures of poverty rates is full of pitfalls in that they can be ad hoc and they may not capture true conceptions of poverty. For more details on alternative poverty measures, see U.S. Census Bureau (2003).

Despite these concerns, the official poverty rate measure is used because it is well known, has been consistent over time, and

Box 1.1 (continued)

is used in both assessing and setting government policy. Even more important is that it is widely reported for various demographic groups and geographical areas. To be sure, the Census Bureau has recently reported a variety of alternative poverty rate thresholds. Yet these are not as widely reported across geographical areas, and their data usually only cover a short time span, dating back to the latter 1990s. Moreover, at least in terms of the change in poverty rates, the alternative poverty rate measures tend to follow the official one quite closely (see, for example, U.S. Census Bureau 2003). That is, while the actual poverty rate percentage may depend on the particular alternative used, the more critical measure, change in poverty rate, is approximately the same over time.

[a] See Slesnick (1993) for a detailed discussion of problems with official poverty thresholds.

1.2 shows that the poverty rate increased for female-headed families during this 20-year period from 32.2 to 35.6 percent, or slightly less than the increases in overall rates in Figure 1.1. This reversal in trend led many experts to question whether economic growth was continuing to trickle down to the poor (Blank and Card 1993; Cutler and Katz 1991).

With the link between growth and poverty seemingly broken and poverty rates stagnant or rising, questions arose as to whether governmental efforts to eliminate poverty had instead made matters worse. Indeed, Stephen Moore (1997) contended that the "War on Poverty, launched by Lyndon Johnson thirty years ago, has probably been the most destructive government concept ever invented." However, the argument that growth was no longer "lifting all boats" also did not go unchallenged. For instance, Bartik (2001) argues that it is counterintuitive to expect economic growth not to reduce the poverty rate unless there is an accompanying increase in income inequality.

Even as the debate raged about the role of economic growth in reducing poverty, the poverty rate began a precipitous decline near the

Figure 1.1 U.S. Family and Person Poverty Rates, 1959–2003 (%)

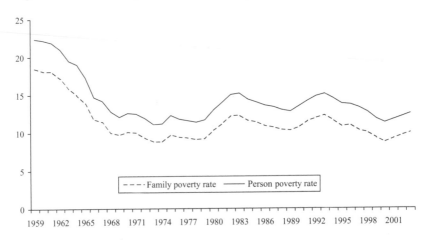

SOURCE: U.S. Census Bureau (2004a).

end of the 1990s economic expansion, as shown in Figure 1.1. It fell from 15.1 percent in 1993 to 11.3 percent in 2000 (the lowest mark since 1974). Subsequently, however, sluggish economic conditions and rising unemployment yielded a modest increase in poverty from 2001 to 2003. One possible explanation for the seemingly closer link with economic conditions is that growth has its strongest influence on lifting households out of poverty when the unemployment rate falls to levels so low that businesses are forced to hire the chronically unemployed and less skilled (Freeman 2001). This reasoning may explain the successes of the 1960s and latter 1990s, as the unemployment rate fell below 4 percent in both cases. The disappointing persistence of the poverty level during the expansions of the latter 1970s and 1980s may have resulted from relatively loose labor markets. Although firms may have been hiring workers during those times, there was a sufficient queue of applicants that employers never had to reach down to hire the more disadvantaged. Such a nonlinear response suggests that the influence of policies on poverty will vary depending on labor market conditions.

Figure 1.3 shows the changes in the U.S. individual and family poverty rates from 1960 to 2003, along with the annual changes in the unemployment rate. While the correlation is not perfect, there appears to be a clear, positive relationship between the change in the unemploy-

Figure 1.2 Female-Headed Family Poverty Rate, 1959–2003 (%)

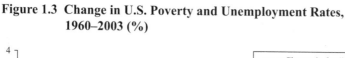

SOURCE: U.S. Census Bureau (2004b).

Figure 1.3 Change in U.S. Poverty and Unemployment Rates, 1960–2003 (%)

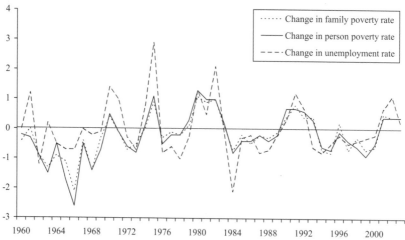

SOURCE: Person rate, U.S. Census Bureau (2004a); family rate, U.S. Census Bureau (2004b); unemployment rate, BLS (2006c).

ment rate and changes in poverty rates. The simple correlation between the change in unemployment and the change in family poverty is 0.66, while the corresponding correlation between the change in unemployment and the change in person poverty is 0.65.

Welfare Reform and Policy Changes in the 1990s

The 1990s was a period of significant public policy change, as it related to the working and nonworking poor. The first change was the expansion of the Earned Income Tax Credit (EITC), which greatly increased work incentives. Then came the Clinton administration's accelerated issuance of state waivers from the Aid to Families with Dependent Children (AFDC) program, beginning in 1993 (Council of Economic Advisers 1999; Ellwood and Blank 2001). Most waivers made welfare more restrictive, such as by adding sanctions for non-compliance with work requirements and by adding time limits for receiving benefits.

A third initiative was the 1996 Personal Responsibility and Work Opportunity Reconciliation Act (PRWORA), which replaced AFDC with the Temporary Assistance for Needy Families (TANF) program. Known as "welfare reform," the 1996 act eliminated the welfare entitlement and placed a strict 60-month federal lifetime limit on most recipients; it also put stringent requirements on states to shift most recipients into work by 2002 (Blank 2002; Ellwood and Blank 2001). New legal immigrants faced restrictions in using TANF, and there were other changes to help reduce births to unwed mothers. Financing was changed to a federal block grant, and states were given great latitude to set program parameters, including those for benefits and eligibility.

Between August 1996, when welfare reform was signed, and September 2001, the number of recipients declined by a remarkable 56 percent (Administration for Children and Families [ACF] 2002a). Even with the sluggish economy, the number of welfare recipients fell slightly in Fiscal Years 2002 and 2003 (ACF 2002b, 2004). Congress has periodically worked on renewing welfare reform, but progress has been slow. Most indications are that the act will remain largely unchanged; however, some likely changes include increased child care support, greater flexibility for states in counting "work-related" activities, and a modest increase in work requirements (U.S. Department of Health and Human Services [DHHS] 2004).

Many economists argue that welfare reform and the work-promotion effects of the expanded EITC were key factors behind the almost 10-percentage-point increase between 1994 and 2000 in the labor force participation of unmarried females with children (Blank and Schmidt 2001). The Council of Economic Advisers (1999) and O'Neill and Hill (2001) hold that welfare reform was the impetus for reducing the number of welfare recipients. Meyer and Rosenbaum (2001) conclude that 60 percent of the increase in employment of single mothers relative to single women without children over the 1984–1996 period was attributable to the federal and state EITC and other tax changes, whereas welfare reforms over the 12-year period were much less important—although they did have significant effects. Yet others contend that welfare reform's supposed initial success had little to do with policy and is more of an artifact of the robust economy of the late 1990s.[3] A comprehensive literature review by Blank (2002) suggests that welfare reform and the strong economy both reduced welfare usage.

Though welfare reform is important, we are ultimately interested in whether it affects poverty. The poverty rate for unmarried women with children—a key welfare-recipient cohort—fell from 41.9 percent in 1996 to 33.0 percent in 2000, before rising to 33.7 percent in 2002 (U.S. Census Bureau 2004b). Yet this could be more economy-driven than welfare-reform driven. Also, even if welfare reform did greatly reduce the rolls, it is still possible that it had little influence on changing the average household income at the lower end of the distribution; it may have merely reallocated income from welfare benefits to labor earnings and the EITC (Blank 2002; Primus 2001).

Welfare reform has also expanded the low-skilled labor supply by encouraging work. The increased labor supply should have a deleterious effect on the wages and employment of low-skilled nonrecipients, which would indirectly increase poverty rates (Bartik 2000, 2002a,b). The possible indirect spillovers suggest that the impact of welfare reform could extend well beyond the most directly affected groups, which means aggregate labor market assessments are necessary to explore how welfare reform affected the overall poverty rate.

PERSON- VS. PLACE-BASED POLICY

Despite declining U.S. poverty in the 1990s, the gains were not spatially uniform, and many high-poverty pockets remain (Jargowsky 2003). It is unclear why all geographic areas did not experience the same favorable developments as the nation as a whole. It could be that some areas experienced lower growth. Alternatively, spatial factors unique to certain areas may have affected the connection between growth and poverty. If so, person-based antipoverty policies alone may be inadequate; instead, what may be required are policies tailored to place.

There is wide debate within the academic and policy communities on whether policies aimed at helping the poor should include place-specific elements to complement person-specific programs (Kraybill and Kilkenny 2003). However, critics contend that policies designed to help distressed communities or regions with concentrations of poverty are misguided and wasteful, and that the best way to aid the disadvantaged is to tailor policies to directly help needy individuals (e.g., Peters and Fisher 2002). Policies such as providing education, training, job and family counseling, relocation assistance, and certain types of health care assistance form the core of person-based approaches.

Critics of place-based subsidies contend that they can induce the disadvantaged not to migrate to localities with better employment opportunities, which creates a culture of dependency in the region (Glaeser 1998; Glaeser, Kolko, and Saiz 2001; Kraybill and Kilkenny 2003). They contend that virtually all of the newly created jobs will instead go to commuters and new residents who already have the necessary skills and experience that employers prefer, and not to the intended disadvantaged beneficiaries (Peters and Fisher 2002). Therefore, policies aimed at improving a distressed local economy (e.g., tax breaks) may primarily help business and property owners instead of the disadvantaged.

Critics of place-based policy also point out that economic development efforts may fail in high-poverty areas. For example, the small-scale economies of remote rural areas may hinder their economic development: not only may there be insufficient public infrastructure for such areas to be economically competitive (Lucas 2001; Jalan and Ravallion 2002; Glasmeier and Farrigan 2003), but there may be a backwash effect of jobs and capital being drawn toward urban centers and

away from these areas (Barkley, Henry, and Bao 1996; Henry, Barkley, and Bao 1997). Further, the exodus of highly mobile, highly skilled labor from high-poverty regions may lower the pay of those remaining (Gibbs 1994).

On the other hand, there are traditional and emerging arguments for place-based policies to be part of the optimal policy mix, based on the "new economic geography." As discussed in Chapter 3 of this book, equilibrating market responses are impeded if labor is not perfectly mobile, particularly the low-skilled segment of labor, which is the most likely to be in poverty (Ravallion and Wodon 1999; Yankow 2003). Such arguments form the core of the urban spatial-mismatch models (Holzer 1991). Rural areas' remoteness and greater distance to potential migration destinations increases the transport and psychic costs for those who may wish to relocate (Greenwood 1997). Therefore, while remoteness, small scale, or social and geographic isolation may be hindrances to successful economic development, they also may lead to disadvantaged residents garnering more of the benefits if economic development is successful, suggesting the potential efficacy of place-based antipoverty policies. That is, if job creation occurred in these distressed areas, more of the benefits would go to the disadvantaged because the area's remoteness would cut down on employment competition from new commuters or migrants.

Other arguments for place-based policies include the notion that geographical space produces monopolistic power, in which entry and exit costs reduce free-market adjustments (Kraybill and Kilkenny 2003). New-economic-geography arguments include agglomeration economies where productivity increases with greater urban scale or arises from the co-location of similar firms in the same industry. Agglomeration economies can arise because of factors such as more specialized input markets, specialized labor supply, and knowledge spillovers across firms. Rural areas also can experience agglomerations when industry "clusters" co-locate to take advantage of enhanced vertical integration of inputs. Place-based policy advocates also argue that economic development policies can effectively enhance local growth and reduce poverty because of factors such as neighborhood effects, economic role models, and knowledge spillovers.

In addition, advocates of place-based policies note that person-based policies are expensive and that programs such as job training may have relatively low returns, depending upon the location of the disadvantaged (Bartik 2001; Carneiro and Heckman 2003). Thus, sole reliance on people-based policies may be inadequate in addressing the spatial concentration of poverty (Blank 2005). Blank argues that place and related contextual effects influence economic vitality and shape the character of the people.

The wide spatial variation in local attributes can thwart "one size fits all" person-based policies. In isolated inner cities and remote rural areas, many of the disadvantaged have less access to job training, counseling, health care, child care, and transportation, suggesting that government service delivery should reflect these spatial differences (Allard, Tolman, and Rosen 2003). Work-support policies such as the provision of child care, transportation, education, and training also may have higher pay-offs if jobs are nearby. Policies that improve a distressed community's vitality and job accessibility may do more for its disadvantaged residents than approaches that give them lengthy training and hope they eventually find work nearby where there are very few jobs, or, failing that, hope they move elsewhere (Kraybill and Kilkenny 2003).

Practically speaking, to ignore the spatial dimension of poverty is also to overlook the basic fact that most politicians and policymakers represent specific jurisdictions. They may have less interest in the necessary person-based human capital development without the added attraction of well-planned (or even poorly planned) policies aimed at particular locations. Place-based policies also have the simple advantage that governments may find it easier to target appropriate poor places than to identify the appropriate poor households with specific attributes (Ravallion and Wodon 1999). Likewise, because of the unpopularity of person-based programs such as welfare assistance with voters, it may be easier to obtain public support for policies aimed at distressed regions than for policies directed at low-income individuals.

OVERVIEW OF THIS BOOK

The following chapters explore the spatial dimension of U.S. poverty, stressing differences across states, metropolitan areas, and counties, with an eye toward state and local policy prescriptions. We find poverty to be very unevenly distributed across the country, varying widely even within states and metropolitan areas. The great diversity in poverty outcomes leads us to explore finer geographical areas: within metropolitan areas, we look at central-city counties and suburbs; beyond metropolitan areas, we look at metro-adjacent and outlying, nonmetropolitan counties. The spatial detail of our study allows us to draw more focused policy conclusions. We conclude that the policy prescriptions should vary greatly across space.[4]

In assessing poverty, we explore the underlying spatial, demographic, and economic contributors to poverty rates. Although we do not need elaborate statistical analysis to know that single-mother-headed households tend to have high poverty rates and that areas with high unemployment also have elevated poverty, we still need to know the relative importance of each factor. If personal characteristics such as race and the prevalence of married-couple households are the overriding factor, policy should be focused more on supports to encourage stronger families and to mitigate racial discrimination. Alternatively, if the uneven geographical location of employment opportunities and an unfavorable industry composition are the important causal factors, then place-based policies aimed at improving employment opportunities in distressed areas would be more effective. Without a detailed statistical assessment, we will not be able to ascertain the proper policy mix and make informed policy prescriptions for different geographic areas. For example, policies that are effective in prosperous suburbs will likely differ from those that prove effective in more remote, rural areas.

Our assessment of the geographical diversity of American poverty begins in Chapter 2, where we examine the spatial variation of state and county poverty rates and their trends over time. Fully understanding the spatial distribution of poverty requires examining multiple geographical aggregations of poverty rates. Analysis of national poverty rates is necessary if one wants to determine the overall effectiveness of national full employment. Yet to understand the relative importance of economic growth versus welfare policies, states should be examined, because they form the political entity that greatly sets and defines differential welfare policies. Understanding the underlying causes and policy solutions that differ within metropolitan areas, or between urban centers and rural communities, requires analysis of disaggregated regions such as counties.

Chapter 2 notes that state poverty rates vary greatly. The South tends to have the highest poverty rates. When examining the state patterns over the period of 1969–1999, we find that there is some persistence. Yet Southern states generally experienced marked reductions in poverty, while others, such as many Western states, had relatively lackluster performances.

When examining counties, we find even more diversity. First, there are homogeneous low-poverty-rate clusters, such as in the upper Midwest, and high-poverty-rate clusters, such as in Appalachia or the Mississippi Delta. Yet poverty can vary greatly within a given state. For example, even in Southeastern states with high average poverty, there are low-poverty pockets within each state. Poverty can also take on a more haphazard pattern, such as the wide range found within larger metropolitan areas. Nevertheless, local poverty rates remain strikingly persistent. For example, areas that had higher poverty rates in the 1950s tend to have higher poverty rates today.

Chapter 3 discusses the elements of local low-wage labor markets that provide the theoretical justification for antipoverty policies. Local labor markets respond differently to policies than does the national labor market. Improving the employment opportunities of the disadvantaged would seem to be a reasonable solution to persistently high poverty rates in certain locales. Yet a major complication is that newly created jobs often go to new migrants or commuters from elsewhere. The intended beneficiaries—the original, poor residents—can end up with few of the new jobs. Hence, the notion that "a rising tide lifts all boats," which seems reasonable in macroeconomic discussions, may not apply at the local level, though this differs by local area.

Chapter 4 provides a statistical assessment of the determinants of state poverty rates. In it, we emphasize roles of economic growth and state public welfare policies. In particular, we try to further determine whether the 1996 welfare reform had a major role in the dramatic poverty rate outcomes in the 1990s. If so, this would give us grounds to be optimistic that Bush administration efforts to further emphasize work-first initiatives will be successful. We find that state economic growth is an important cause of change in state poverty rates, and that this effect is especially large when the labor market is tight. This influence is both direct, through enhanced labor market opportunities, and indirect, through affecting other outcomes such as teen birthrates. In contrast, we find that policies related to welfare reform have virtually no statistically significant effect on state poverty rates. Any favorable effects on the labor force behavior of potential welfare recipients appear to be offset by adverse spillovers on other disadvantaged workers through increased labor market competition. In Chapter 5, we look at case studies of four states, which confirm the results of the statistical analysis and provide context on the nexus between poverty, labor market performance, and welfare reform.

Chapter 6 examines 1989 and 1999 poverty rates for more than 3,000 U.S. counties. One finding is of the importance of family characteristics such as marital status and education. Female labor market participation and male unemployment rates are key labor market factors. Yet we find that, generally, employment growth has only a modest impact on local poverty rates. Without some sort of targeting of the neediest, this suggests that local policies that increase employment will likely have only modest impacts on poverty; it further implies that a strong state and national economy are important reinforcing forces. Another pattern we see is that areas that had higher shares of foreign immigrants arriving in the latter 1990s also had higher 1999 poverty rates. This was a distinct change from the 1980s, when immigrant shares had no detectable influence.

One weakness of the empirical models in Chapter 6 is that they do not fully capture the geographical diversity of low-wage labor markets. Chapters 7 and 8 address this concern by separately considering metropolitan and nonmetropolitan counties. One conclusion of Chapter 7 is that metropolitan areas are not a monolithic block that should be examined in unison. Rather, they are often composed of a mosaic of distinct central-city and suburban counties. Labor market conditions appear to have an even weaker influence on metropolitan poverty rates than on the nation as a whole. But this overlooks the greater responsiveness of poverty rates in central-city counties to changes in labor market conditions. Conversely, new suburban jobs are so regularly filled by in-commuters that poverty rates are hardly influenced by job growth. Thus, we argue that economic development policies can help disadvantaged central-city residents, as job accessibility appears to be a constraint, but that such policies will likely be ineffective in the suburbs. We describe job-creation strategies for central-city counties and indicate how they can be targeted to ensure that the intended disadvantaged beneficiaries capture more of the benefits.

Chapter 8 explores the dimensions of nonmetropolitan and rural poverty. Examination of rural poverty has been a relatively neglected field. A key determinant of rural poverty is whether a nonmetropolitan county is adjacent to a metropolitan area. Residents of nonmetropolitan counties that border on metropolitan areas have significantly better access to jobs, child care, and government services. Because remote nonmetropolitan counties are more isolated, it is not surprising that local labor market conditions are much more important there. Moreover, if local employment growth is concentrated in industries that are faring well at the national level, there will be even more significant declines in rural poverty rates. Hence, all other things being equal, we argue that economic development policies likely have their largest benefits in rural areas, though these policies may be more expensive to implement in remote areas. In contrast, we contend that the countless billions that have been spent on specific resource-based industries, such as agriculture, have had less-than-spectacular results on overall rural economic growth and should be redirected to higher-valued uses for rural America.

Chapter 9 summarizes our empirical findings and policy prescriptions. Our foremost finding is that, while labor market conditions have modest impacts on poverty in general, they can have important impacts in central-city counties and in remote rural counties. Hence, place-based policies aimed at improving the employment prospects of disadvantaged workers in those places are in order. We describe how providing tax credits for newly created jobs and wage subsidies for low-wage workers are two ways of targeting the intended beneficiaries. We also stress the importance of first-source or community-based organizations in brokering and facilitating job creation. Other policies, such as offering relocation assistance to disadvantaged families, are most likely to work in central cities, but even there, the impact will likely be modest. On the other hand, we argue that child care assistance is more likely to be needed in remote rural areas. As with the role of economic development policies, we conclude that a one-size-fits-all geographical approach to person-based policy is misguided. Each area may instead require a unique combination of place-based and person-based antipoverty policies.

Notes

The first epigraph at the beginning of the chapter comes from Gene Koretz (1992), "Trickle-Down Economics May Not Help the Poor," in *Business Week*. The second epigraph comes from the *New York Times* (1996) article "The Welfare Bill." The third comes from a speech made to the Commonwealth Club of California by Quayle (1992).

1. Whether inequality reduces economic growth is a hotly debated topic among economists. For example, Alesina and Rodrik (1994) and Persson and Tabellini (1994) find evidence that it reduces growth, while Forbes (2000) and Partridge (1997, 2005) find the opposite.
2. The 1990s saw the property crime rate drop by nearly 50 percent and the violent crime rate drop by nearly 40 percent (U.S. Department of Justice 2005).
3. For examples of discussion of the link between economic growth and welfare roles, see Bartik and Eberts (1999); Figlio and Ziliak (1999); Hoynes (2000b); and Bennett, Lu, and Song (2002).
4. This book does not empirically examine subcounty poverty rates such as those found in poverty clusters that can exist at the neighborhood level (Weinberg, Reagan, and Yankow 2004). For example, rather than asking why a west-side Chicago neighborhood has higher poverty than a wealthy Highland Park neighborhood in the northern suburbs, we instead ask geographically broader questions, such as "Why do Chicago suburbs have lower poverty rates than the metropolitan area's central-city county?" This focus allows us to more directly consider economic development, which is inherently more widespread than a neighborhood.

2
Recent Spatial Poverty Trends in America

The national poverty trends depicted in Chapter 1 obscure remarkable geographical diversity in the poverty rate outcomes across the United States. This diversity extends beyond the familiar broad regional patterns of high poverty rates in the South and comparatively low rates in the upper Midwest. For one thing, poverty varies greatly within broad regions. Even within narrower areas such as states or metropolitan areas, clusters of high and low poverty often exist in relatively close proximity. Second, at the state or, more broadly, the regional level, there can be large relative changes in poverty rates over time, but at the disaggregated county level, relative poverty is often quite persistent.

Census 2000 data reveal broad regional diversity in poverty rates. In 1999, the South had the highest poverty rate of any region, at 13.9 percent, well above the national average of 12.4 percent.[1] The Midwest had the lowest regional poverty rate, at 10.2 percent, followed by the Northeast at 11.4 percent and the West at 13.0 percent. Yet, within these regions, there is tremendous variation in poverty rates across states and substate areas. Southern poverty rates ranged from 8.5 percent in Maryland to 19.9 percent in Mississippi (the District of Columbia had a 20.2 percent rate). As an example of within-state variation, Virginia's poverty rates ranged from a low of 2.8 percent in Loudoun County to a high of 31.4 percent in Radford. Thus, Virginia's low overall rate of poverty, 9.6 percent, does not mean poverty is not a concern for the state. A similar story can be told for almost every state.

There have been wide disparities in regional poverty trends over time, as well. For example, the South made remarkable gains in reducing poverty over the latter part of the twentieth century, while the West and the Northeast had more lackluster performances. Indeed, during the period from 1969 to 1999, in which the U.S. poverty rate fell by 1.3 percentage points, the poverty rates for Arkansas and Mississippi fell by 12.0 and 15.5 points. By way of contrast, during the same 30-year period, poverty rates rose by 3.2 and 3.5 percentage points in the

District of Columbia and New York. However, as described later in the chapter, while there have been some significant changes at the broad regional level, we see a strong trend of relative persistence when examining counties. Counties that had higher poverty rates in the past tend to have higher poverty rates today, and counties that had lower rates in the past tend to have lower rates today.

The overall national poverty rate also obscures tremendous differences in the rate of poverty across demographic groups. For instance, the 2002 poverty rate for families headed by a married couple stood at 5.3 percent, but it was a remarkable 26.5 percent for families headed by a female. Children also are considerably more likely to live in poverty. The poverty rate for children less than 18 years of age is 16.7 percent, whereas it is only 10.6 percent for adults 18–64 and 10.4 percent for adults 65 years and over. Poverty also varies greatly by racial and ethnic origin. In 2002, poverty rates for White non-Hispanics equaled 8.0 percent. The poverty rate among Asians was 10.1 percent, and among African Americans and American Indians it was 24.1 percent each. Among all Hispanics, it was 21.8 percent.[2]

In addition, as will be seen in this chapter, demographic groups are not equally represented in all geographic areas. The diverse spatial and demographic patterns suggest that poverty eradication efforts need to be tailored to both person and place. This chapter explores in more detail the spatial patterns of poverty, including potentially related spatial differences in the demographic composition of the population, employment growth, and welfare reform.

PATTERNS AND TRENDS IN STATE POVERTY

As shown in Figure 2.1, the historical pattern of high Southern poverty was strongly evident in 1969.[3] Of the 16 states that had poverty rates of 16 percent or greater, all but New Mexico and South Dakota were in the U.S. Census Bureau's South region (Region 3). Nine states had poverty rates below 10 percent, and all but Nevada were in the Census Bureau's Northeast or Midwest regions (Regions 1 and 2). Following the national trend, by 1999 only six states had poverty rates in the high category (16 percent or greater), while 17 states had poverty rates in the low category, below 10 percent (Figure 2.2). Despite these trends, poverty generally remained higher in the South, which contained four of the six high-poverty states, while the low-poverty states were still mostly found in the Northeast or Midwest. In fact, the correlation between the 1969 and 1999 state poverty rates equals 0.80.

The change in poverty rates from 1969 to 1999 is shown in Figure 2.3. All but 16 states experienced reductions in their poverty rates. Except for South Dakota, the largest reductions occurred in the South, where states had had high poverty rates in 1969. Many Northern industrial states experienced the largest increases in poverty. They were joined by states in the West, particularly those on the coast.

As shown in Figure 2.4, even during the robust economic period of the 1990s, 14 states saw their poverty rates rise: 10 Northeastern states (including the District of Columbia, which we count as a state for the purposes of our discussion), Nevada, California, Alaska, and Hawaii. This again illustrates the spatial diversity of poverty outcomes. Within the South, poverty rate declines during the 1990s were less dramatic in the states of the South Atlantic division of the census (Division 5); larger declines occurred in the East South Central and West South Central divisions (Divisions 6 and 7). In contrast to the overall period of 1969–1999, Midwestern states uniformly experienced greater than average reductions in poverty in the 1990s.

To begin to understand spatial poverty trends in the 1990s, we turn to the annual state poverty rates compiled from the Current Population Survey, or CPS (U.S. Census Bureau 2004d). Annual data allows for examination of the relation between economic growth and poverty in the late 1990s. Annual data also then allows for examining the potential link between the timing of the 1996 welfare reform and poverty rates.

One apparent pattern in the decennial census poverty estimates discussed above is the predominance of poverty declines in states with high initial levels of poverty. Using the CPS data for 1984–2000, we fit a regression line through a scatter plot of changes in poverty rates and the average poverty rate over the period (Figure 2.5).[4] The regression line reveals a negative and significant relationship: the states that had higher poverty tended to be those that experienced the greatest reductions.[5]

A comparison of state poverty rate changes to state unemployment rate changes for 1984–2000 (Figure 2.6) confirms the national findings shown in Figure 1.3. As Figure 2.6 shows, states with greater reductions in unemployment rates tended to experience greater poverty rate declines. The positive relationship shown by the regression line fitted through the scatter plot is statistically significant and appears to be consistent throughout the sample.[6] For example, the three states with the largest reduction in poverty rates also experienced dramatic declines in unemployment: Mississippi, Kentucky, and Iowa. Likewise, states with the largest unemployment declines, such as West Virginia and Michigan, experienced large reductions in their poverty rates.

A similar comparison can be made for states that implemented their TANF welfare reforms in 1996 vs. those that implemented them afterwards. Figure 2.7 shows the (unweighted) average poverty rate in states that implemented TANF sometime during 1996 and the average poverty rate of states that first implemented TANF after 1996. Both groups of states experienced significant poverty rate declines in the late 1990s. However, the poverty rate dropped every year beginning with 1993 in states that implemented TANF in 1996, whereas for the remaining states, the average poverty rate leveled off between 1994 and 1996 before again declining.

Although there was a greater total decline for early TANF implementers from 1993 to 2000, most of the relative improvement came during 1994 and 1995, before implementation of TANF. This might be attributable to an announcement effect, in that welfare recipients may have anticipated the policy change and may have begun to transition to work, or it may have been that these states were the ones that had experimented with AFDC waivers. However, the correlation between a state having an AFDC waiver in effect in 1995 and one implementing TANF in 1996 was only 0.1, which calls into question the existence of such effects.[7] The result also may have been due to economic conditions becoming relatively more favorable, around 1994–1995, for states implementing TANF in 1996. The average poverty rate decline for these states is 1.84 percentage points between 1996 and 2000; the corresponding figure for the remaining states is 2.64.[8] This further suggests that welfare reform was not a causal factor in overall reduced poverty rates, but rather that stronger economies in the late TANF-implementing states may have underpinned their greater poverty declines. The narrow window of welfare reform implementation at the state level, combined with other policy changes and with the strengthening of the

U.S. economy, make it difficult to draw definitive conclusions regarding the relative impacts of welfare reform and state economic performance. This issue is explored more extensively in Chapters 4 and 5.

PATTERNS AND TRENDS IN COUNTY POVERTY RATES

As illustrated by the 1979, 1989, and 1999 county poverty rates in Figures 2.8–2.10, considerable variation in poverty rates continued to exist in recent decades within states as well, and this variation showed clear patterns of relative poverty persistence. Solely examining states would mask the considerable variation in substate experiences.[9] The lowest poverty rates are consistently found in the upper Midwest and along the northeast coastline. Poverty is consistently highest in central Appalachia, the lower Mississippi delta, the historic Cotton Belt in the Southeast, counties along the Rio Grande and the Mexican border, and on Native American reservations in the West and Great Plains. Indeed, large regions can be characterized as having high or low poverty clusters that often extend across state boundaries.

However, characterizing the spatial dimension of poverty only in terms of clusters is overly simplistic for many localities, including most large metropolitan areas. The Washington, DC, metropolitan area exhibits one commonly found pattern. Close up, it looks like a doughnut, in that it has high poverty rates in the central city and extremely low poverty rates in almost all surrounding suburban counties. There are also metropolitan areas like St. Louis, which has more of a checkerboard pattern—in its case characterized by high poverty rates in the central city, more moderate rates in its eastern suburban counties in Illinois, and quite low rates in its western suburban counties in Missouri.

Figures 2.11 and 2.12 show the 1989–1999 and 1979–1999 changes in county poverty rates. The maps reveal significant increases in county poverty rates in Western states and in central Appalachia. There are some notable decreases during the 20-year period in the upper Midwestern states and in some Southeastern Atlantic states. However, all regions of the country had some counties with strong performances and others with weak ones. Another overarching feature is one of persistence in relative poverty rates. In fact, the correlation of county poverty

rate levels between 1979 and 1999 equals 0.84. Thus, there are endur-
ing features in most localities that either facilitate or hinder the well-
being of disadvantaged populations.

We explored the spatial dimension of poverty in terms of a place's
metropolitan or nonmetropolitan status. Table 2.1 reports, for both 1989
and 1999, population-weighted poverty rate statistics for the entire sample by five categories: 1) metropolitan vs. nonmetropolitan designation
of the county, 2) age, 3) family type, 4) race/ethnicity, and 5) poverty
severity.[10] Metropolitan counties are further examined in terms of the
size of the metropolitan area (MSA) and whether they are in the central
city or suburbs.[11] Likewise, nonmetropolitan counties are grouped into
those adjacent to an MSA and those nonadjacent. Tables 2.2 and 2.3 report, for 1989 and 1999, population-weighted poverty rate statistics for
these categories of metro and nonmetro counties by age, family type,
race/ethnicity, and poverty severity. Figure 2.13 summarizes the poverty
rate trends for 1989–1999 across the different county types, and Figure
2.14 summarizes the corresponding trends by demographic group.

Table 2.1 and Figure 2.13 reveal that the population-weighted county poverty rate declined from 13.2 percent in 1989 to 12.4 percent in
1999.[12] Although poverty rates were higher in nonmetropolitan counties in both years, over the decade the poverty rate declined by only 0.3
percentage points in metropolitan counties, while in nonmetropolitan
counties it declined by 2.4 points. Yet these statistics mask heterogeneity in poverty trends within metro and nonmetro regions.

From Table 2.2 and Figure 2.13 we see that smaller metropolitan-
area counties (those with a population of less than one million) on average had a poverty rate that declined from 13.7 to 12.8 percent, while
the average poverty rate in larger metropolitan-area counties remained
unchanged at 11.4 percent. The average poverty rate barely changed in
MSA counties containing a central city, inching down from 13.3 to 13.2
percent.[13] Suburban counties fared better; there, poverty declined from
8.5 to 7.8 percent.[14] This shows that the more urbanized areas did not
share equally in the prosperity of the 1990s.

Table 2.3 and Figure 2.13 report population-weighted average overall nonmetro county poverty rates, along with average poverty rates
for nonmetro counties that directly border metro areas and those for
more remote nonmetro counties. Nonmetropolitan counties on average
had higher poverty rates than their metropolitan counterparts, which

somewhat counters the emphasis policymakers and much of the public places on the issue of urban poverty. Among nonmetro counties, those not adjacent to metropolitan areas had higher average poverty rates in both 1989 and 1999. Counties adjacent to metro areas posted a decline in the average poverty rate from 15.9 to 13.7 percent, while nonadjacent counties recorded a decline in the average rate from 18.8 to 16.0 percent. Compared to MSA counties, average poverty rates fell more in nonmetropolitan counties in both relative and absolute terms, especially in more isolated nonmetropolitan counties. The pattern of nonmetropolitan counties faring better is consistent with Jargowsky's (2003) finding that the number of nonmetropolitan residents living in "high poverty" neighborhoods—those with poverty rates exceeding 40 percent—declined by almost one-half during the 1990s, which is a more dramatic decline than that which occurred in MSAs.

DEMOGRAPHIC PATTERNS AND TRENDS IN COUNTY POVERTY

Tables 2.1 to 2.3 also report average county poverty rates for various demographic categories, which are summarized in Figure 2.14. As reported, the average poverty rate of those under the age of 18 declined from 1989 to 1999 across all county categories. For those 18 to 64 years of age, the average all-county poverty rate was unchanged. Yet this group's average poverty rate increased in large MSA and central-city counties while it decreased slightly in suburban counties. The decrease in 18- to 64-year-old poverty rates in nonmetro counties was greater in counties that were not adjacent to metro areas. Because the 18- to 64-year-old group encompasses the prime working years, the rise in poverty rates in large MSAs is somewhat surprising given the robust labor market of the late 1990s and its labor shortages. One explanation for this unexpected pattern is labor market spillovers from welfare reform depressed wages for low-skilled workers (Bartik 2002a,b), which more than offset the benefits derived from the strong labor market at the end of the 1990s. Finally, for those 65 years and older, the average poverty rate declined in all categories, with dramatic declines occurring in nonmetropolitan counties.

Table 2.1 shows that the national-average county poverty rate for all selected family types declined from 1989 to 1999. In terms of percentage points, the greatest reduction occurred among single-female-headed families with children. Besides the importance of a strong economy, this decline underlies the contention of supporters of welfare reform that its work-first emphasis successfully encouraged potential recipients to enter the workforce, which acted to reduce poverty rates (Blank 2002; Haskins 2001; Pear 2003).

The poverty rates by household type in Table 2.2 continue to point to the disappointing performance in large MSAs during the 1990s. Poverty rates for married-couple families and married-couple families with children increased in central-city counties and in counties located in large MSAs. Conversely, poverty rates showed consistent declines across all family types in small MSAs and in suburban counties. Poverty rates across all family types also declined in nonmetropolitan counties regardless of adjacency to MSAs.

Following the overall poverty rate trend, the weighted county average percent of the population living below 50 percent of the poverty line also decreased from 1989 to 1999, from 5.8 to 5.6 percent. It decreased from 6.9 to 6.1 percent in nonmetro counties while remaining unchanged at 5.5 percent in metro counties. The average population share below 50 percent of the poverty threshold increased by 0.1 percentage points in central-city counties and in counties located in large MSAs. These results reinforce the general pattern of larger metropolitan areas not faring as well as nonmetropolitan areas in terms of reducing poverty.

Table 2.1 also indicates that poverty rates declined more rapidly during the 1990s across all racial and ethnic minority groups. However, direct comparisons across the two decades cannot be made because the 2000 census introduced a new racial category of "two or more." Nonetheless, the Hispanic ethnic group is generally comparable across decades, and it, too, suggests a decline between 1989 and 1999. While the results should be cautiously interpreted, it is noteworthy, in Table 2.2, that "white/Caucasian" is the only racial/ethnic group for which average poverty rates increased in large MSAs and central-city counties during the 1990s. This pattern weakly suggests that in large metro areas, minorities were able to buck the overall trend and make some inroads reducing poverty rates. Some of these gains may relate to falling labor market discrimination in the 1990s (Holzer, Raphael, and Stoll 2003). Likewise, spillovers due to welfare reform may have had an adverse impact on less-skilled but employed whites if a disproportionate share of the new job seekers induced to join the labor market were members of minority populations.

COUNTY PATTERNS IN EMPLOYMENT GROWTH

Figure 2.15 addresses the role of economic performance in the differences in poverty trends across metro and nonmetro county types. As shown in Figure 2.15, average job growth equaled 8.6 percent over the 1985–1990 period and 9.2 percent over the 1995–2000 period. MSA counties experienced greater growth in both periods; however, their average growth slowed from 15.4 percent to 13.8 percent. In contrast, average five-year employment growth in nonmetropolitan counties accelerated by 1.5 percentage points in the 1990s, to 7.5 percent. Taken together, these figures show that while MSA counties generally remained more vibrant than nonmetropolitan counties in the 1990s, the five-year employment differential shrank from 9.4 to 6.3 percentage points. Hence, the relative improvement in net nonmetro job creation is likely one reason for MSA counties' better showing in poverty reduction during the 1990s. While it is too strong a statement to assert that the 1990s were a decade of rural renaissance, there was clearly a rebound from the adversity of the 1980s, a decade that included farm crises and other primary-sector shakeouts in energy, mining, and timber.

The largest reduction in MSA employment growth during the 1995–2000 period compared to the 1985–90 period occurred in metropolitan areas of less than one million (13.9 to 11.3 percent) and in central-city counties (13.5 to 11.2 percent), though it also decreased in the suburbs as well. The continuing superior net job creation performance in suburbs is consistent with the growing movement of jobs away from traditional minority residential locations in central cities (Dworak-Fisher 2004; Raphael and Stoll 2002). Somewhat surprisingly, job growth declined more in small metro areas than in large metro areas, which is inconsistent with those two areas' relative performance in poverty rates. Perhaps in small metro areas, access to jobs is a critical ele-

ment that produced better poverty rate declines even though there was
less job growth.

CONCLUSIONS

There is a remarkable spatial dimension to U.S. poverty that is ob-
scured by focusing solely on national poverty rate trends. Poverty rates
vary across broad regions, with the South having the highest poverty
rates and the Midwest having the lowest. Yet within these regions, there
are states with high and low poverty, and there is also significant geographical variation within most states. Likewise, there are wide-rang-
ing differences over time: most Southern states experienced large poverty rate declines between 1969 and 1999, whereas many Western and
Northeastern states experienced modest increases.

At the more detailed county level, the most common pattern is clusters of high and low poverty that often extend across state boundaries.
In metropolitan areas, there are often more irregular patterns between
central-city and suburban counties. Although there are exceptions, another general pattern is that relative county poverty tends to be quite
persistent over time.

Although nonmetropolitan counties consistently had higher poverty
rates than metropolitan counties, nonmetropolitan counties, on average,
experienced larger poverty rate declines in the 1990s. Moreover, it was
the remote nonmetropolitan counties that experienced the greatest declines, not those adjacent to metropolitan areas. For metropolitan counties, the largest poverty rate declines, on average, occurred in small
metropolitan and suburban counties. Poverty rates were unchanged in
large metropolitan-area counties and virtually unchanged for counties
containing the central city of a metropolitan area.

Poverty rate changes among demographic groups generally followed changes in the overall rates for the respective county types.
"White/Caucasian" was the only racial/ethnic group for which the poverty rate increased in large MSA and central-city counties. Poverty rates
for those 18 to 64 years of age and for married families likewise increased in large MSA and central-city counties. A possible explanation

for these results is that welfare reform increased labor market competition for these groups, depressing their wage rates.

Finally, employment growth patterns were not completely consistent with the poverty rate trends in the 1990s. Metro areas continued to grow faster than nonmetro areas, particularly metro areas with more than one million people. Surprisingly, job growth was less rapid in metropolitan areas with a population of less than one million, which contrasts with their better poverty performance. Jobs in suburbs continued to grow much faster than those in the central cities. Although slower than in suburbs, employment growth also accelerated in nonmetro counties, particularly in those not adjacent to metro areas, which may in part explain their greater poverty rate reductions.

Notes

1. The 1970, 1980, 1990, and 2000 decennial censuses report income and poverty data for the year preceding the census, which is why the 10-year census poverty rates are from 1969, 1979, 1989, and 1999 (U.S. Census Bureau 2002a; Bishaw and Iceland 2003). In this chapter, the decennial census state-level data are taken from the U.S. Census Bureau Web site. The county-level poverty data in this chapter are from decennial census data described in Chapter 6.
2. Beginning with the 2002 Current Population Survey, respondents were given the opportunity to identify themselves as belonging to multiple racial categories. While the single-race category poverty rates are almost identical to those for the categories that include multiple designations, the racial groups are not directly comparable to those from earlier years because of the change in method (U.S. Census Bureau 2004a,c).
3. Because they would break up the text too much, the many figures and tables for this chapter have been grouped at the back of the chapter.
4. The t-statistic for the slope equals -3.57. The average poverty rate is used in place of the initial poverty rate to avoid Galton's fallacy of regression to the mean. The relationship remains negative and significant if the dependent variable is defined as the percentage change in the poverty rate rather than as the percentage point change.
5. Black and Sanders (2004) also report a regression to the mean in terms of poverty rates for Appalachian counties.
6. The slope equals 0.66, and the t-statistic is equal to 3.05.
7. This pattern is akin to that noted by Blank (2002) regarding the decline in AFDC caseloads in 1994, predating implementation of TANF, which led her to be skeptical as to whether welfare reform was underlying the decline.

8. Regressing the poverty rate differential on a time trend, on its square, and on a dummy variable that takes a value of unity for 1996–2000 reveals that from 1996 to 2000 the poverty rate was lower by 1.07 percentage points, in the states that did not implement TANF until after 1996, than what would have been expected based on the past trend in the differential. The t-statistic for the 1996 dummy variables was 2.51. The trend variables were jointly significant below the 0.02 level based on a Wald test.

9. As an example of how state data can mask substate trends, Beeson and DeJong (2002), using population data, find that state patterns of growth convergence mask growth divergence at the county level.

10. The metropolitan designation and the counties used in our analysis mostly follow those used by the U.S. Bureau of Economic Analysis (BEA) in its 2000 Regional Economic Information System (REIS). The BEA and Census Bureau definitions are the same except for Virginia, where the BEA combines some of the independent cities with their neighboring counties to form a more coherent measure of labor markets. In five cases in Virginia, we took this one step further by combining the following BEA groups (Federal Information Processing Standards Codes in parentheses): 1) York and Poquoson, (FIPS 51958) with Hampton (FIPS 51650) and Newport News (FIPS 51700); 2) Halifax County (FIPS 51083) and South Boston (FIPS 51780); 3) Fairfax, Fairfax City, and Falls Church (FIPS 51919) and Alexandria (FIPS 51510); 4) Norfolk Independent City (FIPS 51710) and Portsmouth (FIPS 51740); and 5) Roanoke and Salem (FIPS 51944) and Roanoke Independent City (FIPS 51770).

11. For purposes of consistency in this study, we made our 1989–90 MSA areas correspond to the 1999 MSA definitions that were used for the 2000 Census. These also were used by Jargowsky (2003) in his study of poverty concentration.

12. Unless indicated, all of the variables are from the 1990 and 2000 censuses, meaning they reflect characteristics of the county's residents. The county poverty rates used are from the 1980, 1990, and 2000 decennial census of population, with the 1979 poverty measures being taken directly from the U.S. Department of Commerce's CD-ROM *USA Counties 1998* (U.S. Census Bureau 2005f).

13. A central-city county includes the county or counties of the named central city or cities in the MSA definition in a multiple-county MSA. Suburban counties do not include any of the central city or cities. The source of the central-city boundaries is the U.S. Census Bureau publication *County and City Data Book: 2000* (U.S. Census Bureau 2002b). The advantage of this category is that it fully captures the central-city boundaries but also captures the inner-ring suburbs in the "central city" designation. This appears to reflect ongoing patterns in metropolitan areas in that inner-ring suburbs are performing more like their less-vibrant central cities, resulting in a convergence of poverty patterns (Jargowsky 2003). In fact, the descriptive statistics will reveal a sharp distinction between these categories, illustrating that they are indeed a distinct grouping.

14. At first glance, this runs counter to Berube and Frey's (2002) finding that among MSAs with a population above 500,000, central-city poverty rates fell slightly during the 1990s, while suburban poverty rates increased slightly. This pattern

also somewhat counters Jargowsky's (2003) finding that the population residing in neighborhoods with high poverty rates—defined as those neighborhoods having poverty rates exceeding 40 percent—declined by 21 percent in central cities but by only 4 percent in suburbs. This discrepancy is reconciled by the fact that our definition tends to include inner-ring suburbs in central-city counties and that these suburbs lagged behind the more vibrant outer suburbs. Together, the results suggest that poverty became more dispersed in central-city counties, even as the average poverty rate declined only slightly. In fact, Jargowsky's (2003) findings suggest that poverty became more concentrated in the outer fringe of central cities and in the inner ring of suburbs. Conversely, exclusionary zoning and housing affordability in outer suburban counties may have limited the dispersion of household poverty during the 1990s. Thus, our definition captures the performance gap between outer suburbs and the more central parts of metropolitan areas.

Table 2.1 Summary Statistics, 1989 and 1999 County Poverty Rates (%)

Group[a]	1989			1999		
	N	Mean percent (std. dev.)	Max. [min.]	N	Mean percent (std. dev.)	Max. [min.]
Total individual poverty rate	3028	13.2 (6.3)	63.1 [2.2]	3028	12.4 (5.6)	52.3 [2.1]
Metropolitan county total poverty rate	824	12.2 (5.5)	41.9 [2.2]	824	11.9 (5.2)	35.9 [2.1]
Nonmetropolitan county total poverty rate	2204	17.1 (7.6)	63.1 [4.0]	2204	14.7 (6.2)	52.3 [4.0]
By age						
Children <18 years old	3028	18.0 (8.8)	70.1 [1.9]	3028	16.4 (7.8)	61.0 [0.0]
Adults 18 to 64 years old	3028	11.2 (5.5)	57.5 [2.0]	3028	11.2 (5.0)	46.3 [2.0]
Adults > 65 years old	3028	12.6 (6.5)	58.3 [2.8]	3028	9.9 (4.5)	44.1 [1.9]
Selected family types						
Married	3028	5.6 (3.9)	54.4 [0.7]	3028	5.1 (3.4)	43.2 [0.0]
Married with children	3028	7.3 (5.0)	58.6 [0.7]	3028	6.7 (4.5)	48.5 [0.0]
Female-headed with children	3027	40.2 (12.0)	100 [0.0]	3028	32.6 (9.9)	100 [0.0]
Female-headed without children	3027	10.0 (6.5)	100 [0.0]	3027	9.1 (5.1)	66.7 [0.0]

Male-headed with children	3021	18.8 (9.6)	100 [0.0]	3022	17.2 (7.3)	79.5 [0.0]
Racial/ethnic demographic						
Caucasian/White	3028	9.8 (5.0)	56.3 [2.0]	3028	9.3 (4.5)	51.7 [1.9]
African American/Black	2705	27.2 (12.9)	100 [0.0]	2879	23.4 (10.2)	100 [0.0]
Native American	2925	22.5 (13.7)	100 [0.0]	2962	20.3 (11.1)	100 [0.0]
Asian	2760	15.4 (12.7)	100 [0.0]	2906	13.2 (9.6)	100 [0.0]
Other	2688	26.0 (15.8)	100 [0.0]	2923	23.2 (11.1)	100 [0.0]
Hispanic	2980	22.5 (11.7)	100 [0.0]	3020	21.4 (8.6)	100 [0.0]
Two or more[b]				3020	18.8 (7.8)	83.7 [0.0]
Relative to poverty threshold						
Percent of pop. at < 50% of poverty level	3028	5.8 (3.2)	39.3 [0.8]	3028	5.6 (2.7)	26.5 [0.8]
Percent of pop. at 50–100% of poverty level	3028	7.3 (3.4)	32.2 [1.0]	3028	6.8 (3.0)	29.3 [1.3]
Percent of pop. at 100–150% of poverty level	3028	8.6 (3.1)	28.1 [2.2]	3028	8.6 (2.9)	22.0 [1.2]

[a] Weighted by 1990 or 2000 county population. A county is not included when the census did not report any individuals in that group. A nonmetropolitan county uses the 2000 Bureau of Economic Analysis REIS (Regional Economic Information System) county definitions.
[b] Blank = not applicable.
SOURCE: Authors' calculations based on 1990 and 2000 censuses (U.S. Census Bureau 2006e).

Table 2.2 Summary Statistics, 1989 and 1999 Metropolitan County Poverty Rates (%)

Group[a]	1989					1999				
	(1) Total	(2) MSA pop. over 1 million	(3) MSA pop. under 1 million	(4) Central MSA county	(5) Suburban MSA county	(6) Total	(7) MSA pop. over 1 million	(8) MSA pop. under 1 million	(9) Central MSA county	(10) Suburban MSA county
Total individual poverty rate	12.2 (5.5)	11.4 (5.3)	13.7 (5.5)	13.3 (5.2)	8.5 (4.7)	11.9 (5.2)	11.4 (5.3)	12.8 (5.0)	13.2 (5.0)	7.8 (3.5)
By age										
Children < 18 years old	17.0 (8.2)	16.4 (8.4)	18.3 (7.6)	18.8 (7.8)	11.2 (6.5)	15.8 (7.6)	15.3 (7.8)	16.8 (7.0)	17.7 (7.2)	9.9 (5.2)
Adults 18 to 64 years old	10.4 (4.8)	9.6 (4.5)	11.8 (5.0)	11.4 (4.5)	7.0 (4.0)	10.7 (4.7)	10.2 (4.6)	11.8 (4.6)	11.9 (4.4)	6.9 (3.1)
Adults > 65 years old	11.2 (4.9)	10.5 (4.3)	12.5 (5.6)	11.5 (4.7)	10.3 (5.5)	9.2 (3.8)	9.1 (3.8)	9.3 (3.7)	9.7 (3.8)	7.6 (3.2)
Selected family types										
Married	4.8 (3.0)	4.3 (2.4)	5.6 (3.8)	5.1 (3.0)	3.6 (2.7)	4.7 (3.1)	4.7 (3.0)	4.8 (3.5)	5.3 (3.3)	3.0 (1.8)
Married with children	6.4 (4.0)	5.9 (3.4)	7.3 (4.9)	6.9 (4.0)	4.5 (3.5)	6.3 (4.2)	6.2 (4.0)	6.4 (4.7)	7.2 (4.3)	3.7 (2.4)
Female-headed with children	38.0 (10.9)	35.4 (10.6)	43.0 (9.7)	39.8 (9.7)	32.0 (12.3)	30.9 (8.9)	28.9 (8.5)	34.9 (8.2)	32.8 (7.9)	25.2 (9.2)
Female-headed w/out children	8.8 (4.9)	7.8 (4.0)	10.7 (5.8)	9.3 (4.6)	7.0 (5.4)	8.3 (4.0)	7.8 (3.6)	9.3 (4.5)	9.0 (3.7)	6.1 (3.9)
Male-headed with children	17.3 (7.4)	16.2 (6.6)	19.4 (8.4)	18.6 (6.7)	13.2 (8.1)	16.3 (6.1)	15.6 (5.7)	17.9 (6.5)	17.7 (5.7)	12.2 (5.5)

Racial/ethnic demographic										
Caucasian/White	8.7 (4.1)	7.8 (3.3)	10.5 (4.8)	9.3 (4.0)	7.0 (3.8)	8.7 (4.1)	8.1 (3.8)	9.8 (4.4)	9.4 (4.1)	6.3 (2.9)
African American/Black	25.8 (10.0)	23.5 (8.9)	30.4 (10.4)	27.2 (8.8)	21.3 (12.1)	22.4 (7.8)	20.4 (6.9)	26.2 (7.9)	23.8 (6.7)	17.9 (9.0)
Native American	20.9 (10.5)	19.2 (9.1)	24.3 (12.2)	22.2 (9.6)	16.6 (12.0)	19.4 (8.5)	18.4 (7.6)	21.3 (9.9)	21.0 (7.5)	14.3 (9.5)
Asian	15.1 (10.1)	13.3 (7.6)	18.8 (12.9)	16.7 (9.6)	10.2 (10.1)	12.8 (7.3)	11.8 (6.0)	14.9 (9.0)	14.1 (6.9)	8.8 (7.1)
Other	24.9 (11.7)	23.9 (10.8)	26.9 (13.2)	26.5 (10.2)	19.8 (14.6)	22.4 (8.4)	21.4 (8.0)	24.4 (9.0)	23.8 (7.2)	18.1 (10.2)
Hispanic	21.3 (9.3)	20.4 (9.0)	23.1 (9.8)	22.9 (8.5)	16.4 (10.2)	20.5 (7.2)	19.5 (6.9)	22.4 (7.4)	21.9 (6.4)	16.0 (7.6)
Two or more[b]						17.9 (6.4)	16.6 (5.9)	20.6 (6.6)	19.3 (5.9)	13.7 (6.3)
Relative to poverty threshold										
% pop. < 50% poverty level	5.5 (2.9)	5.3 (2.9)	6.0 (2.8)	6.1 (2.8)	3.6 (2.1)	5.5 (2.7)	5.4 (2.8)	5.7 (2.3)	6.2 (2.6)	3.5 (1.6)
% pop. 50–100% poverty level	6.6 (2.8)	6.1 (2.6)	7.7 (3.0)	7.2 (2.6)	4.9 (2.8)	6.4 (2.7)	6.0 (2.6)	7.1 (2.8)	7.0 (2.6)	4.3 (2.1)
% pop. 100–150% poverty level	7.8 (2.6)	7.1 (2.4)	9.0 (2.4)	8.2 (2.3)	6.4 (3.0)	8.0 (2.6)	7.6 (2.6)	8.9 (2.5)	8.6 (2.4)	6.2 (2.5)
N	824	341	483	391	433	824	341	483	391	433

[a] Weighted by 1990 or 2000 county population. For some groups, there are fewer counties than listed when the census did not report any individuals in that category. A metropolitan county employs 2000 Bureau of Economic Analysis REIS county definitions using the MSA population from the 2000 census.

[b] Blank = not applicable.

SOURCE: Authors' calculations based on 1990 and 2000 censuses (U.S. Census Bureau 2006e).

Table 2.3 Summary Statistics, 1989 and 1999 Nonmetropolitan County Poverty Rates (%)

Group[a]	1989			1999		
	(1) Total	(2) Adjacent to MSA[b]	(3) Not adjacent to MSA[b]	(4) Total	(5) Adjacent to MSA[b]	(6) Not adjacent to MSA[b]
Total individual poverty rate	17.1 (7.6)	15.9 (7.0)	18.8 (8.0)	14.7 (6.2)	13.7 (5.7)	16.0 (6.6)
By age						
Children <18 years old	21.8 (9.8)	20.5 (9.2)	23.6 (10.4)	19.0 (8.4)	17.8 (7.8)	20.5 (9.0)
Adults 18 to 64 years old	14.6 (6.8)	13.3 (6.1)	16.2 (7.2)	13.2 (5.7)	12.2 (5.2)	14.6 (6.1)
Adults > 65 years old	18.4 (8.5)	17.5 (8.2)	19.6 (8.8)	12.6 (5.9)	12.1 (5.6)	13.3 (6.2)
Selected family types						
Married	9.0 (5.2)	8.1 (4.6)	10.1 (5.7)	6.6 (3.9)	6.0 (3.4)	7.4 (4.3)
Married with children	11.1 (6.4)	10.0 (5.6)	12.5 (6.9)	8.6 (5.0)	7.8 (4.4)	9.7 (5.6)
Female-headed with children	49.2 (12.3)	46.9 (11.9)	52.0 (12.1)	39.6 (11.0)	37.9 (10.5)	41.9 (11.1)
Female-headed without children	14.7 (9.4)	13.6 (8.6)	16.0 (10.2)	12.1 (7.3)	11.4 (6.5)	13.1 (8.2)
Male-headed with children	24.8 (13.9)	23.3 (12.7)	26.7 (15.2)	20.9 (10.2)	19.3 (8.9)	22.9 (11.5)

	(1)	(2)	(3)	(4)	(5)	(6)
Racial/ethnic demographic						
Caucasian/White	14.2	13.1	15.6	12.1	11.3	13.2
	(5.7)	(5.2)	(6.1)	(4.8)	(4.3)	(5.1)
African American/Black	32.8	31.0	35.3	27.9	26.9	29.2
	(20.4)	(17.6)	(23.3)	(16.2)	(14.2)	(18.6)
Native American	29.0	26.9	31.8	24.0	21.7	27.1
	(21.2)	(18.9)	(23.5)	(17.9)	(15.8)	(19.8)
Asian	16.4	15.6	17.4	14.6	14.5	14.8
	(20.4)	(19.0)	(21.9)	(15.9)	(15.0)	(16.9)
Other	30.9	29.7	32.5	26.7	25.6	28.2
	(26.4)	(24.7)	(28.4)	(18.1)	(16.3)	(20.2)
Hispanic	27.4	26.0	29.2	25.1	24.1	26.5
	(17.5)	(16.0)	(19.1)	(12.2)	(11.1)	(13.4)
Two or more[c]				22.4	20.9	24.4
				(11.3)	(10.0)	(12.6)
Relative to poverty threshold						
% of pop. at < 50% of poverty level	6.9	6.3	7.6	6.1	5.7	6.6
	(4.0)	(3.5)	(4.5)	(3.1)	(2.8)	(3.4)
% of pop. at 50–100% of poverty level	10.3	9.6	11.2	8.6	8.0	9.4
	(4.0)	(3.8)	(4.0)	(3.4)	(3.1)	(3.5)
% of pop. at 100–150% of poverty level	11.9	11.3	12.6	10.8	10.3	11.5
	(2.8)	(2.8)	(2.7)	(2.7)	(2.6)	(2.6)
N	2204	974	1230	2204	974	1230

[a] Weighted by 1990 or 2000 county population. For some groups, there are fewer counties than listed, in cases where the census did not report any individuals in that category. A nonmetropolitan county uses 2000 Bureau of Economic Analysis REIS county definitions.

[b] "Adjacent to MSA" is defined by the U.S. Department of Agriculture as a nonmetropolitan county adjacent to a metropolitan area, using 1993 definitions. Downloaded from http://www.ers.usda.gov/data/NaturalAmenities/natamenf.xls (ERS 1993).

[c] Blank = not applicable.

SOURCE: Authors' calculations based on 1990 and 2000 censuses (U.S. Census Bureau 2006e).

Figure 2.1 1969 State Poverty Rates

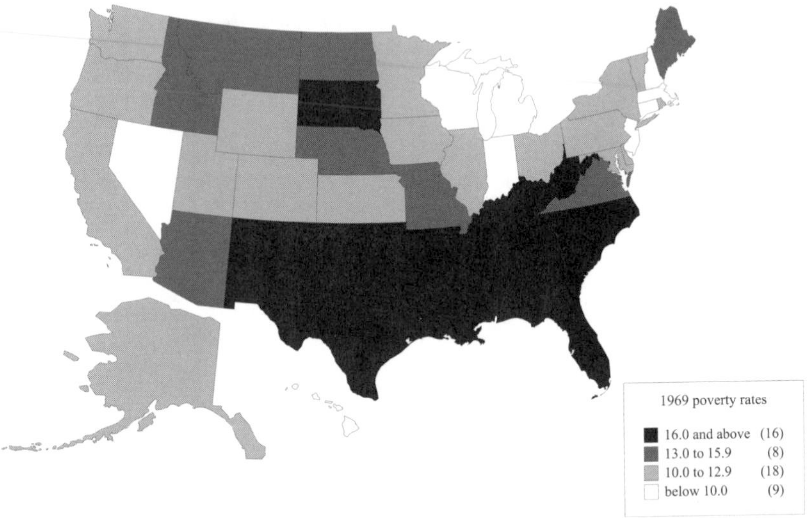

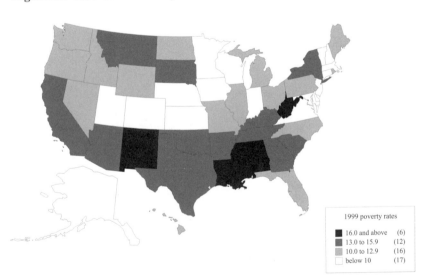

NOTE: Tallies of states for Figures 2.1–2.4 sum to 51 and include the District of
Columbia.
SOURCE: U.S. Census Bureau (2002a); Bishaw and Iceland (2003).

Figure 2.2 1999 State Poverty Rates

SOURCE: U.S. Census Bureau (2002a); Bishaw and Iceland (2003).

Figure 2.3 1969–1999 State Poverty Rate Changes (%)

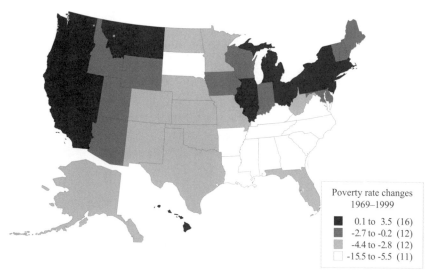

SOURCE: U.S. Census Bureau (2002a); Bishaw and Iceland (2003).

Figure 2.4 1989–1999 State Poverty Rate Changes (%)

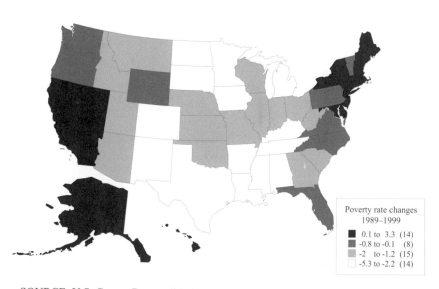

SOURCE: U.S. Census Bureau (2002a); Bishaw and Iceland (2003).

Figure 2.5 1984–2000 Poverty Rate Changes vs. Average Poverty Rate

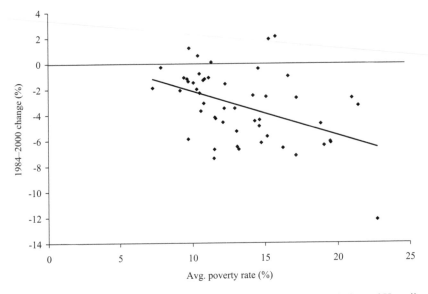

NOTE: Each diamond represents a state. There are 49 diamonds, as Alaska and Hawaii are excluded and the District of Columbia is included.

SOURCE: U.S. Census Bureau (2002a).

Figure 2.6 Changes in State Poverty Rates vs. Unemployment Rates, 1984–2000

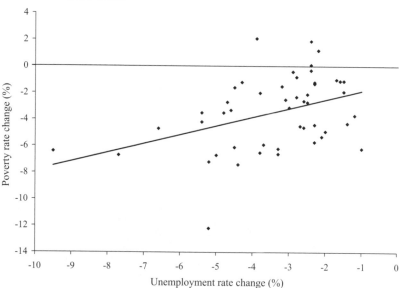

NOTE: Each diamond represents a state. There are 49 diamonds, as Alaska and Hawaii are excluded and the District of Columbia is included.
SOURCE: U.S. Census Bureau (2002a) and unemployment statistics at www.bls.gov.

Figure 2.7 Poverty in States Implementing TANF in 1996 vs. States Implementing TANF after 1996

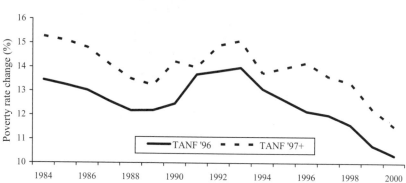

NOTE: TANF '96 indicates states that implemented TANF in 1996. TANF '97+ indicates states that implemented TANF after 1996.
SOURCE: U.S. Census Bureau (2002a) and CEA (1999).

44

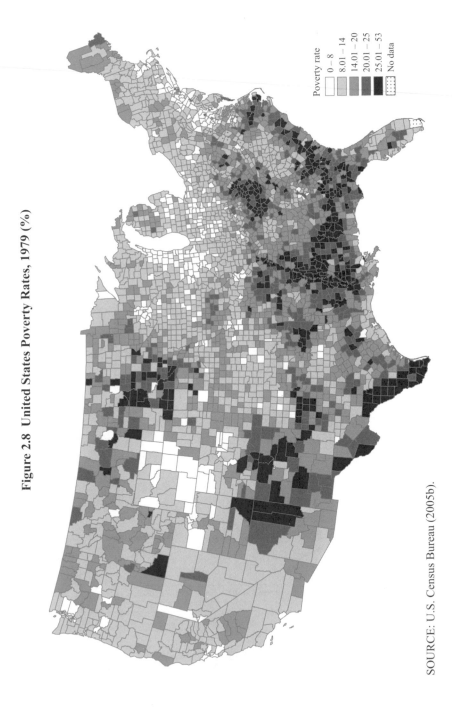

Figure 2.8 United States Poverty Rates, 1979 (%)

Poverty rate

0 – 8
8.01 – 14
14.01 – 20
20.01 – 25
25.01 – 53
No data

SOURCE: U.S. Census Bureau (2005b).

Figure 2.9 United States Poverty Rates, 1989 (%)

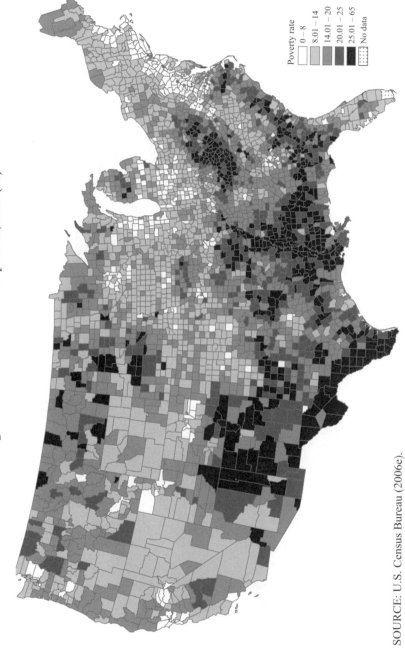

Poverty rate

0 – 8

8.01 – 14

14.01 – 20

20.01 – 25

25.01 – 65

No data

SOURCE: U.S. Census Bureau (2006e).

Figure 2.10 United States Poverty Rates, 1999 (%)

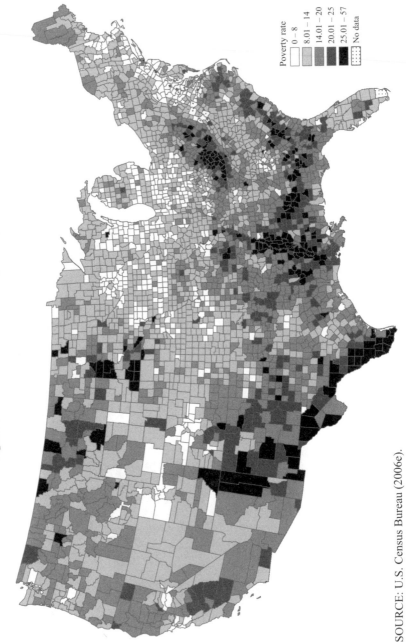

SOURCE: U.S. Census Bureau (2006e).

Figure 2.11 Poverty Rate Change, 1989–1999 (%)

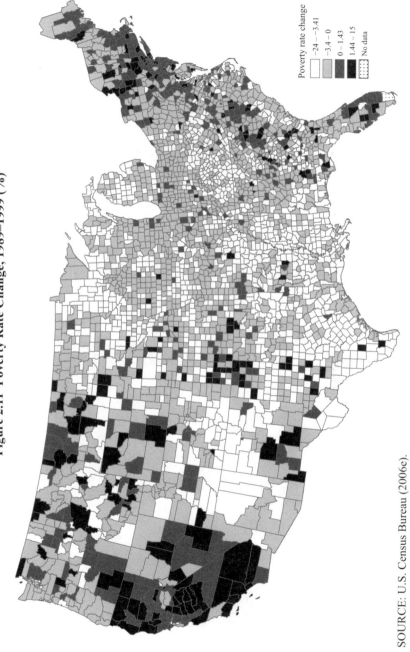

Poverty rate change

- −24 − −3.41
- −3.4 − 0
- 0 − 1.43
- 1.44 − 15
- No data

SOURCE: U.S. Census Bureau (2006e).

48

Figure 2.12 Poverty Rate Change, 1979–1999 (%)

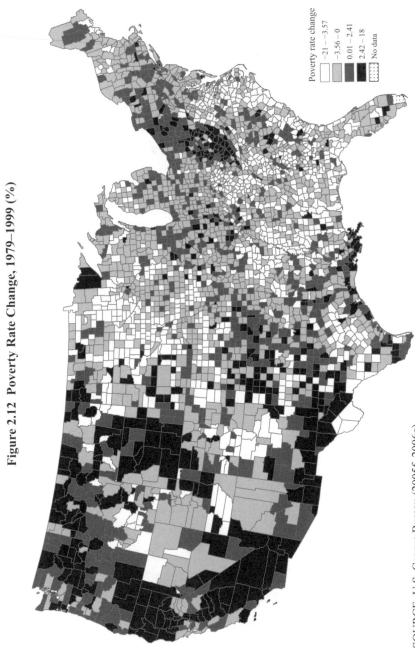

Poverty rate change
- −21 − −3.57
- −3.56 − 0
- 0.01 − 2.41
- 2.42 − 18
- No data

SOURCE: U.S. Census Bureau (2005f, 2006e).

Figure 2.13 Average Weighted County Poverty Rates, MSA and Non-MSA, 1989–1999 (%)

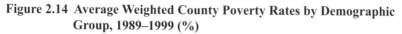

| Total | Total MSA | MSA pop. >1 million | MSA pop. < 1 million | Central MSA city | Suburban MSA city | Total non-MSA | Adjacent to MSA | Nonadjacent to MSA |

SOURCE: U.S. Census Bureau (2006e).

Figure 2.14 Average Weighted County Poverty Rates by Demographic Group, 1989–1999 (%)

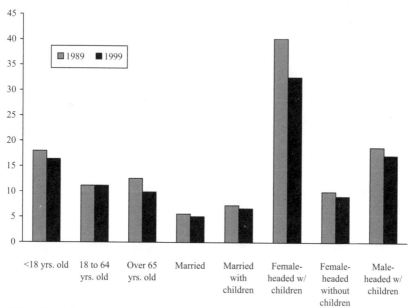

| <18 yrs. old | 18 to 64 yrs. old | Over 65 yrs. old | Married | Married with children | Female-headed w/ children | Female-headed without children | Male-headed w/ children |

SOURCE: U.S. Census Bureau (2006e).

Figure 2.15 Average Weighted County Employment Growth, 1985–1990 and 1995–2000 (%)

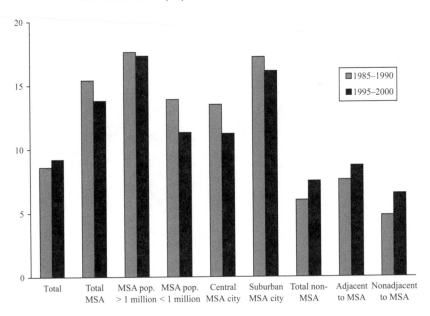

SOURCE: Bureau of Economic Analysis Local Area Personal Income SA25 series at www.bea.gov and authors' calculations.

3

Regional Economic Performance and Poverty

What's the Theoretical Connection?

The lag between job creation and in-migration provides room for jobless locals and working locals on the bottom rungs of the occupational ladder either to become employed or to move up the occupational ladder.
  —Alan Peters and Peter Fisher (2004), "The Failures of Economic Development Incentives," *Journal of the American Planning Association*

Is the world likely to be very far from an equilibrium in which utility is the same everywhere? We believe not, on the grounds that mobility in the United States is quite high and information about alternative locations is good.
  —Philip Graves and Thomas Knapp (1988), "Mobility Behavior of the Elderly," *Journal of Urban Economics*

It is shown that it is difficult to develop a satisfactory explanation for continuing net migration which is compatible with the equilibrium assumption, and that recent relevant research generally fails to support the idea the U.S. economy is in equilibrium.
  —Alan Evans (1990), "The Assumption of Equilibrium in the Analysis of Migration and Interregional Differences," *Journal of Regional Science*

Chapter 2 illustrated the spatial concentration and persistence of poverty in the United States. In many areas, labor market rewards plus transfer payments left significant portions of the population below the federal poverty line. Labor market rewards reflect both the degree of participation in paid work activities and the associated wage rate. The justification and design of antipoverty policies that aim to reduce poverty and eliminate high-poverty clusters depend on the underlying geographical determinants of poverty.

Central to these issues is the debate encapsulated in the three quotations above, regarding whether the geographic distribution of poverty is the result of regions generally being in continuous economic equilibrium, or whether disequilibrium persists for significant periods of time. A continuous interregional economic equilibrium explanation of the spatial distribution of poverty suggests that little can be gained from place-based antipoverty policy. However, this chapter reviews the interregional equilibrium perspective on poverty and concludes, based on both theoretical and empirical considerations, that it is less plausible than a disequilibrium perspective. We argue that policy intervention could effectively reduce and equalize local poverty levels.

INTERREGIONAL EQUILIBRIUM AND DISEQUILIBRIUM PERSPECTIVES ON POVERTY

Simple neoclassical economic theory suggests that capital locates in the place of its highest reward; low-wage regions, then, because they reflect lower production costs, should attract capital. This increases the demand for labor in these regions and narrows regional differences in wages and poverty (Rural Sociological Society Task Force on Persistent Rural Poverty [RSS] 1993). A pure neoclassical interregional equilibrium would be characterized by an absence of differences between the regions in wage rates and the incidence of poverty, because labor movements would quickly eliminate wage differentials.

More complex theories of regional labor markets allow for equilibrium differences in labor market outcomes by emphasizing the productivity and amenity attractiveness of place in wage determination (Beeson and Eberts 1989; Roback 1982). Higher productivity raises nominal wage rates, greater household-amenity attractiveness lowers nominal wage rates, and both increase land costs. Productivity depends on factors such as human and physical capital, location, technology, and regional public policy. Household amenity attractiveness can depend on natural features of the region such as climate and topography, as well as man-made features such as cultural attractions, the quality of schools, and public infrastructure. Assuming full employment and perfect mobility of factors, wages should be such that no firm or household can geographically relocate and improve its economic condition in equilibrium. Differences in wages and poverty across regions can still exist in equilibrium, because they reflect regional productivity and amenity differentials.

Equilibrium-based models can accommodate involuntary unemployment and regional equilibrium differentials in unemployment rates. In equilibrium, a region may have higher unemployment if there are compensating gains in wages or household amenity attractiveness. Higher unemployment requires compensation because it represents a lower probability of workers receiving a given wage rate (Partridge and Rickman 1997a). With frictionless migration, the utility derived from each region's bundle of amenities, wage rates, and unemployment rates should be equalized in equilibrium. These equilibrium-based models leave little scope for regional changes in labor demand to increase regional household utility.

Frictions in migration can create long-run utility differentials. Sense of place, psychic well-being, and moving costs can contribute to equilibrium differentials in unemployment rates. Partridge and Rickman (1997b) argue that these factors hinder households from relocating to areas of higher utility, as amenities and expected labor market rewards create regional utility differentials. Thus, if there were zero adjustment costs, regional shifts in labor demand could increase overall household welfare in the nation since households would relocate to areas that provided higher utility.

These frictions may be greater among those in poverty: historically lower migration rates have been observed for individuals with lower education and skill levels (Schwartz 1976; Yankow 2003), which makes it likely that regional pockets of poverty will persist (Partridge and Rickman 2003b). This follows from human capital theory, in which those with higher levels of human capital are more likely to migrate to take advantage of their increased potential for higher returns (Becker 1962; Borjas 1996; Nord 1998). In addition, job leads and networks tend to be more informal for low-skilled workers, whose information most likely originates from friends and family (Holzer 1996; Ihlanfeldt 1997). Further limiting the mobility of low-skilled individuals is that they may be more reliant on friends and families for support such as transportation or child care, making it risky for them to move (Goetz 1999).

Empirical evidence on whether the U.S. economy tends to continuously hover near interregional equilibrium is mixed. In estimating amenity-compensated wage differentials, studies commonly assume that the U.S. economy continuously remains in interregional equilibrium (Beeson and Eberts 1989; Blomquist, Berger, and Hoehn 1988). Although in their study of internal U.S. migration Greenwood et al. (1991) questioned the assumption of equilibrium, they were not able to statistically reject equilibrium for most states.

Yet the U.S. economy routinely experiences shocks, which may produce heterogeneity in regional fluctuations. Moreover, shocks may arise within particular regions (Clark 1998). Empirical studies examining the length of disequilibrium adjustment provide conflicting evidence. Marston (1985) and Blanchard and Katz (1992) conclude that regional labor markets re-equilibrate quickly as migration flows rapidly dissipate the effects of labor demand shocks. More recently, Partridge and Rickman (2003b) and Gallin (2004) have found that regional labor markets take years to re-equilibrate following shocks to labor demand, although equilibrium typically is obtained within 10 years.[1]

Other theories suggest even more persistent divergence in wages and poverty rates, in which differences across regions may even widen. Such theories involve cumulative causation, growth poles, and agglomeration or localization scale economies (Glaeser et al. 1992; Kaldor 1970; Krugman 1991). According to these theories, the productivity advantages of regions can be endogenous, and expectations of convergence of productivity, incomes, and poverty are replaced with expectations of divergence. For example, regarding rural development, small communities that fall below a population and business-service threshold will experience further population losses because they lose the critical mass necessary to induce new economic activity, whereas those above the threshold will be relatively prosperous.

REGIONALLY ASYMMETRIC LABOR DEMAND SHOCKS AND POVERTY: THE ROLE OF MIGRATION AND COMMUTING

The equilibrium perspective discussed above suggests little role for labor demand in affecting the spatial distribution of poverty. However, the theoretical and empirical support for the disequilibrium perspective of regional economies, along with the observed spatial concentration of poverty, suggests possibilities for relative labor demand shifts to affect regional poverty rates. Below, we outline the potential for this to happen.

The simple labor market representation in Figure 3.1 can be used to illustrate the connection between labor demand shifts and poverty rate changes. Two regional economies are represented, Region A and Region B. Suppose labor demand shifts outward in Region A and inward in Region B, i.e., there are regionally asymmetric shocks to labor demand.

The outward shift of labor demand in Region A causes the wage rate (W) to rise in the short run from its original equilibrium level at point A to its new equilibrium level at point B. The economy moves upward along the short-run supply curve (LS_{sr}) as unemployment falls and labor force participation (L) rises. The combined effect of these labor market outcomes, in the short run, is to reduce poverty in the region. In the longer run, however, the higher regional wage rate induces in-migration, which is represented by the short-run labor-supply curve (LS_{sr}) shifting out. If, as is consistent with the neoclassical interregional equilibrium perspective, labor is perfectly mobile, migration continues until the regional wage, unemployment, and labor force participation rates are driven back to their original levels (point C), making the long-run supply curve (LS_{lr}) horizontal.

Correspondingly, the inward labor demand shift in Region B causes the wage rate to decline from the original equilibrium point (A) to its new equilibrium point (B). In the short run, unemployment rises and labor force participation falls, and, in conjunction with the fall in the wage rate, the poverty rate increases. In the longer run, the out-migration to Region A shifts the short-run supply curve inwards until Region B's wage, unemployment, and labor force participation rates return to their original levels at point C.

When the equilibrium returns to point C, the relative shift in labor demand has no long-run effect on labor market outcomes or the poverty rate in either region. In addition, the faster these adjustments come, the more short-lived the gains (or losses) are from a favorable (or unfavorable) labor demand shock. What the equilibrium relationship suggests is that this adjustment from B to C in both panels is very close to instantaneous, i.e., that poverty changes very little in the long run as a result

Figure 3.1 Illustration of Dynamic Labor Market Responses to a Labor Demand Shift

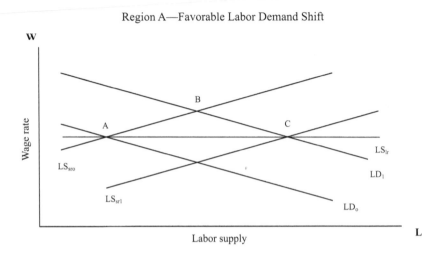

Region A—Favorable Labor Demand Shift

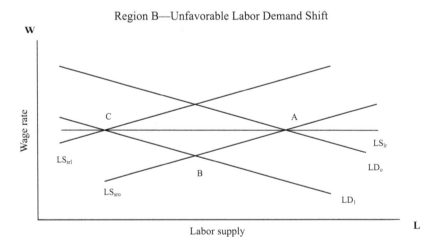

Region B—Unfavorable Labor Demand Shift

SOURCE: Authors' construction.

of labor market shifts. By way of contrast, the disequilibrium approach implies that either the final adjustment ends somewhere between B and C or the movement from B to C is prolonged—perhaps lasting a decade or more. Below, we examine theoretical and empirical considerations regarding the likelihood of these outcomes for poverty.

In finding no relationship between county employment growth and poverty, Levernier, Partridge, and Rickman (1998, 2000) argue that the absence of a relationship likely resulted from significant migration responses. Thus, the original residents, particularly those who are low-skilled or marginal workers, did not benefit from increased employment growth, which supports the equilibrium approach. Likewise, as suggested by Blanchard and Katz (1992), perfectly mobile labor precludes demand-induced changes in wage rates, unemployment rates, and labor force participation rates.

For smaller areas, robust economic growth would also likely attract commuters from neighboring areas where growth may be weaker (Ellwood and Blank 2001; Peters and Fisher 2002). Businesses may simply find it more profitable to hire migrants and commuters that possess higher levels of skills and education (Larson 1989; Sawicki and Moody 1997). Thus, the original residents of the area may receive few benefits of strong growth, and poverty rates may be left relatively unaffected. In this case, it may be more likely that landowners and local businesses largely benefit from growth (Bartik 1991).

In addition, when the national labor market is weak, there is greater likelihood that new migrants will flock to localities where employment is growing (Partridge and Rickman 2002). That is, a growing region will be most attractive to potential migrants when the backdrop is a weak national economy. Greater migration (and commuting) responsiveness implies that differential regional economic growth can produce smaller changes in poverty than what would be expected based on national-level evidence. In particular, when the national economy is weak, it would appear as if changes in local job growth (or unemployment rates), other things being equal, have little influence on poverty rates because of the enhanced migration and commuting responses.

Bartik (2001), however, argues that stronger employment growth should reduce poverty unless there is an accompanying increase in income inequality. He posits that strong employment growth reduces poverty when it disproportionately benefits low-skilled workers because businesses are forced to hire them. Low-skilled workers have historically been overrepresented in cyclically sensitive sectors, or sectors with low profit margins, making the low-skilled the most vulnerable to economic downturns (Pissarides 1991). For example, Holzer and LaLonde (2000) report that unskilled workers are more likely to lose their jobs during a downturn and that they have greater difficulty in finding employment when they are out of work. Moreover, low-skilled individuals have a lower propensity to migrate (Borjas 1996; Yankow 2003), suggesting that they may be less than perfectly mobile. In other words, the long-run supply curve for labor would not be perfectly horizontal as in Figure 3.1. Bound and Holzer (2000) report that low-skilled labor market outcomes depend more on local labor demand, which they attribute to these workers' lower mobility. This makes it more likely that low-skilled workers experience permanent changes in their wage, unemployment, and labor force participation rates in response to labor demand shocks.

A strong national economy also may reduce interstate migration. Partridge and Rickman (2002) report that state net-migration rates converged in the red-hot economy of the late 1990s, as workers appeared to have less reason to relocate for better economic opportunities. With less migration, the original residents of a region are more likely to be hired and benefit from strong regional growth. Low-skilled original residents are most likely to benefit, because they are more likely to be underutilized during sluggish growth; tight labor markets force firms to relax their hiring standards and enhance workplace support (Holzer 1999; Holzer, Raphael, and Stoll 2003). Thus, local economic growth likely reduces subnational poverty rates more during periods of low national unemployment.[2]

The underlying factors driving increased employment growth can also affect its relationship to poverty reduction. This can be addressed using shift-share analysis, where job growth is decomposed into its industry-composition and competitiveness components. Partridge and Rickman (1999a) show that net-migration responds differentially to the source of employment growth. If above-average regional growth is due to having a high composition of industries that are fast-growing nationally (industry-mix growth), then it is much less likely that migrants will be attracted to the region, the reason being that potential migrants in those industries are probably already fully employed. Because employers in the region will then be forced to hire more nonemployed original residents, this type of growth is likely to reduce the local unemployment rate and help disadvantaged residents (Partridge and Rickman 1995). But if job growth is due to the region itself faring well across all or most of its industries (competitiveness growth), then migrants will be more likely to relocate to the area from regions that are not faring as well as the national average. This type of growth produces a smaller impact on unemployment and poverty in the region.[3]

Employment growth may have additional effects on poverty beyond influencing unemployment and labor force participation rates. Job growth also affects the demand for low-skilled workers simply because it is associated with the number of vacancies in a region (Bartik and Eberts 1999). Likewise, strong growth may lead workers to upgrade from lower to higher paying positions (Felsenstein and Persky 1999), particularly if migration is sluggish (Peters and Fisher 2004). Andersson, Holzer, and Lane (2002, 2003) find that about three-quarters of those who escape persistent low-wage status do so after a job change.

LABOR DEMAND AND METROPOLITAN POVERTY: THE SPATIAL MISMATCH HYPOTHESIS

Poverty differences also may exist across smaller areas within regions, even when those areas are in equilibrium. Spatial-skills mismatches between residence and job location are regularly offered as an explanation for the pockets of poverty contained within inner cities.[4] A trend in North American economies has been the movement of jobs in large metropolitan areas from the inner cities to the suburbs (Ingram 1998). In particular, the deconcentration has occurred among manufacturing jobs (Zax and Kain 1996); more generally, it has occurred among low-skilled jobs (Stoll 1999). If original residents, particularly low-skilled workers, are less willing—or are unable—to migrate or commute to areas of newly created jobs, poverty is less likely to be affected by increased metropolitan labor demand, since in-migrants to the region will take the new jobs (Sawicki and Moody 1997). Yet this also means that lessening the poverty among residents in inner city high-poverty pockets depends on having nearby labor demand.

Demand-side explanations for the urban deconcentration of jobs include innovations in transportation, higher inner-city crime and taxes, land price differentials, and suburban proximity to consumer markets (Mieszkowski and Mills 1993; Raphael, Stoll, and Holzer 2000).[5] Supply-side factors such as housing discrimination (Brueckner and Martin 1997; Brueckner and Zenou 2003; Turner 1992) and suburban zoning practices (Holzer, Raphael, and Stoll 2003; O'Regan and Quigley 1991) may prevent the poor and minorities from relocating to the suburbs. Parts of urban areas lack accessible public transportation (Stoll, Holzer, and Ihlanfeldt 2000), and many inner-city residents don't have a car, both of which factors limit their commuting responses to the movement of jobs to the suburbs. Increasing inner-city residents' access to automobiles and public transit has been found to increase employment rates among poor minorities (Raphael and Stoll 2002).

In addition, Holzer, Ihlanfeldt, and Sjoquist (1994) observe that inner-city blacks are less likely to lengthen their commutes to offset the relocation of inner-city jobs to suburban areas. Rogers (1997) finds that unemployment spells are positively related to the distance (hence commuting time) from the unemployed worker's residence to the location of job growth. An increased distance also relates to a deteriorating knowledge by the unemployed worker about work opportunities (Ihlanfeldt 1997; Wasmer and Zenou 2002). For example, suburban firms may only advertise locally (Turner 1997). Housing constraints and a lack of transportation may further reduce the scope of job searches by poor inner-city residents (Stoll and Raphael 2000; Gobillon, Selod, and Zenou 2003). Smith and Zenou (2003) argue that the economic benefit of a suburban job does not offset the benefits of low land rent and large housing consumption in the inner city, which rationally leads to inner-city residents searching less intensively in suburban locations.

In addition to housing discrimination, inner-city residents may face job discrimination by suburban employers (Stoll, Holzer, and Ihlanfeldt 2000). Inner-city residents may be perceived as being unproductive or criminal (Zenou and Boccard 2000); such perceptions may be related to their need to commute (Zenou 2002), or they may be related to race (Holzer and Reaser 2000). Perceived racial discrimination also may cause minorities to search less intensively in the suburbs, which they may perceive as being hostile environments (Sjoquist 2001).

Neighborhood effects such as peer pressure and poor role models closely follow on spatial mismatches in explaining inner-city poverty (Corcoran et al. 1992; Cutler and Glaeser 1997; Kasinitz and Rosenberg 1996). In fact, Cutler and Glaeser (1997) find that blacks are worse off in segregated neighborhoods than in integrated neighborhoods. Weinberg, Reagan, and Yankow (2004) similarly find that the social characteristics of a neighborhood affect the labor market attachment of its residents. One often-cited example of this phenomenon is Chicago's Gautreaux program, which, since the 1970s, has relocated thousands of low-income inner-city blacks to the more affluent suburbs. Studies of this program suggest that families that relocated had higher employment rates, better long-term outcomes for their children, and lower public-assistance usage (Rosenbaum and DeLuca 2000). Yet Page and Solon (2003) argue that neighborhood effects are mostly spurious, relating more to urban-wage advantages and the high propensity to live in an urban area if that is where one spent his or her childhood.[6]

One of the key elements of the spatially concentrated neighborhood phenomenon is the possibility that households self-sort on the basis of income, race, or other preferences (Sethi and Somanathan 2004). Such Tiebout sorting would make it difficult to identify "true" effects of neighborhood characteristics as opposed to factors associated with self-selection.[7] However, this problem is not very germane here because of our focus on much-larger-sized counties rather than on smaller census blocks or census tracts, which resemble neighborhoods.

Closely related to neighborhood effects are sociological explanations, including labor and housing-market discrimination, that underlie the spatial mismatch hypothesis. However, one prominent sociological explanation that will be germane in the county-level analysis in Chapters 6–8 is the connection between the marriage market and poverty (Cancian, Danziger, and Gottschalk 1993; Wilson 1987). Not only does a lack of employment opportunities directly increase poverty rates, but it can indirectly increase poverty rates as well, by reducing the number of marriageable men, which results in more female-headed households—households that often lack the necessary resources to rise above the poverty threshold. Indeed, one could imagine how such poverty-reinforcing patterns could be particularly alarming in distressed communities or neighborhoods.

RURAL LABOR DEMAND AND POVERTY

Rural antipoverty effects of increased labor demand will differ as well, to the extent that migration and commuting responses differ in rural areas. To be sure, although urban spatial-skills job mismatches have received the most attention, mismatches may be even more severe in certain rural settings (Levernier, Partridge, and Rickman 2000). Rural residents' geographic isolation and their unwillingness to migrate to growth centers may contribute to a spatial mismatch between the skills required by the jobs in their area and the skills of these nearby workers (Brown and Warner 1991; Leichenko 2003; RSS 1993).

Several factors may contribute to labor demand having differential poverty effects in rural areas. First, lower economic or population density may hamper skills matching in the labor market. Some studies suggest that low density increases the cost of obtaining information about jobs (Davis, Connolly, and Weber 2003; Davis and Weber 2002), which inhibits the matching of skills. This means that a given shift in labor demand will have less effect on the economic outcomes of the original residents and on the poverty rate. Another factor that potentially reduces labor market matching is that rural residents may have less access to job training and placement assistance services (Fletcher et al. 2002; Kraybill and Lobao 2001). And, just as in the urban spatial mismatch hypothesis, low rural density is often associated with a greater distance between where residents live and where the jobs are located. The absence of public transportation and the lack of dependable automobile transportation (Beale 2004) often limits poor rural residents' access to remotely located jobs (Brown and Stommes 2004; Davis, Connolly, and Weber 2003).

Second, the scarcity of child care centers in rural areas restricts available formal child care options, which may prevent those in poverty from taking newly created jobs (Gordon and Chase-Lansdale 2001; Mills and Hazarika 2003; Weber, Duncan, and Whitener 2001). Third, rural jobs may be more apt to be part-time, low paying, or involve nonstandard hours, which creates additional child care concerns (Findeis and Jensen 1998; Davis and Weber 2002; Fletcher et al. 2002). For these reasons, there may be a weaker relationship between demand-induced employment growth and poverty in rural areas.

On the other hand, there are theoretical reasons to believe that employment growth may have stronger poverty-reducing impacts on rural areas. For one, the smaller scale of rural job markets and the stronger informal communication networks could increase the skills matching process (Gibbs 2002). This could make the poverty rate more responsive to changing labor demand conditions (Gibbs 2002). For another, individuals facing transportation and child care constraints may be more likely to choose to live in metro areas, while those more readily employable may be more likely to remain in rural areas (Kilkenny and Huffman 2003).

There also may be smaller in-commuting responses from outside the area to take newly created jobs in rural areas (Renkow 2003). Low economic density can create a larger-than-normal gap between information available to local residents on job openings and that available to nearby outside residents. Likewise, scarcity of formal child care in neighboring rural areas and a lack of public and private transportation make in-commuting to the area less likely.

Correspondingly, migration responses to changing labor market conditions may be lower in rural areas (Renkow 2003; Renkow and Hoover 2000). The low density of the area may limit in-migration responses to local-area job growth because of a lack of information in distant areas about these jobs. Out-migration responses to job losses also may be smaller because of residents' lack of information about jobs in other areas.

Smaller in-commuting and migration responses mean the residents of the area take a greater share of newly created jobs. The smaller overall supply of responses, then—which implies a steeper short-run labor supply curve and an upward-sloped long-run supply curve, as in Figure 3.1—would lead to larger demand-induced wage rate changes. Both the larger share of new jobs going to original residents and the larger wage gains should lift more individuals above the poverty line. Yet it also means that residents in high-poverty areas are more likely to be adversely affected by job declines. Therefore, a stronger link between employment growth and poverty would be expected in areas that are more rural. Thus, the primary arguments by Peters and Fisher (2002) against place-based policies—in-migration and in-commuting—are probably less applicable in rural areas.

Cultural and sociological factors also may affect the linkage between formal labor market outcomes and poverty in rural areas. For example, Pickering (2004) reports successes for the Rosebud reservation in South Dakota in transitioning TANF recipients into formal market jobs, which she attributes to cooperation between the tribe and the government in providing job placement and support services. In contrast, on the Pine Ridge reservation in South Dakota, she notes, the existence of a strong informal economy weakened the connection between formal labor market demand and poverty. Improved governance and enhanced social capital may also be important in rural communities in improving the prospects for economic development and in ensuring that the benefits of economic development are widely dispersed to all stakeholders (Blank 2005).

Potential neighborhood effects are not just restricted to inner cities; they also exist in rural poverty-stricken areas, such as on many reservations for Native Americans.[8] However, poverty generally is more diffused in rural areas than in the inner city (RSS 1993), which would suggest fewer negative neighborhood effects and a greater prevalence of "middle class values" among low-income households.

POVERTY AND REGIONAL LABOR SUPPLY SHIFTS

Exogenous increases in labor supply are more likely to increase poverty than to reduce it. For a given level of labor demand, increased labor supply reduces the wage rate. If increased regional labor supply is caused by in-migration, then increased unemployment and reduced labor force participation rates should result (Partridge and Rickman 1999b, 2003a). The combined effect of lower average wages and lower employment rates is higher poverty.

Innovations in interregional labor force migration primarily represent a shift in regional labor supply (Partridge and Rickman 2006). Although the transfer of associated assets may provide some shift in demand, those workers who are early in their careers have the highest propensity for migration and are least likely to possess substantial assets. Offsetting the labor-supply-induced wage reduction is a potential composition effect: migrants may possess higher ability or motivation

(Gabriel and Schmitz 1995), although Bartik (1993b) estimates that only one-fifth of labor-force participation-rate increases that follow accelerated employment growth can be attributed to the changing composition of the population associated with migration. On the other hand, retired in-migrants, who often possess substantial assets, act more as a labor demand shift, which may reduce area poverty.

Another notable labor-supply factor that may affect poverty rates is immigration. Immigrants may directly affect poverty by being disproportionately low-skilled compared to native-born workers. The U.S. Census Bureau (2001) puts the poverty rate for the foreign-born at 16.8 percent, compared to 11.1 percent for the entire population. Yet Chapman and Bernstein (2003) argue that during the 1990s this composition effect was offset by greater increases in income among immigrants than among the general population. Hence they conclude that immigration affects poverty less than other labor market factors do.

However, immigrants may have other, indirect effects on poverty rates; for instance, new immigrants might compete for jobs with both natives and previous migrants. Borjas (2003) estimates that immigration significantly lowers the wages of competing workers through increasing the labor supply. Topel (1994) also finds that wages decline for low-skilled males in response to greater immigration and increased labor force participation by females. Likewise, Orrenius and Zavodny (2003) report an inverse association between the foreign-born share of workers in an occupation and the wages of low-skilled natives.

As for employment impacts, if immigration significantly reduces real wages, some individuals may exit the labor force. Yet if immigrants locate in areas where there are labor shortages, they may simply change the size of the economy, not the unemployment rate (Saiz 2003). In addition, at the regional level, less-skilled natives may out-migrate in response to new immigrants (Borjas, Freeman, and Katz 1996; Frey 1995). The offsetting migration mitigates the local wage and unemployment effects of immigration by dispersing the effects to broader regions and across the nation.[9]

SUMMARY AND CONCLUSIONS

To the extent that regional economies are continuously near a neo-classical equilibrium, persistent regional pockets of poverty should be rare, and regional labor demand policies would likely be ineffective at reducing poverty. Yet there are many theoretical reasons why regional economies may not be near a neoclassical equilibrium, so that pockets of high poverty persist. This leaves open the possibility that spatially targeted labor demand policies can reduce poverty.

Frictions in labor supply responses, particularly among the low-skilled, can preclude long-run equalization of labor market outcomes across regions, making it possible for labor demand redistribution to re-duce poverty rates. And even if economies converge towards a long-run interregional equilibrium, significantly long disequilibrium adjustment processes provide avenues for increased labor demand in high poverty areas having long-lasting or even permanent poverty-reducing effects. Migration and commuting responses to asymmetric demand shocks may be sufficiently sluggish or incomplete that the residents of a region are greatly affected by a localized labor demand shock.

In metropolitan areas, incomplete supply responses to deconcentra-tion of job growth underpin the spatial mismatch hypothesis. Incomplete commuting and migration responses can be derived from a number of alternative explanations, including the accessibility of transportation, a lack of information on job opportunities, and discrimination in housing and hiring. Thus, movement of jobs in large metropolitan areas from central cities to their suburbs can create persistent pockets of poverty in inner cities. Policies that effectively stimulate the demand for skills in central cities that are consistent with the skills of their residents have the potential to lift them out of poverty. In our empirical assessment, metropolitan area poverty rates will be touched upon in Chapter 6 and more directly assessed in Chapter 7.

The low density of rural areas and their lack of transportation, lack of formal child care, and constraints on information have been offered as explanations both for and against employment growth affecting ru-ral poverty. To the extent that these factors mostly lead to incomplete migration and commuting responses in rural areas, poverty rates can become greatly affected by localized rural employment growth. This is most likely to be true in the most remote rural areas, which will be a key topic in Chapter 8.

One overriding conclusion that can be drawn from this chapter is that local labor demand can theoretically be expected to influence poverty in an area. This relationship is likely to vary by the size, location, and spatial configuration of the area. Thus, antipoverty policies may likely need to be designed for the particular circumstances of the area. Moreover, given that migration and commuting responses are inversely related to the geographical extent of the labor market—e.g., workers are more likely to travel to the next county for a job than to the next state—we also anticipate different poverty-rate responses to employment growth, depending upon the spatial extent of the labor market. To assess these different issues, our empirical analysis begins in the next two chapters at the state level, followed by county- and metropolitan-area level analysis in Chapters 6 through 8.

Notes

Epigraphs. These three quotations appear in Peters and Fisher (2004), p. 28; Graves and Knapp (1988), p. 3; and Evans (1990), p. 515.

1. These studies do not focus on whether there are persistent effects on poverty, but Partridge and Rickman (2003a) find permanent changes in employment rates, which could translate into a permanent change in poverty.
2. These effects are not related to labor supply shocks (such as welfare reform) that affect labor force participation, which are discussed in the next chapter.
3. The larger industry-mix effect on poverty does not relate to a simple multiplier effect. All else being equal, the creation of an equal-paying job should have the same multiplier response regardless of whether it is attributable to industry mix or competitiveness. In addition, because the multiplier employment response shows up in the competitiveness term regardless of the exogenous source of the increase in jobs, the industry-mix effect is understated when both it and competitiveness are included in a poverty-regression equation.
4. Surveys of the spatial mismatch literature can be found in Gobillon, Selod, and Zenou (2003); Holzer (1991); Ihlanfeldt and Sjoquist (1998); and Kain (1992).
5. These also could underlie the population deconcentration to the extent that it preceded the shift in jobs.
6. A related factor that may contribute to spatial concentrations of poor households is return migration (see Borjas [1996] for a description of return migration). In this case, people who migrated to another location may have failed to establish

themselves or may have been disappointed and returned to their original location (other causes for return migration include returning to established social networks). Yet it would seem that disadvantaged individuals would be more likely to return-migrate because they may be more susceptible to experiencing an economic disappointment in their new destination. Nord (1998) argues that migration can lead to localized persistence of poverty rates, but he disputes the human-capital explanation for this outcome. He instead contends that the poor and nonpoor alike tend to migrate to areas that have a favorable occupational structure for their skill set. For the poor, that implies an occupational structure that requires few skills and many entry-level jobs, all of which may be conducive to a higher poverty rate in a particular place. More affordable housing in low-income nonmetro areas reinforces the attraction of the poor to these areas. In personal correspondence dated March 31, 2004, Nord notes that the existence of job openings for the poor in high-poverty counties is consistent with these locales being "good places to survive but poor places to prosper."

7. Tiebout sorting is the process whereby individuals choose their location of residence based on the combination of location characteristics that most suits their likes and dislikes. The result of Tiebout sorting is a collection of neighborhoods (communities) in which residents of each neighborhood have similar tastes.

8. Leichenko (2003) finds support for the premise that segregation of American Indians leads to lower incomes. But her study argues that the underlying economic mechanisms on tribal reservations are poorly understood, and it questions whether traditional economic measures provide an accurate reflection of tribal community incomes.

9. Card (2001) posits that there are few offsetting native migration effects. Instead, he finds that local labor markets in gateway cities respond to greater foreign immigration through lower wages. Card's study suggests that there is not yet a consensus regarding the response of native migration to foreign immigration.

4

An Empirical Analysis
of State Poverty Trends

Welfare Reform vs. Economic Growth

Our growing economy is giving more and more families a chance to work their way out of poverty.
— President Clinton, quoted in the *New York Times* (1998), "Black and Hispanic Poverty Falls, Reducing Overall Rate for Nation"

The resulting drop in welfare rolls is without precedent. Historically, welfare rolls haven't declined often, even during economic expansions . . . The real reason for the historic decline is that we finally said welfare recipients have to work and that work was preferable to getting a government check.
— Rep. Bill Archer, R-Texas (1998), "Welfare Reform's Unprecedented Success," *Washington Post,* August 10, 1998

If thrown into a job market in which others were being laid off, these would-be workers would find themselves competing for already-scarce jobs.
— Daniel P. McMurrer and Isabel V. Sawhill (1997), "Planning for the Best of Times," *Washington Post,* August 18, 1997

Federal welfare reform and the acceleration of economic growth happened in close proximity. The timing led to competing claims that each was responsible for declining poverty in the late 1990s. Some held that the economy was primarily responsible for the reduction in welfare caseloads, while others emphasized the role of welfare reform. Still others credited both, citing the interaction between a strong economy and welfare reform (Moffitt 1999).

The near-synchronicity of the two events makes it difficult to disentangle their relative effects on welfare caseloads or poverty reduction using national data. Although poverty reduction was not an explicit goal of federal welfare reform (Ellwood and Blank 2001), future attempts to reduce poverty at the national or regional level should be guided by an understanding of the determinants of the 1990s changes. Using regional data along with national data to examine the connections between economic growth, welfare reform, and poverty should help to pin down those determinants more closely.

Despite the close timing at the national level, not all states implemented the welfare reform measures at the same time, and many states experimented with waivers to the AFDC program before passage of the 1996 welfare reform act. In addition, not all states shared equally in the economic prosperity of the late 1990s. This potentially makes state-level analysis more fruitful in disentangling the relative effects of welfare reform and a robust economy on poverty reduction. If welfare reform underlies the reduction in poverty, then, other things being equal, states that took advantage of AFDC waivers and implemented TANF sooner should have experienced greater reductions in poverty. State-level variation in economic performance and welfare policy also makes it possible to examine whether welfare reform was more successful in a strong economy.

It should be cautioned, however, that failure to find effects at the state level does not automatically translate into an absence of such effects at the national level. Migration from economically underperforming states to high-performing states reduces both the adverse effects on poverty in the poorly performing states and the positive effects on poverty in the better performing states. Likewise, strong growth nationwide may reduce poverty in all states, but there could be insufficient variation in poverty-rate performance across states to identify such a trend using only state-level data. A similar case could be made for the assessment of welfare policy at the state level. Nonetheless, state-level analysis remains useful for state policymakers in terms of determining what types of growth and labor market outcomes most affect poverty in their states.

EMPIRICAL EVIDENCE AT THE NATIONAL LEVEL

As shown in Table 4.1, numerous empirical studies have found a positive relationship between the U.S. unemployment rate and the official poverty rate. For samples with ending dates prior to 1984, the aver-

Table 4.1 National Estimates of U.S. Unemployment and Poverty

Study	Time period	Estimated effects[a]
Blank (1993)	1959–1983	0.66
	1983–1989	−0.28
Blank (2000)	1960–1979	0.27
	1980–1989	−0.05
	1990–1998	0.08
Blank and Blinder (1986)	1959–1983	0.69
Cutler and Katz (1991)[b]	1959–1989	0.36–0.45
Richard Freeman (2001)	1959–1999	0.28–0.44
	1969–1999	0.34–0.42
Donald Freeman (2003)	1979–1999	0.72–0.98
Haveman and Schwabish (2000)	1960–1972	0.65
	1973–1981	0.20
	1982–1992	0.11
	1993–1998	0.45
Powers (1995)	1959–1982	0.58
	1983–1992	−0.17
Romer and Romer (1999)	1969–1994	0.44–0.49
Tobin (1994)	1961–1990	0.39

[a] Estimated percentage-point poverty rate change for a 1.00 percentage point increase in the unemployment rate. Some studies simply used the male unemployment rate. Where there was a choice between short-run and steady-state estimates, short-run estimates were selected.

[b] A trend variable for 1983–1989 produced estimates from 0.32 to 0.54, indicating an unaccounted-for rise in unemployment in the 1980s.

SOURCE: Authors' compilation.

age unemployment coefficient suggests that every percentage point reduction in the unemployment rate reduces the poverty rate by about 0.5 percentage points. However, several studies done in the 1980s found a weaker link. To be sure, the average coefficient for samples that primarily consist of years in the 1980s is about zero, while Blank (1993, 2000) and Powers (1995) find a slightly negative relationship. This suggests to researchers that growth no longer benefited those at the bottom of the distribution. Even for 1990–1998, Blank (2000) finds only a slight reversal of the 1980s trend. Freeman (2001) argues that the reason for the weaker link between poverty level and economic growth is the reduction in real wages for workers with low skills and education.

Haveman and Schwabish (2000), however, find that the positive relationship between unemployment and poverty reestablishes itself during the 1993–1998 period, as the estimated coefficient rises nearly to its average pre-1980s level. For samples running from the 1960s to at least the early 1990s, the authors find the average increase in the poverty rate after a one-point increase in the unemployment rate to be about 0.4 percentage points.

To help reconcile these results, we examine, in Table 4.2, three simple models that follow the approaches of Blank and Card (1993) and Bartik (2001) and that are based on U.S. Census Bureau data (though we use national data rather than regional data). Table 4.2 shows regressions of the annual change in the overall U.S. poverty rate for 1960–2002 on the change in the U.S. unemployment rate, the percent change in U.S. real median family income, and three time-period dummies.[1] Poverty rates are expected to be positively related to changes in unemployment rates, while they are expected to be inversely related to changes in median household income.[2]

Column (1) reports that a 1.00-point decline in the unemployment rate is associated with a 0.25-point fall in the poverty rate, whereas a 1.00-point increase in median family income results in a 0.15-point fall in the poverty rate. The poverty rate declined in these two categories an average of 0.57 and 0.26 points faster per year during the 1960–1973 and 1993–2001 periods than during the 1974–1980 and 1981–1992 periods (the latter being the omitted period).

To test whether poverty rates are more sensitive to economic conditions when the labor market is especially tight, column (2) adds a low-unemployment-rate indicator for the 12 years in which the rate was 5 percent or below, and an interaction of this indicator with the change in the unemployment rate. The results are strongly consistent with the arguments made by Freeman (2001). A 1.00-point drop in the unemployment rate is associated with a 0.73-point decline in the poverty rate when the unemployment rate is less than or equal to 5 percent, but with only a 0.23-point decline when the unemployment rate is above 5 percent. To check on whether there was a lagged unemployment response, column (3) reports the results obtained when the lagged change in the unemployment rate is added to the model. These results indicate that the coefficient corresponding to the lagged unemployment rate is marginally significant, but that the other results are essentially unchanged.[3]

Table 4.2 Change in U.S. Overall Poverty Rate Regressions, 1960–2002

	(1) (abs. value t-stat)	(2) (abs. value t-stat)	(3) (abs. value t-stat)
Change in unemployment rate	0.25 (4.22)	0.23 (3.84)	0.23 (4.01)
Lag change in unempl. rate			0.11 (1.52)
(Low unempl. rate) × (change in unempl. rate)[a]		0.50 (2.80)	0.50 (3.19)
% Δ in real median family income[b]	−0.15 (3.57)	−0.13 (3.05)	−0.12 (2.88)
Dummy 1960–1973[c]	−0.57 (3.88)	−0.51 (3.36)	−0.60 (3.89)
Dummy 1974–1980[c]	0.04 (0.24)	0.05 (0.30)	0.06 (0.31)
Dummy 1993–2002[c]	−0.26 (2.65)	−0.16 (1.25)	−0.18 (1.61)
Low unempl. rate[a]		−0.18 (1.16)	−0.09 (0.58)
Constant	0.22	0.20	0.19
R^2	0.77	0.82	0.84
DW	1.95	2.07	2.01
N	43	43	42

NOTE: Numbers in parentheses are absolute value of t-statistic. The dependent variable is the 1960–2002 change in the overall poverty rate except in column (3), where the time period is 1961–2002. The variables are measured in first-difference form to mitigate any spurious trends and unit roots. The t-statistics are adjusted to correct for heteroscedasticity of an unknown form. The mean (std. dev.) for the change in the overall poverty rate is −0.24 (0.78); for the change in the unemployment rate it is −0.01 (0.93); and for the percentage change in real median family income it is 1.4 (2.4). Blank = not applicable.
[a] The low-unemployment-rate indicator variable is for the 12 years when the unemployment rate was 5 percent or below.
[b] When the regression in column (2) included a variable in which the percentage change in real median family income interacted with the low-unemployment indicator, it was insignificant ($t = -0.40$).
[c] The year dummies reflect the War on Poverty and the robust economic growth of the 1960–1973 period, the sluggish economic growth in the latter 1970s, and the rapid economic growth and welfare reform changes that commenced in 1993. The omitted period is 1981–1992, which represents the years of the Reagan and first Bush administrations, a period of rapidly increasing income inequality.
SOURCE: Family poverty rates can be found at U.S. Census Bureau (2004d). Real median family household income can be found at U.S. Census Bureau (2006a,g). Unemployment rates can be found at BLS (2006c).

In sum, these simple models lend support to the notion that the initial strength of the labor market is a key factor in determining whether economic growth reduces the poverty rate. It is especially true that a rising tide lifts all boats when the tide is already high. Yet, because the time dummies only imperfectly control for events such as welfare reform, the results should be interpreted with some caution.

STATE-LEVEL EMPIRICAL STUDIES OF LABOR DEMAND AND POVERTY

Although national studies typically use the unemployment rate as the primary indicator of economic performance, regional studies use a wider variety of labor market indicators. This is at least partly attributable to the added complexity introduced by spatial economic interactions such as migration. Table 4.3 contains a summary of findings for various regional aggregations.

As the table shows, regional studies also find a positive relationship between poverty and unemployment rate; the average coefficient across all samples equals about 0.5. This is remarkably close to the average national estimate, given that regional studies typically include more variables such as additional labor market indicators. As is consistent with the national pattern, Bartik (2001) reports that the poverty-unemployment link is weakened in the 1980s and strengthened in the 1990s, while Freeman (2003) also finds a stronger association in the 1990s.

A smaller number of studies include employment rates or labor force participation rates as indicators of labor demand strength. The corresponding reported coefficients are smaller in absolute value than the average unemployment coefficient. The coefficients range from –0.12 (Albrecht, Albrecht, and Albrecht 2000) to –0.30 (Levernier, Partridge, and Rickman 2000). The studies find different responses across gender lines and across metropolitan vs. nonmetropolitan areas.

Although most studies capture the influence of employment growth indirectly through including unemployment, employment, or labor force participation rates, employment growth has also been examined for its antipoverty role. In panel studies of metropolitan areas, Bartik (1993a, 1996) finds a negative and statistically significant link between

Table 4.3 Previous Studies of Regional Poverty and Economic Performance

Study	Sample	Dependent variable	Estimated effects[a]
Albrecht, Albrecht, and Albrecht (2000)[b]	Nonmetropolitan counties 1990	Household poverty rate	% females employed full time: −0.12 % males employed full time: −0.28
Bartik (1993a)[c]	Metropolitan areas 1973–1989	Person poverty rate	Unemployment rate: 0.33 Employment growth: blacks: −0.4 whites: −0.1
Bartik (1996)	Metropolitan areas 1975–1987	Probability of being in poverty translated into person poverty rate	Unemployment rate equivalent to employment growth effects: female: 0.69 male: 1.09 Employment growth: female: −0.33 male: −0.20
Bartik (2001)	21 States/regions 1967–1997 1967–1979 1980–1989 1990–1997	Person poverty rate	Unemployment rate: 0.37 0.65 0.37 0.58
Blank and Card (1993)	9 census divisions 1967–1991	Family poverty rate	Unemployment rate: 0.28

(continued)

Table 4.3 (continued)

Study	Sample	Dependent variable	Estimated effects[a]
Crandall and Weber (2004)	Census tracts 1990–2000	Person poverty rate	Employment growth: low initial poverty tracts: −0.11 medium initial pov. tracts: −0.35 high initial poverty tracts: −0.77
DeFina (2004)	Panel of states 1991–2001	Person poverty rate	Unemployment rate: 0.32[d]
Richard Freeman (2001)	Panel of states 1959–1999 1989–1998	Person poverty rate	Unemployment rate: 0.27–0.41 0.37
Donald Freeman (2003)	9 census divisions 1979–1989 1990–1999	Person poverty rate	Unemployment rate: 0.45[e] 0.65
Gundersen and Ziliak (2004)	State level 1980–1999	Family poverty	Unemployment rate: 0.50[f] 1% empl./pop. growth: −0.15
Levernier, Partridge, and Rickman (2000)	U.S. metro and nonmetro counties 1990 census	Family poverty rate	Empl./labor force: metro: insignificant nonmetro: −0.81 Employment growth: insignificant Labor force participation rate: female: −0.30 male: −0.13

| Morgan and Kickham (2001) | Panel of states 1987–1996 | Child poverty rate | Female unemployment: 0.63 |
| Tobin (1994) | Changes for states 1979–1987 | Person poverty rate | Unemployment rate: 0.71 |

[a] Estimated percentage-point poverty rate change for a 1-percentage-point increase in the unemployment rate, employment rate, or labor force participation rate, or for a 1 percent increase in employment growth.

[b] Reported effects are direct effects from the poverty regression and do not include simulated indirect effects from other estimated equations.

[c] Unemployment value reported in Bartik (1996, p. 167, Table 5), and employment-growth values reported in the executive summary of Bartik (1993a).

[d] The coefficient was obtained by using the elasticity reported in Table 2 for all persons and calculating the coefficient using the reported mean in Table 1 for the official census poverty rate and mean U.S. unemployment rate for 1991–2001.

[e] For comparability, these estimates are for poverty rates that are unadjusted for regional differences in inflation.

[f] Calculated using the average U.S. family poverty rate of 11.04 percent for 1980–1999 and estimated elasticities from column 1 of Table 1.

SOURCE: Authors' compilation.

job growth and the poverty rate. Using a cross section of counties for 1990, Levernier, Partridge, and Rickman (2000) fail to find a link between lagged employment growth and poverty, even when omitting other measures of labor market strength. Even so, Crandall and Weber (2004), using 1990 and 2000 census tract data, find that employment growth over the decade reduced poverty, and that the largest effects occurred in tracts that had the highest initial levels of poverty.

WELFARE REFORM AND POVERTY

Thirty years of experience with the Great Society should have taught us at least one important lesson: welfare reform is not cruel; welfare is.
  —Stephen Moore (1997), director of fiscal policy studies at the Cato Institute, *Ending Welfare Reform as We Know It*, Cato Institute

The states are ending welfare as we know it—but not poverty.
  —Robert Kuttner (2000), coeditor of the American Prospect, "The States Are Ending Welfare as We Know It—but Not Poverty," *Business Week*, June 12, 2000

Significant public policy changes related to the working and nonworking poor were implemented during the 1990s. One key initiative was a major expansion of the Earned Income Tax Credit in 1993 (Box 4.1). Another major change was the Clinton administration's accelerated issuance of state waivers from AFDC, which also began in 1993 (CEA 1999; Ellwood and Blank 2001). Most waivers made welfare more restrictive, such as by adding sanctions and time limits. Probably the decade's largest initiative was PRWORA, the 1996 welfare reform legislation that replaced AFDC with TANF. This reform eliminated the welfare entitlement and placed a strict 60-month lifetime welfare limit on most recipients, while putting stringent requirements on states to shift most recipients into work by 2002 (Ellwood and Blank 2001). Finally, states were given great freedom to set the parameters of their programs.

The CEA (1999) and O'Neill and Hill (2001) argue that welfare reform was the impetus behind the reduced number of welfare case-

---

Box 4.1 Earned Income Tax Credit

The federal EITC is a refundable tax credit that dates back to 1975. It was originally designed to return to low-income workers their share of Social Security taxes, but it has evolved into a more aggressive antipoverty program for the working poor with children. Its refundable nature gives it powerful effects in reducing poverty.

In 2003, the EITC gave a small maximum tax credit of $382 for childless heads; this credit phased out at an earned income level of $11,230 for singles and $12,230 for married couples. For couples with children, the EITC was considerably more generous. For a single or married couple with two children, the 2003 tax credit equaled 40 percent of earned income until it reached a maximum of $4,204 at an earned income of $10,500. After an earned income of $13,750 for single parents with two children ($14,750 for a married couple), the EITC declined at a rate of about 21 percent of additional earned income until it was phased out at $33,692 ($34,692 for married couples).

In 2004, an additional 18 states had their own EITC, up from 10 states in 1998. Montgomery County, Maryland, also had its own EITC (and Denver had one earlier in the decade). Almost all of the states or localities piggyback on the federal EITC. The 2004 state credit equals between 4 and 43 percent of the federal credit (15 percent is about the median). However, five states—Iowa, Maine, Oregon, Rhode Island, and Virginia—have nonrefundable credits.

SOURCES: Johnson (2001); Johnson and Lazere (1998); Llobrera and Zahradnik (2004); IRS (2003).

---

loads. Yet Figlio and Ziliak (1999) and Bennett, Lu, and Song (2002) conclude that the vast majority of the decline in recipients was due to the strong economy and not to welfare reform, which is consistent with the findings of Bartik and Eberts (1999) and Hoynes (2000a) as well as those cited earlier in this chapter. Blank's (2002) comprehensive review of the literature suggests that welfare reform and the strong economy both reduced welfare usage, but that interaction between the two makes the precise shares difficult to determine.

Even if welfare reform did reduce caseloads, welfare programs may have had only a modest influence on overall poverty rates, for several reasons. For one, welfare recipients compose a small fraction of the total number of people who live below the poverty threshold (less than one-fifth after 1999). For another, the TANF program may have only redistributed the income of poor households from benefits to earnings and the EITC. Despite the high employment rates of women who left welfare (Blank and Schmidt 2001), their incomes are only slightly above what they were when those women were welfare recipients (Moffitt 2002).

Schoeni and Blank (2000) report that initially state AFDC waivers and TANF together reduced state poverty rates by 2.0–2.5 percentage points, all else being equal, though the effects of TANF were not uniform. They further report that low-income, female high-school dropouts did not benefit from implementation of TANF. Likewise, Bennett, Lu, and Song (2002) find that TANF is associated with lower income among poor male and poor female high-school dropouts. Hence, even if TANF reduced poverty rates, it could have done so while at the same time hurting the prospects of the poorest of the poor, many of whom likely have mental or physical disabilities (Freeman 2001). In fact, Moffitt (2002) reports that the women characterized by low job skills, poor health, or disabilities that left welfare have lower income than those that remain on welfare.

Even if welfare reform has a relatively small average effect on poverty rates, there may be certain administrative policies that have stronger effects. For example, the CEA (1999) finds that the various AFDC waivers and TANF rules have differing effects on state caseloads. Policies that sanction recipients for not finding work were found to have large effects in reducing welfare caseloads, while caps on welfare payments to families did not.

Third, welfare reform has spillover effects (Bartik 2002a,b) on other groups that are not current or former welfare recipients. Welfare reform not only pushes current welfare recipients to find employment, it also discourages many qualified households from enrolling in the first place. For example, results from randomized experiments in Florida suggest that potential welfare recipients with very young children are more likely than those with older children to remain off public assistance in order to conserve its availability for future periods (Grogger and Michalopoulos 2003). The combination of those who exited welfare programs and those who were discouraged from enrolling in welfare programs expanded the low-skilled labor supply from what it would have been in the absence of welfare reform. Bartik (2000) estimates that welfare reform ultimately increases the labor supply of females without a bachelor's degree by approximately 3 percent, whereas the resulting decrease in wages causes other less-skilled workers to exit the labor force. His results suggest that for every 10 recipients shifted from welfare to the labor market, two or three low-wage workers exit the labor force. Hence, poverty rates could actually increase through the decline in wages and the related labor force withdrawal. To offset these displacement effects, Bartik argues, the U.S. economy needs an additional 300,000–400,000 jobs.[4]

Extending his analysis, Bartik (2002a,b) finds significant spillover effects from welfare reform concentrated among single women and among male high school dropouts. The spillovers produce wage declines for these groups, and employment gains by single women from welfare reform are almost fully offset by the employment declines of male high school dropouts. A clear implication of Bartik's work is that welfare reform will be felt well beyond those directly affected, reinforcing the need for broader macro studies rather than studies focusing solely on former recipients. In fact, spillovers may explain the findings of Gundersen and Ziliak (2004), which suggest that TANF raised poverty rates for married couples, a group that is less likely to be directly affected by welfare programs.

EMPIRICAL MODEL

Our empirical methodology for examining state poverty trends is outlined in Box 4.2. Because states vary in their poverty rate trends, economic performance, and welfare policies, individual states provide independent information, making it possible to disentangle the separate effects of the various potential factors underlying poverty. In general terms, the approach involves examining whether, on average, changes

Box 4.2 Methodology for Examining State Poverty Trends

Basic Model: The basic model can be written as

$$(i)\ \text{POV}_{st} = \beta 1\ \text{LABORMKT}_{st} + \pi 1\text{WELFARE}_{st} + \eta 1\ \text{DEMOG}_{st} + \varphi 1\text{STATECHAR}_{st}$$
$$+ \sigma_s + \sigma_t + e_{st},$$

where POV is the poverty rate. LABORMKT is a vector of labor market measures including employment growth, unemployment rates
by gender, employment rates by gender, and industry structure.
WELFARE is a vector of variables; it accounts for timing differences
across states in the implementation of AFDC waivers and TANF.
Although endogeneity between poverty rates and welfare policy
adoption would bias the coefficients, Ziliak et al. (2000) found
no statistical difference between states that applied for AFDC
waivers and those that did not. STATECHAR includes the percentage of the state population residing in metropolitan areas. DEMOG
includes demographic controls such as the age distribution of the
population, the educational attainment of the adult population
aged 25 and older, the rate of international immigration, and the
teen birthrate.

The state fixed effects, σ_s, account for unmeasured variables
that cause persistent differences across states in poverty rates,
including long-term demographic effects. Any persistent spatial
spillovers across states also would be captured by the state fixed
effects. The year fixed effects, σ_t, capture common poverty trends
across the nation, such as those attributable to the business cycle,
to aging of the baby-boom generation, or to federal policy changes such as expansion in the EITC (or common national effects from
welfare reform). Some studies that utilize state panel data include
state-specific time trends. We believe that these trends overcontrol
for missing variables, actually picking up much of the time-vary-
ing influence of the other explanatory variables (also see Wallace
and Blank 1999). The final term, e_{st}, is the stochastic term that
reflects random variation in poverty rates.

in a variable over time in a given state affect its poverty rate. Regarding employment growth, the estimated relationship will reflect, on average, how much state poverty rates change over time in response to annual deviations in job growth rates. Likewise, variables are included that reflect the timing of AFDC waivers and the implementation of TANF.

Inclusion of other variables (for example, demographic factors) helps to isolate the effect of the economy and the effect of welfare reform on poverty rates. Time-fixed effects are included to account for uniform national effects, leaving only time-series variation across states to be explained. The empirical approach also accounts for all persistent long-term state differences in poverty rates by including fixed effects for states. Among other things, these fixed effects account for persistent differences in poverty that may relate to equilibrium labor market differences.

Labor Market Variables

Many argue that the unemployment rate, although affected by growth, is the best measure of demand for those in the labor force near or below the poverty line, because they are the most likely to experience unemployment spells (Schoeni and Blank 2000). Though commonly used at the national level, the unemployment rate does not suffice as a sole measure of the strength of regional labor markets. For one thing, regions have different equilibrium unemployment rates (Partridge and Rickman 1997b,c). A 5 percent unemployment rate would be a remarkable achievement for West Virginia but a sign of severe distress in North Dakota. Yet, measured in terms of job growth or per capita incomes, both states have struggled in recent decades. As a comparative measure, their relative unemployment rates are not particularly informative.

Even in the context of changing labor market conditions, the equilibrium unemployment rate can change (Partridge and Rickman 1997b,c), and about one-third of newly created jobs are taken by previously non-employed individuals, residents who were not officially part of the labor force or counted as unemployed (Partridge 2001). This group is particularly important because many less-skilled individuals may only be informally attached to the labor market, particularly females and former welfare recipients.

Therefore, Murphy and Topel (1997), Hoynes (2000a), and Levernier, Partridge, and Rickman (2000) suggest that the employment-population ratio is another important labor market indicator. The employment-population ratio captures unique effects because it is particularly related to the availability of all nonemployed workers and is a measure of the potential size of the untapped labor supply. Because women are more prone to enter and exit the labor force for household reasons, the female employment-population ratio particularly reflects their labor market attachment. A high employment rate also suggests that the employment prospects of marriageable men and women have improved, which may improve the marriage market and eventually reduce poverty among current single-female household heads (Hoynes 2000a; Ellwood and Jencks 2004).

Job growth also is included as an indicator of the labor market. Through vacancy and job-chain effects, job growth may have additional poverty-reducing effects beyond reducing unemployment or increasing labor force participation. Job growth also may be correlated with an increased number of hours worked (such as through overtime) or conversion from part-time to full-time employment status. Strong job growth also allows workers to move up the occupational job ladder and increase their wage rate (Andersson, Holzer, and Lane 2002, 2003; Felsenstein and Persky 1999; Peters and Fisher 2004). Bartik (1996) argues that employment growth is more likely to reflect labor demand and is based on more accurate data than the unemployment rate. But the most important reason to include job growth as an indicator in our model is that job growth is typically the primary goal of economic development policy (Bartik 2001). It is worth knowing whether job growth reduces poverty, even if its primary effects are indirect through reducing unemployment and increasing labor force participation.

Even though creating high-wage jobs is a common policy goal, low-wage jobs often form the entry-level positions that disadvantaged individuals need in the early stages of their careers to get accustomed to the workforce. By providing needed entry points, job growth in low-wage industries such as trade or personal services may have a greater poverty-reducing effect than overall job growth. For example, former welfare recipients are more likely to be employed in food service and retail than in higher-paying jobs (Brauner and Loprest 1999). Andersson, Holzer, and Lane (2002, 2003) find that workers with persistently low-wage jobs—defined as those earning less than $12,000 (1998 $) for at least three consecutive years—tend to be concentrated in various service and retail sectors. A high-wage industry composition may primarily benefit the middle class and may even increase the size of welfare rolls (Bartik 1996, 2001; Bartik and Eberts 1999, p. 138), though Raphael (1998) reports mixed results.

On the other hand, wage premiums may play a role in changing poverty rates. The loss of manufacturing jobs (Bluestone 1990), a shift in demand towards high-skilled occupations (Cutler and Katz 1991), and declining unionization (Freeman 1993) have been noted as possible causes for increased poverty and income inequality. Using 1993–2000 national data, Foster-Bey and Rawlings (2002) find that, holding all else constant, single mothers tend to have higher wages in manufacturing and health services than in other fields. The data left Foster-Bey and Rawlings sufficiently optimistic to conclude that it may be worthwhile to target certain low-wage sectors as possible employment outlets for less-skilled workers.

Greater public-sector employment also may be associated with lower poverty (Bartik 2001), which may be the result of high unionization and administratively set wage rates in the public sector. Levernier, Partridge, and Rickman (2000) also found strong poverty-reducing effects from having a higher employment share in goods-producing industries. Besides the direct effects stemming from the possible loss of higher-paying jobs, greater industry dislocation in general is associated with large declines in postdisplacement earnings (and greater potential for long-term joblessness) as workers are forced to switch to occupations for which they have less training (Carrington and Zaman 1994).

Welfare Reform Variables

The effect of welfare reform on state poverty is examined using three variables. Following the approaches of the CEA (1999) and Figlio and Ziliak (1999), a TANF variable is added that measures the proportion of the year that TANF was in effect. For example, if TANF was in effect for the entire year, the variable takes a value of 1.00, while if TANF was only in effect for half the number of days in the year, the variable takes a value of 0.50. In addition, many states implemented various features of TANF in the form of waivers to the previous program, AFDC.

Thus, a second variable is included; it is calculated as the sum of the yearly proportions that various AFDC waivers were in effect before TANF implementation.[5] The AFDC waivers include five types: 1) the imposition of time limits on receipt of welfare benefits, 2) waiver of job exemptions from work requirements for child care, 3) imposition of a cap on the amount of welfare benefits that a family can receive, 4) increased earnings disregards, and 5) sanctions for not having a job or being engaged in a work-related activity. If these waivers relate to successful features of TANF, their implementation likely reduced poverty rates in these states.

The third variable is the natural logarithm of the average monthly welfare payment to a family.[6] Generosity of welfare benefits mechanically increases income and reduces poverty, but the adverse effects on a person's incentive to work may more than offset this effect and increase poverty (Moffitt 1999).

Person-Based Poverty Factors

As was described in Chapter 2, poverty rates also contain a demographic component. For example, poverty rates are higher for female-headed families nationally, and regions with higher shares of female-headed families are found to have higher rates of poverty, other things being equal (Levernier, Partridge, and Rickman 2000). Female heads of families are the sole potential wage earners, are disproportionately young, less educated, and face child care constraints that limit full participation in the workforce. In a related point, Levernier, Partridge, and Rickman also report a positive relationship between a county's average number of children per family and its poverty rate.

Higher poverty also occurs among minorities. Some possible reasons for higher poverty among blacks include discrimination (Ihlanfeldt and Young 1996; Kirschenman and Neckerman 1991), their residence in inner cities (Corcoran et al. 1992; Cutler and Glaeser 1997; Holzer 1991), more attractive nonmarket opportunities (Viscusi 1986), and low educational attainment (Smith and Welch 1986). Yet Levernier, Partridge, and Rickman (2000) find that after controlling for numerous county characteristics such as labor market performance, education, and other demographic characteristics, counties with greater shares of African Americans had lower poverty. This led the authors to suggest that it is the interaction of race with the other characteristics that underlies higher poverty among African Americans. For example, Levernier, Partridge, and Rickman (2000) found that employment growth and increased educational attainment had greater poverty-reducing effects in counties with high African American population shares. Nevertheless, they report finding higher poverty in counties with greater shares of non–African American minorities.

Other theories suggest there is an interaction between the economy and person-based factors. Higher poverty that results from poor regional economic performance may adversely affect family structure (such as by increasing single female headship because of a lack of opportunities for males), which further perpetuates the poverty cycle. This has been argued to underlie both inner-city poverty (Wilson 1987) and rural poverty (Albrecht, Albrecht, and Albrecht 2000). As was discussed in terms of spatial mismatch in Chapter 3, inner-city poverty may be perpetuated through negative neighborhood effects, such as less exposure to well-educated and employed residents and more exposure to the unemployed and to persons engaged in illicit activities.

REGRESSION RESULTS

Descriptions of the variables included in the model and descriptive statistics can be found in Tables 4.4 and 4.5. The results for alternative specifications of the model shown in Box 4.2 appear in columns (1)–(7) of Table 4.6.[7] Different combinations of explanatory variables produce the alternative sets of results: the interpretation of the regression coefficients varies depending upon what other explanatory variables are included in the estimated equation. For example, when unemployment and employment growth are both included, the employment growth coefficient is interpreted as being the effect employment growth has on poverty other than through its indirect influence on poverty through unemployment. The R^2 statistics reported at the bottom of the table reflect the combined explanatory power of the included variables.

Table 4.4 Variable Definitions and Data Sources

Variable	Notes on calculation and data source
% persons in poverty	U.S. Census Bureau Current Population Survey: *Historical Poverty Tables: Table 21*
Employment growth rate	$[(\text{Total Empl.})_t - (\text{Total Empl.})_{t-1}]/(\text{Total Empl.})_{t-1}$, *BEA Local Area Personal Income SA25 Series*
Male employment rate	U.S. Department of Labor, *Geographical Profile of Employment and Unemployment*, various years
Female employment rate	U.S. Department of Labor, *Geographical Profile of Employment and Unemployment*, various years
Male unemployment rate	U.S. Department of Labor, *Geographical Profile of Employment and Unemployment*, various years
Female unemployment rate	U.S. Department of Labor, *Geographical Profile of Employment and Unemployment*, various years
% female-headed households	The data is interpolated for intervening periods between census years. U.S. Census Bureau: *Household and Family Characteristics, STF1*, from 1980, 1990, and 2000 censuses
Population share ≤ age 19	U.S. Census Bureau
Population share ages 20–24	U.S. Census Bureau
Population share ≥ 65	U.S. Census Bureau
% pop. ≥ 25, h.s. grad, not 4-yr. college grad	U.S. Census Bureau, *USA Counties 1998*
% pop. ≥ 25, 4-yr. college degree	U.S. Census Bureau, *USA Counties 1998*
% workforce union members	Barry T. Hirsch and David A. Macpherson, *Union Membership and Coverage Database from the CPS (Documentation)*. http://www.unionstats.com
% workforce union-covered	Barry T. Hirsch and David A. Macpherson, *Union Membership and Coverage Database from the CPS (Documentation)*. http://www.unionstats.com

# births per 1,000 female teens 15–19	U.S. Census Bureau, *USA Counties 1998*; and National Center for Health Statistics, *National Vital Statistics Reports*
Relative competitiveness wage rate	(Relative Wage Rate)/(Relative Wage Mix). *BEA Local Area Personal Income SA07 Series*
Relative wage mix	Ratio of state employment-weighted U.S. industry wages to U.S. average wage rate. *BEA Local Area Personal Income SA07 Series*
Industry employment shares[a]	*BEA Local Area Personal Income SA25 Series*
Proportion of yr. TANF implemented	Council of Economic Advisers (1999), *Table W-1*
Proportion of yr. time limit in effect, AFDC waiver	Council of Economic Advisers (1999), *Table W-1*
Proportion of year family caps in effect, AFDC waiver	Council of Economic Advisers (1999), *Table B*
Proportion of year job exemption, AFDC waiver	Council of Economic Advisers (1999), *Table B*
Avg. fam. monthly welfare payment	U.S. Department of Health and Human Services
International immigration	"Immigrants Admitted, by State of Intended Residence." Various issues of the *Statistical Yearbook of the Immigration and Naturalization Service*

[a] Industry-mix employment growth is calculated by multiplying state employment in each industry by the corresponding national growth rate and then summing the products across industries. Competitiveness-employment growth is then total-employment growth minus the industry-mix growth.

SOURCE: Authors' compilation.

Table 4.5 Descriptive Statistics of the 48 Contiguous States and the District of Columbia, 1984–2000 (%)

Variable	Mean	Standard deviation
% persons in poverty	13.51	4.21
Employment growth rate	0.022	0.018
Male employment rate	71.55	3.98
Female employment rate	55.71	5.31
Male unemployment rate	5.74	1.81
Female unemployment rate	5.77	1.95
% female-headed households	10.99	2.29
Population share ≤ age 19	0.29	0.03
Population share ages 20–24	0.08	0.01
Population share ≥ age 65	0.13	0.02
% pop. ≥ 25, h.s. grad, not 4-yr. college grad	57.38	5.58
% population ≥ 25, 4-yr. college grad	21.20	4.98
% workforce union members	14.03	5.87
% workforce union-covered	16.11	5.99
# births per 1,000 female teens 15–19	52.60	15.12
Relative competitiveness wage rate	0.94	0.15
Relative wage mix	1.00	0.02
Construction employment share	0.05	0.01
Mining employment share	0.01	0.02
Durable goods employment share	0.08	0.03
Nondurable goods employment share	0.06	0.03
Trade sector employment share	0.21	0.02
Farm employment share	0.03	0.03
Low-paying service employment share	0.04	0.03
High-paying service employment share	0.25	0.04
Trans., comm., and pub. util's empl. share	0.05	0.01
Finance, insurance, and real estate empl. share	0.07	0.02
Proportion of year TANF implemented	0.17	0.36
Proportion of yr. time limit in effect, AFDC waiver	0.01	0.08
Proportion of yr. fam. caps in effect, AFDC waiver	0.03	0.15
Proportion of yr. job exemption, AFDC waiver	0.03	0.15
Average family monthly welfare payment ($)	321.19	115.08
Per capita welfare recipients	0.04	0.02
International immigration/population share	0.007	0.024

SOURCE: Authors' calculations.

Labor Market Results

The results in column (1) of Table 4.6 indicate that current and lagged state employment growth reduce poverty.[8] Summing the three employment growth coefficients yields a sustained acceleration of job growth equal to one percentage point, which reduces the poverty rate by about one-half of a percentage point.

In terms of the other variables, a greater composition of high-wage industries is negatively associated with the poverty rate. High-wage industries may provide above-poverty wage rates for those who otherwise may not be able to obtain them, and may also reduce poverty through positive spillovers on wages in other industries and employment multiplier effects through higher spending in the area.[9] Dropping *Wage mix* and replacing it with variables consisting of employment shares in various Standard Industrial Classification (SIC) aggregates does not change the other results.[10]

Because factors other than job growth may underlie changes in unemployment or labor force participation, unemployment rates and employment rates by gender are added to the column (1) model. For instance, if growth is primarily supply-driven, then strong employment growth increases unemployment rates and lowers employment rates (Partridge and Rickman 1999b), both of which would increase poverty rates; thus, the variables contain independent information. The additional labor market variables caused the lagged-employment variables to become quite insignificant, so these lags were dropped from the model.

The results of adding the employment and unemployment rates in column (2) reveal relatively stronger labor market effects on poverty for females. Morgan and Kickham (2001) likewise found fluctuations in female unemployment rates to be more important than those in male rates in explaining changes in child poverty rates. Given the inclusion of employment growth, the significance of the female employment rate and unemployment rate variables suggests that other poverty-reducing factors underlie their changes.[11] For example, teen birthrates are no longer significant with the inclusion of the additional labor market variables, suggesting that lower teen birthrates reduce poverty through increasing female employment rates. Except for the relative wage mix coefficient becoming insignificant, results for the other variables are qualitatively

Table 4.6 State Econometric Model Results (%)

	Dependent variable: percentage of persons in poverty						
	Specification (1)	Specification (2)	Specification (3)	Specification (4)	Specification (5)	Specification (6)	Specification (7)
Employment growth	-20.22 (3.55)	-11.70 (2.06)			-9.35 (1.61)	-8.92 (1.52)	-8.66 (1.48)
Empl. growth(-1)	-15.09 (2.61)						
Empl. growth(-2)	-13.52 (2.61)						
Empl. growth × DUM96					-20.28 (1.71)	-20.09 (1.66)	-22.33 (1.85)
Industry mix empl. growth				-41.81 (1.26)			
Competitiveness empl. growth				-18.68 (3.12)			
Ind. mix empl. growth(-1)				-76.09 (2.34)			
Comp. empl. growth(-1)				-11.84 (1.95)			
Ind. mix empl. growth(-2)				-28.44 (2.49)			
Comp. empl. growth(-2)				-13.70 (0.62)			
Male unemployment		0.13 (1.26)	0.19 (1.96)		0.15 (1.49)	0.15 (1.45)	0.16 (1.54)

	(1)	(2)	(3)	(4)	(5)	(6)	(7)
Female unemployment		0.23	0.25		0.22	0.22	0.20
		(2.27)	(2.45)		(2.13)	(2.14)	(1.97)
Male empl./pop.		−0.06	−0.05		−0.04	−0.05	−0.05
		(0.90)	(0.83)		(0.67)	(0.69)	(0.72)
Female empl./pop.		−0.18	−0.18		−0.20	−0.20	−0.20
		(3.55)	(3.55)		(3.83)	(3.70)	(3.80)
Metro share	−3.14	−8.39	−10.99	−6.03	−9.96	−10.78	−10.94
	(0.33)	(0.90)	(1.19)	(0.62)	(1.06)	(1.15)	(1.17)
Immigrants/pop.	−1.56	−4.20	−5.34	−0.65	−3.72	−1.43	−3.50
	(0.18)	(0.50)	(0.63)	(0.07)	(0.44)	(0.50)	(0.42)
Pop. share ≤ age 19	55.50	25.87	22.66	56.04	29.86	30.97	30.68
	(3.90)	(1.81)	(1.59)	(3.93)	(2.07)	(2.13)	(2.11)
Pop. share ages 20–24	−10.39	−9.06	−10.25	−1.99	−3.63	−2.63	−2.29
	(4.69)	(0.53)	(0.60)	(0.11)	(0.21)	(0.15)	(0.13)
Pop. share ≥ age 65	120.59	55.77	42.36	115.37	55.51	56.31	56.75
	(6.97)	(2.08)	(1.62)	(4.44)	(2.07)	(2.09)	(2.12)
% pop. h.s. grad, not 4-yr. college grad	−0.30	−0.23	−0.21	−0.29	−0.23	−0.23	−0.23
	(5.67)	(5.36)	(5.11)	(6.74)	(5.50)	(5.41)	(5.38)
% pop. college grad	−0.33	−0.27	−0.26	−0.32	−0.28	−0.27	−0.27
	(2.37)	(4.71)	(4.52)	(5.56)	(4.85)	(4.79)	(4.71)
Teen birthrate	0.04	0.03	0.04	0.04	0.03	0.03	0.02
	(2.37)	(1.45)	(1.96)	(2.01)	(1.35)	(1.33)	(1.12)
Wage mix	−22.89	−14.50	−17.96	−27.74	−12.97	−13.54	−12.73
	(1.92)	(1.22)	(1.52)	(2.27)	(1.09)	(1.13)	(1.07)
Sum of AFDC waivers						−0.03	
						(0.10)	

(continued)

Table 4.6 (continued)

	Dependent variable: percentage of persons in poverty						
	Specification (1)	Specification (2)	Specification (3)	Specification (4)	Specification (5)	Specification (6)	Specification (7)
Proportion of year family caps, AFDC waiver							−0.26 (0.56)
Proportion of year job exemption, AFDC waiver							−0.46 (0.95)
Proportion of year time limit, AFDC waiver							1.35 (1.96)
Proportion of year TANF implemented						−0.30 (0.34)	0.21 (0.22)
Log(monthly welfare payment)						0.65 (1.01)	0.67 (1.05)
State fixed effects	Y	Y	Y	Y	Y	Y	Y
Year fixed effects	Y	Y	Y	Y	Y	Y	Y
R^2	0.86	0.87	0.87	0.86	0.87	0.87	0.87

NOTE: Absolute value of t-statistic is in parentheses. t-statistic = 1.96 corresponds to 0.05 significance level based on a two-tailed test. t-statistic = 1.645 corresponds to 0.05 significance level based on a one-tailed test. Blank = not applicable.

SOURCE: Authors' generated regression results.

unchanged. The coefficient for employment growth is reduced, but some of the poverty-reducing benefits are now captured in the unemployment and employment rate coefficients, suggesting the employment growth coefficients now understate their total poverty effect. Nevertheless, the continued significance of the employment growth coefficient suggests that employment growth reduces poverty through channels other than by reducing unemployment or increasing labor force participation—e.g., it results in fewer part-time workers.[12]

In fact, omitting the employment growth variable in column (3) causes the male unemployment rate coefficient to become significant while the female coefficient increases only slightly. It appears, then, that the effect of male unemployment on poverty derives primarily from the benefits of job growth. The teen birthrate coefficient again becomes significant, which suggests that strong job growth lowers teen birthrates.

Because job growth in association with in-migration likely has limited effects on unemployment and employment rates, state employment growth is separated into two components: growth that is attributable to a state's composition of fast-growing industries nationally, and growth that is idiosyncratic to the state.[13] This tests the proposition that idiosyncratic growth induces greater in-migration (Partridge and Rickman 1999a) and reduces the employment growth effects on poverty. The corresponding results in column (4) indicate stronger poverty-reducing effects in industry-mix employment growth vs. idiosyncratic employment growth, though the difference is not statistically significant at conventional levels.[14]

To examine whether there are any differences in a tight labor market, we interacted job growth with a dummy variable for 1996–2000, a period of strong national economic growth and low unemployment. As shown in column (5), when the interaction variable is added to the regression, the combined effect of employment growth on poverty for 1996–2000 is more than three times the magnitude of the other years.[15] This result accords with Partridge and Rickman (2002), who report lower interstate net migration shifts in the late 1990s; they argue that the uniformly strong economy provided little incentive to regionally migrate, and that new jobs were increasingly likely to be filled by less-skilled original residents.[16]

Welfare Policy Results

The TANF variable is found to reduce poverty, but the estimated relationship is not close to being statistically significant (column [6]). In a sensitivity analysis conducted to examine whether differences in TANF implementation strategies affect poverty, the TANF variable interacted with a variable that measured the overall work incentives of the state's TANF program as assessed by Blank and Schmidt (2001). Blank and Schmidt rated the work incentives as weak, mixed, or strong; these were assigned values of 0, 1, or 2. In results not shown, the interaction term was negative but statistically insignificant (slope = -0.13, $t = 0.64$). Adding separate state-time trend variables or lagged poverty rates (also not shown) did not strongly affect the welfare-reform results. So, as is consistent with the findings of Gundersen and Ziliak (2004) for families, there is no evidence to suggest that implementation of TANF led to a reduction in a state's poverty rate, even if the TANF program contained stronger work incentives.

Nevertheless, the uniform effects of TANF across the nation would be captured in the time fixed effects, and there may be insufficient time-series variation across states to tease out a relationship between TANF and poverty. Twenty-one states implemented TANF during 1996 for an average duration of 0.21 years, whereas 48 states had implemented TANF by the end of 1997 for an average duration of 0.86 years. For 1998, TANF was operational for the entire year in all 49 contiguous states (the number counts the District of Columbia as a state). So some caution should be exercised in drawing conclusions from these results alone, particularly for the effect of welfare reform at the national level.

Nevertheless, the aggregate AFDC waiver and monthly welfare payment variables also are not statistically related to poverty, confirming the insignificance of the TANF variable. The results also barely change when the aggregate AFDC waiver variable is dropped and replaced by the proportion of the year that various individual waivers were in effect (column [7]).[17]

Of the individual AFDC variables, only the time limit variable is significant, but its sign is positive. Although time constraints were unlikely to be binding by 2000, the waiver may have induced individuals to leave welfare, or discouraged others from becoming recipients, to avoid exhausting their allotted time. Families also may have entered and exited welfare as a buffer against adverse labor market outcomes, in a manner akin to unemployment insurance (Moffitt and Pavetti 2000).[18] Omitting the family payment cap variable and the job exemption variable causes the time limit coefficient to lose statistical significance, suggesting that collinearity may partially underlie the result.[19] Even dropping the teen birthrate or employment growth variables does not alter the welfare policy results.[20] TANF and AFDC waiver dummy variables that were interacted with employment growth also had insignificant coefficients.

When the unemployment and employment rate variables are dropped, the coefficient on the generosity of welfare payments becomes positive and significant.[21] Thus, welfare-benefit generosity appears to have adverse labor supply effects on females (Blank and Schmidt 2001; Moffitt 1999), increasing poverty (Gundersen and Ziliak 2004). Overall, besides generosity of welfare benefits or the potentially adverse poverty effects of time limits, there is little evidence to support the hypothesis that welfare reforms altered poverty rates. However, this is not to conclude that welfare reforms did not affect welfare dependency (Bartik 2002b).[22]

Demographic Poverty Effects

Increased educational attainment also reduces state poverty rates. Column (1) results show that a 1.00-percent increase in the adult population holding a high school degree (relative to dropouts) is associated with a 0.30-percentage-point reduction in poverty, while a corresponding change in the college graduate share is associated with a 0.33-point reduction. Higher shares of population at both ends of the age spectrum increase state poverty rates. The share of the state's population that is composed of immigrants is not a significant factor underlying changes in state poverty, which may be related to offsetting internal migration. Likewise, the share of the population that resides in a metropolitan area does not have a statistically significant relationship to poverty.

SIMULATION OF INDIVIDUAL EFFECTS

Because the estimated relationship between employment growth and poverty reduction varies across specifications, a more structured set of equations is needed to isolate the total effect of a particular factor, including any indirect interrelationships. Six equations are specified and econometrically estimated. The equations correspond to the following dependent variables: 1) the poverty rate, 2) the female unemployment rate, 3) the male employment rate, 4) the female employment rate, 5) the male employment rate, and 6) the teen birthrate. The simulation focuses on the predicted quantitative poverty effects regardless of statistical significance.

The estimated poverty equation roughly corresponds to the estimated equation in column (2) of Table 4.6.[23] However, as previously noted, because employment growth may influence the rates for unemployment, employment, and teen births, the coefficients corresponding to the employment growth variables are likely to understate the poverty-reducing effects of job growth. So, separate equations are specified to account for the influence of job growth on these other variables. The welfare variables are included in each equation in an attempt to unravel their effects on poverty. Other control variables generally thought to be exogenous also are added, including state and time fixed effects.

Simulated Employment Growth Effects

The estimated equations (Table 4.7) reveal that employment growth lowers unemployment rates and increases employment rates, particularly for males.[24] Thus, in addition to having a direct poverty-reducing effect, job growth also lowers poverty through reducing unemployment rates and increasing labor force participation. Although job growth has larger effects on male labor market outcomes, female labor market outcomes are most associated with poverty. So, as shown in Table 4.8, the indirect poverty-reducing effects of employment growth are larger for females. Summing the unemployment and employment rate effects reveals that a 1.0-percent acceleration in job growth indirectly lowers poverty rates by nearly 0.3 percentage points, which exceeds the estimated direct reduction of less than 0.2 points. This confirms the estimated employment growth effect in Table 4.6 of 0.5 percentage points when employment and unemployment rates are omitted from the estimated equation.

Employment growth also reduces teen birthrates (column [6] of Table 4.7), and teen birthrates influence poverty both directly and indirectly through affecting unemployment and employment rates. Column (1) of Table 4.8 shows that, through its influence on teen birthrates, acceleration of employment growth reduces poverty.[25]

Simulated Effects of Welfare Policies

Similar calculations can be made for implementation of welfare-reform measures (Table 4.8). Aside from its direct effects, welfare reform can affect poverty through influencing labor market outcomes such as employment and unemployment rates. Likewise, welfare reform can affect poverty through reducing teen birthrates, which can influence poverty both directly and indirectly through measured labor market outcomes.

AFDC waivers directly increased poverty (column [2] of Table 4.8) but indirectly reduced poverty through generally improved labor market outcomes, such as increased employment rates. On the other hand, early implementation of TANF was directly associated with a slight reduction in poverty but was indirectly associated with larger increases in poverty. Although the estimates (not shown) are generally statistically insignificant, implementation of TANF was associated with increased unemployment rates and reduced employment rates. TANF also appeared to be positively related to teen birthrates. It is intuitive that unemployment rates increase when welfare recipients exit and seek employment. However, the employment rate effects are counterintuitive and difficult to reconcile with the fact that many of those leaving welfare found employment. Nevertheless, the results suggest that if there were any poverty benefits of TANF, they are not reflected in the labor market outcome estimates in Table 4.7.

The remaining welfare policy variable, average monthly benefit payment, both directly and indirectly increases poverty (column [4] of Table 4.8). Aside from its influence on poverty through unemployment and labor force participation, a 1.0-percent increase in monthly welfare benefits increases the poverty rate by more than 0.5 percentage points.

Table 4.7 Estimated Simulation Equations (%)

Ind. variable/dependent variable[a]	Poverty	Female unempl.	Male unempl.	Female empl./pop.	Male empl./pop.	Teen birthrate
Employment growth	-10.67	-16.93	-25.10	10.52	12.40	-59.05
Employment growth(-1)	-5.22	-16.74	-23.93	11.05	21.99	-7.90
Employment growth(-2)	-2.78	-20.11	-23.71	17.99	23.16	18.14
Male unemployment[b]	0.11					
Female unemployment	0.19					
Male employment/population	-0.06					
Female employment/population	-0.19					
Population share ≤ 19 years	28.12	36.45	22.84	-86.17	-30.44	58.95
Population share 20–24	-5.63	0.69	6.56	16.13	38.44	18.40
Population share ≥ 65	64.44	73.18	23.21	-174.65	-151.63	221.30
% population h.s. grad, not 4-year college grad	-0.23	-0.12	-0.10	0.13	0.05	-0.19
% population college grad	-0.26	-0.09	-0.05	0.16	-0.02	-0.01
Teen birthrate	0.02	-0.02	-0.03	-0.11	-0.01	
Wage mix	-15.56	10.18	7.17	48.58	31.46	182.35
Proportion of year job exemption, AFDC waiver	-0.44	-0.51	-0.32	1.05	0.65	-1.80
Proportion of year family caps, AFDC waiver	-0.24	0.32	0.38	-0.52	-0.13	0.01
Proportion of year time limit, AFDC waiver	1.23	0.33	-0.20	0.70	1.19	1.67

Proportion of year TANF implemented	-0.08	0.92	0.83	-2.21	-0.52	3.28
Log(monthly welfare payment)	0.59	0.54	0.71	-1.72	-0.83	3.06
R^2	0.869	0.858	0.852	0.944	0.914	0.959

[a] The models include state and year fixed effects.
[b] Blank = not applicable.
SOURCE: Authors' generated regression results.

Table 4.8 Simulated Total Effects (%)

Channel of influence	1% acceleration empl. growth	1 year effects, all AFDC waivers	1 year implement TANF	1% increase in monthly welfare benefit
Direct	−0.187	0.546	−0.075	0.547
Female unempl.	−0.105	0.027	0.175	0.104
Male unempl.	−0.082	−0.015	0.091	0.080
Fem empl./pop.	−0.074	−0.234	0.420	0.321
Male empl./pop.	−0.034	−0.103	0.031	0.049
Teen births	−0.690	−0.041	0.048	0.076
Total	−1.183	0.180	0.690	1.177

SOURCE: Authors' calculations.

Higher welfare payments also increase unemployment and reduce labor force participation, particularly for females. This translates into an additional increase in poverty of more than 0.5 percentage points. Higher welfare payments also increase teen birthrates, and this effect increases poverty by slightly less than 0.1 points. That includes the indirect teen birthrate effects on unemployment and labor force participation. The simulation results (summed together in column [4] of Table 4.8) suggest that a 1.0-percent increase in monthly welfare benefit payments increases the poverty rate by approximately 1.2 percentage points.

CONCLUSION

Regression analysis of reduced-form equations over the 1984–2000 period reveals that state employment growth reduces poverty. There is some evidence that the magnitude of effect was greater during 1996–2000, a period of tight labor markets nationwide. This suggests that state economic development policy is more likely to reduce poverty when national labor markets are strong. A looser national labor market likely engenders greater interregional migration in response to differential state economic performance, reducing potential poverty-reducing effects on disadvantaged original residents. Similarly, there is evidence that job growth that is attributable to a favorable industry composition has a larger estimated effect than competitiveness growth. This likely follows because strong nationwide growth in particular industries induces less interregional migration, forcing firms to hire locally, which reduces poverty more.

Employment growth reduces poverty through reducing unemployment and increasing labor force participation. Beyond working through these channels, job growth also has direct effects such as those associated with more vacancies, increased hours worked among part-time employees, and conversion from part-time to full-time employment status. Simulations reveal that, both through its direct effect and through indirect effects from unemployment and labor force participation, a 1.0-percent acceleration in employment growth reduces poverty by 0.5 percentage points. Yet we find job formation to be associated with lower teen birthrates: lower teen birthrates reduce poverty, including indirectly through increasing employment rates. After accounting for these direct and indirect effects from teen birthrates, the estimated poverty-reducing impact of a 1.0 percent greater employment growth rate rises to 1.2 percentage points.

The simulations also suggest that welfare reform does not contribute to lower poverty rates. Overall, AFDC waivers and TANF increase unemployment as recipients are pushed into the labor market, though the AFDC waivers also increase the overall employment rate. The simulated total impact on poverty of a state implementing AFDC waivers or TANF is positive. There also is no evidence of welfare reform reducing teen birthrates, the estimated effect of which is slightly positive. In addition, there is no evidence that welfare reform reduces poverty when state employment growth is stronger.

Yet increasing the generosity of welfare benefits is found to increase poverty. Generosity of welfare benefits is positively associated with unemployment and negatively associated with labor force participation. The unemployment effect is stronger for males—likely because they have a stronger attachment to the labor force—while labor force participation effects are stronger for females. Welfare benefit generosity also is positively associated with teen birthrates. Through its direct and indirect effects, a 1.0-percent increase in welfare benefit generosity increases the poverty rate by 1.2 percentage points.

In summary, state-level analysis suggests that job creation reduces poverty. There is some evidence to suggest that a stronger national economy increases the likely effectiveness of state and local job growth policies. There is no evidence that AFDC waivers or implementation of TANF reduces poverty; in fact, other things being equal, they may increase poverty. It is more likely that the continued decline in the purchasing power of the median state average monthly welfare payment reduces poverty by increasing the net benefits of being employed (including supplemental government support for such things as housing or child care). In fact, the average median-state monthly welfare payment fell by almost 21 percent on an inflation-adjusted basis between 1990 and 2000.[26] The results also suggest that employment growth, more so than welfare reform, was responsible for the late-1990s decline in poverty.

Although states provide a natural laboratory in which to examine the relationships between economic growth, welfare reform, and poverty, these relationships at the state level should differ from those observed nationally, and added labor market features such as commuting imply that the state results would not apply to local labor markets either. This cautions against the simple extrapolation of state-level results either to national or to local policymaking. Nevertheless, the added nuances of state labor markets make it paramount that state-level data be used to derive insights regarding state economic development policies, welfare reform policies, and poverty. For this reason, the next chapter will consider state case studies in attempting to provide additional context to these findings and help illuminate how poverty rates are linked to economic conditions and state and federal welfare reforms.

Notes

The three epigraphs at the start of the chapter come from the *New York Times* (1998), Archer (1998), and McMurrer and Sawhill (1997). The two epigraphs at the start of the section "Welfare Reform and Poverty" come from Moore (1997) and Kuttner (2000).

1. Other models consider the family poverty rate, but the conclusions are unchanged, so these models are not reported. The variables of the models reported are measured in first-difference form to mitigate any spurious trends and unit roots.
2. The 1960–1973 time-period dummy reflects the War on Poverty and expansion of the safety net during the period. The 1974–1980 dummy reflects the stagflation of that period. The 1993–2002 indicator captures the expansion of the EITC and the wide-scale welfare reform changes. The omitted category is the

1981–1992 period, which represents the Reagan-Bush-I years of scaling back the safety net as well as a period of rapidly increasing income inequality. Since 1981–1992 is the omitted period, the time-period coefficients are interpreted as the effects for the periods relative to the effect for the 1981–1992 period.

3. We also estimated another model (not shown) that added an indicator for the 1997–2002 period to examine whether the TANF era was different. Yet there was no evidence that the effects of the 1993–1996 period differed from 1997–2002. The F-statistic equaled 0.02 for the null hypothesis that the 1993–1996 and 1997–2002 coefficients were equal.

4. The additional workers induced into the labor force as a result of welfare reform complicate efforts to assess how job growth affects poverty rates. In contrast to the 1980s, for people who were both on welfare and above the poverty line, job growth may have helped move large numbers of them off welfare without dropping them into poverty. Yet the increased labor supply may crowd out some welfare-ineligible less-skilled workers from employment, pushing them below the poverty threshold. Consistent with this point is that former recipients who have left welfare in the post-TANF era have only slightly lower poverty rates than those remaining on TANF (Moffitt 2002).

5. We also tried including a binary indicator variable if any AFDC waiver was in effect, but the results were unaffected.

6. Given its representation in nominal log form, the time fixed effects capture any national inflation effects. Note that official state-inflation deflators are unavailable.

7. Each regression includes both time fixed effects and state fixed effects. The coefficients reflect the average effect of within-state time series variation in the corresponding variable on state poverty rates that is not common across the nation.

8. The lagged employment growth variables for periods beyond two years were nowhere near being significant and were omitted from the final model.

9. The wage-composition measure is calculated by weighting national industry wages with state employment shares and dividing this by the average national wage rate. A value in excess of unity indicates that the state has a greater composition of high-paying industries than the national average.

10. The industry employment share variables are statistically significant below the 0.01 level. In order of magnitude, the greatest poverty-reducing effects are found for increased shares in transportation, communications and public utilities, mining, finance, insurance and real estate, trade, manufacturing, low-skilled services, construction, high-skilled services, and government. Low-paying services include hotel and motel services, personal services, and private household services. The remaining categories of services are considered high-paying.

11. For comparison to regional studies that used the unemployment rate as the sole indicator of labor market conditions, a regression also was run replacing employment growth with male and female unemployment rates and using column (1) independent variables (except teen birthrates). The resulting coefficients were 0.27 ($t = 3.34$) for male unemployment and 0.36 for female unemployment (3.73). These estimates lie below the average estimate from the literature of 0.5 reported

in Table 4.3. Slope interactions for male and female unemployment rates for 1993–2000 were jointly significant (p-value = 0.02), in which the 1993–1998 unemployment effects became 0.41 for males and 0.44 for females. Thus, there was evidence that lower unemployment rates became more influential in reducing poverty during the 1990s economic expansion compared to the 1980s.

12. Partridge (2003) finds that strong job growth is associated with falling shares of the workforce that are involuntarily working part-time for various reasons, including economic. Partridge concludes that a strengthening economy means that these part-time workers can increasingly find full-time work. Similarly, he finds that strong employment growth increases the employment share that is voluntarily employed part-time, which also can reduce poverty if this comes from the ranks of the jobless.

13. Employment growth attributable to the state's composition of industries is calculated by multiplying the state employment share in each industry by the corresponding national growth rate and then summing the products across industries. Competitiveness employment growth, then, is total employment growth minus the portion attributable to industry composition.

14. A Wald test fails to reject the equality of the coefficients for the two growth components (for all years jointly) with a p-value of 0.16. Although the coefficient values differ noticeably, a lack of time-series variation in the industry-mix variables likely underlies the large standard errors. Recall from Note 3 in Chapter 3, however, that the coefficient for the industry-mix employment variable understates its effect because part of that effect is picked up in the competitiveness coefficient.

15. This is obtained by summing the coefficients of the employment growth variable and the interaction terms to obtain the 1996–2000 effect, then comparing it to the employment growth coefficient.

16. An alternative formulation, in which employment growth interacts with a dummy variable for 1997–2000, and an additional dummy variable for 1988, 1989, and 1996, produced less significant results. The reason for the alternative formulation was to determine whether unemployment below 5 percent (as happened in 1997 and afterwards) had a differential effect from that of around 5.5 percent (such as occurred in the years 1988, 1989, and 1996).

17. Not all waivers were simultaneously included in the regression because of the high degree of collinearity among some of the waiver variables. Yet experimentation with the other waivers did not yield additional significant results. Ziliak et al. (2000) find that, in terms of changes in welfare caseloads, it did not matter how AFDC waivers were treated. Gundersen and Ziliak (2004) find the same for state family poverty rates.

18. Families in Alabama were observed to leave welfare before their time limits were reached, using it like unemployment insurance (Crowder 2001).

19. Gundersen and Ziliak (2004) likewise find no family poverty-reducing effects of pre-TANF welfare reform measures, though such measures did reduce the depth of poverty for black- and female-headed households.

20. Several additional regressions were performed to test the sensitivity of the results by adding other variables to the column (6) model. When a variable measuring

structural change in the previous two years was added, it was negative but insignificant, while the other results were unchanged. Industrial structure change is defined as one-half the sum of absolute changes in the share of one-digit industry employment shares between periods t and t-2. It is interpreted as the share of the workforce that would have to shift one-digit shares such that the two years have the same industrial composition (Levernier, Partridge, and Rickman 2000). In another case, a variable measuring percent of employment covered by unions was negative and significant when it was added to the model, yet the other results were essentially unchanged. Nevertheless, replacing union coverage with the percentage of employees that are union members produced an insignificant result. The share of the population that was African American and the share that was Caucasian were insignificant when added, while the other results were not notably affected. The sample is limited to 1984–1999 when racial categories are included because racial categories for 2000 are not directly comparable to those used in previous years.

21. The t statistic equals 2.76; the largest change results from dropping the female employment rate.

22. We again caution that identifying the effects from TANF is very problematic, and almost all of the identification comes from pre- and post-1997 effects, since that is the year when almost all states implemented TANF (Bitler, Gelbach, and Hoynes 2003). With separate time-period effects for the strong economy and other changes such as the EITC, it is virtually impossible to identify possible trend effects, such as whether the response to TANF changes with the passage of time.

23. The interaction of employment growth with the 1996–2000 indicator is not used because of the marginal significance of the interaction term, and because in the remaining four equations the interaction term was insignificant or the wrong sign. See Note 20 for results.

24. Although Hoynes (2000b) reports that metropolitan female employment rates are more cyclically sensitive, she examined responses to U.S. cycles, not local cycles.

25. Earlier in the chapter we reported that employment growth reduced poverty rates more from 1996 to 2000 relative to the rest of the sample, but the simulation results are not strongly affected by replacing lagged employment growth variables with employment growth that interacts with a dummy variable for 1996–2000. When we calculate the effects for the 1996–2000 period, we find that the estimated overall effects of employment growth rise only 0.07 percentage points. Despite larger direct poverty-reducing effects (e.g., the final column in Table 4.7), employment growth generally affected unemployment and employment rates less in the 1996–2000 period—though it reduced teen birthrates more—which overall slightly lowered the indirect poverty-reducing effects of employment growth.

26. The 1980s somewhat contradict falling real benefits as a primary causal factor because poverty rates did not decline, even as the inflation-adjusted median-state average welfare payment fell almost 20 percent.

5

State Economic Performance, Welfare Reform, and Poverty

Case Studies from Four States

[The Minnesota Family Investment Program], unlike welfare reform programs in many other states, was designed as an antipoverty approach to welfare reform, with goals of economic independence and self-sufficiency in addition to job placement.
 —Office of the Legislative Auditor, State of Minnesota (2000), *Welfare Reform*

If you look at the number of jobs that we're creating today, we're leading just about the Southeast in jobs created. We're going to have a positive job increase this year for the first time in four years, and they are good paying jobs. I think this administration has made great progress in moving people out of poverty.
 —Alabama Governor Bob Riley (AP 2004), responding to a report from the U.S. Census Bureau that Alabama had the eighth highest poverty rate in the nation in 2003

To provide more context and an in-depth understanding of the nexus between poverty, the economy, and welfare reform, we examine four states as case studies. The four states are Alabama, Minnesota, New Jersey, and Washington—one from each of the four major census regions. We chose these states not only for their geographic diversity but because they had varied economic experiences and approaches to welfare reform.

REGRESSION SAMPLE PERIOD ANALYSIS

Table 5.1 contains economic, poverty, and welfare-caseload statistics for the 1984–2000 sample period and the welfare reform subperiod of 1996–2000. Despite having the largest decline over the entire sample period, Alabama experienced a more modest poverty rate decline during 1996–2000, when poverty decreased from 14.0 to 13.3 percent compared to the U.S. decline from 13.7 to 11.3. For the 1996–2000 period, Minnesota's poverty rate declined the most of any state's; it went from 9.8 to 5.7 percent, greatly exceeding the national percentage-point decline. Because of that, Minnesota had the second lowest poverty rate in the nation in 2000. Washington experienced a more modest poverty rate decline during the late 1990s, a decade in which its poverty rate actually increased. In fact, Washington's poverty rate declined to 8.9 percent in 1998 before climbing back up to 10.8 percent in 2000. New Jersey's poverty rate only declined from 9.2 to 7.3 percent, falling short of the national decline in percentage points. Even so, this gave New Jersey the third lowest poverty rate in the nation in 2000.

As shown in Table 5.1, using the coefficients from column 7 of Table 4.4 and the 1996–2000 reported statistics for employment rates, unemployment rates, and employment growth, the predicted poverty changes for Alabama, Minnesota, New Jersey, and Washington are −0.7, −1.1, −1.4, and −1.2 percentage points.[1] Except for Minnesota, these estimates are remarkably close to the corresponding actual poverty rate changes. In addition, for comparability to the poverty studies that solely use unemployment rates, we multiply the unemployment coefficients reported in Note 11 of Chapter 4 for 1996–2000 (i.e., 0.41 for males and 0.44 for females) by the respective changes in state rates. The predicted changes in poverty rates then become −0.4, −0.6, −2.1, and −1.2 percentage points, respectively. Although these predicted effects are modestly smaller for Alabama and Minnesota and greater for New Jersey, they are similar to the first set of estimates.

Alabama

Alabama did not experiment with AFDC waivers; its only pre-TANF experimentation occurred with the Avenues to Self-Sufficiency

Table 5.1 State Case Study Statistics by Regression Sample Period (% change)

	Ala.	Minn.	N.J.	Wash.	U.S.
1984–2000					
Poverty rate[a]	−5.8	−3.4	−2.8	−0.5	−3.1
Empl. growth[b]	2.1	2.3	1.4	2.6	2.3
Male empl./pop.	0.1	1.9	−0.8	3.4	0.7
Fem. empl./ pop.	11.2	8.9	5.1	11.5	8.6
Male unempl.	−5.3	−3.5	−2.5	−4.3	−3.3
Fem. unempl.	−8.1	−2.4	−2.4	−4.2	−3.5
1996–2000					
Pred. poverty rate[c]	−0.7	−1.1	−1.4	−1.2	
Actual poverty rate	−0.7	−4.1	−1.9	−1.1	−2.4
Empl. growth	1.4	2.4	2.1	2.9	2.2
Male empl./pop.	−0.8	0.0	1.9	−1.2	0.6
Fem. empl./pop.	0.9	1.8	0.4	2.7	1.5
Male unempl.	−0.4	−1.0	−2.5	−0.7	−1.2
Fem. unempl.	−0.6	−0.4	−2.4	−2.0	−1.3
Welfare cases[d]	−45	−31	−55	−46	−53

NOTE: Blank = not applicable.

[a] The poverty rate, employment growth, and welfare cases are reported for the nation. The remaining variables are unweighted averages across states in the sample.

[b] "Empl. growth" is the annual percentage change in nonfarm employment; "Welfare cases" is the percentage change in welfare cases; and the remaining variables give the percentage-point difference between the beginning and the end of the period. Thus all categories measure percentage change.

[c] Predicted 1996–2000 change in poverty rates, based on 1996–2000 employment growth and changes in male and female unemployment and employment rates. See text for more details.

[d] Measured as the change in the total number of TANF recipients between August 1996 and June 2000 (ACF 2000).

SOURCE: Authors' compilation.

through Employment and Training and Services (ASSETS) program in three counties from 1991 to 1994 (Holcomb et al. 2001). Alabama implemented TANF on November 15, 1996. Welfare rolls declined 45 percent from August 1996 to June 2000 (DHHS 2000), and subsequently leveled off, partly because the cases that remained were the most difficult (AP 2000).

According to Holcomb et al. (2001), federal welfare reform led Ala-bama to initially replace education activities with job search activities as the primary focus. Compared to its AFDC program, Alabama im-posed harsher sanctions and increased enforcement for noncompliance, became less lenient in granting exemptions from work requirements to care for dependent children, and set the time limit for receiving cash assistance at the federal maximum of 60 months. Starting in 1998, a broader variety of activities were counted as "work" activities. In fed-eral Fiscal Year 1998, Alabama had an above-average share of TANF recipients engaged in job search or education activities and a below-average share in unsubsidized employment or in "any activity" (House Ways and Means Committee 2000). Overall, Blank and Schmidt (2001) rate Alabama as having mixed work incentives and give it low marks for low-earnings disregards.

Despite a larger percentage change in TANF program expenditures from 1995 to 2000, Alabama's average expenditure per family in 1999 was just under 50 percent of the U.S. average. Its average monthly wel-fare payment rose from $144 in 1996 to $162 in 2000, compared to an average increase across the sample of states of $319 to $338 over the same period. Only South Carolina ($141) and Mississippi ($117) had lower average monthly cash payments in 2000. Yet with the implemen-tation of welfare reform Alabama began spending significantly more on child care subsidies for working-poor families than it did on direct welfare benefits (AP 1999, 2001).

During the 1996–2000 period, Alabama's average annual employ-ment growth decelerated to 1.4 percent, while the average growth across states was 2.2 percent. This was associated with a 0.8 percentage-point decline in the male employment rate, compared to an unweighted aver-age employment-rate increase of 0.6 points for "all 49" states (counting the District of Columbia and excluding Alaska and Hawaii). The Ala-bama female employment rate increased 0.9 percentage points, while the unweighted state average increased 1.5 points. Although Alabama male and female unemployment rates declined by 0.4 and 0.6 percent-age points, they were well below the corresponding average declines across all states.

Accompanying the deceleration of employment growth in Alabama was a decline in manufacturing employment of 5.1 percent from the 1995 peak to 2000. By comparison, U.S. manufacturing employment growth peaked in 1998 and actually gained 0.1 percent between 1995 and 2000. The larger percentage decline in Alabama manufacturing, combined with a much greater share of employment in manufacturing (20.4 vs. 14.7 percent), likely contributed to its less favorable labor market performance and weak poverty reduction in the late 1990s. The WAGEMIX variable used in the regression models in Chapter 4 declined from a peak of 1.4 percent above-average wage composition of industries in 1994 to only 0.6 percent above by 2000. On a favorable note, from 1989 to 1999 the real median hourly wage increased 8.8 percent in Alabama, compared to 2.4 percent for the nation. The 20th percentile hourly wage increased 9.4 percent, compared to 5.6 percent for the nation (Mishel, Bernstein, and Schmitt 2001).

Minnesota

Minnesota has traditionally been known for its progressive and generous social policies. Minnesota did not implement AFDC waivers statewide, but in April 1994 Minnesota began its widely praised Minnesota Family Investment Program (MFIP) in seven counties (Bartik 2001; DHHS 2000). MFIP was expanded statewide in January 1998, when it became the state's TANF program.

MFIP merged the AFDC and Food Stamp programs into the state's cash assistance program. The program also increased the earned-income disregard and mandated employment of its recipients. MFIP's average monthly welfare benefit and income eligibility for child care and health benefits were significantly above their corresponding U.S. averages, while sanctions for noncompliance with the work program were less severe than in other states (Tout et al. 2001). Nevertheless, the maximum monthly benefit remained at $532 during the 1996–2000 period.

MFIP also subsidized child care costs through the state general fund, the federal Child Care Development Fund (CCDF), and federal TANF funds. The 2001 annual family income cutoff for child care assistance in Minnesota for a one-parent family of three was $42,304, the fourth highest in the nation. The maximum benefit level for a four-year-old in center care in 2001 was $8,208, the sixth highest in the nation (National Center for Children in Poverty 2004).

Early results from the MFIP pilot program in seven counties suggest that it increased employment levels and earnings of long-time welfare recipients and reduced poverty (Gennetian, Knox, and Miller 2000), while the results for short-term recipients are not as favorable (Tout et al. 2001). MFIP was modified, however, when it was expanded statewide under TANF. The State of Minnesota lowered the income standard for disenrollment from 137 percent of the federal poverty level to 120 percent, adopted the 60-month time limit, strengthened sanctions for noncompliance, and limited education and training possibilities (Tout et al. 2001).

In a critique of the work incentives of Minnesota's welfare system by the Minnesota Office of the Legislative Auditor, the office notes that from 1994 to 1999, welfare caseloads dropped 39 percent, which compared to 50 percent for the nation. Nine of ten neighboring states experienced larger declines (Office of the Legislative Auditor 2000, p. 25). The report (p. 52) further reveals that although welfare recipients' employment rates and the hours they worked significantly increased, during 1998 and 1999 less than one-half of welfare cases had a working adult in the home. In many of those that did, the adult worked only part time. Only one in four had jobs with health benefits, and those that had first left MFIP were among the more advantaged. Blank and Schmidt (2001) similarly rate Minnesota as having weak overall work incentives. Yet a study by the Minnesota Department of Human Services finds that 34 percent of welfare recipients left welfare within twelve months after MFIP was expanded statewide, and that 64 percent of those who left reported that they felt life was better under the new welfare system (Hopfensperger 2000). Another evaluation of MFIP concluded that employment and earnings increased more for those receiving housing subsidies (Center on Budget and Policy Priorities 2000).

Between 1996 and 2000, Minnesota's annual job growth averaged 2.4 percent. Surprisingly, this was associated with no change in Minnesota's male employment rate. Yet the female employment rate in Minnesota increased 1.8 percentage points, which was better than the average across all states. Although the male and female unemployment rates in Minnesota declined by 1.0 and 0.4 percentage points, this was less than the corresponding average decline across all states.

Accompanying overall strong employment growth in Minnesota was a smaller-than-average decline in manufacturing employment. As in the nation, manufacturing employment in Minnesota peaked in 1998; it then declined 0.9 percent from 1998 to 2000. This compares favorably to the larger U.S. decline of 1.7 percent over the same two-year period. Minnesota's wage composition of industries increased throughout the 1990s, reaching 0.9 percent above the national average by 2000. Median average hourly wages increased 12.8 percent from 1989 to 1999, while average hourly wages at the 20th percentile increased 13.6 percent (Mishel, Bernstein, and Schmitt 2001).

Thus it appears that income growth, more than increased employment rates or reduced unemployment rates, was responsible for Minnesota's greater-than-average reduction in poverty in the late 1990s. Minnesota's labor market was remarkably tight: its employment rate was the third highest in the nation in 1996 and by far the highest in 2000 (by more than a full percentage point). The 2000 female employment-population rate was nearly two percentage points above the closest state (Nebraska). Thus, strong job growth appears to have more directly affected those at the bottom and manifested itself more in increasing wage rates than in states with initially looser labor markets. And although Minnesota had lower-than-average reduction in welfare caseloads, its more generous assistance programs may have had a greater poverty-reducing effect than those of other states. To be sure, the significantly larger-than-predicted decline in Minnesota's poverty rate from 1996 to 2000 may have at least partly resulted from Minnesota's unique approach to welfare reform.

New Jersey

Along with Michigan, New Jersey was the first to implement a major AFDC waiver; it did so on October 1, 1992, under its Family Development Program. New Jersey changed its work exemptions, jobs sanctions, and caps on family welfare payments. The state first implemented TANF on July 1, 1997, as Work First New Jersey (WFNJ). The program sought to "help people get off of welfare and into a job" (New Jersey Department of Human Services 2006a). WFNJ was combined with other assistance programs to shift program focus from education and training to immediately placing recipients into work (Koralek et al. 2001). According to Blank and Schmidt (2001), New Jersey's TANF program contains strong work incentives, and compared to other states New Jersey has medium benefit generosity, medium earnings disregards, strict sanctions, and moderate time limits. If a recipient is unsuccessful in obtaining a job during an initial search, he or she must continue to seek work while participating in activities countable as "work" activities under federal law (Koralek et al. 2001).

From August 1996 to September 2000, New Jersey's welfare caseloads declined by 55 percent, slightly better than the U.S. average of 53 percent. Under contract from the state, Mathematica Policy Research Inc. tracked a sample of WFNJ families in a series of four surveys over approximately four-and-one-half years (Wood, Rangarajan, and Deke 2003). The firm found that 50 percent had left TANF, up from 34 percent three years earlier. Their monthly real income increased from $1,157 a year and a half after leaving TANF to $1,543 three years later, and the poverty rate among the former recipients declined from 65 to 45 percent over the final three years. On a less positive note, about one-tenth were off TANF and were not able to replace the lost welfare benefits with alternative income sources, though they tended to either go back on TANF or obtain employment within a year. Progress also slowed in later years with the weak economy and the greater difficulty in placing the remaining recipients. Because of temporary extensions to the five-year time limit, very few WFNJ recipients who reached the mandated limit had their benefits terminated. Individuals who reached their five-year limit on cash assistance may have qualified for Supportive Assistance to Individuals and Families (SAIF), which provided up to 24 more months of cash assistance, as well as child care and transportation support (New Jersey Department of Human Services 2006b).

Beginning in 2000, the state created a number of initiatives to assist former and current TANF recipients and low-income families. For example, New Jersey phased in a state Earned Income Tax Credit. In 2001, career advancement vouchers for up to $4,000 were made available to former recipients for additional training while they are working, and a program was started that provides monthly support payments of $200 for working recipients to close their cases.

Over the 1996–2000 period, New Jersey's average annual employment growth accelerated to 2.1 percent, 50 percent higher than the 1.4 percent posted for the entire 1984–2000 sample period. This was associated with a 1.9 percentage-point increase in the male employment rate and a 0.4 point increase in the female rate. The reduction in New

Jersey's male and female unemployment rates from 1996 to 2000 was approximately double the unweighted average for all states.

New Jersey experienced a smaller decline in manufacturing employment from 1998 to 2000 than the nation, though its manufacturing employment continued a long-term trend of decline. New Jersey's real median hourly wage decreased 0.5 percent from 1989 to 1999, while its 20th percentile real hourly wages fell 4.2 percent. Yet the state's 80th percentile real hourly wages increased 4.0 percent, exceeding the national increase of 3.4 percent (Mishel, Bernstein and Schmitt 2001). Its wage composition of industries increased throughout the 1990s until, in 2000, it was only 0.4 percent below the national average. Thus, New Jersey's income gains appeared to occur primarily near the top of the income ladder.

Washington

The State of Washington has long provided generous support for low-income families (Thompson et al. 2001). The only AFDC waiver that Washington implemented prior to TANF was a termination limit at the beginning of 1996 (DHHS 2000). Washington replaced its AFDC program, Success Through Employment Program (STEP), with Work-First. WorkFirst shifted the focus from education and training to immediate employment (Thompson et al. 2001). WorkFirst contained the federal 60-month time limit, generous income disregards, graduated sanctions, and a maximum monthly benefit for a family of three of $546 from 1996–2000. Blank and Schmidt (2001) characterize the overall work incentives in Washington's TANF program as being mixed: its high welfare-benefit generosity and lenient time limits provide weak incentives for welfare recipients to obtain employment. WorkFirst also initially included sufficient child care funding so that there was not a child care waiting list (Thompson et al. 2001).

The stated aim of WorkFirst is to help "financially struggling families find jobs, keep their jobs, get better jobs and build a better life for their children" (Washington WorkFirst 2006). A year after its implementation, Governor Gary Locke declared that the primary aim of Work-First was not to get people off of welfare but to "help [them] liberate themselves from dependency and poverty" (McDermott 2001). Yet the initial authorizing legislation set specific goals only for welfare caseload reduction, leaving the development of other outcome measures of the status of former recipients to the governor (McDermott 2001).

Welfare caseloads in Washington declined 46 percent from August 1996 to June 2000, or a little less than the national decline (DHHS 2000). The first evaluation of WorkFirst compared outcomes for female heads of households three quarters after leaving WorkFirst (fourth quarter 1998) to those for female heads three quarters after leaving AFDC (fourth quarter 1996). Compared to AFDC, WorkFirst was found to significantly reduce welfare use while increasing employment rates, hours worked, and total earnings (Washington State Institute for Public Policy 1999). But according to exit surveys given in 1998, half of leavers used Food Stamps after leaving TANF, more than half reported monthly cash incomes below the federal poverty threshold, 43 percent were cutting back on meal portions sometimes or often, and 24 percent were skipping meals altogether (McDermott 2001). Nevertheless, in a study of the postwelfare experiences of 1999 and 2000 TANF recipients, the 1999 recipients reported higher employment rates, wage rates, hours worked, and greater likelihood of fringe benefits such as health insurance than the 2000 recipients. This suggests that it takes time for former recipients to improve their postwelfare economic well-being (Klawitter, Griffey, and VanNynatten 2002).

For 1996–2000, Washington's annual job growth averaged a robust 2.9 percent. As in the nation, manufacturing employment in the state peaked in 1998, but over the next two years Washington experienced a steep 8.0 percent decline. One of the hardest-hit sectors was aerospace product and parts manufacturing, where employment declined from 112,000 in 1998 to 86,100 in 2000, a 23.1 percent drop. The losses appear to have had particularly adverse effects on males. Conversely, strong overall employment growth for the four-year period was associated with significant improvements in the female employment and unemployment rates.[2] Welfare reform likely contributed to an increased supply of females, which facilitated greater job growth, but given the hourly wages of these jobs, this growth had much more modest effects on income.[3] Thus, it appears that Washington's strong employment growth and welfare reform in the late 1990s had a more modest effect on reducing poverty than did the nation's.

CASE STUDY EPILOGUE: POST-2000 TRENDS

Given the change in economic fortunes brought about by the 2001 U.S. recession and the subsequent long-lasting weakness of the labor market, an examination of post-2000 trends in poverty rates, employment, and welfare caseloads for the case study states may provide additional insights. In a general way, they provide a limited out-of-sample test of the regression conclusion that the economy—not welfare reform—was responsible for the poverty decline in the late 1990s.

As Table 5.2 shows, poverty rates increased after 2000 in all case study states, while nonfarm employment ("Empl. growth") decreased, and manufacturing employment declined precipitously. These trends held true nationally as well. From the beginning of the recession in Feb-

Table 5.2 State Case Study Statistics for Postsample Period (% change)

	Ala.	Minn.	N.J.	Wash.	U.S.
Poverty rate[a]	1.7	1.7	1.3	1.8	1.2
Empl. growth[b]	−2.9	−0.9	−0.4	−2.0	−1.4
Mfg. empl. growth	−16.4	−13.4	−16.9	−19.5	−15.9
Male empl./pop.[c]	−2.0	−1.2	−3.8	−4.0	−3.0
Female empl./pop.	−1.4	−1.4	−0.2	−2.9	−1.4
Male unempl.	0.9	1.9	2.6	3.0	2.4
Female unempl.	1.5	1.4	1.6	1.6	1.6
Welfare cases, Feb. '01–Feb. '04[d]	2.9	4.0	−7.8	2.9	−4.6
Welfare cases, 2002–2003	6.3	0.3	−1.6	1.9	−0.7
Food Stamp cases, May '02–'03[e]	6.1	9.1	8.1	17.8	10.9

[a] "Poverty rate" is the cumulative percentage change in the poverty rate for persons from 2000 to 2003.

[b] "Empl. growth" is the cumulative percentage change in average annual total nonfarm employment over the 2000–2003 period, and "Mfg. empl. growth" is the comparable measurement for average annual manufacturing employment.

[c] Male and female employment-population rate change and male and female unemployment rate change statistics come from BLS (2005).

[d] "Welfare cases" is measured as the percentage change in the total number of TANF cash recipients over the relevant periods. Data from NCSL (2005).

[e] "Food Stamp cases" is measured as the percentage change in the number of Food Stamp caseloads over the period (Llobrera 2004).

SOURCE: Authors' compilation.

ruary 2001 to three years later in February 2004, welfare caseloads continued to decline nationally while poverty rose. Thus, as suggested by our regression results, a reduction in welfare caseloads does not appear to reduce poverty. For example, from Federal Fiscal Year (FY) 2001 to FY 2002, the number of U.S. single mothers without jobs increased by 181,000 (Children's Defense Fund 2003a). Even the number of welfare caseloads barely budged in 2003, decreasing only slightly, which suggests the economy drove both poverty rates and welfare caseloads.

Despite the reduction in welfare caseloads nationally, Food Stamp caseloads increased dramatically, a divergence that appeared with the implementation of welfare reform (Ziliak, Gundersen, and Figlio 2003). Unlike Food Stamps, welfare caseloads are less variable because they are not as tied to the economy; this is due to time limits for welfare caseloads and other state policies. The state-specific post-2000 experiences follow below.

Alabama

Following its pattern from 1996–2000, Alabama's economy underperformed compared to the nation's from 2000 to 2003, including a slightly greater-than-average percentage loss of manufacturing jobs. Despite continued investment by Honda, Mercedes-Benz, and Hyundai, Alabama lost 57,700 manufacturing jobs over the 2000–2003 period, and its losses were widespread across sectors (Wingfield 2004). The decline in Alabama's female civilian employment rate (and the increase in the female civilian unemployment rate), which the regression analysis shows to be strongly related to higher poverty, followed the national trend. This development likely underlies Alabama's increase in poverty.

Alabama's increase in the poverty rate exceeded the national increase. Correspondingly, in contrast to the national trend, Alabama's welfare caseloads increased for the three-year period beginning with the onset of the 2001 recession, particularly from 2002 to 2003. One likely reason for the increase in welfare caseloads is that Alabama raised the maximum family welfare payment from $164 to $215, which made more families eligible for payments since families previously making between $164 and $215 were ineligible because their income was above the maximum payment (Crowder 2003). Food Stamp usage increased

6.1 percent from May 2002 to May 2003, less than the national average (AP 2003).

Alabama also found that subsidizing child care was more expensive than paying welfare. In 2002, Alabama was one of seven states not to use available federal day care dollars because they were not matched with state money. In fact, a family of three earning $20,000 would not qualify for assistance (Children's Defense Fund 2003b). The next year, Alabama's Department of Human Resources trimmed enrollment in its child care subsidy program by not replacing those who had departed because of insufficient resources (Chandler 2003). Moreover, with the September 2003 defeat of Governor Riley's tax and accountability plan, the state scaled back its ALL Kids health care plan for poor children (Birmingham News 2003). Therefore, lackluster economic performance appears to increase poverty through reducing both employment opportunities and state financial assistance for those most likely to be affected by the economic downturn.

Minnesota

Post-2000, Minnesota's poverty rate increased more than the nation's, and its welfare caseloads also increased, whereas the nation's dropped. In contrast, Minnesota's labor market performance was not as weak, with both nonfarm and manufacturing employment declining less than that of the nation (Table 5.2). Minnesota's male employment rate declined less than the nation's, and its male and female unemployment rates both increased less than the nation's.

Welfare caseloads in Minnesota increased from February 2001 to February 2004, differing markedly from the continued nationwide drop. This is consistent with the late 1990s experience, in which welfare caseloads declined relatively less in Minnesota.

In 2003, the Minnesota legislature approved several major changes to MFIP proposed by incoming governor Tim Pawlenty (Minnesota Public Radio 2003). The governor's proposal was based on a pilot project in Dakota County that reported success in holding down welfare caseloads (Rosario 2003). Among the changes enacted were these three: 1) a significant reduction in child care assistance, 2) counting $50 of federal housing subsidy and $125 of Social Security Insurance as income against MFIP grants, 3) increasing the maximum sanction from 30 to 100 percent of welfare money withheld after the sixth occurrence of noncompliance, and 4) reducing the MFIP exit level from 120 to 115 percent of the federal poverty line (Minnesota Department of Human Services 2003). The child care funding cuts amounted to nearly $90 million, and eligibility for assistance for child care was reduced from 290 to 170 percent of the federal poverty line for a family of three (Children's Defense Fund 2003a). In terms of income eligibility, this reduced Minnesota's ranking from fourth to twenty-ninth in the nation (Howe 2004).

In contrast to Minnesota's superb record on reducing poverty in the late 1990s despite lower-than-average reduction in welfare caseloads, Minnesota's post-2000 reforms were associated with relatively poor poverty performance. The post-2000 reforms also did not appear to have successfully reduced welfare caseloads; they may have simply reduced the income of those receiving assistance. Early results suggest the changes have been counterproductive. Yet Minnesota more recently has implemented even more sweeping reforms with the state's Diversionary Work Program. Under the program, participants must wait four months before receiving welfare checks, during which time welfare checks are replaced with paid rent, Food Stamps, and a small amount of expense money. Participants in the program also must spend 35 hours a week looking for a job, and unlike diversion programs in other states all families applying for welfare assistance must participate (Hopfensperger 2005). The uniqueness of the program will help shed light on the relative effectiveness of various features of state welfare reform efforts.

New Jersey

Despite New Jersey's lower rate of decline in payroll employment relative to the nation's, only its female employment rate fared better than that of the nation. As was consistent with the relatively worse outcomes for male employment and unemployment rates, New Jersey's decline in manufacturing employment exceeded the national decline.

From February 2001, the beginning of the recession, to February 2004, New Jersey's welfare caseloads declined 7.8 percent, which was greater than the decline nationally. The decline from 2002 to 2003 also exceeded the nation's, and Food Stamp cases increased less than the national average. In response to high profile reports of child abuse, including the death of a 7-year-old boy, New Jersey recently overhauled its child welfare system (New Jersey Department of Human Services 2004). The focus of the plan is on providing more resources to handle child welfare caseloads and increasing accountability within the system.

Washington

Among the case study states, Washington's poverty rate increased the most from 2000 to 2003, perhaps reflecting its dramatic employment losses. In particular, there was a 23.9 percent decline in aerospace product and parts manufacturing employment from 2000 to 2003, which was part of a broader decline over the 1998–2003 period of more than 40 percent. Despite the job losses, Washington maintained strong population growth of 12 percent from April 1, 2000, to July 1, 2004 (U.S. Census Bureau 2005a). Of this growth, 4.4 percent was attributable to immigration, while 2.1 percent was attributable to internal in-migration. The combination of job losses and population growth dramatically reduced employment rates (and increased unemployment rates), particularly for males.

Correspondingly, Washington has experienced an increase in welfare caseloads since the recession, which continued into 2003. Eligibility for child care assistance was reduced from 225 to 200 percent of the federal poverty line (Children's Defense Fund 2003c). Because of a budget shortfall, there were a number of cuts made to WorkFirst in 2003, including funding cuts to the Child Care Career and Wage Ladder Pilot Program (Cook 2003). According to a support services staff memo, among the reductions implemented on July 1, 2003, were lower allowances for clothing, car repairs, and license fees, and a six-month limit for post-TANF recipients to receive support services (Washington WorkFirst 2003). Moreover, in May 2004 the sanction for noncompliance with WorkFirst requirements for first-time offenders increased to a 40 percent benefit reduction for a minimum of one month, and welfare checks were to be immediately sent to a protective payee to pay rent and utilities (J. Martin 2004). Yet in 2003 Washington expanded its Targeted Wage Initiative, which does more in-depth assessment to help transition TANF recipients into higher-paying jobs, rather than simply push them into the first available job (Stevens 2003).

The case of Washington illustrates the strong influence of the economy on poverty outcomes, and even its success in reducing welfare caseloads. It also reinforces the notion that a declining economy hurts the impoverished both directly, through a loss of employment opportunities, and indirectly, through the loss of state financial assistance.

CONCLUSIONS

Case studies of Alabama, Minnesota, New Jersey, and Washington generally confirm the empirical results examined in Chapter 4. For example, despite Alabama's stricter welfare program and fair success in reducing its caseloads, the state's progress in reducing poverty stagnated in the late 1990s as its economy faltered. On the other hand, although Minnesota was perceived as having been less successful at reducing its welfare caseloads, its strong economy in the late 1990s—particularly as evidenced by strong wage growth—helped that state achieve the second lowest poverty rate in the nation in 2000. The significantly greater actual decline in Minnesota poverty relative to that predicted by our regression results for 1996–2000 also suggests that Minnesota's welfare program may have played a role in reducing poverty. However, Minnesota's scaling back of financial assistance for welfare recipients correlated with an increase in poverty above that for the nation. Washington's sluggish economy, particularly in manufacturing, led to the worst poverty performance among the case study states and an increased number of post-2000 welfare caseloads.

The most positive aspects of welfare reform appear to be those that provide work support such as child care and transportation subsidies. These help to facilitate transitions from welfare to work and to lift families above poverty status. However, the adverse effects of the sluggish economy on state budgets made matters worse, as many of the low-income support programs were cut.[4] This made it less likely that those who left welfare would be lifted out of poverty, as was evidenced by the nationwide post-2000 rise in poverty and by a dramatic rise in Food Stamp use. For example, both Minnesota and Washington have made their programs stricter. On a favorable note, Washington is increasing its efforts to place former recipients into higher-paying jobs.

In short, the increasing emphasis on pushing welfare recipients into jobs makes it imperative that there are sufficient job vacancies, particularly if state and federal assistance for former recipients is not enough to provide training and placement. Otherwise, many former recipients will simply be replacing welfare payments with equivalently small gross-labor-market rewards. In this case, those with the fewest job skills and cognitive abilities may experience even more severe forms of poverty. Thus, in contrast to recent welfare reforms, given the importance of job creation in reducing poverty rates, economic development policies appear to be an important part of the mix that could be used to reduce poverty, as well as to level out geographic pockets of high poverty. Because economic development often occurs at the local level, the next three chapters' emphasis on counties or metropolitan areas will shed light on the potential effectiveness of these policies in reducing poverty.

Notes

The first epigraph to this chapter comes from the Office of the Legislative Auditor's program evaluation report on welfare reform in Minnesota (Office of the Legislative Auditor 2000, p. xii). The second epigraph comes from the Associated Press (2004) story "Census: 15.1 Percent of Alabama Residents Live in Poverty," August 26, 2004.

1. These were obtained by first summing the results of multiplying the coefficients in column (7) by the corresponding changes in employment and unemployment rates by gender. To this was added the product of the coefficient for the employment-growth interaction term and the 1996–2000 employment-growth rate. A final adjustment to the estimate was made by adding the result obtained by multiplying the employment-growth coefficient by the change in job growth. Thus, the result assumes that all changes in employment and unemployment rates were attributable to the strong economy, an assumption supported by the general lack of significance of the welfare variables.
2. For the decade, however, Washington's median average hourly wages increased 4.0 percent from 1989 to 1999, while 20th percentile average hourly wages increased 7.5 percent. The corresponding national average increases were 2.4 and 5.6 percent (Mishel, Bernstein, and Schmitt 2001).
3. This confirms a trend found by Waldfogel and Mayer (2000) that the gender gap for low-skilled workers narrowed because of decline in male earnings, not increases in the real earnings of low-skilled women.
4. At least 13 states decreased spending for child care assistance in 2002, while others enacted cuts in 2003 (Weinstein and Blank 2003).

6
County Employment
Growth and Poverty

In previous chapters we found that economic growth reduces poverty at the state and national levels, especially when U.S. unemployment rates are low. This supports the belief that a "rising tide lifts all boats," particularly approaching high tide, when the tide reaches the boats stranded on the beach. We found less evidence that the 1996 federal welfare reform affected poverty rates.

However, we have yet to answer some critical questions. For one, does economic growth evenly reduce poverty in all localities? Are the growth effects on poverty greater in urban areas? Does metropolitan growth affect poverty in all parts of the area? Can poverty be reduced in remote rural areas?

Examination of national or even state data overlooks these important localized effects. Moreover, understanding how labor markets affect local poverty is complicated by factors such as commuting or migration within states or metropolitan areas, which affect the ability of the poor to get the jobs that lie beyond their immediate vicinity. Local responses to economic growth may differ completely from the corresponding national or state responses found in Chapters 1 and 4. Indeed, the county-level descriptive statistics in Chapter 2 reveal how poverty rates vary greatly across county types. Analysis of smaller geographical units is necessary to fully assess the effects of local economic development policies on poverty outcomes.

This chapter describes an empirical methodology for the assessment of county poverty. The resulting empirical analysis focuses on the "average" county response across the entire country; we then use the model to assess the poverty outcomes of various demographic subgroups within the county. In a more spatially focused discussion, Chapters 7 and 8 present separate analyses of metropolitan and nonmetropolitan counties. Most of this chapter's discussion dwells on the links between labor markets and county poverty rates; Appendix A describes in more detail the empirical approach and findings for other key demographic factors. The appendix also presents several simulations to ascertain the influence of economic development policies and employment growth on poverty rates.

WHY EXAMINE COUNTIES OR METROPOLITAN AREAS?

Along with the phenomenon that poverty is locally persistent, there are related policymaking and labor market considerations that need to be weighed in deciding a study's geographical scale. For our purposes, we believe the optimal local scale on which to assess poverty outcomes is the county and metropolitan statistical area (MSA) level.[1] One advantage of examining these geographical units is that they are large enough to represent an area in which most residents live and work. Correspondingly, economic development policies are usually limited in geographical scope, rarely exceeding the size of counties, with an entire MSA being about the largest scale in use. Hence, states or nations are not the optimal-sized unit for assessing the effects of such policies. Decentralization in both the 1996 Personal Responsibility and Work Opportunity Reconciliation Act and the 1998 Workforce Investment Act (Bartik 2001) means that counties and MSAs have a greater role in designing welfare and training programs that affect labor markets for disadvantaged workers.

Any definition of a local labor market has a somewhat arbitrary nature, which has drawbacks. An illustration of the complications that arise in practice can be seen in the view that a labor market can be defined as a commuting zone. Under this definition, a neighborhood is far too small to frame a labor market, because its residents don't need to commute—they can simply walk to neighboring job opportunities if necessary. At the other extreme, a labor market can extend far beyond the boundaries of a commuting zone. Indeed, for university professors, one could argue that the appropriate market is national, because the participants typically have high mobility and reliable information about national employment opportunities.

In most cases, "local" labor markets fall somewhere in between a neighborhood and the nation, depending on commuting and information flows. Yet there is considerable room between a neighborhood and the entire nation. The example of university professors illustrates that the geographic scope of a labor market likely varies by skill and occupation. Fortunately, analysis of poverty focuses more on the low-skilled end of the labor market, which is unlikely to be far-ranging because migration rates are typically lower for that end than for skilled professionals (Borjas 1996), and because low-income residents often have commuting limitations stemming from a lack of reliable auto or public transportation. Additionally, child care needs further limit the accessibility of jobs for many low-income residents, especially single mothers.

Given these considerations, counties should be the units that most closely approximate nonmetropolitan labor markets, especially for low-income households. For one thing, the largest city is usually the county seat, which is often centrally located in the county. As well, commuting data support the argument that nonmetropolitan counties generally reflect labor markets. Statistics reported in Appendix Table A.2 show that in 1999 fully 69 percent of employed residents in a typical non-metropolitan county worked in their county of residence. Moreover, the lower mobility of less-skilled workers implies that the figures are likely higher for them. It should be kept in mind that residents who live near the border of their county would likely view employment options in neighboring counties as being almost as desirable as a job opportunity in their own county. So although conditions in the county of residence appear to generally reflect the labor market options available to most nonmetropolitan low-skilled residents, labor market conditions in surrounding counties (with the exception of remote counties) also play a role.

In MSAs, the appropriate labor market more likely crosses county boundaries, because commuting patterns are more widespread. Yet this assumption should not be exaggerated. In the typical MSA county in 1999, 63 percent of employed residents—five out of eight—worked in their county of residence. Job accessibility constraints likely mean that less-skilled MSA workers have a higher employment share in their county of residence.

The issue of job accessibility in larger urban areas spawned the spatial mismatch literature described in Chapter 3 (e.g., Kain 1992). It becomes increasingly likely in large MSAs that vacant jobs are more distant from job seekers; an MSA population of 800,000 appears to reflect a point beyond which job accessibility becomes increasingly problematic (Bartik 2001). This suggests that aggregate MSA data obscure the disparities that often exist between central cities and suburbs, particularly for large MSAs. Thus, we primarily examine individual MSA counties rather than aggregate MSAs; this enables us to explore potential intra-MSA distinctions.

CONCEPTUAL MODEL OF COUNTY POVERTY

While the county and metropolitan trends and statistics examined in Chapter 2 help us understand the underlying patterns from the 1990s, they are insufficient alone to inform policymaking. To fully analyze the degree to which local economic development policies can reduce overall poverty or chip away at persistent pockets of poverty, we return to regression analysis. We first briefly outline the conceptual determinants of county and MSA poverty rates. In particular, as was described in Chapter 3, the smaller geographical size of these local labor markets means that the underlying responses differ somewhat from those at the state and national levels. The following section outlines the empirical methodology used to ascertain the underlying causes of county poverty rates.

Labor Demand Factors

As noted in Chapter 3, theory alone does not provide clear guidance as to whether greater employment reduces poverty in small geographic areas. In responding to an exogenous labor demand shock within a region, commuters and migrants may eventually take most of the newly created jobs (Bartik 2001; Partridge and Rickman 2006). Thus, the region's "original" residents may receive few benefits, and the poverty rate would be left relatively unaffected. The strength of the business cycle also complicates how local economic activity affects the low-wage labor market. It is not surprising that past poverty studies have produced inconsistent findings, as their final conclusions appear sensitive to both the geographic scope and the time period used in the study (Bartik 1994, 2001; Blank and Card 1993; Freeman 2001; Levernier et al. 2000).

As is consistent with the methodology in previous chapters, labor market conditions are measured by variables for employment growth, unemployment rates, and employment-population ratios. While these three labor market tightness measures capture their own independent effects, they are interrelated, which can make it difficult to draw ceteris paribus conclusions. For example, faster job growth likely raises employment-population ratios and reduces unemployment rates. Thus, we conduct various sensitivity tests and simulations to test the robustness of the results. For some specifications we omit the unemployment- and employment-rate measures, which means that the employment growth coefficient should then reflect its direct effects in reducing poverty plus its indirect effects through changing the unemployment- and employment-population rates.

A further complicating factor is the question of whether local poverty rates should be modeled as being in equilibrium. If poverty rates follow an equilibrium process, they immediately reflect the underlying socioeconomic conditions. But if modeled as a disequilibrium process, poverty rates may respond sluggishly to changes in the underlying determinants, making them dependent upon past poverty rates. Neither the theory in the field nor the literature offers clear guidance on this question, and the equilibrium/disequilibrium issue is typically ignored by most research.[2]

Sluggish disequilibrium adjustment can occur when there are self-perpetuating effects. For one thing, there is tremendous persistence for households that fall into poverty in any given year, and there is also persistence for workers in low-wage jobs.[3] Chapter 3 describes how, at the neighborhood level, residents in persistently high-poverty areas often have few employed role models, which could further inhibit them from obtaining long-term employment (Weinberg 2004; Weinberg, Reagan, and Yankow 2004). Further reinforcing the persistence of local poverty rates are migration patterns: migration flows are inversely related to education, which implies that disadvantaged households will be less likely to leave their current location (Borjas 1996; Bound and Holzer 2000).

Slow adjustment is reinforced by other delayed responses. For instance, in counties that are faring well economically, it may take time for employers to realize that the economic upswing is permanent or to recognize that job openings are going unfilled and begin offering jobs to those on the lower rungs of the ladder (Freeman 2001; Holzer,

Raphael, and Stoll 2003). Similarly, rapid economic growth may attract new migrants, but only after a delay stemming from imperfect information being relayed across regions and from raising the money for moving costs.

Related to the equilibrium/disequilibrium issue is the timing of the county's growth-poverty linkage. Poverty rates may be more affected by recent economic performance than by conditions that existed for many years in the past (Bartik 1993b). Even so, Bartik (1996, 2001) contends that lags of economic growth from the distant past can benefit less-skilled individuals through hysteresis effects.[4] A strong economy can have persistent effects if, over time, low-skilled workers gain experience and confidence, receive training, and acquire good work habits (Gladden and Taber 2000). However, Levernier et al. (2000) did not find such local effects for the 1980s, which they attributed to the relatively soft labor market of that decade. It may be, though, that persistent effects from economic growth only emerge if the local labor market has been sufficiently tight for many years, such as in the 1990s expansion.

A final point is that besides the overall employment growth effect from the loss of higher-paying jobs, greater industry dislocation is associated with large declines in employees' postdisplacement earnings and more long-term joblessness (Carrington and Zaman 1994). Indeed, adjustments that are due to restructuring and job search could further slow the response of poverty rates to current conditions.

Other Factors Affecting County Poverty

Numerous other supply and demand factors potentially affect county poverty rates. Examples include demographic factors such as the immigrant, racial, and ethnic composition of the population, as well as the share of families with children that are headed by single men or women. Especially for counties, racial composition varies greatly. Higher concentrations of minorities tend to reside in inner cities (Corcoran et al. 1992; Cutler and Glaeser 1997; Holzer 1991), and these minority groups usually have below-average levels of education. This deficiency reduces their labor market opportunities (Smith and Welch 1986).

County poverty also may be related to population size because of factors such as agglomeration economies and skills-matching in the labor market, which generally increase wages and reduce poverty

(Glaeser et al. 1992; Henderson et al. 1995). Yet congestion may reduce productivity, which could increase poverty. Population's role also depends on how the scale of the urban center affects the distance between residence and employment and, hence, how it affects an inhabitant's access to jobs.

EMPIRICAL MODEL OF COUNTY POVERTY RATES

The empirical model nests the equilibrium outcome within the disequilibrium approach and tests for the appropriate specification. The particular disequilibrium process we implement is the partial adjustment model (Greene 1997). Appendix A more fully develops the empirical model and describes the exact specification. Descriptive statistics also are reported in Appendix Table A.2.

We separately examine 1989 and 1999 patterns in county poverty rates for the lower 48 states and the District of Columbia. Considering both decades allows us to compare outcomes when economic growth is geographically more uneven, as in the 1980s, versus more widespread, as in the late 1990s. The 1990s also straddle the historic 1996 welfare reform and other federal policy changes, such as the expansion of the EITC. As detailed in Box 6.1, the poverty rate (POV) in county i, state s, year t (for 1989 or 1999) will be regressed on various explanatory variables intended to capture the direct effects and the interrelationships of the person-specific and place-specific effects described above.

EMPIRICAL ASSESSMENT OF LOCAL POVERTY: LOCAL ATTRIBUTES

Sluggish or Rapid Poverty Rate Adjustment?

Table 6.1 presents the regression results for the models described above. Columns (1) to (3) report the 1989 results, and columns (4) to (6) report the 1999 results. Most of the discussion will focus on the 1999 labor market results, but comparisons with 1989 will be drawn

Box 6.1 County Regression Model

The base county model has the poverty rate (POV) in county i, state s, year t (1989 or 1999) being regressed on various explanatory factors:

$$(6.1) \quad \text{POV}_{ist} = \alpha 1 \text{POV}_{ist\text{-}1} + \beta 1 \; \text{CTY\_TYPE}_{ist} + \gamma 1 \; \text{DEMOG}_{ist} + \varphi 1 \; \text{ECON}_{ist} + \sigma_{st} + \varepsilon_{ist},$$

In Equation (6.1), the X vector from Equation (A.3) is decomposed into three subcomponents: CTY_TYPE represents the type of county, DEMOG denotes demographic characteristics of the population, and ECON contains measures related to area economic performance. $\alpha 1$ is $(1-\alpha_t)$ in Equation (A.3) of the appendix, and reflects the sluggish poverty adjustment, while $\beta 1$, $\gamma 1$, and $\varphi 1$ represent corresponding regression coefficients. The specific explanatory variables included in the model closely follow the specification used by Levernier et al. (2000). Closing out Equation (6.1) is σ_s, which denotes the state fixed effect, and ε, which is the error term carrying the usual assumptions. By state fixed effects, we simply mean 48 zero-one dummy variables that take on a value of 1 when the county observation is from that state.[a]

The specific explanatory variables are described in the appendix. Note that the state fixed effects account for the poverty effects of omitted or nonincluded state-level factors that have a common effect across the entire state (i.e., they either raise or lower the poverty rate a set amount across all counties in a given state). Omitted factors may include cost-of-living differences, amenity effects, and cultural influences. State-level factors also include state government policies such as welfare programs. Even in the old AFDC welfare program that existed until the 1996 federal reform, there was significant state variation in benefits and in the administration of the program. The inclusion of state fixed effects means that the slope coefficients reflect cross-county variation within states.[b]

[a] One state category is omitted so that all of the state poverty-rate effects are measured relative to that omitted state.

[b] Including state fixed effects or dummies is the equivalent of first-differencing the explanatory variables around the state mean. In general, if these common state effects were correlated with the included independent variables, omitting the state dummy variables would bias the coefficients of the remaining variables. However, the state fixed effects may in essence overcontrol for other factors if they are common across the state. For example, if a state has faster-than-average employment growth across most counties, some of the influence of job growth should be reflected in the state fixed effect, or the explanatory-variable results may not fully reflect their total impact.

when pertinent. Many of the explanatory variables are included to account for other independent factors. Although interesting, their discussion will be left to Appendix A.[5]

Because the matter is closely related to the spatial persistence of poverty, it should first be determined whether local poverty adjustment is a rapid or a slow process. Columns (1) and (4) present the base disequilibrium adjustment model. Columns (2) and (5) report the equilibrium model, in which the only difference is that the lagged poverty rate from the previous decade has been omitted. Comparing the disequilibrium and equilibrium models indicates that key results are different. For example, the five-year employment growth variables take on the expected inverse relationship with poverty rates in the disequilibrium models, but they are positive and statistically insignificant in the equilibrium approach.

The empirical findings strongly support a sluggish disequilibrium adjustment process for county poverty rates. Columns (1) and (4) reveal that the 10-year lagged poverty rate is highly statistically significant in both the 1989 and 1999 models. The large values of the lagged poverty rate coefficients indicate that the underlying determinants of local poverty rates have half-lives of almost one decade. Indeed, such persistence is consistent with the spatial patterns identified in the 1979, 1989, and 1999 county poverty rate maps shown in Figures 2.8 through 2.10. Hence, the remaining discussion focuses on the models that include the 10-year lagged poverty rate.[6]

The persistence in county poverty rates likely has two explanations. One, households in poverty choose to remain in their original counties, and household poverty is persistent. Two, the communities themselves have characteristics that are conducive to higher poverty rates regardless of an individual's or a household's characteristics. Statistics regarding the persistence of individual poverty indicate that place plays a key role because individual persistence is less than what would be expected if individual behavior were the sole source of the large 10-year lagged-poverty-rate coefficient. For example, a study by the U.S. Census Bureau (2003) found that only 51 percent of the population that was in poverty in 1996 remained in poverty in 1999, while about 4 percent of the population that was not in poverty in 1996 was in poverty in 1999.

The spatial persistence supports the argument that policies designed to reduce poverty should include a component to provide development

Table 6.1 Poverty Rate Regression Model for all Counties, 1989 and 1999

Group	1989 poverty rate			1999 poverty rate		
	(1) Base	(2) Base equivalent	(3) Base + broad labor market	(4) Base	(5) Base equivalent	(6) Base + broad labor market
Lagged poverty rate	0.47 (28.1)		0.44 (22.74)	0.39 (27.31)		0.38 (23.94)
Weighted surrounding-city poverty			0.09 (5.57)			0.06 (4.17)
Single-county MSAs[a]	-0.78 (1.47)	-1.53 (2.21)	-1.18 (2.14)	-0.58 (1.40)	-1.36 (2.25)	-0.89 (2.04)
Big-MSA central county[b]	-0.79 (1.30)	-1.69 (2.11)	-1.16 (1.81)	-0.59 (1.27)	-1.50 (2.17)	-0.74 (1.49)
Big-MSA suburban county[b]	-0.49 (0.83)	-1.66 (2.14)	-1.07 (1.71)	-1.15 (2.54)	-1.83 (2.77)	-1.40 (2.93)
Small-MSA central county[b]	-0.68 (1.24)	-1.76 (2.47)	-1.10 (1.90)	-0.47 (1.09)	-1.43 (2.27)	-0.72 (1.59)
Small-MSA suburban county[b]	-0.57 (1.04)	-1.53 (2.16)	-1.15 (1.99)	-0.99 (2.41)	-1.75 (2.87)	-1.25 (2.89)
Population	5.2e-7 (2.43)	1.2e-6 (3.55)	4.8e-7 (2.35)	2.9e-7 (1.56)	2.3e-7 (0.89)	2.9e-7 (1.44)
MSA population	-6.3e-8 (1.13)	-8.6e-8 (1.18)	-4.0e-8 (0.74)	6.9e-8 (1.75)	-2.3e-8 (0.40)	8.6e-8 (2.19)
Nonmetro county × population	-1.3e-5 (4.93)	-2.3e-5 (6.42)	-1.1e-5 (4.22)	-8.7e-7 (0.46)	-1.2e-5 (5.16)	-3.7e-7 (0.19)

1985–90 or 1995–2000 empl. growth	-0.016 (3.30)	0.008 (1.40)	-0.012 (2.45)	-0.014 (3.06)	0.006 (1.22)	-0.014 (2.92)
1988–90 structural change^c	5.86 (2.17)	7.16 (2.15)	5.91 (2.22)	6.59 (3.55)	5.64 (2.89)	6.90 (3.80)
1995–2000 structural change^c						
Pop. × structural change^c	-4.2e-5 (3.05)	-8.5e-5 (4.20)	-3.9e-5 (3.06)	-1.1e-5 (1.71)	-1.4e-5 (1.55)	-1.2e-5 (1.67)
% male employment/population	-0.08 (6.02)	-0.16 (9.13)	-0.09 (6.26)	-0.03 (2.03)	-0.06 (4.16)	-0.02 (1.30)
% female employment/population	-0.16 (9.14)	-0.21 (9.73)	-0.15 (8.62)	-0.19 (11.98)	-0.30 (15.39)	-0.18 (11.31)
% civilian male unemployment rate	0.17 (5.12)	0.23 (5.39)	0.18 (5.29)	0.15 (5.74)	0.23 (6.61)	0.15 (5.83)
% civilian female unemployment rate	0.07 (2.02)	0.08 (2.00)	0.07 (2.03)	-0.04 (1.25)	-0.01 (0.29)	-0.04 (1.17)
% residential employment in agriculture-forestry-fisheries	0.13 (5.64)	0.25 (8.86)	0.13 (6.06)	0.21 (10.14)	0.29 (10.22)	0.21 (9.91)
% residential employment in goods	0.01 (0.85)	-3.7e-4 (0.02)	0.03 (1.57)	0.05 (3.70)	0.03 (1.71)	0.06 (4.29)
% residential employment in transportation or public utilities	0.11 (3.83)	0.08 (2.44)	0.12 (4.10)	0.02 (0.82)	-0.02 (0.80)	0.03 (1.11)
% residential employment in trade or trade & entertainment	0.12 (5.49)	0.12 (4.54)	0.12 (5.35)	0.10 (5.34)	0.15 (6.29)	0.09 (4.97)
% residential employment in information				0.02 (0.43)	0.11 (1.86)	0.03 (0.64)

(continued)

Table 6.1 **(continued)**

	1989 Poverty rate			1999 Poverty rate		
	(1)	(2)	(3)	(4)	(5)	(6)
Group	Base	Base equivalent	Base + broad labor market	Base	Base equivalent	Base + broad labor market
% residential employment in finance, insurance, and real estate	-0.04 (1.18)	-0.03 (0.57)	-0.05 (1.27)	0.05 (1.70)	0.03 (0.83)	0.07 (2.43)
% residential employment in services	0.06 (2.63)	0.08 (2.73)	0.06 (2.69)	0.10 (5.13)	0.15 (5.78)	0.11 (5.43)
% residential employment in public administration						
1985–90/1995–2000 commuting zone employment growth[d]			-0.02 (2.93)			-0.005 (0.61)
1985–90/1995–2000 MSA employment growth (# MSA counties ≥ 2)[e]			0.004 (0.43)			-0.005 (0.42)
% of workers employed in county of residence			-0.003 (0.73)			0.01 (2.9)
% education < high school graduate (age ≥ 25 yrs.)						
% high school graduate (age ≥ 25 yrs.)	-0.16 (10.30)	-0.33 (18.87)	-0.16 (10.02)	-0.14 (9.08)	-0.25 (13.29)	-0.14 (9.04)
% some college, no degree (age ≥ 25 yrs.)	-0.20 (9.03)	-0.39 (13.92)	-0.20 (8.92)	-0.12 (6.15)	-0.29 (12.07)	-0.13 (6.45)
% associate college degree (age ≥ 25 yrs.)	-0.16 (4.36)	-0.34 (7.45)	-0.16 (4.44)	-0.18 (5.35)	-0.31 (7.56)	-0.20 (5.71)

% bachelor's degree or more (age ≥ 25 yrs.)	0.03 (1.48)	-0.03 (1.32)	0.03 (1.69)	-0.03 (1.91)	-0.10 (5.84)	-0.04 (2.69)
% of HHs female-headed with children	0.73 (14.61)	0.85 (14.47)	0.73 (14.77)	0.61 (11.99)	0.97 (17.26)	0.61 (12.18)
% of HHs male-headed with children	0.48 (4.24)	0.50 (3.84)	0.52 (4.63)	0.24 (2.88)	0.21 (2.15)	0.26 (3.21)
% population white[f]						
% population African American[f]	-0.04 (4.84)	0.01 (1.42)	-0.04 (5.03)	-0.03 (1.91)	-0.03 (3.59)	-0.03 (3.89)
% population other race[f]	0.03 (2.32)	0.04 (3.14)	0.03 (2.65)	-0.009 (0.95)	0.002 (0.15)	-0.003 (0.34)
% population Hispanic[f]	0.01 (1.33)	0.01 (0.93)	0.01 (1.20)	-0.01 (2.15)	-0.03 (3.22)	-0.02 (2.59)
% population children < 7 yrs. old	0.06 (0.90)	0.32 (4.05)	0.08 (1.27)	0.03 (0.48)	0.07 (0.97)	0.03 (0.49)
% population children 7–17 yrs. old	0.08 (1.78)	0.20 (3.81)	0.05 (1.16)	0.08 (1.65)	0.14 (2.49)	0.07 (1.55)
% population adults 18–24 yrs. old	0.24 (9.81)	0.36 (10.50)	0.25 (10.10)	0.25 (10.32)	0.41 (13.30)	0.25 (9.90)
% population adults 25–59 yrs. old						
% population adults 60–64 yrs. old	-0.11 (1.13)	-0.09 (0.81)	-0.08 (0.84)	0.24 (3.25)	0.47 (5.43)	0.25 (3.36)
% population over 65 yrs old	-0.009 (0.31)	0.30 (0.80)	-0.004 (0.13)	-0.10 (4.36)	-0.16 (5.36)	-0.10 (4.04)
% lived in same house 5 yrs. before	0.08 (6.21)	0.08 (5.08)	0.07 (5.99)	0.06 (4.96)	0.11 (8.12)	0.05 (3.88)

Table 6.1 (continued)

Group	1989 poverty rate			1999 poverty rate		
	(1) Base	(2) Base equivalent	(3) Base + broad labor market	(4) Base	(5) Base equivalent	(6) Base + broad labor market
% lived in same county but different house 5 yrs. before	0.07 (4.46)	0.04 (2.27)	0.06 (3.22)	0.04 (3.04)	0.05 (2.74)	0.003 (0.16)
% lived in same MSA but different house 5 yrs. before if current resident of MSA	−0.01 (0.57)	0.002 (0.10)	5.2e−4 (0.03)	0.01 (0.92)	0.01 (0.53)	0.03 (1.76)
R^2	0.94	0.91	0.94	0.94	0.91	0.94
N	3028	3028	3028	3028	3028	3028

NOTE: Absolute values of robust t-statistics are in parentheses. A metropolitan county is defined using 2000 Bureau of Economic Analysis REIS county definitions. Blank indicates the variables were not included in the regression for that column, so there is no result to report.

[a] Single-county MSA/PMSA, with the exception of Los Angeles and San Diego, which are included as central-county MSAs.

[b] Central county includes the county or counties of the named central city or cities in the MSA definition in a multiple-county MSA. Suburban counties do not include any of the central city or cities. A large MSA had a 2000 population of greater than one million.

[c] The structural change index is the share of the county's employment that would have to change sectors in each year so that there would be an equivalent industry structure in each of the two years. It is a similarity index defined as one-half the sum of the absolute value of the difference in one-digit industry employment shares between the two years.

[d] For nonmetropolitan counties, the broader labor market employment growth was defined using 1990 commuting zone definitions from the Department of Agriculture (http://www.ers.usda.gov/Briefing/Rurality/lmacz).

[e] For multiple-county MSAs, the broader labor market employment growth was defined using the entire metropolitan area.

[f] Hispanics form an ethnic category; thus, Hispanics are also included in white, African American, and "other race" groups. In the 2000 census, individuals who claim two or more racial categories are classified in the "other race" group. Because of the two-or-more racial category in the 2000 census, the 1990 and 2000 figures are not comparable.

SOURCE: U.S. Census Bureau (2006e).

assistance to communities with high poverty rates. At the very least, poverty reduction programs should account for the need to tailor their assistance to individuals to fit the characteristics of their community, as well as to recognize that specific services need to be delivered differently in particular communities (Allard 2004).

Locational Differences in Poverty Determination

Among the county type indicators, only the two 1999 suburban county indicators are significant, and no county indicators are significant in the 1989 model. Suburban counties had about 1 percentage point lower short-run poverty rates in 1999 compared to nonmetropolitan counties.[7] Even when one accounts for faster job growth, a popular view is that suburbs have other advantages, such as favorable neighborhood effects. Thus it is surprising that suburban counties possess such a small overall advantage. The specific causes for differing central-county and suburban-county poverty rates are examined in detail in Chapter 7.

Given that job seekers may have superior opportunities to find better employment matches with higher wages in the suburbs, one might expect that poverty rates would be lower in the most populated metropolitan areas (MSAs), ceteris paribus. However, greater overall MSA population is positively related to 1999 MSA-county poverty rates (at least at the 10 percent level). Thus, job accessibility and labor market information appear to erode in larger MSAs for low-skilled workers, which supports claims that job creation needs to be spatially targeted in large metro areas.

EMPLOYMENT GROWTH AND POVERTY

Direct Job Growth Impacts

The beginning of this chapter noted that employment growth both directly and indirectly affects poverty rates. First we examine employment growth's direct impacts, by holding the unemployment- and employment-population rates constant. In the next subsection, we summarize the indirect effects, by allowing the unemployment and employment rates to be affected. In assessing how local job growth affects poverty rates, we take into account the underlying variability of county employment growth by simulating the impact from a one standard deviation change in job growth. Roughly speaking, a one standard deviation change in a variable would generally take a county from the middle of the distribution to either one-third above or one-third below the mean.

For five-year employment growth, Table A.2 shows that a one standard deviation increase equaled 12.2 percent between 1985 and 1990 and 10.1 percent between 1995 and 2000. Using the results in columns (1) and (4) of Table 6.1, we find that a one standard deviation increase in five-year employment growth reduced the typical county's short-run poverty rate by 0.20 percentage points in 1989 and by 0.14 points in 1999. This yields 1989 and 1999 long-run poverty-rate reductions of 0.37 and 0.23 percentage points, suggesting a moderate response.[8] In other analysis, we find that it takes time for job growth to significantly affect poverty, as we discover no evidence that two-year job growth reduced county poverty rates.[9]

Our conclusion is that strong job growth does not immediately reduce poverty; poverty reduction will be delayed until job growth has persisted long enough to ensure that employers have to reach down and hire the lowest-skilled workers. Earlier in the chapter, we noted that long-run job growth allows low-skilled workers to gain work experience and also allows these same low-skilled workers more time to find stable employment with longer work hours (a better job match). Hence, the findings support various hysteresis arguments. It may not so much have been the strength of the red-hot economy of the late 1990s that reduced poverty as it was the length of the expansion: the long duration of the 1990s economic expansion allowed low-skilled workers the opportunity to acquire labor market skills and find suitable employment matches.

The finding that a long duration of economic growth is more important than current conditions is somewhat at odds with Richard Freeman's (2001) argument that national unemployment needs to fall below 5 percent before poverty rates sharply decline. However, Freeman did not explicitly consider the duration of the economic expansion. One way to reconcile these two views is to say that the extremely low national unemployment rates of the late 1990s were consistent with the economic expansion lasting long enough to reach those lows and to reduce poverty rates.[10] This interpretation has discouraging implications for national poverty rates in the near future: a seemingly positive outcome of the 2001–2003 economic sluggishness is that the overall poverty rate increased only 0.8 percentage points between 2000 and 2002, compared to the 1.4 and 2.0 point increases for the 1989–1991 and 1980–1982 periods (i.e., the analogous points in the business cycle). But if economic growth influences poverty rates over a lengthier span, such as five years, the sluggish job growth of the 2001–2003 period will have negative ramifications for poverty rates that will last until near the end of the decade—especially for local pockets of poverty. Even in the case of the more mild "jobless" recovery after the 1990–1991 recession, poverty rates did not start to decline until 1994.

In terms of "generic" local economic development policies, the results are a little cautionary. First, policies aimed at increasing economic activity need to be of sufficient duration (greater than two years) to help the most disadvantaged households. Second, the poverty-reducing impacts of a generic 10 percent increase in employment are relatively modest. Even this response would require annual employment growth to rise about 2 percentage points more than expected for five consecutive years.

In terms of policy priorities, generic employment growth is more effective in reducing poverty rates when it occurs nationally and even statewide, at least when the aggregate economy is strong. Using the results for national poverty rates in Chapter 4, a one standard deviation, 1.7 percentage-point increase in annual U.S. employment growth immediately reduces poverty rates about 0.2 percentage points when the national unemployment rate is above 5 percent. The U.S. poverty rate falls about 0.6 points when the unemployment rate is below 5 percent, as was the case in the late 1990s.[11] Even the state-level data indicate that a one standard deviation increase in employment growth (1.8 percent) would have immediately reduced poverty rates about 0.5 points in the late 1990s. These results illustrate that if economic growth is statewide or national in scope and the economy is already quite strong, poverty rates will fall much more quickly and dramatically than if growth is isolated to smaller geographical areas like counties or MSAs. Yet national growth alone is less useful for redressing poverty in spatially isolated poverty pockets than in the nation as a whole.

These results clearly reveal that state and national estimates should not be simply extrapolated to assess poverty outcomes in local areas. This further illustrates the conundrum facing local policymakers: at the county or sub-MSA level, commuters and in-migrants can quickly take the newly created jobs, leaving fewer jobs for the disadvantaged original residents. Moreover, when growth is isolated to a local area, low-skilled residents need more time than these outside competitors to acquire the necessary training and experience to pull themselves out of poverty. The county results suggest that two to five years of local economic growth is necessary for that growth to trickle down. The good news in a strong national or state economy is that local employers are forced to hire low-skilled residents almost immediately because potential commuters and migrants likely already have suitable job opportunities in their current location.

The upshot of the dampened poverty-rate response to local conditions is that if local policymakers want their economic development activities to help their disadvantaged residents, they need to find ways to focus their strategies directly on their needy residents. For example, rather than giving businesses a tax break for expanding in a specific location—in, say, an enterprise zone—give employers a tax break for hiring residents (preferably disadvantaged residents) of these zones. Chapter 9 describes how an employer tax credit for creating new jobs can be targeted towards disadvantaged workers, by including a specific residential requirement for hired workers to boost the credit's poverty-rate reducing effect. During the early days of the Clinton administration, there were efforts to include enticements to help the residents of targeted low-income communities, but these provisions were not implemented (Bartik 2001).

Indirect Effects of Job Growth

To some extent, the overall effect of job growth on reducing poverty rates may have been understated. Greater job growth may reduce poverty rates by also reducing the unemployment rate and increasing the employment-population ratio, both of which are implicitly held constant in the employment-growth simulations described above. Appendix Table A.1 presents the results of four different scenarios that factor in various indirect effects of job growth on unemployment rates and employment-population ratios. After adjusting for the various indirect effects of job growth, the four simulations suggest that the total (direct + indirect) short-run response of poverty rates ranges from −0.13 to −0.37 percentage points after a 10 percent increase in 1995–2000 employment growth, which is comparable to the −0.14 percent short-run direct impact described above.[12]

The Effects of Targeted Employment Growth

Chapter 4 described how targeting state employment growth to sectors that are faring well at the national level might have stronger poverty-reducing impacts. For counties, we also find that targeting employment growth to rapidly growing industries at the national level has stronger poverty-reducing impacts. Specifically, we decomposed the five-year employment growth rate into its industry-mix and competitiveness components (not shown).[13] On average, when using these employment measures, a 10-percentage-point increase in 1995–2000 industry-mix and competitiveness employment growth induced 0.67 ($t = 1.88$) and 0.12 ($t = 2.56$) percentage point declines, respectively, in 1999 county poverty. This shows that if job growth comes primarily from a favorable composition of industries, poverty rates would decline about sixfold more than if it originated from competitiveness effects.[14]

These estimates again likely understate the poverty-reducing effects of industry-mix employment growth if it indirectly affects unemployment, employment-population, and industry structural change in the county. In a quasireduced form model that omitted these other labor market variables, a 10-percentage-point increase in the five-year industry-mix and competitiveness growth rates yielded larger short-run poverty rate changes of −1.04 ($t = 2.71$) and −0.13 ($t = 2.29$) percentage points in 1999.[15]

Thus, although merely creating jobs in general may not have large impacts on poverty rates, there appears to be promise in directing economic development efforts toward creating jobs in industries that are faring well nationally. Further focusing incentives and efforts on increasing employment among the low-skilled in nationally fast-growing industries would likely reinforce these impacts.

Other Labor Market Measures

Besides the influence of long-run employment growth, other labor market variables in Table 6.1 have important roles. First, it appears that local labor market churning or restructuring leads to higher poverty rates, even after controlling for job growth, though the interaction between population and structural change shows that the influence of structural change declines as county population increases. For 1999, greater industry realignment increases poverty until the county population reaches about 600,000.

With employment growth already included in the regression models, the unemployment rate and employment-population rate variables essentially measure how labor supply availability affects poverty rates. As these measures are allowed to change, and job growth is held constant, original residents are increasingly assumed to fill the new jobs. At the margin, when the unemployment rate falls and the employment-population rate rises, the available local labor pool shrinks and the newly employed will increasingly be less-skilled workers.

With the exception of the female unemployment rate, Table 6.1 shows that results for the male and female employment-population rates and unemployment rates are as expected in the 1999 model. To give a sense of the magnitude of the responses, a one standard deviation increase in the female employment-population ratio and a one standard deviation decrease in the female unemployment rate would have reduced short-run poverty rates by 1.31 and 0.11 percentage points in 1999.[16] For men, a one standard deviation decrease in the employment-population rate and a one standard deviation increase in the unemployment rate produces a 0.26 and a 0.44 percentage-point increase in the 1999 short-run poverty rate.[17]

These results show that increasing the labor market attachment of females is particularly effective in reducing poverty rates. This may be accomplished by reducing barriers to female participation, such as by providing better child care, transportation, treatment for drug abuse, and programs for family violence. Welfare reform has taken steps in this direction: 56 percent of welfare expenditures went toward noncash work support in Fiscal Year 2003 vs. only 23 percent in 1996 (Pear 2003). In a result that illustrates child care's critical role, Blau and Tekin (2003) found that among single mothers with a child under the age of

13, receiving child care subsidies increased the probability of employment by about 13 percentage points, after controlling for family characteristics.[18]

There are still many workplace support needs going unfilled. For example, only about 15 percent of federally eligible children receive child care subsidies (Waller and Berube 2002). Nevertheless, results from the late 1990s illustrate why the work-first approach to welfare reform did not dramatically increase poverty rates: the associated increase in female participation likely offset other adverse effects. For enough female-headed households, labor earnings and the Earned Income Tax Credit formed a greater sum than welfare payments alone (Haskins 2003).

In terms of its impact on poverty reduction, the rather small influence of female unemployment rates compared to that of female employment rates indicates that there is no clear distinction between female unemployment and nonemployment.[19] Hence, it is not so much that there are barriers that impede the job search of low-skilled unemployed women, but rather that there are barriers inhibiting them from entering the labor force. Besides pointing to the need for improved access to child care and other supports, such findings support those who argue that more direct forms of intervention, such as public employment and wage subsidies, are necessary if the goal is to employ more low-skilled women (Bartik 2001).

The relatively modest poverty response to changes in the male employment-population ratio suggests that increasing male labor force participation would have only modest impacts on reducing poverty. This finding is consistent with male-headed households already having the resources to be above the poverty line, whether because they are in married families or because single male-headed households are much less likely to include children than are female-headed households. Compared to the female rate, the male unemployment rate has a more important impact on poverty rates, illustrating a sharper divide between male unemployment and nonemployment. For reducing poverty, it is not so much a question of inducing more men into the labor force as it is helping unemployed men in their job search to reduce the duration of their unemployment spell. Yet it is not clear whether the relatively large poverty response to male unemployment is due to a lack of skills or whether less-skilled men do not have knowledge of, or access to, jobs.

The literature cited in Chapter 3 indicates that all of these factors likely play some role.

The size and the significance of the industry-share results indicate that the county's industry composition of employment strongly affects poverty. With one exception, the positive industry share coefficients suggest that a larger public-administration employment share (the omitted group) is most associated with lower poverty rates, while larger shares in trade and services are associated with higher poverty rates.[20] These patterns are inconsistent with the argument that a greater number of entry-level jobs in low-skilled trade and service industries reduce poverty, but it does support claims that public-sector employment is one avenue to reducing poverty. Because trade and service jobs are generally "secondary sector" jobs characterized by lower wages and benefits, fewer hours, and more erratic spells of employment, this is not an entirely unexpected finding.

Our findings suggest that goods employment is less of a high-wage outlet for low-skilled blue-collar workers. Over the 1990s the goods-employment share impact went from being insignificantly different from public administration in 1989 to being positive and significant in 1999. Clearly, this pattern could relate to declining unionization, ongoing skill-based technological change, and increasing global competition, which is pressuring low-skilled intensive manufacturers to cut labor costs or relocate abroad. In terms of employment, manufacturers began struggling in early 1998, well before the 2001 recession.[21] A greater agricultural share also became more associated with higher 1999 poverty rates.[22] Ongoing consolidation in agriculture is likely making it more difficult for many family farmers to have a sustainable livelihood. Likewise, the emergence of larger-scale operations such as intensive-livestock facilities may not be creating stable employment that offers adequate wages.

Community Demographic Attributes

It is not surprising that factors such as female headship, education, and immigration are statistically related to county poverty rates. Because most of the results are as expected, they are not described in the chapter, but interested readers can consult Appendix A for a detailed discussion of their effects.

NEIGHBORING COUNTY SPILLOVERS

Labor and social conditions in neighboring counties likely spill over and affect poverty rate outcomes in a given county. We assessed the importance of these spillovers by adding the following four variables to the base poverty model: 1) the average surrounding-county poverty rate from the previous decade, 2) the five-year commuting-zone employment growth rate for nonmetropolitan counties, 3) the five-year MSA employment growth rate for MSA counties (only for MSAs with two or more counties), and 4) the percentage of the county's workers who are employed in the county. The regression results for these models are reported in columns (3) and (6) of Table 6.1. With few exceptions, the previous results do not change with inclusion of the spatial spillover variables.

Clustering of poverty occurs at the county level, even after accounting for the particular state. That is, past poverty rates in surrounding counties (1989) have a positive and significant impact on current poverty rates (1999). This clustering likely relates to push and pull factors associated with household mobility and the spatial persistence of poverty. Nearby counties with low poverty rates are the most logical relocation choices for residents of a high-poverty county, for whom low poverty serves as a pull factor and high poverty as a push factor.[23]

To explore the clustering push-pull pattern, the four poverty spill-over variables and the previous decade's poverty rate were added to the auxiliary employment-population and unemployment rate regressions described in Appendix A (not shown). The results show how localized poverty can have persistent effects as well as cross-county spillovers. Namely, for every one point the weighted 1989 surrounding county poverty rate increased, the 1999 male and female employment-population rate fell about 0.25 percentage points, while the male and female unemployment rates increased about 0.10 point (all are significant at the 0.01 level).

There is also support for the argument that localized employment growth is a more important determinant of individual metro-county poverty rates than economic conditions in the broader metro area. Specifically, overall MSA employment growth had an insignificant impact on poverty rates, or overall MSA labor market conditions had no additional influence on county poverty rates after accounting for the MSA's own labor market conditions. Spatial mismatch proponents would not be surprised by these findings. Chapter 3 described their general contention that factors such as information and transportation constraints, as well as exclusionary zoning, limit the ability of the disadvantaged to find or take work across an entire metro area (especially a larger one).

The spatial clustering of county poverty rates was clearly revealed in Figures 2.8–2.10. Counties with high poverty rates tend to border counties with high poverty rates, and vice versa. Although we include several variables in an attempt to capture this dependence, spatial autocorrelation of the residuals may still exist.[24] Various tests of spatial autocorrelation in the residuals for the expanded models in columns (3) and (6) uniformly suggested that this could be a concern, especially for nonmetropolitan counties.[25] Yet when we reestimated the models to correct for spatial autocorrelation, the coefficients were essentially unchanged, which indicated that the spatial dependence was relatively harmless, arising out of the spatial heterogeneity of the model.[26]

POVERTY RESPONSES ACROSS KEY DEMOGRAPHIC GROUPS

As indicated in the previous chapters, local economic and demographic characteristics should affect various groups differently. For example, while all female-headed families should be similarly affected by labor market characteristics associated with female employment, female-headed households with children should be more influenced by welfare policies and responsibilities related to child rearing. Similarly, both married families with children and female-headed households with children have child care responsibilities. Yet the former group will be less affected by welfare policies, and the latter group may be more affected by labor market treatment and discrimination of women.

To examine demographic differences, Tables 6.2 and 6.3 report the base 1989 and 1999 model results using poverty rates for various subgroups. Columns (1) to (3) report the poverty rate results for female-headed families with children, female-headed families without children, and married families with children. We primarily focus on the 1999 results in Table 6.3.

Compared to the overall 1999 results in Table 6.1, five-year job growth has a much larger influence for the female-headed family with children category in column (1), but it has a smaller influence on poverty rates for female-headed families without children and married-couple families with children. The employment-growth response on single female–headed families was also larger in 1999 compared to 1989. The greater 1999 poverty effect for female–headed families is consistent with welfare reform increasing their exposure to labor market forces.[27] By contrast, the potential for two earners enables married families to be more diversified to protect against labor market conditions that may result in dramatic income loss. Compared to 1989, the smaller 1999 employment effects on females without children and on married-couple families with children suggest that there were some welfare reform–related supply spillover effects from the increased labor force participation of single female heads with children. Gundersen and Ziliak (2004) also find that welfare reform is positively (although weakly) associated with married-couple poverty rates, though they attribute this to the changing composition of married-couple households.

It is unsurprising that the female employment rates have much stronger impacts on female-head poverty rates than on other groups. Conversely, the female-head poverty rates are not statistically affected by male unemployment and employment rates. Given the differing occupational structures of low-skilled men and women, these results are consistent with low-skilled men and women not directly competing in the labor market. One argument that has been raised to explain high female-head poverty rates is the lack of marriageable men, especially for minority women (Wilson 1987). Yet if this strongly were the case, we would expect that male labor market conditions would affect female-head poverty rates. For married-couple families, female employment rates and male unemployment rates have the strongest impact on poverty rates—the same pattern as shown in Table 6.1.

Poverty rate models for children, adults 18–64 years of age, and seniors 65 and over are reported in Tables 6.2 and 6.3. It is striking the extent to which child poverty, compared to poverty in other age groups, is affected by labor market conditions, demographic characteristics, and suburban residence. Short-run child poverty rates appear to be even

Table 6.2 Poverty Rate Regression Results for Selected Subgroups, 1989

Group	(1) Female head w/ children	(2) Female head w/o children	(3) Married family w/ children	(4) Children <18 yrs.	(5) Age 18-to-64 yrs.	(6) Age 65 yrs. and over	(7) Under 50% of poverty line	(8) 50–100% of poverty line
Lagged poverty rate[a]	0.20 (5.75)	0.08 (2.68)	0.39 (17.02)	0.36 (17.73)	0.42 (25.26)	0.44 (25.60)	0.21 (17.94)	0.26 (19.74)
Single-county MSA	-0.26 (0.14)	1.61 (1.05)	-0.60 (1.02)	-1.10 (1.45)	-1.38 (2.14)	0.81 (1.07)	0.23 (0.59)	-1.01 (3.17)
Big-MSA central county	-0.05 (0.02)	0.17 (0.10)	-0.35 (0.51)	-0.79 (0.90)	-1.57 (2.16)	1.02 (1.20)	0.25 (0.58)	-1.04 (2.94)
Big-MSA suburban county	-0.46 (0.23)	0.99 (0.56)	-0.36 (0.54)	-1.05 (1.26)	-1.10 (1.57)	1.17 (1.39)	0.52 (1.24)	-1.00 (2.93)
Small-MSA central county	0.97 (0.51)	1.02 (0.64)	-0.53 (0.87)	-0.90 (1.16)	-1.38 (2.09)	1.24 (1.59)	0.27 (0.68)	-0.95 (2.91)
Small-MSA suburban county	0.58 (0.32)	0.83 (0.52)	-0.39 (0.64)	-0.92 (1.19)	-1.28 (1.97)	1.25 (1.61)	0.24 (0.62)	-0.81 (2.55)
1985–90 empl. growth	-0.037 (1.79)	-0.034 (1.91)	-0.011 (1.75)	-0.023 (3.00)	-0.009 (1.86)	-0.004 (0.53)	-0.007 (2.00)	-0.009 (2.27)
1988–90 structural change	25.6 (1.92)	9.01 (0.87)	6.50 (1.75)	10.16 (2.34)	5.65 (2.13)	4.79 (1.17)	3.54 (1.86)	2.32 (0.90)
Pop. × structural change	-1.7e-4 (2.74)	-1.0e-4 (2.79)	-8.0e-6 (0.42)	-5.9e-5 (2.60)	-4.1e-5 (3.04)	-4.1e-5 (2.01)	-2.4e-5 (2.67)	-1.8e-5 (1.92)
% male employment/ population	-0.008 (0.11)	-0.07 (1.19)	-0.09 (4.72)	-0.08 (3.46)	-0.10 (6.78)	-0.02 (0.81)	-0.05 (4.54)	-0.03 (3.05)
% female employment/ population	-0.74 (8.55)	-0.25 (3.31)	-0.18 (8.42)	-0.28 (9.71)	-0.17 (9.60)	0.02 (0.84)	-0.11 (8.30)	-0.05 (3.94)

	(1)	(2)	(3)	(4)	(5)	(6)	(7)	(8)
% civilian female unemployment rate	8.0e−4	0.21	0.09	0.08	0.06	0.04	0.02	0.04
	(0.01)	(1.76)	(1.94)	(1.50)	(1.74)	(0.75)	(0.96)	(1.69)
% high school graduate (age ≥ 25 yrs.)	−0.03	−0.13	−0.20	−0.24	−0.12	−0.22	−0.06	−0.10
	(0.46)	(2.13)	(9.28)	(9.00)	(7.77)	(9.82)	(5.82)	(8.39)
% some college, no degree (age ≥ 25 yrs.)	−0.16	−0.31	−0.16	−0.29	−0.14	−0.32	−0.05	−0.16
	(1.51)	(3.17)	(5.22)	(7.70)	(5.92)	(8.80)	(2.88)	(8.80)
% associate college degree (age ≥ 25 yrs.)	−0.23	−0.11	−0.24	−0.28	−0.13	−0.14	−0.05	−0.12
	(1.25)	(0.66)	(4.78)	(4.27)	(3.25)	(2.46)	(1.74)	(3.98)
% bachelor's degree or more (age ≥ 25 yrs.)	−0.13	0.008	−0.04	−0.06	0.11	−0.16	0.08	−0.05
	(1.89)	(0.14)	(1.90)	(2.00)	(6.02)	(5.86)	(7.04)	(3.95)
% households female-headed with children	1.34	0.43	−0.03	1.38	0.55	0.13	0.48	0.26
	(6.51)	(2.25)	(0.40)	(16.07)	(11.21)	(1.54)	(12.61)	(6.42)
% households male-headed with children	−0.25	0.39	0.29	0.60	0.55	0.05	0.33	0.15
	(0.50)	(0.76)	(2.06)	(3.01)	(4.86)	(0.27)	(4.30)	(1.80)
% pop. African American	0.02	0.007	−0.12	−0.03	−0.06	0.04	−0.009	−0.03
	(0.66)	(0.25)	(10.15)	(2.20)	(7.33)	(3.22)	(1.73)	(4.54)
% pop. other race	−0.04	0.11	0.01	0.02	0.03	0.01	0.03	−0.003
	(0.83)	(2.32)	(0.84)	(0.86)	(2.26)	(0.64)	(3.12)	(0.28)
% pop. Hispanic	0.01	−0.07	0.05	0.03	0.003	0.006	−0.005	0.02
	(0.40)	(2.95)	(4.93)	(2.39)	(0.41)	(0.43)	(0.74)	(2.30)
R^2	0.66	0.47	0.86	0.91	0.92	0.88	0.89	0.89
N	3027	3027	3028	3028	3028	3028	3028	3028

NOTE: The specification is the same as used in column (1) of Table 6.1, with some of the results suppressed for brevity. Absolute values of robust t-statistics are in parentheses. A metropolitan county is defined using 2000 Bureau of Economic Analysis REIS county definitions. See the notes to Table 6.1 for more details on variable definitions.

[a] Because of data availability, the total county lagged poverty rate is used in columns (3), (5), (7), and (8), while the overall female-head poverty rate is used in columns (1) and (2).

SOURCE: U.S. Census Bureau (2006e) and 1969–2000 U.S. Bureau of Economic Analysis REIS data (BEA 2002).

Table 6.3 Poverty Rate Regression Results for Selected Subgroups, 1999

Group	(1) Female head w/ children	(2) Female head w/o children	(3) Married family w/ children	(4) Children <18 yrs.	(5) Age 18-to-64 yrs.	(6) Age 65 yrs. and over	(7) Under 50% of poverty line	(8) 50–100% of poverty line
Lagged poverty rate	0.17 (6.97)	0.08 (3.01)	0.29 (15.03)	0.32 (19.86)	0.41 (25.35)	0.36 (22.96)	0.31 (18.17)	0.33 (19.91)
Single-county MSA	-0.72 (0.45)	-1.50 (0.88)	-0.24 (0.54)	-1.23 (1.89)	-0.57 (1.29)	0.53 (0.88)	-0.47 (1.57)	-0.24 (0.91)
Big-MSA central county	-0.04 (0.02)	-2.47 (1.27)	-0.19 (0.38)	-1.30 (1.73)	-0.54 (1.09)	0.46 (0.65)	-0.44 (1.33)	-0.31 (1.00)
Big-MSA suburban county	-0.22 (0.12)	-1.86 (0.97)	-0.78 (1.70)	-2.20 (3.10)	-1.00 (2.08)	0.17 (0.26)	-0.80 (2.48)	-0.47 (1.60)
Small-MSA central county	0.69 (0.41)	-2.20 (1.21)	-0.31 (0.68)	-0.90 (1.33)	-0.47 (1.02)	0.35 (0.55)	-0.48 (1.55)	-0.15 (0.55)
Small-MSA suburban county	-0.43 (0.27)	-1.01 (0.55)	-0.50 (1.18)	-1.74 (2.65)	-0.95 (2.19)	0.24 (0.39)	-0.70 (2.36)	-0.42 (1.60)
1995–2000 empl. growth	-0.044 (2.58)	-0.003 (0.22)	-0.007 (1.09)	-0.017 (2.13)	-0.014 (3.07)	$-2.3e{-4}$ (0.04)	$-5.7e{-4}$ (0.21)	-0.010 (2.93)
1995–2000 structural change	7.75 (1.34)	12.31 (1.94)	5.15 (2.12)	8.83 (3.07)	6.14 (3.34)	3.21 (1.13)	2.09 (1.95)	4.28 (3.36)
Pop. × structural change	$-1.9e{-5}$ (0.80)	$-4.6e{-5}$ (2.29)	$5.3e{-6}$ (0.54)	$-5.4e{-6}$ (0.48)	$-1.4e{-5}$ (2.11)	$-4.9e{-6}$ (0.45)	$-3.0e{-6}$ (0.78)	$-8.4e{-6}$ (2.09)
% male employment/population	-0.07 (1.44)	-0.007 (0.17)	-0.05 (2.69)	-0.05 (2.52)	-0.02 (1.88)	0.03 (1.69)	-0.01 (1.64)	-0.02 (2.04)
% female employment/ population	-0.52 (7.54)	-0.41 (6.47)	-0.23 (9.28)	-0.31 (11.51)	-0.18 (10.85)	-0.10 (4.42)	-0.09 (9.05)	-0.12 (9.39)

% civilian male unemployment rate	0.12 (1.27)	0.12 (1.38)	0.18 (4.42)	0.19 (4.51)	0.15 (5.48)	0.09 (2.70)	0.06 (3.24)	0.11 (5.42)
% civilian female unemployment rate	−0.03 (0.28)	−0.17 (1.70)	−0.04 (0.94)	−0.06 (1.01)	−0.03 (1.05)	−0.05 (1.09)	0.008 (0.40)	−0.04 (1.75)
% high school graduate (age ≥ 25 yrs.)	−0.10 (1.74)	−0.10 (1.80)	−0.19 (9.02)	−0.21 (8.12)	−0.11 (7.40)	−0.19 (8.83)	−0.05 (5.48)	−0.11 (8.74)
% some college, no degree (age ≥ 25 yrs.)	−0.008 (0.09)	−0.09 (1.22)	−0.12 (4.58)	−0.12 (3.98)	−0.09 (4.33)	−0.26 (9.59)	−0.06 (4.62)	−0.09 (5.78)
% associate college degree (age ≥ 25 yrs.)	−0.21 (1.56)	−0.08 (0.61)	−0.20 (4.52)	−0.30 (5.49)	−0.16 (4.40)	−0.10 (2.35)	−0.10 (4.58)	−0.10 (4.39)
% bachelor's degree or more (age ≥ 25 yrs.)	−0.18 (3.14)	0.03 (0.65)	−0.09 (4.60)	−0.07 (2.86)	6.0e−4 (0.04)	−0.15 (7.54)	0.01 (1.28)	−0.05 (4.86)
% households female-headed with children	1.18 (6.78)	0.46 (2.93)	0.13 (1.85)	1.16 (13.42)	0.48 (9.89)	0.23 (3.40)	0.39 (12.96)	0.29 (7.74)
% households male-headed with children	0.21 (0.55)	−0.39 (1.24)	−0.05 (0.39)	0.31 (2.08)	0.27 (3.42)	−0.04 (0.35)	0.15 (2.50)	0.09 (1.41)
% pop. African American	−0.10 (4.08)	0.03 (1.64)	−0.05 (5.15)	−0.04 (3.36)	−0.03 (4.16)	0.01 (1.55)	−0.006 (1.42)	−0.02 (4.41)
% pop. other race	−0.06 (2.06)	0.05 (1.61)	−0.01 (0.91)	−0.03 (2.14)	−0.01 (1.29)	0.01 (0.72)	−6.4e−4 (0.10)	−0.007 (1.02)
% pop. Hispanic	0.01 (0.48)	−0.04 (2.00)	−0.006 (0.74)	−0.02 (1.91)	−0.01 (2.18)	−0.001 (0.12)	−0.02 (3.26)	−0.001 (0.27)
R^2	0.71	0.46	0.83	0.90	0.92	0.85	0.89	0.89
N	3027	3026	3028	3028	3028	3028	3028	3028

NOTE: The specification is the same as used in column (4) of Table 6.1, with some of the results suppressed for brevity. Absolute values of robust *t*-statistics are in parentheses. A metropolitan county is defined using 2000 Bureau of Economic Analysis REIS county definitions. See the notes to Table 6.1 for more details on variable definitions.

SOURCE: U.S. Census Bureau (2006e) and 1969–2000 U.S. Bureau of Economic Analysis REIS data (BEA 2002).

more affected by a county's labor market conditions than those for the 18–64 age group, the group actually in the labor market. Not surprisingly, poverty rates for seniors are not very responsive to labor market conditions, or to county type.

The child poverty findings illustrate how the welfare of children is affected by the broader well-being of their parents and their communities. In fact, they may reflect the strongest hysteresis effects of all, because current local conditions can have a strong impact on children through their family's income. For this reason, there is a growing literature on how a child's family income has long-term impacts on that child's health, education, nutrition, income, and future welfare as an adult (Carneiro and Heckman 2003; Case et al. 2003; Karoly et al. 1998). These results relate to the emerging literature suggesting that early-childhood intervention programs have large short- and long-term future returns (Carneiro and Heckman 2003; Currie 2000; Karoly et al. 1998). A lack of labor market opportunities for poor children's parents, along with the corresponding lack of early-childhood enrichment and well-being, may underlie some of the high spatial persistence of poverty rates described earlier in this chapter and in Chapter 2.

The last set of results examines whether the strong labor market conditions of the late 1990s and the 1996 federal welfare reform lessened the number of people who were very poor vs. the number who were less poor. The corresponding dependent variables are 1) the share of the population whose household income is less than one-half of the poverty threshold, and 2) the share whose household income falls between 50 and 100 percent of the threshold. If anything, there is weak evidence that MSA counties had higher relative shares of the very poor in 1999 compared to 1989, all else being constant. Suburbs of large metropolitan areas had lower shares of the very poor in 1999—about 0.8 percentage points lower than nonmetropolitan counties, again all else being equal.

In terms of labor market effects, it is notable that there were few differences between the very poor and the less poor in 1989, as both groups benefited from stronger labor markets. By 1999, this had changed. The less poor cohort was much more strongly affected by labor market conditions than the very poor group. Indeed, this is consistent with welfare reform primarily prodding those who have some minimum level of skills to obtain work. Increasing the exposure of disadvantaged groups to labor markets was one goal of the 1996 federal welfare reform. However, this would leave a very poor cohort that lacks labor market skills, many of whom possess physical and mental disabilities that further limit their ability to take work (Freeman 2001; Moffitt 2002; Schoeni and Blank 2000). It may be the case that the five-year (or less) time limits in TANF eventually leave a large number of very poor households without reliable support and having little realistic opportunity to find employment.

With the exception of the population share that has an associate degree, the very poor poverty share was considerably less affected by average educational attainment. Conversely, the very poor share was more strongly affected by the share of female-headed and male-headed households with children. This is particularly alarming because of the short- and long-run implications for the well being of children and their community.

SUMMARY OF OVERALL COUNTY FINDINGS

This chapter has examined overall U.S. county-level poverty rates using 1990 and 2000 census of population data. The analysis produced five key findings:

1. Local poverty rates are highly persistent. We find the half-life of a county's poverty rate to be almost one decade, a duration that seems likely to underlie much of the persistence of local poverty rates identified in Chapter 2. These long-lasting effects suggest that economic shocks have lengthy impacts on localized poverty rates, which illustrates the need to tailor poverty reduction policies not just to people but also to high-poverty places.

2. Employment growth reduces poverty rates after a long duration. County employment growth in the previous five years had a statistically significant influence on poverty rates, while two-year job growth did not. This pattern implies a long-term cumulative effect for job creation that is consistent with the views of those who argue that greater labor market experience and the associated increase in wages have independent effects. Thus, the 1990s economic expansion may have had its greatest impact on poverty through its longevity, not through the remarkable labor shortages experienced near its conclusion. Child (and their parents') poverty rates were even more affected by labor market conditions than rates for the adult age groups. Because early childhood experiences have such a long-running influence on a variety of measures of well-being, these findings may have the biggest long-term impact of all.

3. The link between generic county employment growth and poverty rates is moderate. Compared to larger responses found at the state and national levels, these results suggest that a five-year employment growth increase totaling about 2 percent a year would have directly reduced the average overall 1999 county poverty rate by a modest 0.14 percentage points in the near term (and almost double that rate over the course of many years). There is another approximately 0.10-percentage-point indirect decline in the near term poverty rate that comes through increasing the employment-population rate and decreasing the unemployment rate.

4. Targeted employment growth can more effectively reduce poverty rates. When local job growth is concentrated in industries that are faring well at the national level, there is a much stronger poverty-reducing effect than from generic job growth. We believe that strong national performance in an industry reduces the incentive for migration for workers in that industry and makes it more likely that current residents will benefit from employment growth. Thus, assuming economic development efforts are worthwhile, targeting job growth can have a much greater poverty-reducing impact, which would be further enhanced if firms had incentives to hire the least-well-off original residents.

5. Poverty rates for female-headed families with children are most affected by employment growth. Compared to female-headed families without children and married-couple families with children, female-headed families with children had their poverty rates most affected by five-year employment growth. Because this influence was greater in the 1990s, this was taken as evidence that welfare reform increasingly exposed these families to labor market forces.

CONCLUSION

Although the results are suggestive of strong employment growth—possibly in conjunction with welfare reform—helping to reduce poverty during the 1990s, the results are equally cautionary about the future. For example, welfare reform exposed female-headed households more to the labor market. With a strong labor market such as occurred in the late 1990s, this can be good. But the jobless recovery after the 2001 recession will likely have detrimental poverty impacts that last well into the decade. In fact, there are early signs of adverse effects: fewer welfare leavers report that they were employed in 2002 than did in 1999, and a larger percentage of leavers report no source of income (Loprest 2003).

The results in this chapter suggest how county poverty rates are influenced by local labor markets and other local attributes. This chapter also shows why it is important to examine different-sized geographical groupings. Compared to the national- and state-level responses identified in Chapters 1 and 4, we found that county poverty rates are only about one-half as responsive to greater job growth. These findings suggest that 1) extrapolating results to larger or smaller geographical regions can lead to inaccurate conclusions, and 2), it can be challenging to eliminate smaller geographic pockets of poverty.

Beyond what was examined in this chapter, there are a host of metro and nonmetro distinctions that may affect local poverty rates. For example, unlike their rural counterparts, metropolitan counties are likely to have their own labor market effects, which relate to transportation, housing availability, and information constraints between suburban and central counties. Rural labor markets appear to be more spatially isolated than their urban cousins, which means labor market shocks in rural areas appear to have larger impacts on local wages and produce smaller commuting and migration responses (Renkow 2003; Renkow and Hoover 2000). As described in Chapter 3, each of these factors likely influences local poverty dynamics. To further capture the geographical diversity of poverty rates, Chapters 7 and 8 provide more detailed analyses of how local labor market conditions affect poverty in metropolitan and nonmetropolitan counties.

Notes

1. Metropolitan areas are generally defined by strong commuting patterns. The government definition of a metropolitan area is given in Box A.1.
2. One exception is Gundersen and Ziliak (2004), who examine annual poverty rates using state data. There are other examples of a dynamic specification following from the welfare caseload literature that present evidence that current caseloads are affected by past caseload levels (e.g., Ziliak et al. 2000).
3. Illustrating the persistence in low-skilled labor markets, Andersson et al. (2002) find that 53 percent of all workers who earned below $12,000 (1998 $) each year between 1993 and 1995 also earned below $12,000 each year between 1996 and 1998. Likewise, 54 percent of low-wage workers from 1996 to 1998 remained in low-wage jobs from 1999 to 2001 (Andersson et al. 2003). Stevens (1999), also, finds that about 30 percent of the white households and 50 percent of the black households that fall into poverty for any one year remain in poverty for at least 5 of the following 10 years.
4. Hysteresis refers to a state in which the underlying initial conditions have long-run effects, and the effects from forces of change are slow to take shape. The result is a persistent process with sluggish adjustment.
5. Not including these variables could create what is called an omitted variable bias, in which the included explanatory variables would inadvertently pick up some of the excluded variables' impact.
6. Gundersen and Ziliak (2004) find much smaller persistence using state data. Yet there are so many differences between our study and theirs that the results are not comparable. Besides differences in the use of annual data, using states may result in different offsetting aggregation patterns compared to those gotten by using counties. As well, Gundersen and Ziliak's study included measures of state income distribution. We do not include income distribution measures because there is a high likelihood of reverse causality between the poverty rate and income distribution.
7. The R^2 equaled about 0.94 in both the 1989 and 1999 poverty models. In other models that omitted all of the variables except for population measures and the state and county type indicators, the R^2 value declined to 0.48 and 0.45, respectively, for those two variables, suggesting that the other explanatory variables besides state of residence explain a significant share of the variation of the regression.
8. As described in this chapter's appendix, the more immediate impact of a variable can be derived from the corresponding variable's regression coefficient in columns (1) and (4) of Table 6.1. The disequilibrium model implies that the long-run response is larger. While we will not regularly discuss the long-run impact, using the lagged poverty-rate coefficient in column (1) indicates that the 1989 long-run effect is approximately 1.887 times larger than the short-run response, while the corresponding measure in column (4) indicates that the 1999 long-run response is about 1.639 times larger.

9. Moreover, when the two-year 1988–1990 and 1998–2000 job growth rates were added to the respective base models, they were actually positively related to poverty rates in both decades, and neither was considered further. In fact, the two-year job growth term was statistically significant in the 1999 model. The unexpectedly positive two-year employment growth response indicates that the currently employed and new commuters can fill the labor supply needs for short-term job growth spurts but that low-skilled workers will increasingly benefit if the local economy remains strong.

10. To further examine whether the influence of labor market conditions on poverty rates differs in strong or weak conditions, the 1989 and 1999 models were reestimated on subsamples that included counties in either the lower one-third in terms of five-year job growth or the upper two-thirds in terms of five-year job growth. There is no clear evidence suggesting the labor market variables had a larger effect in the strong employment growth counties.

11. The derivation of the national response is as follows. First, using the same USDOL sources as in Table 4.2, we regressed the 1960–2002 change in the national annual unemployment rate on the percentage change in national annual employment from the household survey along with the three time-period dummies shown in the table. Annual growth rates are used because at the national level lagged changes in the unemployment rate were insignificant. The results from this auxiliary regression suggest that a one standard deviation change in job growth (1.74 percent) is associated with a 0.87-point fall in the national unemployment rate (i.e., the unemployment rate falls by about 0.50 points for every one point increase in job growth). If we go by the results in column (2) of Table 1.1, a 1.00 percentage point decline in the unemployment rate reduces poverty rates by 0.23 percentage points when the unemployment rate is above 5 percent and by 0.73 points (0.23 + 0.50) when the unemployment rate falls below 5 percent. Hence, a 0.20 and a 0.64 percentage point decline in U.S. poverty rates after a one standard deviation increase in national employment growth follow from taking 0.87 × 0.23 and 0.87 × 0.73.

12. The scenario we prefer is the implicit reduced-form model that omits the unemployment and employment rate variables from the regression model, allowing the five-year employment growth coefficient to reflect the direct and indirect effects of job growth. This approach suggests short-run poverty rates would decline by −0.20 percent.

13. See Note 13 in Chapter 4 for the formal definitions of industry-mix and competitiveness employment growth. We constructed the industry-mix and competitiveness employment terms using the 11 industries in the BEA 2000 REIS data; we used overall U.S. growth rates to calculate industry-mix totals. In many counties, employment was not reported for all industries in a given year because of disclosure restrictions. In these cases, industry employment was interpolated and extrapolated, while ensuring the sum of employment in the 11 industries equaled total county employment. The unweighted mean of the 1985–1990 industry mix and competitiveness growth rates equaled 9.0 percent and −0.4 percent (std. dev. = 3.0 and 11.1). The corresponding 1995–2000 industry-mix and competitive-

ness growth rates equaled 10.1 percent and −0.9 percent (std. dev. = 2.0, 9.5).

14. For 1989, a 10-percentage-point increase in 1985–1990 industry-mix and competitiveness employment growth induced 0.72 ($t = 2.79$) and 0.12 ($t = 2.41$) percentage-point reductions in 1989 poverty. The industry-mix response is significantly different from the competitiveness effect in the 1989 model ($F = 4.89$, $p = .027$), but not in the 1999 model ($F = 2.24$, $p = .134$).

15. The competitiveness and industry-mix coefficients are significantly different from each other. The F-statistic for testing the null hypothesis that the industry-mix coefficient equals the competitiveness employment growth coefficient is 5.41 ($p = .020$).

16. The corresponding 1999 long-run poverty rate responses resulting from a one standard deviation change in the female employment-population rate and the female unemployment rate were 2.15 and −0.18 percentage points. By way of comparison to earlier chapters, a one-point decline in the 1990 and 2000 female unemployment rates is associated with a −0.07 and a 0.04 point change in the 1989 and 1999 short-run poverty rates.

17. The corresponding 1999 long-run poverty rate responses resulting from a one standard deviation change in the male employment-population rate and the male unemployment rate were 0.43 and 0.71 percentage points. In earlier chapters we saw that a one-point decline in the 1990 and 2000 male unemployment rates is associated with −0.17 and −0.15 point changes in the 1989 and 1999 short-run poverty rates.

18. Encouraging the disadvantaged to work by improving child care access could have adverse effects if the children suffer from poor-quality care. In their assessment of this issue, Loeb et al. (2003) find that children from disadvantaged backgrounds experienced positive cognitive effects when enrolled in stable arrangements, involving center-based day care or, to a smaller degree, licensed family home–based care. Hence, public support for stable child care arrangements in high-quality centers would appear to have the most favorable outcomes for disadvantaged children.

19. Unemployment is defined as both being out of work and actively seeking work, whereas nonemployment is defined as not working regardless of whether the person is seeking employment.

20. The industry-share coefficients are measured relative to public administration, the omitted category.

21. Based on USDOL employment data accessed at http://www.bls.gov/data and at http://www.bls.gov/cpi/home.htm (BLS 2006b,c).

22. Additional analysis indicated that this increase was not related to the large share of foreign immigrants engaged in agricultural production. In other analysis (not shown), two variables representing the share of the population that had immigrated to the United States between the periods of 1990–1994 and 1995–2000 were added to the 1999 poverty model, but the agricultural share coefficient was only slightly smaller than reported in Table 6.1.

23. A good example of low-income residents making short moves to neighboring areas follows from the welfare literature. Compared to the population share of

welfare recipients in the interior of a high- (low-)welfare-benefit state, McKinnish (2005) finds that there is a significantly higher (lower) share of welfare recipients in bordering counties when those counties share a border with neighbor states that pay relatively low (high) benefits.

24.   Spatial dependence can arise for several reasons. For one, spatial autocorrelation may exist because a labor-demand shock in a county spills over and affects the labor market in neighboring counties. This problem can be corrected by including weighted averages of neighboring-county characteristics (e.g., their labor market variables) as independent variables and adjusting for the autocorrelation in the residuals to improve efficiency. Another type of spatial dependence arises when there is slight spatial heterogeneity in the underlying parameters, which is mostly harmless. For instance, the determinants of poverty rates in rural Mississippi and rural Iowa counties are slightly different. Similarly, there is usually a positive spatial correlation in the explanatory variables (e.g., rural Mississippi counties tend to have low educational attainment and more minorities, and the opposite is true for rural Iowa). In this case, there will also be a positive correlation between the residuals (e.g., the model consistently overforecasts [underforecasts] poverty in rural Iowa [Mississippi]), although this has more to do with a slight misspecification due to pooling than a mechanism of shocks spilling over into nearby counties. We pool all counties to obtain the average national effect and increase efficiency, but estimating a uniform national effect does produce a loss of information when there is spatial heterogeneity. Nonetheless, standard spatial autocorrelation tests will be unable to identify whether the spatial autocorrelation in the residuals is due to spatial heterogeneity in both the specification and the explanatory variables, to omitted neighboring-county variables, or to an economic process of shocks spilling over into nearby counties. For a similar discussion, see McMillen (2003, 2004).

25.   Spatial autocorrelation of the residuals was tested with a Lagrange multiplier test (Bera and Yoon 1993), using both a Delaunay Triangulation and nearest-neighbor routines to compute the spatial contiguity weight matrices. The Delaunay Triangulation was computed using a MATLAB program (xy2cont) written by Kelly Pace that relied on a Delaunay routine provided by MATLAB. We employed the w2 matrix, which is a row-stochastic spatial weight matrix. The nearest-neighbor-based contiguity matrices were computed using the MATLAB program make_neighborsw, written by James LeSage, in which the number of prespecified nearest neighbors ranged between four and eight. All programs can be found at http://www.spatial-econometrics.com.

26.   A spatial error model was estimated using the sem.m MATLAB routine written by James LeSage and accessed at http://www.spatial-econometrics.com.

27.   Evidence consistent with welfare reform being a strong impetus for a greater 1999 labor market response for female-headed families with children is provided in analogous 1989 and 1999 regressions using the percentage of the population between 100 and 150 percent of the poverty line (not shown). First, the five-year employment growth had similar statistically significant negative effects in both periods. Yet the percentage of households that were female-headed families with

children had virtually no effect in the 1989 model, while it had a positive and significant response in the 1999 model. Hence, female heads with children—the group most affected by welfare reform—was more concentrated among the near-poor, suggesting that welfare reform may have helped lift many of these families above poverty, though this does not rule out offsetting adverse effects on other demographic groups.

7
Poverty in Metropolitan America

That wealth is not their wealth.
   —Secretary of Housing and Urban Development Andrew Cuomo,
   during a 1999 visit to Guadalupe, Arizona, contrasting the tremendous growth in the Phoenix metro area with the persistent poverty
   in Guadalupe

Chapter 2 illustrated the wide variation in poverty rates across
U.S. counties—both across metropolitan and nonmetropolitan counties
and across central-city and suburban counties. Chapter 6 assessed the
causes of poverty rates using regression analysis for all U.S. counties.
While this analysis discovered a multitude of findings for the "typical"
U.S. county, it may have overlooked heterogeneities that exist between
densely populated metropolitan and nonmetropolitan counties. For example, metropolitan areas may attract more migrants in response to job
growth, and they are often home to higher shares of minorities. Large
metro areas also include a disproportionate share of welfare recipients
(Waller and Berube 2002). Having more than twice as many long-term
welfare recipients as what would be expected based on population further reinforces this high share, giving large MSAs an especially hard-
to-serve disadvantaged population.[1]

Even within metropolitan areas, there is often significant heterogeneity between central cities and their suburbs. Chapter 3 described how
factors such as spatial mismatch and neighborhood effects can produce
entirely different poverty dynamics. For example, Berube and Frey
(2002) find that among the 102 largest MSAs, central cities had poverty
rates that were more than double those found in the suburbs, which
was also the pattern revealed in Chapter 2.[2] This chapter more directly
assesses the underlying determinants of poverty rates for metropolitan
areas, leaving it to the next chapter to focus on nonmetropolitan counties.

TRENDS IN 1989 AND 1999 METROPOLITAN AREA POVERTY RATES

The 2000 census defined 318 U.S. metropolitan areas, but we will not consider Anchorage or Honolulu, which leaves 316. As in Chapters 2 and 6, to ensure consistency we use the same MSA boundaries as the 2000 census for our definition of 1990 metro areas. We classify metropolitan areas by size groupings; again, we use the same size categories for each of the two periods to further ensure consistency.

Tables 7.1 and 7.2 present 1999 and 1989 descriptive statistics for the 15 metropolitan areas with the lowest poverty rates in the top panel and the 15 with the highest poverty rates in the bottom panel. Comparing the overall poverty rates in both decades, we see there was little change in the overall average for the 15 lowest poverty rates between the decades, but the average poverty rate among the 15 highest poverty rate MSAs declined by about 3 percentage points. In fact, it is remarkable that the Brownsville and McAllen-Edinburg metropolitan areas in Texas had poverty rates in 1989 above 40 percent, which is the rate applied by researchers and federal programs to assess whether an individual neighborhood or census track has chronically high poverty.[3] While these two MSAs still had high poverty rates in 1999, they both had declined by more than 6 percentage points, falling well below the 40 percent line.

In 1989, the metropolitan areas with the five lowest poverty rates were concentrated just outside of New York City, and four others in the top 15 were on the northeast coast. The metro areas with the highest poverty rates were all located in Sun Belt states, particularly Texas and Louisiana. Consistent with the historically high poverty rates in the South, 9 of the 15 highest-poverty MSAs were southeastern metropolitan areas, stretching from Gainsville, Florida, to Monroe, Louisiana.

The poverty rate patterns had changed somewhat by 1999. No longer do the MSAs surrounding New York City dominate the low-poverty rankings; the lowest metropolitan-area poverty rates are now more typically found in the Upper Midwest and Plains states. While certain Texas metropolitan areas are still in the 1999 highest poverty rate group, MSAs in central and southern California are now almost as prominent, and there are fewer high poverty rate MSAs in the Southeast. In both decades, college towns such as Athens, Georgia; Auburn-Opelika, Alabama; Flagstaff, Arizona; Bryan–College Station, Texas; Gainesville, Florida; and Las Cruces, New Mexico, were among the metropolitan areas with the highest poverty rates.[4]

For the key socioeconomic characteristics of these high and low poverty rate MSAs, we look at the values in Table 7.1, some of which are for 1999 and some of which are for 2000. The 2000 minority population share (defined as 100 minus the percent white [only] share) was, on average, about three times higher in high poverty rate counties than in low ones. However, Middlesex-Somerset-Hunterdon, New Jersey, had the third-lowest 1999 MSA poverty rate even though more than one-fourth of its population is minority. Not surprisingly, median household income in low poverty rate MSAs, on average, was almost two-thirds higher than it was in high poverty rate MSAs. The median household income was uniformly low in high poverty rate counties, but there are metropolitan areas, such as Sioux Falls, South Dakota, that had a relatively low median household income and a low poverty rate.

In high poverty rate counties, both the average share of the 2000 population that did not graduate from high school and the average 2000 unemployment rate were more than twice the level found in low poverty rate MSAs. There is more uniformity among low poverty rate metropolitan areas, though York, Pennsylvania, had a relatively low high-school completion rate. Among high poverty rate metro areas, non–high school degree attainment ranged from 11.9 percent in Gainesville, Florida, to a remarkably high 49.5 percent in McAllen-Edinburg, Texas. Likewise, unemployment rates varied from a relatively low 5.8 percent in Auburn-Opelika, Alabama, to a high 13.1 percent in Merced, California.

Between 1990 and 2000, there were some unexpected changes. In 2000, there was a much larger gap between low and high poverty rate metropolitan areas in terms of percent minority, less-than-high-school education, and unemployment rate. The average unemployment rate in high poverty rate MSAs was higher in 2000 despite the widespread "labor shortages" of the period. While other indicators such as race, educational attainment, and unemployment strongly delineated low and high poverty rate metro areas in 1999–2000, population and median household income were distinguishing features in 1989–1990. Illustrating how the 1990s boom filtered down to high poverty MSAs, median household income increased, on average, by about 50 percent over the

Table 7.1 Highest and Lowest Metropolitan Area Poverty Rates, 1999

Rank/MSA county[a]	State	Poverty rate (%)	Population	% minority	Median household income ($)	% education <12 years	Unempl. rate (%)
Lowest poverty rates							
1 Sheboygan	WI	5.2	112,646	7.5	46,237	15.6	2.6
2 Appleton-Oshkosh-Neenah	WI	5.4	358,365	5.3	47,687	12.8	3.3
3 Middlesex-Somerset-Hunterdon	NJ	5.4	1,169,641	26.3	67,308	13.5	4.4
4 Nassau-Suffolk	NY	5.6	2,753,913	18.0	68,555	13.6	3.8
5 New London-Norwich	CT	6.4	259,088	13.1	50,646	14.0	4.1
6 Rochester	MN	6.4	124,277	9.7	51,316	8.9	3.7
7 Cedar Rapids	IA	6.5	191,701	6.0	46,206	9.4	3.5
8 Wausau	WI	6.6	125,834	5.8	45,165	16.2	3.8
9 Monmouth-Ocean City	NJ	6.6	1,126,217	11.7	56,183	14.4	4.8
10 Minneapolis-St. Paul	MN-WI	6.7	2,968,806	13.9	54,481	9.4	3.5
11 York	PA	6.7	381,751	7.2	45,268	19.3	3.6
12 Barnstable-Yarmouth	MA	6.9	222,230	5.7	45,933	8.2	5.2
13 Green Bay	WI	6.9	226,778	8.8	46,447	13.7	3.8
14 Sioux Falls	SD	7.1	172,412	6.5	43,374	11.4	2.8
15 Janesville-Beloit	WI	7.3	152,307	8.9	45,517	16.1	5.6
Highest poverty rates							
302 Bakersfield	CA	20.8	661,645	38.6	35,446	31.5	12.0
303 Lafayette	LA	20.9	385,647	30.3	31,177	28.7	7.8

304	Albany	GA	21.4	120,822	53.0	34,554	24.8	8.6
305	Athens	GA	21.4	153,444	27.1	34,317	19.9	7.9
306	Merced	CA	21.7	210,554	44.2	35,532	36.2	13.1
307	Auburn–Opelika	AL	21.8	115,092	26.0	30,952	18.6	5.8
308	Fresno	CA	22.7	922,516	44.7	34,933	32.8	12.0
309	Gainesville	FL	22.8	217,955	26.5	31,426	11.9	7.0
310	El Paso	TX	23.8	679,622	25.9	31,051	34.2	9.5
311	Visalia–Tulare–Porterville	CA	23.9	368,021	42.1	33,983	38.3	12.7
312	Las Cruces	NM	25.4	174,682	32.1	29,808	30.0	9.2
313	Bryan–College Station	TX	26.9	152,415	25.4	29,104	18.7	8.5
314	Laredo	TX	31.2	193,117	17.8	28,100	47.0	9.3
315	Brownsville–Harlingen–San Benito	TX	33.1	335,227	19.6	26,155	44.8	11.4
316	McAllen–Edinburg	TX	35.9	569,463	22.3	24,863	49.5	12.0
Avg. pov. rate, all MSAs (std. dev. = 4.4)			12.6					

NOTE: Poverty rates and median household income are measured for 1999; the other variables are for 2000. Anchorage and Honolulu are not included. Percent minority is 100 minus the percentage of persons that consider white/Caucasian to be their single racial group.
a Metropolitan area definitions follow those in place for the 2000 census as defined by the Bureau of Economic Analysis. For details, see Chapters 2 and 6.

SOURCE: U.S. Census Bureau (2006e).

Table 7.2 Highest and Lowest Metropolitan Area Poverty Rates, 1989

Rank/MSA county[a]	State	Poverty rate (%)	Population	% minority	Median household income ($)	% education <12 years	Unempl. rate (%)
Lowest poverty rates							
1 Nassau-Suffolk	NY	4.2	2,609,212	11.5	51,671	16.8	4.5
2 Middlesex-Somerset-Hunterdon	NJ	4.2	1,019,835	15.1	48,906	18.2	4.4
3 Dutchess County	NY	5.4	259,462	11.5	42,250	20.2	4.2
4 Monmouth-Ocean City	NJ	5.4	986,327	9.1	40,289	20.7	5.5
5 Bergen-Passaic	NJ	6.1	1,278,440	18.2	45,119	22.7	5.4
6 York	PA	6.3	339,574	4.8	32,605	27.2	3.8
7 New London-Norwich	CT	6.4	254,957	8.2	37,488	19.1	6.0
8 Sheboygan	WI	6.5	103,877	3.5	31,603	22.6	4.1
9 Washington	DC-MD-VA-WV	6.6	4,223,485	32.6	46,538	15.7	3.7
10 Rochester	MN	6.9	106,470	4.1	35,789	12.0	3.4
11 New Haven-Bridgeport-Stamford-Danbury-Waterbury	CT	7.0	1,631,864	14.8	44,263	20.7	5.6
12 Elkhart-Goshen	IN	7.0	156,198	6.3	30,973	27.2	3.7
13 Hartford	CT	7.1	1,123,678	13.7	41,446	20.9	4.9
14 Appleton-Oshkosh-Neenah	WI	7.2	315,121	2.6	32,125	19.1	4.1
15 Ventura	CA	7.3	669,016	20.8	45,612	20.6	4.8

Highest poverty rates

302 Flagstaff	AZ-UT	22.7	101,760	33.9	25,859	20.8	8.9
303 Albany	GA	22.8	112,561	46.7	24,653	32.1	9.4
304 Gainesville	FL	23.5	181,596	22.4	22,084	17.3	5.6
305 Houma	LA	23.6	182,842	19.0	21,601	42.0	8.2
306 Pinebluff	AR	23.9	85,487	43.9	21,322	34.1	9.9
307 Monroe	LA	24.7	142,191	32.0	21,129	28.4	8.7
308 Hattiesburg	MS	24.7	98,738	25.8	19,612	27.5	7.8
309 Auburn–Opelika	AL	24.9	87,146	25.5	21,227	26.8	6.7
310 Las Cruces	NM	26.5	135,510	8.7	21,859	29.6	9.4
311 Lafayette	LA	26.6	344,953	28.4	20,074	36.4	9.5
312 Bryan–College Station	TX	26.7	121,862	22.2	20,411	20.2	5.7
313 El Paso	TX	26.8	591,610	23.4	22,644	36.3	10.7
314 Laredo	TX	38.2	133,239	29.5	18,074	52.2	11.6
315 Brownsville–Harlingen–San Benito	TX	39.7	260,120	17.6	17,336	50.0	13.3
316 McAllen–Edinburg	TX	41.9	383,545	25.2	16,703	53.4	14.3
Avg. pov. rate, all MSAs (std. dev. = 5.1)		13.6					

NOTE: Poverty rates and median household income are measured for 1989; the other variables are for 1990. Anchorage and Honolulu are not included. Percent minority is 100 minus the percentage that consider white/Caucasian to be their single racial group.
[a] Metropolitan area definitions follow those in place for the 2000 census as defined by the Bureau of Economic Analysis. For details, see Chapters 2 and 6.
SOURCE: U.S. Census Bureau (2006e).

decade for the high poverty rate metro areas, while the corresponding increase for low poverty rate areas was only about 25 percent.[5] Hence, despite a relative weakening in some indicators over the decade, the 3-percentage-point average decline in the poverty rate in the high poverty group appears to relate to greater household income.

POVERTY RATES BY METROPOLITAN SIZE

Tables 7.3 and 7.4 report 1999–2000 and 1989–1990 socioeconomic indicators in large, medium, and small metro areas for the highest and lowest poverty rate MSAs in each size classification. Following the classification criteria used in Chapters 2 and 6, "large" metropolitan areas are the 61 MSAs with a 2000 population greater than 1 million. For these 61 MSAs, the lowest and highest five poverty rates are reported. Cities with a 2000 population of less than one million were divided into 160 "small" metropolitan areas of less than 300,000 people and 95 "medium" metropolitan areas of between 300,000 and 1,000,000 people. For the small and medium MSA groups, the lowest and highest 10 metropolitan areas in terms of poverty rates are reported.

On the positive side, among the largest metropolitan areas in 1999, Minneapolis–St. Paul broke into the lowest poverty group. A more discouraging finding for large metro areas in 1999 is that the two largest U.S. metropolitan areas—New York and Los Angeles–Long Beach—had the highest and fourth-highest poverty rates. The three other high-poverty-rate large metro areas in the top five in 1999—Memphis, Miami, and New Orleans—were also in the top five in 1989, as was New York.

The medium-sized metropolitan areas with the lowest poverty rates in 1999 tend to be concentrated in Pennsylvania, Delaware, and the Midwest. Nine of the ten highest poverty rate medium-sized MSAs were in Louisiana, Texas, and California, with the highest rates found near the Rio Grande. The one outlier—an MSA encompassing Huntington, West Virginia, and Ashland, Ohio—is located in Appalachia. Among the smaller metropolitan areas, the lowest poverty rates tend to be concentrated in the Upper Midwest. Eight of the ten highest poverty rates among small metro areas were located in the Deep South and Texas, including a strong representation of college towns.

Not surprisingly, a consistent pattern across the three size groups is that the highest-poverty metropolitan areas tend to have two to four times greater minority population shares than the lowest poverty rate MSAs. Yet there are exceptions, such as Huntington-Ashland, which had only about a 4 percent minority share even though its 1999 poverty rate was over 18 percent. One distinction across the size categories is that the highest-poverty large metropolitan areas tend to have lower unemployment rates than the corresponding medium and small metropolitan areas.

Table 7.5 reports the largest and smallest decreases in poverty rates between 1989 and 1999 using the same three size categories. One pattern that emerges in Table 7.3 is that areas with high poverty rates in 1989 had among the largest declines— a reversion to the mean. Across the size groupings, the largest declines often occurred in Texas metro areas or in other historically high-poverty southern MSAs. Michigan's Rust Belt metropolitan areas were among the group with the greatest declines in poverty rates (Detroit, Flint, and Saginaw–Bay City–Midland), and there were rapid declines in high-amenity magnets in Arizona, Colorado, and Utah. Consistently, MSAs that experienced the largest poverty rate declines tended to be less populated.

A troubling pattern is that the greatest poverty rate increases were clustered near heavily populated New York and Los Angeles. Both areas struggled in the early 1990s, and their 2000 unemployment rates had grown from their 1990 levels. They also experienced large influxes of foreign immigrants, which may have placed further pressure on the wages and opportunities of disadvantaged native workers. Like the New York City and Los Angeles MSAs, small and medium-sized New York and California metropolitan areas experienced among the highest increases in poverty rates. A feature they have in common with the two largest cities is that these smaller areas did not appreciably gain from the 1990s economic boom.

Perhaps the clearest way an area's overall health is revealed is through its net migration flows (Partridge and Rickman 2003a). Table 7.5 shows that among medium and large metropolitan areas, those having the largest decreases in poverty rates in the 1990s also had population growth rates about 2 percentage points greater on average than

Table 7.3 Highest and Lowest Poverty Rates for Large, Medium, and Small Metropolitan Areas, 1999

Rank/MSA county[a]	State	Poverty rate 1999 (%)	Population 2000	% minority 2000	Median household income 1999 ($)	% education <12 years 2000	Unempl. rate 2000 (%)
Large: MSA pop. ≥ 1 million							
Lowest poverty rates							
1 Middlesex-Somerset-Hunterdon	NJ	5.4	1,169,641	26.3	67,308	13.5	4.4
2 Nassau-Suffolk	NY	5.6	2,753,913	18.0	68,555	13.6	3.8
3 Monmouth–Ocean City	NJ	6.6	1,126,217	11.7	56,183	14.4	4.8
4 Minneapolis–St. Paul	MN-WI	6.7	2,968,806	13.9	54,481	9.4	3.5
5 Washington	DC-MD-VA-WV	7.4	4,923,153	40.0	63,675	13.3	4.3
Highest poverty rates							
57 Memphis	AR-MS-TN	15.3	1,135,614	47.1	40,101	20.2	6.4
58 Los Angeles–Long Beach	CA	17.9	9,519,338	51.4	42,189	30.1	8.2
59 Miami	FL	18.0	2,253,362	30.3	35,966	32.1	8.7
60 New Orleans	LA	18.4	1,337,726	42.7	35,784	22.3	6.8
61 New York	NY	19.5	9,314,235	51.2	42,137	26.0	8.8
Medium: MSA pop. > 300,000 & < 1 million							
Lowest poverty rates							
1 Appleton-Oshkosh-Neenah	WI	5.4	358,365	5.3	47,687	12.8	3.3
2 York	PA	6.7	381,751	7.2	45,268	19.3	3.6
3 Des Moines	IA	7.5	456,022	10.2	46,709	11.4	4.4
4 Lancaster	PA	7.8	470,658	8.4	45,507	22.6	3.0

5 Colorado Springs	CO	8.0	516,929	18.7	46,844	8.7	4.7
6 Santa Rosa	CA	8.1	458,614	18.5	53,076	15.1	4.3
7 Harrisburg–Lebanon–Carlisle	PA	8.1	629,401	12.2	43,172	16.9	3.9
8 Fort Wayne	IN	8.2	502,141	11.9	42,876	14.7	4.2
9 Ann Arbor	MI	8.2	578,736	14.6	55,101	9.9	3.8
10 Wilmington–Newark	DE-MD	8.2	586,216	23.9	52,139	15.2	5.0
Highest poverty rates							
86 Corpus Christi	TX	18.2	380,783	27.0	35,761	26.1	7.6
87 Huntington–Ashland	KY-OH-WV	18.3	315,538	4.0	29,380	24.4	7.9
88 Shreveport–Bossier City	LA	19.2	392,302	40.3	33,079	21.1	8.2
89 Bakersfield	CA	20.8	661,645	38.6	35,446	31.5	12.0
90 Lafayette	LA	20.9	385,647	30.3	31,177	28.7	7.8
91 Fresno	CA	22.7	922,516	44.7	34,933	32.8	12.0
92 El Paso	TX	23.8	679,622	25.9	31,051	34.2	9.5
93 Visalia–Tulare–Porterville	CA	23.9	368,021	42.1	33,983	38.3	12.7
94 Brownsville–Harlingen–San Benito	TX	33.1	335,227	19.6	26,155	44.8	11.4
95 McAllen–Edinburg	TX	35.9	569,463	22.3	24,863	49.5	12.0
Small: MSA pop. ≤ 300,000							
Lowest poverty rates							
1 Sheboygan	WI	5.2	112,646	7.5	46,237	15.6	2.6
2 New London–Norwich	CT	6.4	259,088	13.1	50,646	14.0	4.1
3 Rochester	MN	6.4	124,277	9.7	51,316	8.9	3.7
4 Cedar Rapids	IA	6.5	191,701	6.0	46,206	9.4	3.5
5 Wausau	WI	6.6	125,834	5.8	45,165	16.2	3.8

(continued)

Table 7.3 (continued)

Rank/MSA county[a]	State	Poverty rate 1999 (%)	Population 2000	% minority 2000	Median household income 1999 ($)	% education <12 years 2000	Unempl. rate 2000 (%)
6 Barnstable-Yarmouth	MA	6.9	222,230	5.7	45,933	8.2	5.2
7 Green Bay	WI	6.9	226,778	8.8	46,447	13.7	3.8
8 Sioux Falls	SD	7.1	172,412	6.5	43,374	11.4	2.8
9 Janesville-Beloit	WI	7.3	152,307	8.9	45,517	16.1	5.6
10 Kenosha	WI	7.5	149,577	11.5	46,970	16.5	5.8
Highest poverty rates							
151 Alexandria	LA	20.5	126,337	33.8	29,856	25.4	7.1
152 Monroe	LA	20.7	147,250	35.6	32,047	21.4	8.2
153 Albany	GA	21.4	120,822	53.0	34,554	24.8	8.6
154 Athens	GA	21.4	153,444	27.1	34,317	19.9	7.9
155 Merced	CA	21.7	210,554	44.2	35,532	36.2	13.1
156 Auburn-Opelika	AL	21.8	115,092	26.0	30,952	18.6	5.8
157 Gainesville	FL	22.8	217,955	26.5	31,426	11.9	7.0
158 Las Cruces	NM	25.4	174,682	32.1	29,808	30.0	9.2
159 Bryan-College Station	TX	26.9	152,415	25.4	29,104	18.7	8.5
160 Laredo	TX	31.2	193,117	17.8	28,100	47.0	9.3

NOTE: Large: MSA pop. ≥ 1 million in 2000, avg. 1999 pov. rate = 10.6 (std. dev. = 2.9). Medium: MSA pop. > 300,000 & < 1 million in 2000, avg. 1999 pov. rate = 12.7 (std. dev. = 4.9). Small: MSA pop. ≤ 300,000, avg. 1999 pov. rate = 13.3 (std. dev. = 4.3). Poverty rates and median household income are measured for 1999; the other variables are for 2000. Anchorage and Honolulu are not included. Percent minority is 100 minus the percentage that consider white/Caucasian to be their single racial group.

[a] Metropolitan area definitions follow those in place for the 2000 census as defined by the Bureau of Economic Analysis. For details, see Chapters 2 and 6.

SOURCE: U.S. Census Bureau (2006e).

those that had the largest poverty rate increases (or smallest decreases). For the smallest MSAs, those with the greatest declines in poverty rates averaged approximately 4 percentage points larger population growth than the least successful ones. This pattern is consistent with metro areas that had the most rapid declines in poverty rates becoming generally more attractive to the overall population. Yet, as column (10) shows, it was only in the small and medium-sized MSAs that the more rapid average population growth translated into a significant advantage in average employment growth. In these MSAs, it appears that favorable economic conditions attracted new migrants while also improving wage and job opportunities for the disadvantaged.

There is no clear relationship between the minority population share and whether an MSA experienced one of the largest or smallest declines in poverty rates. For example, poverty rates declined rapidly in Memphis, Tennessee, which had a 47 percent minority population share in 2000, and also in Grand Junction, Colorado, which had an 8 percent minority population share. The same can be said about metro areas that experienced the largest increases in poverty rates. New York and Los Angeles are prime examples of cities having high minority population shares, while Elmira and Binghamton, New York, have the opposite characteristics. But all experienced large increases in poverty rates.

However, a more telling demographic was recent immigrant population. Metro areas with the largest poverty rate declines tended to have about half the share of recent immigrants as those with the smallest declines.[6] One surprising pattern is that the MSAs with the most rapid declines in poverty rates had approximately the same adult population share that did not graduate from high school as those that had the greatest increases (or slowest declines). Similarly, MSAs with the fastest increases in poverty rates tended to have higher median household incomes than those with the greatest declines.

The above finding demonstrates that economic conditions are important. MSAs with the largest poverty rate declines consistently had lower unemployment rates in 2000 than in 1990, and the opposite applied for those with the largest increases (or smallest decreases). While the link is not as strong, metropolitan areas with the largest poverty rate declines tended to have faster job growth.

Table 7.4 Highest and Lowest Poverty Rates for Large, Medium, and Small Metropolitan Areas, 1989

Rank/MSA county[a]	State	Pov. rate 1989 (%)	Population 2000	Population 1990	% minority 1990	Median household income 1989 ($)	% education <12 Years 1990	Unempl. rate 1990 (%)
Large: MSA pop. ≥ 1 million								
Lowest poverty rates								
1 Nassau-Suffolk	NY	4.2	2,753,913	2,609,212	11.5	51,671	16.8	4.5
2 Middlesex-Somerset-Hunterdon	NJ	4.2	1,169,641	1,019,835	15.1	48,906	18.2	4.4
3 Monmouth–Ocean City	NJ	5.4	1,126,217	986,327	9.1	40,289	20.7	5.5
4 Bergen-Passaic	NJ	6.1	1,373,167	1,278,440	18.2	45,119	22.7	5.4
5 Washington	DC-MD-VA-WV	6.6	4,923,153	4,223,485	32.6	46,538	15.7	3.7
Highest poverty rates								
57 New York	NY	17.5	9,314,235	8,546,846	43.5	32,490	29.7	8.3
58 Miami	FL	17.9	2,253,362	1,937,094	26.9	26,909	35.0	7.7
59 Memphis	AR-MS-TN	18.5	1,135,614	1,007,306	42.0	26,890	26.9	7.3
60 San Antonio	TX	19.5	1,592,383	1,324,749	24.6	26,060	27.5	8.3
61 New Orleans	LA	21.3	1,337,726	1,285,270	37.8	24,456	28.1	9.2
Medium: MSA pop. >300,000 & < 1 million								
Lowest poverty rates								
1 York	PA	6.3	381,751	339,574	4.8	32,605	27.2	3.8
2 Appleton-Oshkosh-Neenah	WI	7.2	358,365	315,121	2.6	32,125	19.1	4.1

3	Ventura	CA	7.3	753,197	669,016	20.8	45,612	20.6	4.8
4	Vallejo–Fairfield–Napa	CA	7.3	518,821	451,186	27.8	38,539	17.8	5.8
5	Trenton	NJ	7.4	350,761	325,824	24.8	41,227	22.9	5.2
6	Allentown–Bethlehem–Easton	PA	7.5	637,958	595,081	5.7	31,971	26.5	4.7
7	Wilmington–Newark	DE-MD	7.5	586,216	513,293	17.5	38,256	20.5	3.9
8	Santa Rosa	CA	7.6	458,614	388,222	9.3	36,299	15.6	4.8
9	Fort Wayne	IN	7.6	502,141	456,281	8.4	31,318	20.0	4.8
10	Harrisburg–Lebanon–Carlisle	PA	7.8	629,401	587,986	8.6	31,755	23.1	3.8
Highest poverty rates									
86	Mobile	AL	19.9	540,258	476,923	28.9	23,554	29.2	8.2
87	Huntington–Ashland	KY-OH-WV	20.3	315,538	312,529	2.6	21,172	33.3	9.4
88	Fresno	CA	21.0	922,516	755,580	35.5	26,493	34.1	9.8
89	Corpus Christi	TX	21.6	380,783	349,894	24.1	24,922	32.4	8.6
90	Shreveport–Bossier City	LA	22.4	392,302	376,330	35.7	22,822	26.5	10.7
91	Visalia–Tulare–Porterville	CA	22.6	368,021	311,921	34.1	24,450	39.8	10.7
92	Lafayette	LA	26.6	385,647	344,953	28.4	20,074	36.4	9.5
93	El Paso	TX	26.8	679,622	591,610	23.4	22,644	36.3	10.7
94	Brownsville–Harlingen–San Benito	TX	39.7	335,227	260,120	17.6	17,336	50.0	13.3
95	McAllen–Edinburg	TX	41.9	569,463	383,545	25.2	16,703	53.4	14.3
Small: MSA pop. ≤ 300,000									
Lowest poverty rates									
1	Dutchess County	NY	5.4	280,150	259,462	11.5	42,250	20.2	4.2
2	New London–Norwich	CT	6.4	259,088	254,957	8.2	37,488	19.1	6.0

(continued)

Table 7.4 (continued)

Rank/MSA county[a]	State	Pov. rate 1989 (%)	Population 2000	Population 1990	% minority 1990	Median household income 1989 ($)	% education <12 Years 1990	Unempl. rate 1990 (%)
3 Sheboygan	WI	6.5	112,646	103,877	3.5	31,603	22.6	4.1
4 Rochester	MN	6.9	124,277	106,470	4.1	35,789	12.0	3.4
5 Elkhart-Goshen	IN	7.0	182,791	156,198	6.3	30,973	27.2	3.7
6 Barnstable-Yarmouth	MA	7.5	222,230	186,605	3.8	31,766	11.6	7.1
7 Punta Gorda	FL	7.5	141,627	110,975	5.1	25,746	24.3	4.5
8 Sioux Falls	SD	7.8	172,412	139,236	2.5	27,850	17.3	2.8
9 Wausau	WI	7.9	125,834	115,400	2.6	30,143	24.1	3.9
10 Portland	ME	8.0	265,612	243,135	2.0	32,286	15.0	5.2
Highest poverty rates								
151 Albany	GA	22.8	120,822	112,561	46.7	24,653	32.1	9.4
152 Gainesville	FL	23.5	217,955	181,596	22.4	22,084	17.3	5.6
153 Houma	LA	23.6	194,477	182,842	19.0	21,601	42.0	8.2
154 Pinebluff	AR	23.9	84,278	85,487	43.9	21,322	34.1	9.9
155 Monroe	LA	24.7	147,250	142,191	32.0	21,129	28.4	8.7
156 Hattiesburg	MS	24.7	111,674	98,738	25.8	19,612	27.5	7.8
157 Auburn-Opelika	AL	24.9	115,092	87,146	25.5	21,227	26.8	6.7
158 Las Cruces	NM	26.5	174,682	135,510	8.7	21,859	29.6	9.4
159 Bryan-College Station	TX	26.7	152,415	121,862	22.2	20,411	20.2	5.7
160 Laredo	TX	38.2	193,117	133,239	29.5	18,074	52.2	11.6

NOTE: Large: MSA pop. ≥ 1 million in 2000, avg. 1989 pov. rate = 10.9 (std. dev. = 3.4). Medium: MSA pop. > 300,000 & < 1 million in 2000, avg. 1989 pov. rate = 13.6 (std. dev. = 5.8). Small: MSA pop. $\leq$ 300,000 in 2000, avg. 1989 pov. rate = 14.6 (std. dev. = 4.8). Poverty rates and median household income are measured for 1989; the other variables are for 1990 or 2000. Anchorage and Honolulu are not included. Percent minority is 100 minus the percentage that consider white/Caucasian to be their single racial group.

[a] Metropolitan area definitions follow those in place for the 2000 census as defined by the Bureau of Economic Analysis. For details, see Chapters 2 and 6.

SOURCE: U.S. Census Bureau (2006e).

Table 7.5 Change in Poverty Rates from 1990 to 2000 for Large, Medium, and Small Metropolitan Areas

Rank/MSA county[a]	State	(1) % change in poverty rate 1990–2000	(2) Population 2000	(3) Population change % 1990–2000	(4) % foreign immigrants 1995–2000[b]	(5) % minority 2000	(6) % education <12 years 2000	(7) Median hh. income 1999 ($)	(8) Unempl. rate (%) 1990	(9) Unempl. rate (%) 2000	(10) Empl. growth (%) 1995–2000
Large: MSA pop. ≥ 1 million in 2000											
Largest decrease in poverty rates											
1 Austin–San Marcos	TX	-4.8	1,249,763	32.3	4.4	27.6	15.2	48,991	5.9	4.0	28.1
2 San Antonio	TX	-4.4	1,592,383	16.8	2.1	29.3	22.7	39,059	8.3	5.7	15.7
3 Memphis	AR-MS-TN	-3.1	1,135,614	11.3	1.2	47.1	20.2	40,101	7.3	6.4	11.4
4 New Orleans	LA	-2.9	1,337,726	3.9	0.8	42.7	22.3	35,784	9.2	6.8	6.5
5 Detroit	MI	-2.4	4,441,551	3.9	2.0	28.8	17.9	49,249	8.9	5.9	10.0
Largest increase in poverty rates											
57 Bergen-Passaic	NJ	1.5	1,373,167	6.9	5.4	27.5	17.9	59,532	5.4	5.1	7.2
58 Orange County	CA	1.9	2,846,289	15.3	5.8	35.3	20.5	58,820	4.8	5.0	18.7
59 New York	NY	2.0	9,314,235	8.2	7.2	51.2	26.0	42,137	8.3	8.8	12.4
60 Los Angeles–Long Beach	CA	2.8	9,519,338	6.9	6.3	51.4	30.1	42,189	7.4	8.2	9.6
61 Riverside–San Bernardino	CA	2.9	3,254,821	20.5	3.0	38.1	25.4	42,456	7.4	7.9	24.4
Medium: MSA pop. > 300,000 & < 1 million in 2000											
Largest decrease in poverty rates											
1 Brownsville–Harlingen–San Benito	TX	-6.6	335,227	22.4	4.3	19.6	44.8	26,155	13.3	11.4	18.5
2 McAllen–Edinburg	TX	-6.0	569,463	32.6	5.6	22.3	49.5	24,863	14.3	12.0	27.9

3	Lafayette	LA	−5.7	385,647	10.6	0.5	30.3	28.7	31,177	9.5	7.8	12.8
4	Biloxi-Gulfport-Pascagoula	MS	−4.4	363,988	14.2	0.7	24.1	19.8	36,836	8.3	6.4	14.2
5	Mobile	AL	−3.6	540,258	11.7	0.8	30.7	21.8	35,410	8.2	6.7	11.6
6	Corpus Christi	TX	−3.4	380,783	8.1	0.9	27.0	26.1	35,761	8.6	7.6	10.6
7	Flint	MI	−3.4	436,141	1.3	0.4	24.8	16.9	41,951	10.9	7.1	−0.3
8	Provo-Orem	UT	−3.4	368,536	28.5	2.7	7.7	9.1	45,833	5.2	4.8	25.6
9	Shreveport-Bossier City	LA	−3.2	392,302	4.1	0.3	40.3	21.1	33,079	10.7	8.2	7.8
10	Saginaw–Bay City–Midland	MI	−3.1	403,070	0.9	0.5	15.3	16.7	40,086	9.8	6.7	5.6

Largest increase in poverty rates

86	Reading	PA	1.4	373,638	9.9	1.0	11.8	22.0	44,714	4.5	5.1	10.0
87	Santa Barbara–Santa Maria–Lompoc	CA	1.6	399,347	7.4	4.3	27.3	20.8	46,677	5.4	6.7	12.5
88	Fresno	CA	1.7	922,516	18.1	4.1	44.7	32.8	34,933	9.8	12.0	9.6
89	Syracuse	NY	1.7	732,117	−1.4	1.1	11.2	16.2	39,698	5.8	6.2	3.7
90	Modesto	CA	1.9	446,997	17.1	3.2	30.9	29.6	40,101	10.0	11.7	17.1
91	Salinas	CA	1.9	401,762	11.5	6.6	44.1	31.6	48,305	8.4	8.7	17.4
92	Ventura	CA	2.0	753,197	11.2	3.6	30.2	19.9	59,666	4.8	5.2	13.3
93	Stockton-Lodi	CA	2.0	563,598	14.7	3.7	42.1	28.8	41,282	8.8	10.3	13.9
94	Providence-Warwick-Pawtucket	RI	2.6	962,886	4.8	2.2	15.6	22.9	41,599	6.7	5.7	7.4
95	Bakersfield	CA	3.8	661,645	17.9	3.1	38.6	31.5	35,446	9.7	12.0	12.2

(continued)

Table 7.5 (continued)

Rank/MSA county[a]	State	(1) % change in poverty rate 1990–2000	(2) Population 2000	(3) Population change % 1990–2000	(4) % foreign immigrants 1995–2000[b]	(5) % minority 2000	(6) % education <12 years 2000	(7) Median hh. income 1999 ($)	(8) Unempl. rate (%) 1990	(9) Unempl. rate (%) 2000	(10) Empl. growth (%) 1995–2000
Small: MSA pop. ≤ 300,000 in 2000											
Largest decrease in poverty rates											
1 Laredo	TX	-7.0	193,117	31.0	5.9	17.8	47.0	28,100	11.6	9.3	24.3
2 Houma	LA	-5.7	194,477	6.0	0.4	21.8	33.3	35,085	8.2	5.9	18.7
3 Hattiesburg	MS	-5.6	111,674	11.6	0.8	28.4	19.4	30,991	7.8	6.6	14.3
4 Pueblo	CO	-5.4	141,472	13.0	0.8	20.6	18.7	32,775	9.0	6.3	15.5
5 Flagstaff	AZ-UT	-5.0	122,366	16.8	1.2	35.0	16.1	38,058	8.9	6.9	19.2
6 Grand Junction	CO	-4.9	116,255	19.9	0.7	7.8	15.0	35,864	7.0	5.7	21.7
7 Lawrence	KS	-4.7	99,962	18.2	2.4	14.1	7.6	37,547	5.3	4.6	18.4
8 Victoria	TX	-4.7	84,088	11.6	0.9	25.9	23.8	38,732	6.5	4.7	11.3
9 Sumter	SC	-4.4	104,646	1.9	0.5	49.8	25.7	33,278	7.9	7.6	6.1
10 Monroe	LA	-4.0	147,250	3.4	0.2	35.6	21.4	32,047	8.7	8.2	12.1
Largest increase in poverty rates											
151 Chico-Paradise	CA	0.9	203,171	10.4	1.5	15.7	17.7	31,924	9.5	9.3	12.3
152 Yolo	CA	0.9	168,660	16.3	5.8	32.5	20.2	40,769	7.2	7.1	12.4
153 Santa Cruz–Watsonville	CA	1.2	255,602	10.1	3.7	24.9	16.8	53,998	5.2	6.1	10.9
154 Elmira	NY	1.6	91,070	-4.5	0.3	9.3	17.9	36,415	7.3	7.8	7.6
155 Binghamton	NY	1.6	252,320	-4.8	1.0	7.3	16.0	36,357	5.7	5.3	5.1
156 Redding	CA	1.6	163,256	9.9	0.5	10.9	16.7	34,335	8.8	8.7	11.0

157 Merced	CA	1.8	210,554	15.3	4.2	44.2	36.2	35,532	10.6	13.1	8.8
158 Bellingham	WA	1.9	166,814	23.4	2.5	11.7	12.5	40,005	4.8	7.4	11.0
159 Vineland-Millville-Bridgeton	NJ	2.0	146,438	5.7	1.9	34.2	31.5	39,150	7.4	9.9	4.5
160 Dutchess County	NY	2.2	280,150	7.4	1.6	16.5	16.0	53,086	4.2	5.7	9.9

NOTE: Poverty rates and median household income are measured for 1989 and 1999; the other variables are for the period stated in the column headings. Anchorage and Honolulu are not included. Percent minority is 100 minus the percentage of persons that consider white/Caucasian to be their single racial group. See discussion of census and BEA statistics in Appendix A.

[a] Metropolitan area definitions follow those in place for the 2000 census as defined by the Bureau of Economic Analysis. For details, see Chapters 2 and 6.

[b] Percentage of the population that immigrated to the United States between 1995 and 2000.

SOURCE: U.S. Census Bureau (2006e) and Bureau of Economic Analysis REIS data for employment growth (BEA 2002).

REGRESSION ANALYSIS OF MSA POVERTY RATES

Although the general patterns above are suggestive of the determinants underlying metropolitan variation in poverty rates, regression analysis is needed to draw more definitive conclusions. In the remainder of this chapter we use the empirical model from Chapter 6, in which counties remain one unit of analysis, to further examine metropolitan and nonmetropolitan poverty rates. We experimented with using the entire metropolitan area as the unit of observation, but the results were completely unsatisfactory.[7]

Table 7.6 reports regression results that divide the sample into metropolitan and nonmetropolitan counties.[8] Columns (1) and (2) report the 1989 metro county results, while columns (5) and (6) contain the 1999 metro county results. Columns (3) and (4) and columns (7) and (8) report the corresponding nonmetropolitan county results. The nonmetropolitan results are only reported to facilitate comparison. A full assessment of those results will be given in Chapter 8.

The discussion stresses the 1999 findings, though the 1989 results will be highlighted when there are key differences. Consider the 1999 results in column (5): after we account for the poverty effects of differences in their socioeconomic characteristics, big metropolitan suburban counties have approximately a half-percentage-point lower poverty rate than single-county MSAs (significant at the 0.01 level).[9] There is evidence that small-MSA (less than one million in population) suburban counties have slightly lower poverty, but this is measured imprecisely. Along with other results that suggest that poverty rates are positively related to overall metropolitan area population (not shown), these results are consistent with moderate spatial mismatch effects, especially in larger MSAs with more accessibility concerns.[10]

Metropolitan county poverty rates appear to be less affected by labor market conditions than nonmetro poverty rates. For example, industrial structural change appears to be statistically unrelated to metropolitan area poverty rates. This may be a scale effect in that metro areas may be large enough for dislocated workers to obtain a suitable employment match. Likewise, five-year employment growth has a very small influence on metropolitan county poverty rates.[11] For comparison to Chapter 6, we assess the impacts of an overall one standard deviation change, which equals 10.1 percent for 1995–2000 employment growth (from column [4] of Table A.1). This increase in five-year job growth reduces short-run metro county poverty rates by 0.07 percentage points, or less than half of the corresponding nonmetro response.

As indicated in Chapters 4 and 6, an avenue through which job growth reduces poverty rates is by reducing male and female unemployment rates and increasing employment-population rates. The quasi-reduced form model that omitted the unemployment rate and employment-population variables was one way to allow employment growth to affect poverty rates while allowing the employment and unemployment rates to vary. Using this model, a 10.1 percent increase in 1995–2000 job growth is now estimated to reduce poverty rates by about 0.13 percentage points ($t = 2.10$), with a long-run impact almost twice as large (see Note 8 in Chapter 6). While the quasireduced form results are stronger, they still indicate that overall MSA poverty rates are only modestly affected by new job growth.

The employment-population rate and the unemployment rate findings also indicate a larger nonmetropolitan labor market influence compared to the corresponding MSA models. One difference, however, is that the male unemployment rate is relatively more important and the female employment rate is relatively less important in affecting MSA poverty rates. Holding job growth constant, a one standard deviation increase in the female employment rate and a corresponding one standard deviation decline in the male unemployment rate would reduce the typical 1999 short-run MSA-county poverty rate by 0.55 and 0.67 percentage points.[12]

This pattern is further supported by the smaller single-mother coefficient in the MSA model, compared to its corresponding nonmetropolitan coefficient in Table 7.6. The relative metro or nonmetro female-headed household share pattern is similar in both the 1989 and 1999 models, suggesting that it was not caused by welfare reform or other policy changes such as the EITC expansion but, rather, reflects a factor associated with metro areas. Finally, the 1999 MSA female-head share response remains smaller than in the 1989 model, which continues a pattern that emerged in Chapter 6.

Labor market linkages with surrounding counties are assessed in the models reported in columns (2) and (6) by including the previous decade's surrounding-county average poverty rate, the overall five-year

Table 7.6 MSA and Nonmetropolitan Poverty Rate Regression Results, 1989 and 1999

Group	1989 (1) MSA base	(2) MSA broad labor mkt.	(3) Nonmetro base	(4) Nonmetro broad lab.	1999 (5) MSA base	(6) MSA broad labor mkt.	(7) Nonmetro base	(8) Nonmetro broad lab.
Lagged poverty rate	0.49 (14.97)	0.49 (14.67)	0.47 (24.25)	0.42 (19.14)	0.43 (13.01)	0.44 (13.28)	0.38 (23.65)	0.35 (19.89)
Weighted surrounding-city poverty		-0.003 (0.15)		0.11 (5.39)		-0.01 (0.88)		0.08 (4.75)
Single-county MSA								
Big-MSA central county	-0.13 (0.62)	0.13 (0.47)			-0.11 (0.67)	0.16 (0.67)		
Big-MSA suburban county	-0.10 (0.46)	0.15 (0.51)			-0.54 (2.85)	-0.27 (1.13)		
Small-MSA central county	0.14 (0.89)	0.36 (1.61)			0.10 (0.82)	0.31 (1.61)		
Small-MSA suburban county	-0.02 (0.12)	0.17 (0.65)			-0.19 (1.20)	0.06 (0.29)		
1985–90/1995–2000 empl. growth	-0.006 (0.76)	-0.003 (0.40)	-0.020 (3.37)	-0.016 (2.53)	-0.007 (1.35)	-0.005 (0.91)	-0.017 (3.05)	-0.017 (2.83)
1988–90/1995–2000 structural change	1.16 (0.31)	0.65 (0.17)	12.31 (2.54)	11.46 (2.44)	1.11 (0.53)	0.49 (0.23)	10.58 (3.49)	10.65 (3.68)
Pop. × structural change	$-2.5e{-}5$ (2.09)	$-2.3e{-}5$ (1.95)	$-4.8e{-}4$ (2.80)	$-4.3e{-}4$ (2.56)	$-2.6e{-}6$ (0.48)	$-9.6e{-}7$ (0.17)	$-2.4e{-}4$ (2.66)	$-2.2e{-}4$ (2.60)
% male employment/population	-0.06 (2.16)	-0.06 (2.12)	-0.09 (5.19)	-0.09 (5.34)	-0.03 (2.08)	-0.03 (1.91)	-0.03 (1.88)	-0.02 (1.19)
% female employment/ population	-0.14 (5.00)	-0.14 (5.02)	-0.16 (8.27)	-0.16 (7.90)	-0.08 (3.12)	-0.08 (3.08)	-0.21 (11.50)	-0.20 (10.73)

	(1)	(2)	(3)	(4)	(5)	(6)	(7)	(8)
% civilian male unemployment rate	0.32 (4.91)	0.30 (4.74)	0.15 (4.27)	0.16 (4.40)	0.23 (3.81)	0.23 (3.78)	0.14 (5.19)	0.15 (5.32)
% civilian female unemployment rate	0.02 (0.33)	0.02 (0.35)	0.07 (1.86)	0.07 (1.85)	-0.02 (0.30)	-0.02 (0.40)	-0.05 (1.36)	-0.04 (1.31)
1985–90/1995–2000 MSA empl. growth (#MSA counties ≥ 2)		-0.017 (1.41)				-0.019 (1.50)		
1985–90/1995–2000 commuting zone empl. growth				-0.02 (1.87)				-0.005 (0.55)
% of workers employed in county of residence	-0.004 (0.53)	-0.004 (0.53)		-0.003 (0.54)		0.004 (0.87)		0.01 (2.36)
% high school graduate (age ≥ 25 yrs.)	-0.10 (3.82)	-0.10 (3.79)	-0.17 (9.13)	-0.16 (8.80)	-0.15 (5.58)	-0.15 (5.54)	-0.14 (7.79)	-0.14 (7.57)
% some college, no degree (age ≥ 25 yrs.)	-0.23 (7.12)	-0.24 (7.09)	-0.19 (6.56)	-0.18 (6.43)	-0.20 (6.62)	-0.21 (6.52)	-0.11 (4.42)	-0.11 (4.57)
% associate college degree (age ≥ 25 yrs.)	-0.05 (0.68)	-0.04 (0.67)	-0.19 (4.37)	-0.18 (4.33)	-0.15 (3.18)	-0.16 (3.33)	-0.19 (4.89)	-0.21 (5.17)
% bachelor's degree or more (age ≥ 25 yrs.)	0.06 (2.07)	0.06 (2.03)	-0.004 (0.16)	0.003 (0.13)	-0.10 (4.24)	-0.11 (4.29)	-0.02 (0.96)	-0.03 (1.69)
% households female-headed w/ children	0.59 (7.61)	0.59 (7.41)	0.77 (13.43)	0.75 (13.26)	0.43 (6.55)	0.43 (6.59)	0.62 (10.50)	0.61 (10.69)
% households male-headed w/ children	0.18 (0.72)	0.18 (0.74)	0.54 (4.40)	0.57 (4.75)	-0.14 (1.02)	-0.13 (0.97)	0.28 (3.03)	0.30 (3.30)
% pop. African American	-0.03 (1.74)	-0.03 (1.68)	-0.04 (4.21)	-0.04 (4.54)	-0.01 (1.59)	-0.01 (1.51)	-0.03 (3.50)	-0.03 (3.46)
% pop. other race	0.02 (0.82)	0.02 (0.71)	0.02 (1.78)	0.03 (2.36)	-0.04 (2.48)	-0.04 (2.45)	-0.009 (0.75)	-4.6e-5 (0.00)
% pop. Hispanic	0.02 (1.96)	0.02 (2.09)	0.01 (1.27)	0.009 (0.96)	0.002 (0.26)	0.003 (0.31)	-0.02 (1.98)	-0.02 (2.52)

(continued)

Table 7.6 (continued)

	1989				1999			
	(1) MSA base	(2) MSA broad labor mkt.	(3) Nonmetro base	(4) Nonmetro broad lab.	(5) MSA base	(6) MSA broad labor mkt.	(7) Nonmetro base	(8) Nonmetro broad lab.
Group								
R^2	0.96	0.96	0.93	0.93	0.96	0.96	0.93	0.93
N	824	824	2204	2204	824	824	2204	2204

NOTE: The specifications follow those in columns (1), (3), (4), and (6) of Table 6.1, with some of the results suppressed for brevity. Blank = not applicable. Absolute values of robust t-statistics are in parentheses. A metropolitan county is defined using 2000 Bureau of Economic Analysis REIS county definitions. See the notes to Table 6.1 for more details on variable definitions.

SOURCE: Authors' compilation.

metropolitan area employment growth rate, and the corresponding share of workers that were employed in their county of residence. Focusing on the 1999 results, column (6) shows that all three of these measures are statistically insignificant. In terms of the surrounding-county poverty rate, the insignificance could represent heterogeneity in county responses. For example, low-income residents from neighboring counties may relocate to counties with lower poverty rates, which would tend to produce a positive surrounding-county effect. Yet, in other cases, wealthier residents of neighboring counties with higher poverty rates may "flee" those counties, reducing the poverty rate of the destination county. This can occur if the middle and upper classes want to avoid possible ramifications such as a deteriorating tax base, declining public services, and falling property values.

In sum, the generally different metro and nonmetro poverty responses illustrate Allard's (2004) claim that the delivery of public assistance programs needs to be differentiated for urban and rural communities. For instance, the unemployment results suggest metropolitan programs should place more emphasis on disadvantaged men than nonmetropolitan programs. Finally, although the demographic variables will not be discussed in detail, note that greater concentrations of minorities are not directly linked to higher MSA-county poverty rates (ceteris paribus), although we find evidence that greater shares of immigration increased 1999 (but not 1989) poverty rates.[13]

SUBURBAN/CENTRAL COUNTY POVERTY RATE DISPARITIES

General Regression Results

The spatial mismatch hypothesis described in Chapter 3 is one reason why different poverty patterns may exist between central counties and suburbs. Namely, factors such as limited transportation and information about suburban job opportunities reduce the likelihood that disadvantaged central city workers will be able to take these positions, while affordability, zoning, and housing discrimination limit their ability to relocate to the suburbs. Yet if employment growth occurs closer to poor communities, the spatial mismatch hypothesis implies that a greater share of disadvantaged workers will take these jobs. Hence, central county job growth would have stronger impacts on poverty than corresponding growth in suburban counties. Conversely, if disadvantaged workers lack the requisite hard and soft skills to acquire work or to remain in a job, there are fewer reasons to expect that nearby employment opportunities will make a noticeable dent in poverty rates, regardless of location.

To examine spatial differences within metropolitan areas, we divide the MSA sample into the 391 central counties and 433 suburban counties using the definitions outlined in Chapter 2.[14] The corresponding descriptive statistics for key variables are reported in Table 7.7. Table 7.8 reports the regression results. In it, columns (1) and (2) report the 1989 suburban county results, followed by the 1989 central county results in columns (3) and (4). Columns (5) to (8) report the analogous 1999 suburban and central county results. As before, most of the emphasis will be on the base 1999 suburban and central county results in columns (5) and (7).

The considerably smaller lagged 1989 suburban poverty rate coefficient suggests that central county poverty rates adjust more slowly to socioeconomic shocks, making them more persistent. To put it into perspective, a shock to a central county poverty rate would have a half-life of more than 10 years, while a shock to a suburban county has a half-life of more than six years.[15] As noted before, this persistence likely not only reflects individual household persistence of poverty rates but also "place" persistence, because central county labor markets may not adjust as quickly through migration and commuting. While place persistence may be generated by individual spatial mismatch factors such as a reduced tendency to relocate where there is more vibrant job growth, it can be exacerbated by the relocation of jobs to faster growing suburbs. For example, in the 1990s, firm relocation worsened the spatial mismatch between jobs and the residences of African Americans (Dworak-Fisher 2004; R. Martin 2004; Raphael and Stoll 2002). Consistent with this point, suburban counties in large metro areas have about a 0.5-percentage-point lower poverty rate than small metropolitan suburban counties, all else being equal.

Five-year job growth is now weakly associated with reduced suburban poverty rates (at the 0.10 level), though the link to greater job growth is much stronger in central counties (at the 0.05 level). For example, a 10.1 percent (one standard deviation) increase in employment growth reduces short-run central county poverty rates by about 0.2 percentage points, while the suburban response is just over half that size. Using the lagged 1989 poverty rate coefficient, greater persistence in central counties suggests that long-run poverty rates would fall about 0.45 percentage points and that the suburban response would be only about one-third that size.[16]

There appear to be some key gender roles in how labor market effects are transmitted. First, the short-run poverty-reducing impacts of the female employment-population rate are about twice as large in suburban counties as in central counties. Again using the overall one standard deviation changes reported in Table A.1, a 6.9-percentage-point increase in the female employment-population rate reduces short-run suburban poverty rates by about 0.9 percentage points, and the corresponding response in central-city counties is a little less than half the size. Likewise, a 2.9-percentage-point reduction in the male unemployment rate reduces short-run suburban poverty rates by about 0.84 percentage points but central county rates by only 0.35 points.

These labor market findings suggest that, compared to suburbs, central county poverty rates are more affected by job growth than by whether labor supply is tight, as reflected through their smaller responsiveness to the male unemployment rate and the female employment rate. These findings further support those who argue that public assistance policies cannot be a one-size-fits-all approach, as significant differences even exist within a given metro area. For example, transportation and household mobility constraints may be why disadvantaged persons in central counties benefit more from employment growth than their suburban counterparts. Disadvantaged suburban residents appear to benefit more from policies that enhance their ability to enter the labor force and find work. Rather than policies that enhance job growth, the suburbs may benefit more from policies that augment job-hunting and job-retention skills as well as improve child care assistance to increase labor force participation among disadvantaged females. Since jobs are more accessible to suburban dwellers, there is less need to improve work transportation.[17]

In general, the finding that minority shares are not positively related to 1999 poverty rates counters claims that urban poverty is an issue of

Table 7.7 Summary Statistics for Metropolitan Counties, 1989/90 and 1999/2000ᵃ

Group	1989–1990					1999–2000				
	(1) Total MSA	(2) MSA pop. over 1 million	(3) MSA pop. under 1 million	(4) Central MSA city	(5) Suburban MSA city	(6) Total MSA	(7) MSA pop. over 1 million	(8) MSA pop. under 1 million	(9) Central MSA city	(10) Suburban MSA city
Single-county MSAᵇ	0.17 (0.37)	0.01 (0.12)	0.28 (0.45)	0.36 (0.48)		0.17 (0.37)	0.01 (0.12)	0.28 (0.45)	0.36 (0.48)	
Big-MSA central countyᵇ	0.12 (0.32)	0.28 (0.45)		0.24 (0.43)		0.12 (0.32)	0.28 (0.45)		0.24 (0.43)	
Big-MSA suburban countyᵇ	0.29 (0.46)	0.71 (0.46)			0.56 (0.50)	0.29 (0.46)	0.71 (0.46)			0.56 (0.50)
Small-MSA central countyᵇ	0.19 (0.39)		0.33 (0.47)	0.40 (0.49)		0.19 (0.39)		0.33 (0.47)	0.40 (0.49)	
Small-MSA suburban countyᵇ	0.23 (0.42)		0.40 (0.49)		0.44 (0.50)	0.23 (0.42)		0.40 (0.49)		0.44 (0.50)
Population	239,597 (478,619)	383,433 (704,857)	138,048 (125,351)	385,526 (645,131)	107,822 (154,923)	272,984 (528,087)	439,496 (774,102)	155,425 (141,460)	433,856 (711,111)	127,716 (173,764)
MSA population	1,200,309 (1,554,358)	2,427,554 (1,788,952)	333,868 (223,534)	825,282 (1,388,983)	1,538,958 (1,618,273)	1,371,422 (1,745,655)	2,788,184 (1,963,929)	371,183 (244,702)	938,897 (1,545,049)	1,761,994 (1,824,308)
1988–90 or 1998–2000 empl. growth	5.1 (4.8)	5.4 (5.1)	4.9 (4.5)	4.5 (4.1)	5.7 (5.2)	4.7 (3.7)	5.9 (4.1)	3.8 (3.1)	4.0 (2.9)	5.3 (4.1)
1985–90 or 1995–2000 empl. growth	15.4 (11.8)	17.6 (12.7)	13.9 (10.9)	13.5 (9.8)	17.2 (13.1)	13.8 (10.8)	17.3 (12.8)	11.3 (8.3)	11.2 (7.4)	16.1 (12.7)
1988–90 or 1998–2000 structural change	0.029 (0.015)	0.030 (0.015)	0.028 (0.015)	0.023 (0.009)	0.034 (0.018)	0.022 (0.012)	0.022 (0.012)	0.022 (0.012)	0.019 (0.01)	0.025 (0.013)
1985–90 or 1995–2000 structural change	0.06 (0.024)	0.062 (0.022)	0.058 (0.025)	0.051 (0.016)	0.068 (0.027)	0.048 (0.024)	0.048 (0.026)	0.047 (0.022)	0.040 (0.016)	0.055 (0.027)

% male employment/ population	70.0	72.3	68.4	68.9	71.0	68.0	70.3	66.3	66.4	69.4
	(6.3)	(6.6)	(5.6)	(5.5)	(6.8)	(6.6)	(6.7)	(6.0)	(5.9)	(6.8)
% female employment/ population	53.4	55.7	51.9	53.4	53.5	55.4	57.2	54.2	54.8	56.1
	(6.6)	(6.5)	(6.2)	(5.9)	(7.2)	(6.1)	(5.7)	(6.0)	(5.6)	(6.4)
% civilian male unemployment rate	5.9	5.5	6.2	6.4	5.5	5.2	4.6	5.6	6.0	4.5
	(2.1)	(2.1)	(2.0)	(2.0)	(2.1)	(2.0)	(1.9)	(2.0)	(1.9)	(1.8)
% civilian female unemployment rate	6.1	5.5	6.5	6.3	5.8	5.3	4.9	5.7	6.0	4.8
	(2.2)	(1.9)	(2.3)	(2.1)	(2.3)	(2.1)	(2.0)	(2.2)	(2.1)	(2.0)
1985–90/1995–2000 MSA employment growth (# MSA counties $\geq$ 2)	12.9	13.4	8.8	12.5	13.2	11.6	13.7	6.7	11.2	11.8
	(7.0)	(7.7)	(7.7)	(7.8)	(6.5)	(5.8)	(6.2)	(5.7)	(6.0)	(5.7)
% of workers employed in county of residence	65.9	57.9	71.6	81.3	52.0	63.2	55.4	68.7	78.9	49.0
	(20.5)	(17.7)	(20.5)	(15.0)	(13.8)	(20.5)	(17.1)	(20.9)	(15.3)	(12.8)
% workers with 20–45 minute commute	35.8	38.6	33.7	33.8	37.5	37.4	39.7	35.7	35.5	39.1
	(8.1)	(7.1)	(8.2)	(8.1)	(7.8)	(7.7)	(6.5)	(8.0)	(7.7)	(7.2)
% workers with 45–90 minute commute	11.6	16.1	8.5	8.2	14.7	14.2	19.2	10.6	10.5	17.5
	(7.4)	(8.1)	(4.8)	(5.6)	(7.5)	(8.0)	(8.5)	(5.3)	(6.3)	(8.0)
N	824	341	483	391	433	824	341	483	391	433

NOTE: Unweighted descriptive statistics. Blank = not applicable. For some groups, there are fewer counties than listed, if the census did not report any individuals in that category. A metropolitan county employs 2000 Bureau of Economic Analysis REIS county definitions using the MSA population from the 2000 census.

[a] All values are in percentages except for the rows on "Population" and "MSA Population."

[b] See the text and Table A.1 for definitions of various MSA groups.

SOURCE: U.S. Census Bureau (2006e).

Table 7.8 Suburban and Central County Poverty Rate Regression Results, 1989 and 1999

	1989				1999			
Group	(1) Suburban base	(2) Suburban broad lab.	(3) Central city base	(4) Central city broad lab.	(5) Suburban base	(6) Suburban broad lab.	(7) Central city base	(8) Central city broad lab.
Lagged poverty rate	0.41 (10.21)	0.42 (9.44)	0.53 (12.44)	0.53 (12.5)	0.35 (8.70)	0.34 (8.43)	0.53 (17.86)	0.53 (17.45)
Weighted surrounding-city poverty		−0.009 (0.25)		−0.001 (0.05)		0.007 (0.27)		−0.004 (0.24)
Single-county MSA[a]								
Big-MSA central county			0.06 (0.24)	0.47 (1.40)			0.07 (0.37)	0.18 (0.67)
Big-MSA suburban county								
Small-MSA central county			0.12 (0.74)	0.44 (1.81)			0.07 (0.53)	0.16 (0.80)
Small-MSA suburban county[b]	0.41 (1.98)	0.41 (1.95)			0.46 (2.59)	0.47 (2.62)		
1985–90/1995–2000 empl. growth	−0.006 (0.67)	−0.005 (0.57)	−0.016 (1.51)	−0.008 (0.74)	−0.012 (1.66)	−0.012 (1.71)	−0.021 (2.18)	−0.180 (1.69)
1985–90/1995–2000 structural change	−0.83 (0.18)	−1.44 (0.30)	−1.19 (0.15)	−3.26 (0.40)	1.39 (0.46)	1.60 (0.52)	−1.34 (0.41)	−1.46 (0.44)
Population × structural change	−2.79e−5 (0.59)	−2.12e−5 (0.45)	−1.24e−5 (0.89)	−7.15e−6 (0.51)	−7.64e−6 (0.40)	−7.67e−6 (0.38)	−4.70e−6 (0.87)	−4.16e−6 (0.75)
% male employment/population	−0.03 (1.04)	−0.03 (1.10)	−0.05 (1.46)	0.05 (1.24)	−0.02 (1.11)	−0.02 (1.05)	−0.04 (1.40)	−0.04 (1.32)

	(1)	(2)	(3)	(4)	(5)	(6)	(7)	(8)
% female employment/population	-0.12 (3.30)	-0.12 (3.38)	-0.18 (4.52)	-0.18 (4.61)	-0.13 (4.16)	-0.12 (3.99)	-0.06 (1.84)	-0.07 (1.84)
% civilian male unemployment rate	0.45 (5.37)	0.44 (5.22)	0.24 (2.57)	0.25 (2.70)	0.29 (3.54)	0.30 (3.61)	0.12 (1.75)	0.12 (1.75)
% civilian female unemployment rate	0.061 (0.75)	0.070 (0.88)	0.054 (0.54)	0.035 (0.35)	-0.088 (1.15)	-0.087 (1.12)	0.049 (0.70)	0.047 (0.67)
1985–90/1995–00 MSA empl. growth (# MSA counties ≥ 2)		-0.007 (0.38)		-0.024 (1.75)		0.005 (0.23)		-0.008 (0.63)
% of workers employed in county of residence		-0.012 (1.11)		0.005 (0.50)		0.005 (0.60)		0.001 (0.11)
% high school graduate (age ≥ 25 yrs.)	-0.14 (4.04)	-0.14 (4.00)	-0.13 (3.71)	-0.13 (3.79)	-0.14 (4.24)	-0.14 (4.26)	-0.21 (6.71)	-0.11 (6.59)
% some college, no degree (age ≥ 25 yrs.)	-0.29 (6.63)	-0.28 (6.25)	-0.19 (4.13)	-0.20 (4.32)	-0.15 (3.39)	-0.15 (3.45)	-0.21 (6.38)	-0.21 (6.37)
% associate college degree (age ≥ 25 yrs.)	-0.54 (0.49)	-0.50 (0.47)	0.05 (0.61)	-0.04 (0.57)	-0.23 (3.56)	-0.23 (3.55)	-0.17 (2.85)	-0.17 (2.87)
% bachelor's degree or more (age ≥ 25 yrs.)	0.54 (1.58)	0.06 (1.82)	0.03 (1.11)	0.02 (0.78)	-0.10 (3.01)	-0.10 (3.09)	-0.13 (5.31)	-0.13 (5.17)
% households female-headed w/ children	0.60 (5.82)	0.59 (5.75)	0.52 (4.85)	0.51 (4.71)	0.34 (3.67)	0.34 (3.81)	0.36 (4.15)	0.36 (4.11)
% households male-headed w/ children	0.07 (0.25)	0.06 (0.19)	0.25 (0.73)	0.29 (0.83)	0.01 (0.03)	0.01 (0.04)	-0.16 (0.76)	-0.14 (0.69)
% of pop. African American	-0.008 (0.48)	-0.007 (0.39)	-0.044 (2.76)	-0.040 (2.40)	0.004 (0.33)	0.004 (0.27)	-0.024 (2.21)	-0.024 (2.12)
% of population other race	0.042 (0.79)	0.036 (0.68)	-0.007 (0.32)	-0.007 (0.32)	0.010 (0.34)	0.013 (0.45)	-0.017 (1.04)	-0.017 (1.02)

(continued)

Table 7.8 (continued)

	1989				1999			
	(1) Suburban base	(2) Suburban broad lab.	(3) Central city base	(4) Central city broad lab.	(5) Suburban base	(6) Suburban broad lab.	(7) Central city base	(8) Central city broad lab.
Group								
% of population Hispanic	0.53	0.53	0.01	0.01	−0.04	−0.04	−0.02	−0.02
	(1.92)	(1.90)	(0.87)	(0.98)	(1.72)	(1.80)	(1.58)	(1.54)
R^2	0.959	0.960	0.972	0.972	0.956	0.956	0.980	0.980
N	433	433	391	391	433	433	391	391

NOTE: The specifications follow those in columns (1), (3), (4), and (6) of Table 6.1, with some of the results suppressed for brevity. Absolute values of robust t-statistics are in parentheses. Blank = not applicable. A metropolitan county is defined using 2000 Bureau of Economic Analysis REIS county definitions. The central counties include single-county MSAs. See Chapters 2 and 6 for details of the suburban/central county definitions.

[a] In the central county regressions, the single-county metropolitan area is the omitted category.
[b] In the suburban county regression, the large metropolitan area suburb is the omitted category.

SOURCE: Authors' compilation.

race, not space. One of the factors that could be influencing the race and ethnic results is that a disproportionate share of immigrants that arrived in the 1990s were Hispanic and thus more likely to be less skilled and to face language barriers. Moreover, recent immigrants are considerably more likely to concentrate in central counties than in outer suburbs.[18] To examine whether recent immigration affects metropolitan poverty, we added the shares of the population that immigrated to the United States between 1990–1995 and 1995–2000 to the base 1999 suburban and central county models (not shown). Despite the larger share of recent immigrants in central counties, the 1995–2000 central county immigrant share was insignificant. In the suburban model, there was a strong direct relationship in which a 1-percentage-point increase in the 1995–2000 immigrant population share raised suburban county poverty rates by 0.66 percentage points ($t = 3.98$).[19]

While a complete explanation for the spatial difference between central county and suburban immigration responses is hard to trace, one likely reason for the difference is that less-skilled workers are more likely to out-migrate in response to greater immigrant competition in central counties than they are in the suburbs.[20] One possible reason for such a differential response is that a labor market–driven relocation from the central city to the suburbs is a short move towards what is likely greater access to jobs. Yet if one relocates from the suburbs for labor market reasons, the central city may not be an appealing economic option, which means that such a person would consider more-distant moves. However, the added relocation costs would dampen this migration response.

The results are robust when the lagged average surrounding-county poverty rates, the 1995–2000 metropolitan area job growth rate, and the share of workers employed in their county of residence are added to the model (shown in columns [6] and [8]). In neither central counties nor suburbs is there any evidence that these variables are significant determinants of poverty rates, which is consistent with the overall MSA results in Table 7.6.

Intrametropolitan Area Differences By Race

Racial composition may alter the way labor market conditions affect poverty rates in both suburban and central county MSAs. For example, Raphael and Stoll (2002) find that the spatial mismatch between employment and residence in metropolitan areas is considerably greater for African Americans than for whites. Hispanics and Asians fall almost exactly in the middle. Together, this suggests that the responsiveness of poverty rates to labor market conditions may be modified by the community's racial composition.

To examine whether the racial and ethnic composition of the metropolitan county alters the determination of poverty rates, the base 1999 suburban and central county regression models were reestimated after adding interactions of the race and Hispanic population shares with various labor market indicators. Panel A of Table 7.9 presents the results of adding interactions of the population shares with five-year employment growth.[21] The estimates suggest that job growth reduces poverty rates more in counties with higher African American population shares, although only the central county coefficient is significant at conventional probability levels. Suburban job growth reduces poverty rates more when there are greater non–African American minority population shares. These are rather large effects considering the scale of the share measures.[22] By contrast, suburban job growth does not appear to reduce poverty rates when the Hispanic population share is above 1 percent. Supporting these results, Weinberg, Reagan, and Yankow (2004) also find that job access has smaller impacts on Hispanic employment rates.

Our earlier analysis indicated that the male unemployment rate and the female employment rate best reflect the availability of less-skilled labor. Panel B reports regression results when we have the race and Hispanic shares interact with the male unemployment rate and the female employment-population rate. The unemployment results almost exactly correspond to the job growth findings. For example, a higher central county unemployment rate has greater adverse poverty effects when the African American share is larger.[23] The influence of the suburban female employment-population rate also appears to be strongly affected by racial composition, but not in central counties. In particular, a greater female employment rate has greater poverty-reducing impacts when the suburban county has greater shares of African Americans and Hispanics.

In summary, central counties with higher shares of African Americans experience greater poverty rate declines as a result of job growth.

Table 7.9 Alternative Metropolitan Labor Market Effects by Race and Ethnicity

Panel A: Dependent variable: 1999 county poverty rate		
	Suburban	Central county
1995–2000 employment growth × % African American	−6.9e−4 (1.31)	−1.29e−3 (2.19)
1995–2000 employment growth × % non– African American minority	−5.5e−3 (2.61)	−1.27e−3 (0.85)
1995–2000 employment growth × % Hispanic	6.3e−3 (2.77)	1.4e−3 (1.63)
1995–2000 employment growth	−5.5e−3 (0.68)	−8.5e−3 (0.58)
F-interactions[b]	3.74	2.56
(p-value)	($p = 0.0113$)	($p = 0.0555$)

Panel B: Dependent variable: 1999 county poverty rate[a]		
	Suburban	Central county
2000 male unemployment rate × % African American	−1.25e−3 (0.37)	6.1e−3 (2.19)
2000 male unemployment rate × % non–African American minority	0.048 (3.17)	4.7e−3 (0.74)
2000 male unemployment rate × % Hispanic	−0.029 (2.13)	4.3e−3 (0.85)
2000 male unemployment rate	0.224 (2.40)	−0.033 (0.40)
F-interactions[b]	3.60	3.04
(p-value)	($p = 0.0138$)	($p = 0.0293$)
2000 female empl./pop. × % African American	−3.0e−3 (2.52)	1.5e−3 (1.29)
2000 female empl./pop. × % non–African American minority	0.016 (2.64)	−7.6e−5 (0.03)
2000 female empl./pop. × % Hispanic	−8.5e−3 (1.69)	9.2e−4 (0.56)
2000 female empl./pop	−0.154 (4.43)	−0.093 (2.28)
F-interactions[b]	3.69	0.68
(p-value)	($p = 0.0122$)	($p = 0.5634$)

NOTE: The coefficients reflect the estimates when the interaction variables are added to the model shown in columns (5) and (7) of Table 7.8. In parentheses are the robust t-statistics and F-statistic p-values.
[a] In Panel B, all six race–labor market interactions were simultaneously added to the respective models.
[b] The F-statistics test the joint significance of the corresponding three interactions.
SOURCE: Authors' compilation.

Yet in suburban counties with higher African American shares, poverty rates are more affected by having a tighter female labor market than by simple job creation (i.e., higher female employment rates). For other minorities, greater job growth and lower male unemployment rates have stronger poverty-reducing impacts in suburban counties but a smaller impact in central counties. Finally, there is evidence that greater job growth and lower male unemployment rates have smaller poverty-reducing impacts in suburban counties with greater Hispanic population shares.

Stoll's (1999) study helps explain these disparate racial findings. He finds that increasing Latino and African American access to employment induces more extensive job search but that the impact is much greater for Latinos. Stoll's results are consistent with Latinos already having significant job opportunities in ethnic enclave economies, which would explain why greater job opportunities and tighter labor supplies have a smaller impact for Hispanics. He suggests that one possibility is that African Americans have weaker skills and less knowledge about more distant job opportunities. These tendencies are likely reinforced by their greater spatial isolation from employment and by a general reluctance to migrate away from family ties (Spilimbergo and Ubeda 2004). Therefore, creating jobs in central counties may have strong poverty-reducing impacts for African Americans. The large male unemployment rate response in central counties with large African American populations (holding job growth constant) supports adding structural policies, including more job counseling. Moreover, if the suburban responses relate to a general reluctance of suburban employers to hire African Americans (Holzer and Reaser 2000), then enhanced affirmative action policies are needed.

CASE STUDIES OF METROPOLITAN POVERTY TRENDS

The statistical analysis provides an assessment of the typical causes of county poverty rates, both on average and for central and suburban counties in isolation. For context on these results in specific instances, we examine three metropolitan areas as case studies: Decatur, Alabama, an example of a small metropolitan area in the South; Philadelphia, a larger and older metro area in the Northeast; and Phoenix, Arizona, a fast-growing western Sun Belt metro area.

Decatur, Alabama

Decatur, a metropolitan area of nearly 150,000 people located in northern Alabama, ranked 245 out of 316 metropolitan areas in 2000 population (U.S. Census Bureau 2006e). It consists of Lawrence and Morgan counties; the city of Decatur is the Morgan county seat. Like many regions in the South, Decatur's post–World War II economic growth was spurred by startups of chemical plants, paper mills, and other factories seeking a nonunionized, low-cost labor force (Davis 2002). In 2000, 28 percent of employed residents in the Decatur MSA worked in manufacturing, compared to an unweighted national metro average of 14 percent.

Decatur entered the 1990s economic recovery inauspiciously; its unemployment rate peaked at 8.1 percent in 1992 and 1993 (BLS 2006a). National economic growth appeared to bypass Decatur despite the fact that it set aside prime property for industrial development and despite its close proximity to rail lines and an interstate highway (Davis 2002). Like many areas of the South, Decatur suffered from a less-educated labor force and a perceived lack of the amenities that executives demand. Yet as the national economy continued to expand, booming areas began to price themselves out of the market. Real estate prices soared in these booming areas, which not only directly increased business costs but also indirectly increased costs through discouraging workers from locating there, creating labor shortages and higher wages. This made places like Decatur more economically attractive to firms seeking low-cost employees.

By 1996, the Decatur metro area unemployment rate had dropped to 5.1 percent, and it reached a low of 4.1 percent in 1998 (Davis 2002). The employment boom was fueled by high-profile openings of manufacturing facilities, such as the one by Trico Steel Company. This was accompanied by a boom in the retail and local service sectors, as a result of which occupancy at Decatur's only mall jumped from 70 percent in 1995 to 90 percent in 2000.

The tight labor market caused wages to rise. McDonald's began paying new hires $6 an hour instead of the $5.15 minimum wage, while mall security guards saw their starting wages rise 25 percent. Accompanying the increase in wages across occupations were increases associated with workers moving up the job chain. For example, McDonald's workers reportedly quit to take higher-paying jobs elsewhere or to start their own businesses.

The poverty rate in Lawrence County rose from 16.5 percent in 1989 to 17.8 percent in 1993, before falling to 16.6 in 1995, 15.2 in 1998, and 14.0 percent in 2000. Morgan County's poverty rates rose from 11.5 percent in 1989 to 12.9 percent in 1993, before steadily falling to 11.1 percent in 2000 (U.S. Census Bureau 2005b). Thus, Lawrence County was left with poverty above national and statewide rates in 2000, while Morgan County had lower relative poverty. Median household income increased in the two counties; the largest annual increases occurred during the 1993–1995 period in both metro counties, and the smallest occurred during the 1998–2000 period. In fact, in Lawrence County the median household income decreased at an annual rate of 0.5 percent from 1998 to 2000.[24] The decline may have been partly attributable to falling manufacturing employment. For instance, Courtland Mill, a subsidiary of International Paper and the largest employer in Lawrence County, in 1998 began the first of two rounds of layoffs that eventually totaled 600 workers (Decatur Daily 2003). Median household income growth also may have slowed because of an increased proportion of below-average-paying jobs at the end of the 1990s expansion.

Following the national economy, Decatur's boom ended by 2001. In that year its unemployment rate climbed to 7.4 percent in August, up from 4.3 percent the previous August (BLS 2006a). Included in the layoffs was the shutdown of the Trico Steel plant in response to fierce global competition (Davis 2002). Consistent with state and national trends, the layoffs in manufacturing were widespread across industries and continued into 2003 (ADECA 2006). Manufacturing employment dropped to 14,552 in 2002, the lowest it had been since 1982 (BEA 2006). The unemployment rate rose to an average of 7 percent in 2002, its highest rate since 1993. Low-cost advantages relative to the rest of the nation were offset by increased globalization and even lower costs in developing nations.

Decatur's large employment share in manufacturing meant that losses in that sector greatly affected the secondary economy. Laid-off workers who were more experienced, or educated, moved down the job ladder, squeezing out less-qualified workers (Davis 2002). Others who were laid off enrolled in a community college for training in new careers such as cosmetology and child care. Yet the availability and profitability of careers in secondary sectors often depend on basic employment sectors such as manufacturing, making it difficult for the region to offset the income losses associated with the layoffs. Annual wages in the Decatur metro area dropped 1.7 percent from 2001 to 2002, in contrast to a 1.4 percent gain nationally (BLS 2002).

The experience of Decatur demonstrates the importance of strong sustained national economic growth for poverty reductions. Poverty and welfare caseload declines coincided with reductions in the unemployment rate post-1993, prior to implementation of welfare reforms, and did not accelerate after their implementation. Sustained national growth forced firms to move to where there was low-cost labor, making poverty reductions geographically widespread. Conversely, high real estate prices and a lack of informal support networks likely precluded disadvantaged households from being able to make utility-improving moves to booming areas. Thus, the Decatur experience suggests that place needs to be taken into account in the design of antipoverty programs. In addition, sustained growth is required for those at the bottom of the skill distribution to benefit, as workers move up the job ladder and wage increases occur across occupations. The 2001 recession and subsequent jobless recovery have unraveled some of the 1990s' progress in reducing poverty rates, particularly in the face of strict work requirements in Alabama's welfare program. Lawrence County's poverty rate climbed to 15.1 in 2001 before before settling back down to 14.4 percent in 2002, while Morgan County's poverty rate climbed to 12.4 percent in 2001 before inching down to 12.3 percent in 2002 (U.S. Census Bureau 2005b).

Philadelphia

Encompassing Greater Philadelphia, the Philadelphia–New Jersey metropolitan area (PMSA) was the sixth largest metro area in the country, registering just over five million people in the 2000 census. Even so, it grew only 3.6 percent in the 1990s.[25] Median household income increased 34 percent from 1989 to 1999, while the poverty rate increased from 10.4 to 11.1 percent. By comparison, median U.S. household income increased 40 percent, while the poverty rate decreased from 13.1 to 12.4 percent. The Philadelphia PMSA unemployment rate began the 1990s at 4.9 percent and climbed to 7.9 percent in 1992 before dropping to 3.9 percent in 2000. At the same time, the U.S. unemployment rate dropped more substantially, from 5.6 to 4.0 percent from 1990 to 2000 (BLS 2006a,d).

In the midst of lackluster growth, the Philadelphia metro area continued to extend farther from its core in the 1990s (Brookings Institution 2003a). The suburbs experienced 7.4 percent population growth, although population losses occurred in most inner suburbs and the city of Philadelphia lost over 4 percent of its population (U.S. Census Bureau 2006b). Among the 10 largest U.S. cities, this made Philadelphia just one of two to lose population (Perry and Mackun 2001). A large population decline in the 1990s among whites, combined with modest increases in other racial categories, changed the racial composition of the city from majority white to majority minority (Brookings Institution 2003a). Nine percent of the city of Philadelphia's populace in 2000 was foreign-born, with nearly half arriving in the 1990s (U.S. Census Bureau 2006b). This is a lower immigration rate than in most large cities and may be partly attributable to more than twice as many foreign-born persons living in the suburbs as do in other metropolitan areas (Brookings Institution 2003a). Having lost married-couple families in the 1990s, Philadelphia had more single-parent families than married couples with children in 2000.

Not surprisingly, the poverty rate in the city of Philadelphia increased from 20.3 to 22.9 percent from 1989 to 1999, while the child poverty rate increased from 30.3 to 31.6 percent (Brookings Institution 2003a). Poverty in excess of 40 percent was present in several neighborhoods. Median household income increased only 25 percent, failing to keep pace with the 34 percent increase in the region's average price level and leaving it at 73 percent of the national average (BLS 2006e; U.S. Census Bureau 2006b). Only 56 percent of people 16 years and older were in the labor force in 1999, down from 58.4 percent in 1989 (U.S. Census Bureau 2006b). This meant the city of Philadelphia had the fourth-lowest labor force participation rate among the 100 largest U.S. cities, potentially reflecting an increasing distance between inner-city residents and job growth in outer suburbs (Brookings Institution 2003a). The unemployment rate for males was 6.8 percent, while it was 5.5 percent for females (U.S. Census Bureau 2006b). Additional evidence of weak central city vitality is that only 9.9 percent of work-commutes are from the suburb to the central city and more than half of metro workers commute between suburbs. Conversely, almost one-quarter of the city of Philadelphia's employed residents work outside the central city (Brookings Institution 2003a).

A study by the Manpower Demonstration Research Corporation (MDRC) suggests that welfare reforms implemented in Pennsylvania had little effect on the city of Philadelphia's poverty between 1992 and 2000. The area's weak economy was listed as a prime factor (MDRC 2003). The study found that welfare caseloads declined but that this began before the implementation of welfare reform measures, suggesting that the economy was the primary impetus for the decline. Although TANF appeared to increase the exit rate of long-term recipients, former recipients experienced marginal work placements, with pay rates near minimum wage, few fringe benefits, or only part-time hours. The percentage of women in the MDRC sample that were neither working nor receiving welfare doubled with implementation of welfare reform. Most women faced multiple barriers to working. Nearly three-fourths of the surveyed women did not have a valid driver's license or access to an automobile, which was noted as a sizable barrier considering that job creation mostly occurred in the suburbs.

Employment outcomes were better for those with a high school diploma, a level not attained by nearly 50 percent of the sampled women. Some good news was that the high school completion rate increased in the 1990s. Despite the dramatic drop in the number of welfare recipients, those who remained on welfare were geographically and socially isolated from nonrecipients. Yet the MDRC found that social conditions improved in Philadelphia's poorest neighborhoods in the 1990s and that welfare recipients in high-welfare neighborhoods were just as likely as others to work. Jargowsky (2003, p. 18) reports that the percentage of people living in neighborhoods with over 40 percent poverty fell by 3.4 percent in the 1990s; during the same decade, the corresponding drops for blacks and Hispanics were 7.5 and 12.1 percent.

The Philadelphia experience points to the importance of the economy for poverty reduction, particularly during a time of welfare reform. It also highlights the difficulties for inner-city residents of improving their economic fortunes in a large, relatively stagnant, increasingly dispersed metro area. Increased employment and lower poverty are likely to follow when there is increased job creation in the inner city, more education, or reduced barriers for inner-city residents to gain access to jobs in growing suburbs through commuting or relocating.

Phoenix

The city of Phoenix is located within the Phoenix-Mesa metropolitan area, which consists of Maricopa and Pinal counties. Its 2000 population of 3,251,876 people made it the twelfth largest metro area in the nation. It grew 45.3 percent in the 1990s, eighth fastest among the 316 MSAs in our sample. Only two of the seven metro areas that grew faster than Phoenix-Mesa had populations over one million—Las Vegas, Nevada, and Austin–San Marcos, Texas.

Except for a few neighborhoods in South Phoenix, the entire metro area experienced robust growth in the 1990s; the fastest growth (53.8 percent) occurred in the suburbs (Brookings Institution 2003b). The city of Phoenix registered a population of 1,321,045 in the 2000 census, making it the sixth largest city in the nation (Perry and Mackun 2001). And Phoenix grew 34 percent in the 1990s, making it the fastest growing city among the 10 largest U.S. cities.

A recent Brookings Institution (2003b) study highlights several notable characteristics of Phoenix MSA residents. Approximately three-fourths were employed in the four central cities (Mesa, Phoenix, Scottsdale, and Tempe). Slightly over 30 percent of the metro population moved there during the five years prior to the census. About one in five residents were foreign-born, which is about the same share as in the 100 largest U.S. cities. However, the number of foreign-born residents tripled in the 1990s, which meant that 6 of 10 foreign-born residents arrived in the 1990s. Thus, only one in five of the foreign-born residents were naturalized citizens, and three-fourths of the foreign-born originated from Mexico. In contrast to the Dallas and Denver MSAs, more immigrants resided in the city of Phoenix than in its suburbs. Phoenix's high immigration rate contributed to a younger, less educated, and poorer population. Yet nearly two-thirds of its adults were in the labor force. Immigration from Mexico during the 1990s grew the Latino population share from one-fifth to over one-third. Those over 64 years old disproportionately resided in the suburbs.

Despite the high immigration rate, during the 1989–1999 period median household income in the metro area grew from \$30,797 to \$44,752, a 45 percent increase, while the poverty rate declined from 12.3 to 12.0 percent. This was accompanied by a decrease in the unemployment rate from 6.0 to 3.1 percent. The poverty rate was 13.4 percent in the cities of Mesa, Phoenix, Scottsdale, and Tempe, and 9.6 percent outside these cities (U.S. Census Bureau 2006b).

Moreover, the number of people that lived in neighborhoods with extreme poverty—again, defined as those with a rate in excess of 40 percent—declined by 829, which when combined with population growth resulted in a reduction from 15.2 to 10.5 percent of the MSA population living in such areas (Jargowsky 2003, p. 18). Even the town of Guadalupe in Maricopa County, which then–Secretary of Housing and Urban Development Andrew Cuomo described during a visit as an example of extreme poverty in America, saw its person poverty rate decline from 40.1 percent in 1989 to 26.7 percent in 1999 (Herbert 1999; U.S. Census Bureau 2006b). Yet the number of neighborhoods defined as having extreme poverty increased from 27 to 30 over the period (Jargowsky 2003, p. 18). Most of the commuting occurred from central city to central city (57.3 percent); 18.4 percent occurred from suburb to central city, and 14.5 percent between suburbs (Brookings Institution 2003b).

Median household income grew 40.6 percent in the city of Phoenix from 1989 to 1999. In contrast to the metropolitan area, where it dropped slightly, poverty in the city of Phoenix increased from 14.2 to 15.8 percent during 1989–1999. Related child poverty also ratcheted up, from 20.0 to 21.0 percent over the period. In that same time, unemployment declined only 1.0 point, to 5.6 percent, which was less than for the entire metro area (Brookings Institution 2003b).

In November 1995, Arizona implemented a set of welfare reforms through federal waivers to the AFDC program. The reforms were called EMPOWER—Employing and Moving People Off Welfare and Encouraging Responsibility (Mills et al. 2001, p. 1). Except for exemptions to work requirements, most of the reforms were along the lines of those that later became part of the federal welfare reform implemented in August 1997. An evaluation of a sample of Phoenix metropolitan area welfare recipients when EMPOWER was implemented reveals that, while caseloads decreased dramatically and earned income increased significantly, total household income did not increase, as earned income simply replaced reductions in cash assistance and Food Stamps (Mills et al. 2001, p.8). In addition, caseloads had begun to decrease before the implementation of welfare reform measures, suggesting the economy was partly responsible for caseload reductions (p. 15). For example, metro unemployment declined from a peak of 6.6 percent annual unemployment in 1992 to 3.5 percent by 1995, eventually reaching a low of 2.7 percent in 2000 (BLS 2006a). The reasons listed by welfare recipients for not working included illness, disability, or a desire to stay at home to care for their children (Mills et al. 2001, p. 2). This further points to the benefits of a strong economy for implementing welfare reform, as well as a continuing need to improve child care supports.

The case of Phoenix points to the antipoverty benefits of strong growth in a metropolitan area. Yet the poverty rate in the city of Phoenix increased, as did the number of extreme-poverty neighborhoods in the metro area. Thus, growth is not a panacea for reducing poverty. Overall metro area improvement may mask persistent pockets of poverty and countertrends within it, particularly for an area experiencing high immigration rates of younger and less-educated cohorts. Even in the midst of this robust growth, welfare reform appears to be more effective at reducing welfare caseloads and increasing self-sufficiency than at reducing poverty.

A POLICY FRAMEWORK TO ALLEVIATE METROPOLITAN POVERTY

The findings in this chapter reinforce the conclusion that the underlying causes of poverty have a strong element of place. Not only are average poverty rates about two-thirds higher in central counties than in suburban counties, but the gap actually widened slightly in the 1990s. Besides these differences, the underlying determinants, such as for job growth, can differ. The influence of labor market conditions is even affected by county racial composition. The strong persistence of both place and person poverty rates suggest that policies need to be tailored to fit the community.

One conclusion is that job creation in central counties can help reduce poverty rates, especially when there are greater African American population shares. To be sure, job growth can mitigate poverty rates in suburban counties with high non–African American population shares as well, but its effects in such cases are more limited. Simple job growth will likely be ineffective when there are large shares of Hispanics. Nevertheless, in the cases where employment growth has been identified as being effective, we must ask what the optimal way is to achieve it.

The conventional way of encouraging economic growth is through various incentives and business tax breaks.[26] For across-the-board tax breaks at the state or regional level, Bartik (1991, 2004) contends that lost tax revenue can be justified through enhanced economic activity, especially when there are underutilized workers and infrastructure. Yet our analysis suggests that incentives need to be geographically targeted. Since the early 1980s, a common method to target economic growth in a local area has been through various types of enterprise zones. The incentives are typically state corporate-tax credits for investment and jobs, as well as local property-tax abatements (Peters and Fisher 2002). These incentives can be used in conjunction with customized training and the provision of infrastructure. Initially, enterprise zones were only utilized by states and localities, but in 1993 the federal government began to implement enterprise zones with the Empowerment Zone and Enterprise Community Act, passed that year.

Enterprise zones are typically located in distressed communities or neighborhoods (Peters and Fisher 2002). A key feature is that their incentives are aimed at encouraging firms to locate in particular places that have seen economic distress, but they generally provide few incentives to actually employ the specific residents of these distressed zones. For this and other reasons, spatially targeted enterprise zones have come under attack in recent years.

Peters and Fisher provide the most cogent criticism of enterprise zones. First, they argue that they are expensive: using early 1990s data, they find that the present discounted value of subsidies costs at least $52,000 per induced job (Peters and Fisher 2002, p. 230). Peters and Fisher argue that more cost-effective programs could be developed for disadvantaged workers, including programs that raise their skill level and enhance their mobility. A second criticism the authors level at a typical enterprise zone is that it has a design flaw that usually favors the use of capital over labor, which runs counter to the goal of hiring disadvantaged workers. Third, they say that in the 75 enterprise zones they examined, the vast majority of zone residents worked outside of the zone, while the vast majority of those working in the zone resided outside of it. The diffusion of economic activity has already been discussed in the case of generic job creation. This disappointing outcome likely relates to the lack of restrictions that would force firms to hire residents of the enterprise zones. Overall, Peters and Fisher contend that it is much better to focus efforts on directly helping the people in need rather than on targeting firms.[27]

Notwithstanding, we believe an effective policy aimed at reducing poverty rates must have some orientation toward place in terms of creating more job opportunities in distressed areas. Our primary rationale is that poverty rates are geographically persistent and low-income households are less mobile. Indeed, there is evidence that high-poverty areas actually have net in-migration of low-income households, which further exacerbates the already high poverty rates (Nord 1998).[28] Although efforts to induce residential relocation and enhance reverse commuting in urban areas have potential benefits, we are skeptical that they ever can be sufficiently implemented to make an appreciable dent in poverty. By contrast, our evidence indicates that certain types of job growth can reduce poverty. Moreover, the evidence suggests that while standard business tax incentives have modest impacts at the state level, they have far larger impacts at the intrametropolitan level.[29] Intrametropolitan development efforts have been criticized because it is presumed they primarily redistribute growth within the region. But this is precisely the goal in this case. Simply redistributing growth can reduce overall poverty in the broader region. Chapter 9 will provide more specific recommendations for antipoverty policies.

CONCLUSION

This chapter has examined trends in inter- and intrametropolitan poverty rates found by comparing the 1990 and 2000 censuses. We use basic descriptive statistics to conduct regression analysis. The primary findings can be summarized under the following six headings:

1. The lowest and highest metropolitan area poverty rates shifted west during the 1990s. The lowest metropolitan poverty rates in 1989 occurred near New York City, while the highest poverty rates were in the Deep South and Texas. By 1999, the lowest MSA poverty rates were typically found in the Upper Midwest, and the highest were found in Texas and in southern and central California.

2. Across small, medium, and large metropolitan areas, there were considerable geographical disparities. Among large MSAs, the lowest 1999 poverty rates tended to be in the Northeast. The lowest poverty rates in small and medium-sized MSAs tended to be more dispersed—in Delaware, Pennsylvania, and the Midwest. Among the 61 largest metropolitan areas, the two biggest—New York and Los Angeles—had the first- and fourth-highest poverty rates in 1999. Across all MSA size groupings, many of the highest poverty rates in 1999 were clustered in the Deep and Middle South, Texas, central and southern California, and a sampling of college-town MSAs. The largest metropolitan poverty rate declines occurred in some of these same places: the South, Texas, and certain college towns. In what likely reflects a rebound in the Rust Belt's economic fortunes, there were also large declines in metropolitan areas in Michigan.

3. There are clear socioeconomic patterns for high and low poverty rate metropolitan areas. The largest poverty rate decreases consistently occurred in MSAs that had lower unemployment rates in 2000 than in 1990. Higher shares of both minorities and recent immigrants were associated with higher poverty rates, but this was not universal. There was a strong positive link between greater shares of the population that did not complete high school and higher metropolitan poverty rates.

4. The labor market linkages within metropolitan areas differ between central-city and suburban counties. With the exception of male unemployment rates, MSA-county poverty rates tend to be less affected by labor market conditions. Further investigation suggests that suburban county poverty rates are less affected by new job growth, while central county rates are less affected by labor supply tightness measures such as male unemployment and female employment rates.

Hence, new jobs are critical in centralized cores, and efforts to increase labor market participation and reduce the length of job searches are more appropriate in suburban counties.

5. The racial and ethnic composition of the metropolitan counties modifies how labor market conditions affect poverty rates. Job growth reduced poverty rates more in central counties with greater African American population shares. There was evidence that in metro counties with larger Hispanic population shares, stronger labor markets had smaller poverty rate–reducing effects, especially in the suburbs.

6. Programs aimed at reducing poverty rates need a targeting mechanism for the most distressed communities. We argue that a set of targeted efforts to reduce poverty in distressed urban cores is a necessary component of an effective antipoverty policy. These efforts should focus more on central counties with high African American population shares. They should also target residents of the zones rather than encourage firms to locate there. Examples of possible programs that fit these criteria are described in Chapter 9.

We conclude that, in general, metropolitan counties are not dramatically different from other counties. Yet they do vary in terms of the role played by labor market conditions, as well as in terms of other factors such as the influence of female-headed families. Moreover, place-based policies appear to be necessary, but they need to be carefully targeted to certain parts of metropolitan areas, and they need to consider racial composition. More sparsely populated nonmetro counties are also likely to have unique trends that call for their own tailored policies. That is the topic of the next chapter.

Notes

The epigraph at the start of the chapter comes from Herbert (1999).

1. Long-term recipients are defined as those who have accumulated 48 months of assistance towards the federal five-year time limit.
2. In Berube and Frey's (2002) analysis, "central city" is defined as the largest or best-known city in the MSA. Besides not counting as many central cities in their definition as we do, they do not include the inner-ring suburbs that are included in our central-county definition. As noted in Chapter 2, our suburban definition better reflects the newer, more vibrant suburbs at the exurban edge. The formal definition of a metropolitan area is given in Figure A.1.
3. A census track is a reasonably homogenous grouping set up by the U.S. Census Bureau and has about 4,000 people on average. Jargowsky (2003) provides more discussion on the 40 percent poverty rate threshold and on high poverty rate metropolitan-area census tracks.
4. Berube and Frey (2002) also find regional distinctions in poverty rate changes for central cities and suburbs during the 1990s. Rust Belt and south Texas central cities fared well, but northeastern and California cities did not. Southern suburbs tended to fare well, while suburbs in New England, New York, and California tended to fare poorly.
5. By comparison, the U.S. Department of Labor (USDOL) reports that the consumer price index increased by 34.4 percent between 1989 and 1999. Data can be accessed from the U.S. Bureau of Labor Statistics (2006e) Web site at http://data .bls.gov/cgi-bin/surveymost?cu (accessed March 30, 2006). Note that there is a composition effect, as the precise high- and low-poverty-rate metropolitan areas changed between the decades, but this pattern still illustrates trends between the two categories.
6. Slower population growth and greater recent immigration shares in areas with rising poverty rates are consistent with native out-migration, which likely mitigated any further poverty rate increases that would have occurred otherwise.
7. The regression coefficients were consistently estimated with less precision when using MSA-level observations. One likely cause is that there are only 316 MSA observations, while there are 824 metropolitan counties. Also, as indicated in Chapter 2, aggregating metropolitan area counties into one MSA-level observation loses much of the intra-MSA variation that improves the precision of the results. Finally, we also would lose the richness of being able to separately consider central counties and suburban counties.
8. Key descriptive statistics are reported in Table 7.7. Variable definitions are detailed in Appendix A.
9. The interpretation of the county-type results differs from Chapter 6 because the omitted county group is now single-county MSAs—in other words, the central-city and suburban coefficients are measured relative to the effects of a single-MSA county. The results show no clear evidence that big or small metropolitan

area central counties have different poverty rates than single-county MSAs, ceteris paribus.

10. The metropolitan area population coefficient equals 9.94e − 8 ($t = 2.48$). Conversely, the county population coefficient is insignificant, further indicating that in MSAs it is the size of the entire metropolitan area that limits employment access.

11. The 1995–2000 employment growth coefficient is only significant at the 20 percent level.

12. In Table A.1, a one standard deviation change in the overall female employment-population rate equals 6.9 percentage points, and the corresponding change in the overall 1999 male unemployment rate equals 2.9 percentage points.

13. When the percent of the population that immigrated to the United States between 1990–1995 and 1995–2000 is added to the metropolitan model, the racial and ethnic share variables became even more inversely related to poverty rates (not shown). The 1995–2000 immigrant share result suggests that a one-percentage-point greater share immigrating in the five-year period increases the MSA-county poverty rate by just over a quarter of a percentage point ($t = 2.91$). As before, the 1990–1995 immigrant share is insignificant in the 1999 model and both of the corresponding immigrant shares are insignificant when added to the 1989 MSA-county model.

14. In interpreting the results, recall that there are 139 metropolitan areas that are each located in a single county and are thus classified as central county MSAs. As shown in Table 7.6 and the corresponding results in Chapter 6, poverty rates in single-county MSAs are essentially the same as central county poverty rates (ceteris paribus). While these MSAs may appear to differ because they are smaller and more suburban than other central-county MSAs, they are similar in terms of poverty rates. Specifically, the 1989 average poverty rate in single-county MSAs equals 14.5 percent (std. dev. = 6.0) and the average equals 13.5 percent (std. dev. = 5.3) in 1999. This compares to the overall population-weighted average central county poverty rate of 13.3 percent in 1989 and 13.2 percent in 1999 (from columns (4) and (9) of Table 2.2).

15. A "half-life" refers to the period of time that elapses before one-half of the effect of a shock dissipates.

16. To examine whether job growth has additional indirect effects through affecting unemployment and employment rates, the quasireduced form model was estimated. It indicates that the direct and indirect effects of job growth through unemployment and employment rates are about one-third greater than these direct figures (not shown).

17. Andersson, Holzer, and Lane (2003) report that the prevalence of medium- and high-paying jobs for disadvantaged persons tends to be concentrated in central counties. But the overall lack of nearby job creation remains a concern.

18. The share of the population that immigrated to the United States between 1995 and 2000 equaled 2.0 percent (std. dev. = 1.9) in central counties and 1.0 percent (std. dev. = 1.2) in suburban counties. Note that this migration pattern is consistent with foreign immigrants locating in central county enclaves where there are

already well-established immigrant communities, rather than individual immigrants choosing to locate where there are greater job opportunities, which would have implied a greater likelihood of locating in the suburbs.

19. The results suggest that greater 1990–1995 immigrant shares had no statistical impact on either suburban or central county poverty rates. When the shares of the population that immigrated to the United States between 1980–1985 and 1985–1990 were added to the 1989 central-county and suburban models, they had an insignificant impact.

20. To assess this issue, we examined African American migration and residential-choice decisions during the 1990s. We focused on this group because their population share should be much less confounded by new immigrants than the Hispanic or other-minority population shares. Specifically, we regressed the change in African American population shares between 1990 and 2000 on the share of the population that immigrated to the United States between 1990–1995 and 1995–2000, on the beginning 1990 African American population share, and on the county's 1990 population. Focusing on the 1995–2000 immigration share, for central counties there appears to be almost a one-for-one inverse tradeoff between the change in the African American population share and the recent immigrant share (significantly different from zero at the 0.01 level). This relationship applies regardless of whether the regression is or is not weighted by the 1990 county population. Hence, African American location decisions almost completely offset recent immigration patterns in central counties, which helps explain why central county rates on balance were unaffected by recent immigration. Conversely, there is little statistical evidence that the change in the African American suburban population share is related to the 1995–2000 recent immigrant share. The lack of an African American migration response in suburban counties is consistent with a greater supply of low-skilled workers competing for suburban jobs (which likely increased unemployment and reduced wages for low-skilled groups).

21. The F-statistic suggests the three interactions are jointly significant at about the 0.05 level in both cases.

22. The race and ethnic shares are measured in percentages. For a county with a 10 percent share of one of the groups, one calculates the influence of job growth by multiplying the interaction coefficient by 10 and adding that value to the main employment growth (or unemployment rate, or employment-population rate) coefficient. Hence, in counties with large minority population shares, employment growth's overall effect can vary considerably from the average result.

23. These racial effects can be rather large. In a suburban county, a 2.9-percentage-point increase in the male unemployment rate increases the poverty rate by about 0.65 points when the Hispanic population share is zero (and the other minority shares are assumed to be zero), but it reduces the poverty rate when the Hispanic population share rises above 7.7 percent. In this simulation, the other-race population shares are assumed to be zero for ease of presentation. In reality, the other-race group shares will be greater than zero and their corresponding effect will be added to the total effect.

24. A study of a four-county region that includes Lawrence and Morgan counties reports that monthly welfare caseloads dropped from 1,577 in 1993 to 1,167 in 1996 and to 645 in 1998, a 59 percent decline in five years (Farrell, Opcin, and Fishman 2001).

25. U.S. Census Bureau Summary File 3 (SF3) files from the 1990 and 2000 censuses (U.S. Census Bureau 2006b). Follow same link to SF3 files for all later text citations of U.S. Census Bureau (2006b) in this chapter.

26. A general overview of the various business incentives can be found in Bartik (1991, 2001, 2004) and in Fisher (2004).

27. The Peters and Fisher (2002) view appears to reflect a large share of the economic and public-policy profession. However, a recent, widely cited study by Greenstone and Moretti (2003) suggests that blockbuster incentive packages (e.g., Chicago's efforts to lure Boeing) are economically worthwhile (see Fisher [2004] for a critique).

28. In terms of central counties, we are also concerned by evidence that job growth increasingly became more distant from African American residences in the 1990s (Raphael and Stoll 2002).

29. The general rule of thumb in the literature is that a 10 percent decrease in business taxes increases economic activity in a state by about 2–3 percent, while the same 10 percent reduction in a small suburb's taxes increases economic activity 10–30 percent (see Bartik 1991, p. 43; 2004; Fisher 2004). In more-populated central counties, it is less clear whether tax cuts will have as large of an impact on business location decisions (Bartik 2004). However, in heavily populated metropolitan areas with relatively small central cities (e.g., Atlanta), a tax cut in the central city would be much more effective because that area is just one of several possible business locations.

8
Poverty in Rural America

Some of the same signs of despair and breakdown that wore out aging American industrial cities in the 1960s have come to the rural plains. Among teenagers, there is now a higher level of illicit drug use in rural areas than in cities or suburbs, recent surveys indicate. The middle class is dwindling, leaving pockets of hard poverty amid large agribusinesses supported by taxpayers.
  —Timothy Egan, "Amid Dying Towns of Rural Plains, One Makes a Stand," *New York Times*, December 1, 2003

Fundamental structural changes in technology, markets, and organizations are redrawing our nation's economic map and leaving many rural areas behind.
  —Robert D. Atkinson, *Reversing Rural America's Economic Decline*, Progressive Policy Institute, 2004

Chapter 7 showed that larger population and other characteristics help produce different poverty rate patterns and dynamics for metropolitan areas than for the nation as a whole. Low population densities and differing demographic characteristics also suggest that nonmetropolitan patterns may vary from national patterns. These variations likely mean that nonmetro regions have different commuting patterns and responses to job growth, which translate into different poverty rates. As reported in Table A.1, average nonmetro county poverty rates were more than 6 percentage points higher than metro county poverty rates in 1989, and more than 4 points higher in 1999. Yet these averages obscure tremendous diversity in poverty rates across nonmetro counties.[1] Some nonmetro counties in the Northeast and Midwest possess very low poverty rates, while others, such as those in the South, have persistently high poverty rates. This chapter assesses the underlying causes of higher nonmetropolitan poverty rates as well the sources of nonmetro counties' tremendous diversity.

WHAT IS DIFFERENT ABOUT RURAL OR NONMETROPOLITAN COUNTIES?

What Is Rural?

The meaning of the word "rural" is ambiguous and is regularly applied in confusing or contradictory ways that often depend on the user's purpose or agenda. The U.S. Census Bureau defines rural areas as being those with less than 500 people per square mile (Box 8.1). The U.S. Department of Agriculture's Economic Research Service says "rural areas comprise open country and settlements with fewer than 2,500 residents" (ERS 2004a). However, this latter definition means that relatively small towns and communities would be classified as "urban," which would be misleading in most cases and would be inconsistent with popular notions. Thus, we follow the convention of referring to nonmetropolitan counties as rural, and we will use the two terms interchangeably.

Chapter 7 describes how metropolitan areas comprise economically linked counties surrounding an urbanized area of at least 50,000 people. Outlying counties are included when a 25 percent commuting threshold is surpassed. Nonmetro counties are the remaining counties. In 2003, the federal government divided nonmetro counties into noncore and micropolitan areas.[2] Micropolitan areas include an urbanized cluster of at least 10,000 people but less than 50,000, while outlying counties are included if the 25 percent commuting threshold is exceeded (Box A.1).

Micropolitan counties now account for approximately 60 percent of the nonmetropolitan population. During the 1990s, population in these counties grew about 10 percent on average, compared to about 8 percent for the less-populated noncore rural counties. Average metro county population grew about 14 percent (ERS 2004b). So while rural areas grew less than metropolitan counties during the 1990s, it should be noted that even noncore rural counties experienced almost double-digit growth on average. Yet there is tremendous diversity within that category, as many noncore rural counties suffered significant population loss during the decade.

Box 8.1   Official Definitions of Rural and Urban

The following is taken from the U.S. Census Bureau (2004f) Web page "Census 2000 Urban and Rural Classification":

URBAN AND RURAL CLASSIFICATION

For Census 2000, Census Bureau classifies as "urban" all territory, population, and housing units located within an urbanized area (UA) or an urban cluster (UC). It delineates UA and UC boundaries to encompass densely settled territory, which consists of

- core census block groups or blocks that have a population density of at least 1,000 people per square mile, and

- surrounding census blocks that have an overall density of at least 500 people per square mile.

In addition, under certain conditions, less densely settled territory may be part of each UA or UC.

The Census Bureau's classification of "rural" consists of all territory, population, and housing units located outside of UAs and UCs. The rural component contains both place and nonplace territory. Geographic entities, such as census tracts, counties, metropolitan areas, and the territory outside metropolitan areas, often are "split" between urban and rural territory, and the population and housing units they contain often are partly classified as urban and partly classified as rural.

Distinctions in Rural Labor Markets and Demographics

Nonmetropolitan counties possess several distinguishing poverty-related characteristics. For one thing, depending on household size, the official poverty rate threshold is a fixed nominal dollar figure for each year that applies across the country. Yet rural areas are estimated to have a 16 percent lower cost of living than urban areas, primarily because of lower housing costs, though housing costs alone would overstate the rural/urban difference in cost of living (Nord 2000). A lower cost of living means that rural poverty rates are generally overstated relative to urban areas. Low-income rural residents are also believed to be more reliant on informal economic arrangements in which individuals agree to do unpaid work for each other, which also suggests that measured rural poverty rates are overstated (Harvey et al. 2002).[3]

Despite these advantages, low-income nonmetropolitan residents can suffer from the effects of living in an area with low population density. Low population density means that workers may have to commute long distances for work. Commuting is further hampered by the lack of public transportation, making owning a reliable automobile paramount. Small population and low density can limit the quantity and quality of child care; licensed centers are especially scarce in poor nonmetropolitan areas (Gordon and Chase-Lansdale 2001; Whitener, Weber, and Duncan 2002). Child care solutions are further complicated because workers may have to travel longer distances not only to work but also to their care provider. Key social services for training, disabilities, and health care are also more dispersed or, worse yet, nonexistent. Hence, rural low-income families and households that are already under tremendous stress may find it more difficult to escape poverty.

Rural labor markets have offsetting factors that both hinder and improve the well being of low-income households. On one hand, we expect that job growth has stronger poverty-reducing effects in rural communities, especially when those communities are more isolated. This follows because rural migration and commuting responses are relatively muted in response to labor demand shocks compared to such responses in metro areas (Renkow 2003; Renkow and Hoover 2000). If fewer commuters and migrants take the new jobs, more of the jobs go to disadvantaged rural residents. One reason for this outcome may be that potential workers are less informed about a given rural county's economic conditions, while a larger metro area's economic conditions (e.g., Las Vegas's) may be well known. For example, in the case of a city with 1 million total jobs and a town with a total of 1,000 jobs, it would be big news if a new firm created 10,000 jobs in the city (1 percent of the city's employment), but it would hardly be known outside of the county if a new firm created 10 jobs in the small rural town (1 percent of the town's jobs). Relocation costs are also greater between urban and remote regions than between urban and nearby suburban or exurban communities.

On the other hand, despite higher shares of poor rural female heads that work either part-time or full-time, there is a larger share of single working mothers who are in poverty in rural areas than in metro areas (Lichter and Jensen 2002). Moreover, nonmetro residents tend to have less educational attainment than their metro counterparts (see Table A.1). There is a considerably higher share of the rural adult population that did not complete high school, and there is a lower share with a college degree. Finally, reliance on agriculture and other extractive industries may exacerbate rural poverty rates (Brown and Warner 1991).

It is not surprising that with lower average education and lower cost of living, rural wages are considerably below the metropolitan average. For example, in 1993, average nonmetropolitan wages were about 72 percent of the average MSA wage, and by 2001 they had fallen to 66 percent.[4] For nonemployed rural residents, finding a suitable employment match is further hindered because low population density reduces the diversity of job opportunities, meaning that a person may find it harder to obtain a job that requires his or her particular skill set (Gibbs 2002). Nevertheless, smaller communities may facilitate the formation of informal labor market networks that help low-income residents identify a larger share of suitable employment opportunities over a wider geographical area. Simply put, in small communities, disadvantaged persons may be more likely to personally know someone employed at the nearby firms that are hiring workers.

Overall Trends in Rural Poverty Rates

Poverty rates in rural areas have historically been higher than in urban centers. In the late 1950s, nonmetropolitan poverty rates were almost 20 percentage points higher.[5] But over the next 15 years rural poverty rates declined so dramatically that by the mid-1970s the gap was less than 5 points. The gap somewhat increased in the 1980s because of the economic fallout in the resource and farm sectors, but subsequent improvements in the rural economy reduced the gap to 3.1 percentage points in 2001.

In that year, nonmetropolitan poverty tended not only to be highest in the South, at 17.6 percent, but the gap between rural and metropolitan poverty rates was also greatest in that region of the country, at 5.4 percentage points (ERS 2004a). The West had the second-highest rates in both categories, followed by the Northeast. The Midwest's nonmetro poverty rate was only 9.8 percent, and the rural/metropolitan gap was a barely perceptible 0.6 percentage points. Among racial groups, the rural/metropolitan poverty gap was largest among black non-Hispanics (at more than 10 percentage points) and "other" minorities (at about 13 points). The metro/nonmetro gap was only 3 percentage points for Hispanics.

Another trait is the persistence of pockets of extreme rural poverty. The Economic Research Service of the USDA uses a 20 percent threshold in defining a high poverty county. Miller and Weber (2004) report that out of just over 3,000 counties, a remarkable 382 had 20 percent or greater poverty rates in 1959, 1969, 1979, 1989, and 1999 (using income from the year preceding the decennial census). Only 19 of these are metropolitan area counties. The remaining 363 persistent-poverty counties are nonmetropolitan, and 229 of them are not adjacent to an MSA. There are 2,248 total nonmetropolitan counties. Thus, about one-sixth (363 out of 2,248) rural counties have struggled with consistently high poverty for at least the last 40 years.

Figures 2.8 through 2.12 showed the tremendous diversity in nonmetropolitan poverty outcomes over the 1979–1999 period. The pockets of highest rural poverty are generally found in the Southeast, and the lowest nonmetro poverty rates are centered in the northern Great Plains and the Upper Midwest. Further illustrating the diversity, by 1999 there were even pockets of low poverty in the Piedmont regions of North Carolina and Virginia, despite those areas being near high poverty counties. In the 1979–1999 span, rural poverty increased the most in the Mountain and Pacific states; it also rose in central Appalachia and New England. The largest reductions occurred in the Upper Midwest and the Southeast. Highlighting the tremendous variations that occurred even among stronger performing states like Iowa, there were isolated counties that experienced marked increases in poverty rates.

CHARACTERISTICS OF HIGH AND LOW POVERTY RATE RURAL COUNTIES

Tables 8.1 (for 1999) and 8.2 (for 1989) present the 15 counties with the lowest and the highest poverty rates among the 2,248 nonmetropolitan counties.[6] The counties in the bottom half of the two tables were all among the 363 persistently high nonmetro poverty rate counties over the 1959–1999 period. Illustrating the depths of their problems, all 15 of these counties were just at or above the 40 percent poverty rate threshold used by federal agencies to define chronically high poverty rates for not counties but neighborhoods.

Focusing on the 1999 patterns in Table 8.1, we see that the 15 lowest poverty rate counties were geographically dispersed. In contrast, the 15 highest poverty rate counties were located in or near Native American Indian reservations, areas with high concentrations of African Americans or Hispanics, and predominantly white areas of Appalachia. The 15 lowest poverty rate counties tended to have more inhabitants. Compared to the highest poverty rate counties, the lowest poverty rate counties generally have lower minority population shares, more than twice the median household income, considerably lower population shares that did not complete high school, and an average unemployment rate about 13 percentage points lower than in the highest poverty rate counties. Very often, a majority of the population in the highest poverty rate counties were members of national minority populations. Nevertheless, there is diversity even among the highest poverty rate counties. For example, the two Appalachian counties had very few minorities. In another example, Brooks County, Texas, and Owsley County, Kentucky, did not suffer from exceedingly high unemployment rates.

Tables 8.3 (for 1999) and 8.4 (for 1989) report the 10 lowest and highest nonmetropolitan county poverty rates for the 984 counties adjacent to a metropolitan area, for the 1,264 counties not adjacent to a metropolitan area, and for the 243 nonadjacent counties that had a 2000 population of less than 5,000 (using 2000 population to ensure comparability across decades).[7] As before, the counties in the highest poverty rate group all were persistently high poverty counties.

Concentrating on the 1999 figures in Table 8.3, we see that the distinguishing characteristics between the lowest and the highest poverty

Table 8.1 Highest and Lowest Nonmetropolitan County Poverty Rates, 1999

Rank/Non-MSA county[a]	State	(1) Poverty rate 1989	(2) Population 1990	(3) % minority 1990	(4) Median hh. income 1989 ($)	(5) % education < 12 yrs. 1990	(6) Unempl. rate 1990
Lowest poverty level							
1 Loving County	TX	0.0	67	17.9	40,000	13.7	0.0
2 Elbert County	CO	4.0	19,872	4.6	62,480	7.5	2.4
3 Gilpin County	CO	4.0	4,757	7.3	51,942	5.9	2.1
4 Litchfield County	CT	4.5	182,193	4.1	56,273	14.1	3.8
5 Union County	OH	4.6	40,909	4.5	51,743	14.0	2.3
6 Grundy County	IO	4.6	12,369	0.9	39,396	13.5	3.6
7 McLeod County	MN	4.8	34,898	3.1	45,953	15.3	3.8
8 Piatt County	IL	5.0	16,365	1.7	45,752	11.3	2.9
9 Iowa County	IO	5.0	15,671	1.0	41,222	13.0	2.3
10 Bremer County	IO	5.1	23,325	1.9	40,826	12.3	5.8
11 Scott County	KS	5.1	5,120	3.5	40,534	15.5	2.2
12 Green County	WI	5.1	33,647	1.7	43,228	15.9	3.2
13 Wasatch County	UT	5.2	15,215	5.1	49,612	10.7	4.3
14 Morgan County	UT	5.2	7,129	2.0	50,273	7.4	3.8
15 Columbia County	WI	5.2	52,468	3.0	45,064	13.8	3.5

Highest poverty level[b]

	County	State						
2234	Bennett County	SD	39.2	3,574	58.6	25,313	28.7	10.5
2235	Sioux County	ND	39.2	4,044	83.2	22,483	21.5	23.3
2236	Clay County	KY	39.7	24,556	6.4	16,271	50.6	10.7
2237	Wilcox County	AL	39.9	13,183	72.6	16,646	40.5	15.2
2238	Brooks County	TX	40.2	7,976	24.3	18,622	50.1	8.5
2239	East Carroll Parish	LA	40.5	9,421	68.7	20,723	42.1	15.0
2240	Corson County	SD	41.0	4,181	62.3	20,654	24.0	13.2
2241	Holmes County	MS	41.1	21,609	79.6	17,235	40.3	17.3
2242	Zavala County	TX	41.8	11,600	35.5	16,844	56.6	16.7
2243	Owsley County	KY	45.4	4,858	0.9	15,805	50.8	8.8
2244	Todd County	SD	48.3	9,050	86.2	20,035	25.9	18.4
2245	Ziebach County	SD	49.9	2,519	73.5	18,063	28.6	17.4
2246	Starr County	TX	50.9	53,597	12.0	16,504	65.3	20.9
2247	Shannon County	SD	52.3	12,466	95.0	20,916	30.0	33.0
2248	Buffalo County	SD	56.9	2,032	83.3	12,692	36.1	21.7

NOTE: All 1999 Non-MSA unweighted avg. poverty rates = 15.4 (std. dev. = 6.7); avg. lowest pov. = 4.5; avg. highest pov. = 44.4. Poverty rates and median household income are measured for 1999 and the other variables are for 2000, excluding Alaska and Hawaii. Percent minority is 100 minus the percentage of persons that consider white/Caucasian to be their single racial group.

[a] Nonmetropolitan-area definitions follow those in place for the 2000 census as defined by the Bureau of Economic Analysis. For details see Chapters 2 and 6.

[b] All counties on this page are persistent-poverty counties, defined as having a 20 percent or higher poverty rate in 1959, 1969, 1979, 1989, and 1999.

SOURCE: U.S. Census Bureau (2006e).

Table 8.2 Highest and Lowest Nonmetropolitan County Poverty Rates, 1989

Rank/Non-MSA counties[a]	State	(1) Poverty rate 1989	(2) Population 1990	(3) % minority 1990	(4) Median hh. income 1989 ($)	(5) % education <12 yrs. 1990	(6) Unempl. rate 1990
Lowest poverty level							
1 Loving County	TX	0.0	107	16.8	26,563	44.0	0.0
2 Litchfield County	CT	4.0	174,092	2.1	42,565	19.1	4.7
3 Merrimack County	NH	5.5	120,005	1.3	35,801	16.8	5.9
4 Clark County	KS	5.6	2,418	3.4	24,003	16.5	0.5
5 Steuben County	IN	5.6	27,446	0.8	29,203	21.0	4.8
6 Nantucket County	MA	5.7	6,012	2.8	40,331	10.6	2.1
7 Putnam County	OH	5.8	33,819	1.8	32,492	22.5	3.8
8 Piatt County	IL	6.1	15,548	0.2	31,369	17.0	4.4
9 Dubois County	IN	6.1	36,616	0.5	31,227	27.8	3.2
10 Roberts County	TX	6.2	1,025	2.8	30,203	18.6	3.2
11 Pitkin County	CO	6.3	12,661	3.4	39,991	5.3	3.4
12 Belknap County	NH	6.5	49,216	0.7	31,474	19.6	6.9
13 Moore County	TN	6.5	4,721	3.9	28,056	33.3	2.7
14 York County	NE	6.6	14,428	1.4	25,722	18.2	3.0
15 Ottawa County	OH	6.6	40,029	2.7	31,360	24.1	7.7
Highest poverty level[b]							
2234 Sioux County	ND	47.4	3,761	75.9	14,838	31.7	23.0
2235 Sharkey County	MS	47.5	7,066	66.7	13,304	48.7	10.1

2236	Presidio County	TX	48.1	6,637	15.7	13,016	56.1	10.3
2237	Dimmit County	TX	48.9	10,433	27.1	12,222	60.2	13.7
2238	Issaquena County	MS	49.3	1,909	56.4	13,005	56.3	10.0
2239	Todd County	SD	50.2	8,352	82.9	13,327	32.8	20.6
2240	Zavala County	TX	50.4	12,162	47.0	11,822	61.4	19.7
2241	Maverick County	TX	50.4	36,378	34.7	12,262	64.3	21.1
2242	Ziebach County	SD	51.1	2,220	64.4	14,129	37.5	15.6
2243	Owsley County	KY	52.1	5,036	0.1	8,595	64.5	17.2
2244	Holmes County	MS	53.2	21,604	76.0	9,809	52.0	15.8
2245	East Carroll Parish	LA	56.8	9,709	65.3	9,791	50.9	24.1
2246	Tunica County	MS	56.8	8,164	75.6	10,965	54.1	17.0
2247	Starr County	TX	60.0	40,518	38.1	10,182	68.4	18.8
2248	Shannon County	SD	63.1	9,902	94.9	11,105	40.6	30.5

NOTE: All 1989 Non-MSA unweighted avg. poverty rates = 18.4 (std. dev. = 8.0); avg. lowest pov. = 5.5; avg. highest pov. = 52.4. Poverty rates and median household income are measured for 1989 and the other variables for 1990, excluding Alaska and Hawaii. Percent minority is 100 minus the percentage of persons that consider white/Caucasian to be their racial group.

[a] Nonmetropolitan area definitions follow those in place for the 2000 census as defined by the Bureau of Economic Analysis. For details see Chapters 2 and 6.

[b] All counties on this page are persistent-poverty counties, defined as having a 20 percent or higher poverty rate in 1959, 1969, 1979, 1989, and 1999.

SOURCE: U.S. Census Bureau (2006e).

Table 8.3 Highest and Lowest Poverty Rates for Adjacent, Nonadjacent, and Small Nonadjacent Nonmetropolitan Counties, 1999

Rank/Non-MSA county[a]	State	(1) Poverty rate 1999	(2) Population 2000	(3) % minority 2000	(4) Median hh. income 1999 ($)	(5) % education < 12 years 2000	(6) Unempl. rate 2000
Adjacent to MSA							
Lowest poverty level							
1 Elbert County	CO	4.0	19,872	4.6	62,480	7.5	2.4
2 Gilpin County	CO	4.0	4,757	7.3	51,942	5.9	2.1
3 Litchfield County	CT	4.5	182,193	4.1	56,273	14.1	3.8
4 Union County	OH	4.6	40,909	4.5	51,743	14.0	2.3
5 Grundy County	IO	4.6	12,369	0.9	39,396	13.5	3.6
6 McLeod County	MN	4.8	34,898	3.1	45,953	15.3	3.8
7 Piatt County	IL	5.0	16,365	1.7	45,752	11.3	2.9
8 Iowa County	IO	5.0	15,671	1.0	41,222	13.0	2.3
9 Bremer County	IO	5.1	23,325	1.9	40,826	12.3	5.8
10 Green County	WI	5.1	33,647	1.7	43,228	15.9	3.2
Highest poverty level[b]							
975 Macon County	AL	32.8	24,105	86.2	21,180	30.0	12.3
976 Luna County	NM	32.9	25,016	25.6	20,784	40.2	17.1
977 Tunica County	MS	33.1	9,227	73.0	23,270	39.5	9.3
978 Willacy County	TX	33.2	20,082	29.4	22,114	51.3	13.8
979 Bullock County	AL	33.5	11,714	73.6	20,605	39.5	8.6

980	Greene County	AL	34.3	9,974	81.2	19,819	35.2	13.1
981	Hudspeth County	TX	35.8	3,344	12.8	21,045	53.9	8.2
982	Zapata County	TX	35.8	12,182	14.8	24,635	46.9	11.1
983	Holmes County	MS	41.1	21,609	79.6	17,235	40.3	17.3
984	Starr County	TX	50.9	53,597	12.0	16,504	65.3	20.9

Nonadjacent to MSA

Lowest poverty level

1	Loving County	TX	0.0	67	17.9	40,000	13.7	0.0
2	Scott County	KS	5.1	5,120	3.5	40,534	15.5	2.2
3	Dubois County	IN	5.3	39,674	2.2	44,169	19.8	2.5
4	Leelanau County	MI	5.4	21,119	6.3	47,062	9.3	5.0
5	Daggett County	UT	5.5	921	5.8	30,833	16.3	7.7
6	Wyandot County	OH	5.5	22,908	2.2	38,839	17.5	2.9
7	Putnam County	IL	5.5	6,086	2.4	45,492	16.2	4.9
8	Polk County	NE	5.8	5,639	0.7	37,819	13.4	1.8
9	Grand Traverse County	MI	5.9	77,654	3.8	43,169	10.7	4.6
10	Dickinson County	IO	6.0	16,424	1.1	39,020	10.8	2.8

Highest poverty level[b]

1255	Wilcox County	AL	39.9	13,183	72.6	16,646	40.5	15.2
1256	Brooks County	TX	40.2	7,976	24.3	18,622	50.1	8.5
1257	East Carroll Parish	LA	40.5	9,421	68.7	20,723	42.1	15.0
1258	Corson County	SD	41.0	4,181	62.3	20,654	24.0	13.2
1259	Zavala County	TX	41.8	11,600	35.5	16,844	56.6	16.7

(continued)

Table 8.3 (continued)

Rank/Non-MSA county[a]	State	(1) Poverty rate 1999	(2) Population 2000	(3) % minority 2000	(4) Median hh. income 1999 ($)	(5) % education <12 years 2000	(6) Unempl. rate 2000
Highest poverty level							
1260 Owsley County	KY	45.4	4,858	0.9	15,805	50.8	8.8
1261 Todd County	SD	48.3	9,050	86.2	20,035	25.9	18.4
1262 Ziebach County	SD	49.9	2,519	73.5	18,063	28.6	17.4
1263 Shannon County	SD	52.3	12,466	95.0	20,916	30.0	33.0
1264 Buffalo County	SD	56.9	2,032	83.3	12,692	36.1	21.7
Small nonadjacent to MSA[c]							
Lowest poverty level							
1 Loving County	TX	0.0	67	17.9	40,000	13.7	0.0
2 Daggett County	UT	5.5	921	5.8	30,833	16.3	7.7
3 Hooker County	NE	6.9	783	2.2	27,868	10.3	1.3
4 Roberts County	TX	7.2	887	2.1	44,792	10.0	1.3
5 Hinsdale County	CO	7.2	790	3.2	37,279	6.9	2.2
6 Ouray County	CO	7.2	3,742	3.5	42,019	6.6	3.6
7 Logan County	KS	7.3	3,046	2.5	32,131	13.3	3.8
8 Gosper County	NE	7.9	2,143	1.2	36,827	11.1	0.8
9 Wahkiakum County	WA	8.1	3,824	6.5	39,444	15.8	8.1
10 Garfield County	UT	8.1	4,735	3.8	35,180	14.2	8.1

Highest poverty level[b]

	County	State						
234	Edwards County	TX	31.6	2,162	14.7	25,298	32.9	4.9
235	Issaquena County	MS	33.2	2,274	63.9	19,936	41.2	13.5
236	Mellette County	SD	35.8	2,083	55.1	23,219	21.9	11.5
237	Jackson County	SD	36.5	2,930	50.3	23,945	17.3	15.7
238	Bennett County	SD	39.2	3,574	58.6	25,313	28.7	10.5
239	Sioux County	ND	39.2	4,044	83.2	22,483	21.5	23.3
240	Corson County	SD	41.0	4,181	62.3	20,654	24.0	13.2
241	Owsley County	KY	45.4	4,858	0.9	15,805	50.8	8.8
242	Ziebach County	SD	49.9	2,519	73.5	18,063	28.6	17.4
243	Buffalo County	SD	56.9	2,032	83.3	12,692	36.1	21.7

NOTE: Adjacent-to-MSA unweighted average 1999 poverty rate = 14.5 (std. dev. = 6.1). Nonadjacent-to-MSA unweighted average 1999 poverty rate = 16.1 (std. dev. = 7.0). Small nonadjacent-to-MSA with 2000 pop. < 5,000 unweighted average 1999 poverty rate = 15.8 (std. dev. = 7.2). Poverty rates and median household income are measured for 1999 and the other variables for 2000, excluding Alaska and Hawaii. Percent minority is 100 minus the percentage of persons that consider white/Caucasian to be their single racial group.

[a] Nonmetropolitan area definitions follow those in place for the 2000 census as defined by the Bureau of Economic Analysis. For details see Chapters 2 and 6.

[b] All counties listed under "highest poverty level" category are persistent-poverty counties, defined as having a 20 percent or higher poverty rate in 1959, 1969, 1979, 1989, and 1999.

[c] For consistency, small nonadjacent nonmetropolitan counties are defined as having a population of less than 5,000 in 2000. Note that the 243 small nonadjacent counties are a subset of the 1,264 nonadjacent counties.

SOURCE: U.S. Census Bureau (2006e).

Table 8.4 Highest and Lowest Poverty Rates for Adjacent, Nonadjacent, and Small Nonadjacent Nonmetropolitan Counties, 1989

Rank/Non-MSA county[a]	State	(1) Poverty rate 1989	(2) Population 1990	(3) Population 2000	(4) % minority 1990	(5) Median hh. income 1989 ($)	(6) % education <12 years 1990	(7) Unempl. rate 1990
Adjacent to MSA								
Lowest poverty level								
1 Litchfield County	CT	4.0	174,092	182,193	2.1	42,565	19.1	4.7
2 Merrimack County	NH	5.5	120,005	136,225	1.3	35,801	16.8	5.9
3 Steuben County	IN	5.6	27,446	33,214	0.8	29,203	21.0	4.8
4 Putnam County	OH	5.8	33,819	34,726	1.8	32,492	22.5	3.8
5 Piatt County	IL	6.1	15,548	16,365	0.2	31,369	17.0	4.4
6 Belknap County	NH	6.5	49,216	56,325	0.7	31,474	19.6	6.9
7 Ottawa County	OH	6.6	40,029	40,985	2.7	31,360	24.1	7.7
8 Kosciusko County	IN	6.6	65,294	74,057	1.9	31,666	22.5	3.6
9 Dodge County	WI	6.6	76,559	85,897	2.4	29,166	27.7	4.3
10 Adams County	PA	6.8	78,274	91,292	2.5	30,304	30.0	3.9
Highest poverty level[b]								
975 Clay County	WV	39.2	9,983	10,330	0.1	12,855	50.6	19.9
976 Yazoo County	MS	39.2	25,506	28,149	53.0	14,234	46.6	9.4
977 Zapata County	TX	41.0	9,279	12,182	28.0	14,926	49.9	14.5
978 Claiborne County	MS	43.6	11,370	11,831	82.5	12,876	41.3	20.3
979 Willacy County	TX	44.5	17,705	20,082	21.8	14,590	57.1	15.1

980 Greene County	AL	45.6	10,153	9,974	80.6	11,990	46.2	10.5
981 Lee County	AR	47.3	13,053	12,580	58.2	11,949	55.8	14.9
982 Holmes County	MS	53.2	21,604	21,609	76.0	9,809	52.0	15.8
983 Tunica County	MS	56.8	8,164	9,227	75.6	10,965	54.1	17.0
984 Starr County	TX	60.0	40,518	53,597	38.1	10,182	68.4	18.8
Nonadjacent to MSA								
Lowest poverty level								
1 Loving County	TX	0.0	107	67	16.8	26,563	44.0	0.0
2 Clark County	KS	5.6	2,418	2,390	3.4	24,003	16.5	0.5
3 Nantucket County	MA	5.7	6,012	9,520	2.8	40,331	10.6	2.1
4 Dubois County	IN	6.1	36,616	39,674	0.5	31,227	27.8	3.2
5 Roberts County	TX	6.2	1,025	887	2.8	30,203	18.6	3.2
6 Pitkin County	CO	6.3	12,661	14,872	3.4	39,991	5.3	3.4
7 Moore County	TN	6.5	4,721	5,740	3.9	28,056	33.3	2.7
8 York County	NE	6.6	14,428	14,598	1.4	25,722	18.2	3.0
9 Mercer County	OH	6.7	39,443	40,924	0.9	29,618	24.5	4.7
10 Dukes County	MA	6.7	11,639	14,987	7.7	31,994	9.6	6.1
Highest poverty level[b]								
1255 Presidio County	TX	48.1	6,637	7,304	15.7	13,016	56.1	10.3
1256 Dimmit County	TX	48.9	10,433	10,248	27.1	12,222	60.2	13.7
1257 Issaquena County	MS	49.3	1,909	2,274	56.4	13,005	56.3	10.0
1258 Todd County	SD	50.2	8,352	9,050	82.9	13,327	32.8	20.6
1259 Zavala County	TX	50.4	12,162	11,600	47.0	11,822	61.4	19.7
1260 Maverick County	TX	50.4	36,378	47,297	34.7	12,262	64.3	21.1

(continued)

Table 8.4 (continued)

Rank/Non-MSA county[a]	State	(1) Poverty rate 1989	(2) Population 1990	(3) Population 2000	(4) % minority 1990	(5) Median hh. income 1989 ($)	(6) % education <12 years 1990	(7) Unempl. rate 1990
Highest poverty level								
1261 Ziebach County	SD	51.1	2,220	2,519	64.4	14,129	37.5	15.6
1262 Owsley County	KY	52.1	5,036	4,858	0.1	8,595	64.5	17.2
1263 East Carroll Parish	LA	56.8	9,709	9,421	65.3	9,791	50.9	24.1
1264 Shannon County	SD	63.1	9,902	12,466	94.9	11,105	40.6	30.5
Small nonadjacent to MSA[c]								
Lowest poverty level								
1 Loving County	TX	0.0	107	67	16.8	26,563	44.0	0.0
2 Clark County	KS	5.6	2,418	2,390	3.4	24,003	16.5	0.5
3 Roberts County	TX	6.2	1,025	887	2.8	30,203	18.6	3.2
4 King County	TX	7.3	354	356	12.1	27,625	21.8	2.0
5 Haskell County	KS	7.6	3,886	4,307	11.8	26,761	23.9	2.4
6 Gosper County	NE	8.5	1,928	2,143	0.1	25,669	20.9	2.0
7 Greeley County	KS	9.2	1,774	1,534	5.0	25,709	17.6	1.4
8 Clark County	ID	9.3	762	1,022	10.6	24,583	25.3	1.9
9 Ouray County	CO	9.6	2,295	3,742	2.5	27,500	12.5	7.0
10 Hemphill County	TX	9.6	3,720	3,351	5.8	28,697	27.1	4.1
Highest poverty level[b]								
234 Guadalupe County	NM	38.5	4,156	4,680	25.9	13,350	42.2	6.4
235 Jackson County	SD	38.8	2,811	2,930	42.5	17,246	31.1	10.6

	County	State							
236	Mellette County	SD	41.3	2,137	2,083	47.0	14,539	32.0	7.8
237	Edwards County	TX	41.7	2,266	2,162	6.7	14,639	41.7	4.6
238	Corson County	SD	42.5	4,195	4,181	48.7	14,324	36.7	14.8
239	Buffalo County	SD	45.1	1,759	2,032	77.7	14,566	38.8	20.4
240	Sioux County	ND	47.4	3,761	4,044	75.9	14,838	31.7	23.0
241	Issaquena County	MS	49.3	1,909	2,274	56.4	13,005	56.3	10.0
242	Ziebach County	SD	51.1	2,220	2,519	64.4	14,129	37.5	15.6
243	Owsley County	KY	52.1	5,036	4,858	0.1	8,595	64.5	17.2

NOTE: Adjacent-to-MSA unweighted average 1989 poverty rate = 17.4 (std. dev. = 7.4). Nonadjacent-to-MSA unweighted average poverty rate = 19.1 (std. dev. = 8.3). Small nonadjacent-to-MSA with 2000 pop. < 5,000 unweighted average 1989 poverty rate = 18.6 (std. dev. = 8.1). Poverty rates and median household income are measured for 1989 and the other variables for 1990, excluding Alaska and Hawaii. Percent minority is 100 minus the percentage of persons that consider white/Caucasian to be their racial group.

^a Nonmetropolitan area definitions follow those in place for the 2000 census as defined by the Bureau of Economic Analysis. For details see Chapters 2 and 6.

^b All counties listed under "highest poverty level" category are persistent-poverty counties, defined as having a 20 percent or higher poverty rate in 1959, 1969, 1979, 1989, and 1999.

^c For consistency, small nonadjacent nonmetropolitan counties are defined as having a population of less than 5,000 in 2000. Note that the 243 small nonadjacent counties are a subset of the 1,264 nonadjacent counties.

SOURCE: U.S. Census Bureau (2006e).

rate counties are the same in all three subgroupings as they were for the overall nonmetropolitan poverty rates. There is considerable geographical diversity in the lowest poverty rate category, although there are fewer representatives from Southern and Pacific Coast states. There is more spatial concentration in the highest poverty rate counties. Adjacent counties with the highest poverty rates tend to be those with high shares of African Americans or Hispanics and are located in Gulf Coast states or the Southwest. Conversely, the highest-poverty-rate nonadjacent counties include five in South Dakota with high shares of Native Americans and one primarily white Appalachian county.

The lowest- and highest-poverty-rate adjacent rural counties tend to have lower poverty rates than their nonadjacent counterparts, illustrating the benefits of being closer to larger labor markets. Nonetheless, as shown in the high poverty rate group, being near a metro area is not a guarantee of economic prosperity. In this group, the average median household income hovered in the $20,000 range, the average 2000 unemployment rate was about 13 percent, and the average high-school noncompletion rate was about 44 percent. There are few differences in the characteristics of the lowest poverty rate counties, regardless of adjacency to metro areas. Two exceptions are that low-poverty-rate adjacent counties tend to have about twice the population and about $7,000 more in median household income for 1999.

The nonadjacent group with less than 5,000 people is included so we can examine the 243 rural counties whose isolation and small scale mean that many are unlikely to have sufficient critical mass to attract and retain businesses. Their small population also may mean they have fewer cultural and urban recreational amenities to retain young adults and professionals. Nevertheless, with an average poverty rate of about 6.5 percent, the 10 lowest poverty rate counties illustrate that it is possible to have low poverty despite some locational disadvantages. The lowest poverty rate counties tend to be agricultural and in the Great Plains. While their median household incomes are relatively low, they tend to have greater high school completion rates and relatively low unemployment rates. Despite their success in some measures, it is not clear whether most of these counties have a viable future, given their reliance on a declining farm base. It is possible that many unemployed and low income residents leave these counties relatively quickly, which would contribute to the counties' "success" in having low poverty and unemployment.

Among the 10 nonadjacent less-populated high poverty rate counties, seven are in the Dakotas and have high shares of Native Americans. They tend to have low median household incomes and relatively high unemployment rates, although their high school noncompletion rates are often not very high. Nevertheless, their small size, geographical isolation, and inherent risk for any private sector investor mean that most of these counties cannot realistically expect lower poverty rates without policy intervention. Either the policies need to encourage relocation of low income residents, or they need to create a positive stimulus for job creation. Likewise, as is the case for most high poverty rural counties, these areas need help in improving their community's capacity to offer services, such as transportation and child care, and their ability for governmental and nongovernmental governance. And, they may need to be better integrated into their larger economic regions to achieve a critical economic mass.

Improving institutional cooperation between the various levels of government would help ensure a more efficient use of resources and a more certain direction for private investment. Likewise, by better governmental and nongovernmental coordination across larger economic regions, these counties can more fully participate in economic growth that may be taking place outside their boundaries. Finally, given the economic and social duress in these counties, their nonprofit service organizations and other nongovernmental arrangements may need financial and organizational assistance.

CHANGES IN 1989–1999 RURAL POVERTY RATES

To help us consider the underlying causes for large declines or increases in poverty rates, Table 8.5 presents various characteristics of counties that experienced the 10 largest poverty rate declines and the 10 largest increases over the 1989–1999 period, using the same three adjacent/nonadjacent categories used in Table 8.3. The best news in Table 8.5 is that seven of the ten largest declines in adjacent county poverty

Table 8.5 Change in Poverty Rate from 1989 to 1999 for Adjacent, Nonadjacent, and Small Nonadjacent Nonmetropolitan Counties

Rank/Non-MSA county[a]	State	(1) Change in poverty rate 1989–1999	(2) Population 2000	(3) Population change in % 1990–2000	(4) % minority	(5) % education <12 Years	(6) Median hh. income 1999 ($)	(7) Unempl. rate 2000	(8) Unempl. rate 1990	(9) Empl. growth 1995–2000
Adjacent to MSA										
Largest decrease in poverty rate										
1 Tunica County[b]	MS	−23.7	9,227	11.5	73.0	39.5	23,270	9.3	17.0	52.9
2 Lee County[b]	AR	−17.4	12,580	−3.8	57.1	43.8	20,510	13.3	14.9	6.3
3 Karnes County[b]	TX	−14.6	15,446	19.4	32.2	40.9	26,526	6.5	8.9	10.8
4 Concho County	TX	−13.9	3,966	23.2	11.9	40.7	31,313	3.6	4.0	24.8
5 West Feliciana Parish	LA	−13.9	15,111	14.5	51.3	46.7	39,667	5.6	9.5	7.9
6 Elliott County[b]	KY	−12.1	6,748	4.3	0.6	47.4	21,014	10.5	17.6	0.3
7 Holmes County[b]	MS	−12.1	21,609	0.0	79.6	40.3	17,235	17.3	15.8	−12.7
8 Clay County[b]	WV	−11.7	10,330	3.4	2.1	36.3	22,120	11.5	19.9	18.0
9 Madison County	TX	−11.5	12,940	15.5	33.7	27.2	29,418	5.8	6.4	4.4
10 Lafayette County[b]	AR	−11.4	8,559	−12.7	37.9	34.7	24,831	7.9	10.6	−0.8
Largest increase in poverty rate										
975 Colusa County	CA	2.8	18,804	13.4	35.9	36.0	35,062	10.7	8.3	14.0
976 Ulster County	NY	2.9	177,749	7.0	11.0	18.3	42,551	6.3	5.0	11.0
977 Sullivan County	NY	2.9	73,966	6.3	14.7	23.8	36,998	9.2	6.3	5.5
978 Liberty County	FL	3.2	7,021	20.7	23.4	34.4	28,840	5.0	3.5	−0.9
979 Oldham County	TX	3.7	2,185	−4.3	9.2	19.5	33,713	6.9	1.9	18.0
980 Skamania County	WA	3.7	9,872	16.0	6.5	14.1	39,317	11.1	10.7	9.9

981	Chouteau County	MT	4.2	5,970	8.7	15.7	12.9	29,150	5.7	3.5	8.8
982	DeSoto County	FL	4.3	32,209	25.9	25.7	36.5	30,714	5.3	5.9	7.8
983	Hendry County	FL	5.2	36,210	28.8	33.4	45.8	33,592	7.8	7.9	14.6
984	Judith Basin County	MT	6.0	2,329	2.0	1.4	12.4	29,241	2.5	2.6	12.7

Nonadjacent to MSA

Largest decrease in poverty rate

1	San Saba County	TX	−17.2	6,186	12.7	16.9	30.0	30,104	3.7	5.2	15.3
2	McPherson County	NE	−16.9	533	−2.4	2.3	11.4	25,750	0.0	0.0	−3.7
3	Guadalupe County[b]	NM	−16.8	4,680	11.2	45.6	31.7	24,783	7.7	6.4	−0.5
4	Billings County	ND	−16.8	888	−24.8	0.3	22.2	32,667	2.8	4.8	−8.2
5	East Carroll Parish[b]	LA	−16.4	9,421	−3.1	68.7	42.1	20,723	15.0	24.1	1.8
6	Issaquena County[b]	MS	−16.1	2,274	16.1	63.9	41.2	19,936	13.5	10.0	23.5
7	Dimmit County[b]	TX	−15.6	10,248	−1.8	22.9	45.7	21,917	14.2	13.7	9.1
8	Maverick County[b]	TX	−15.6	47,297	23.1	28.9	57.9	21,232	17.6	21.1	26.0
9	Mason County	TX	−14.6	3,738	8.4	8.5	21.9	30,921	1.6	1.8	5.2
10	Dickens County	TX	−13.9	2,762	6.9	22.0	29.4	25,898	5.1	8.1	9.1

Largest increase in poverty rate

1255	Rock County	NE	6.4	1,756	−15.0	2.2	12.6	25,795	2.3	1.1	−4.7
1256	Modoc County	CA	6.4	9,449	−2.4	15.2	22.9	27,522	11.9	10.6	9.1
1257	Hidalgo County[b]	NM	6.5	5,932	−0.4	15.4	31.2	24,819	9.7	7.0	−23.5
1258	Wheeler County	NE	6.6	886	−7.0	1.8	9.2	26,771	3.2	0.5	11.6
1259	Clark County	KS	7.1	2,390	−1.2	3.9	12.6	33,857	2.6	0.5	16.0
1260	San Juan County	CO	8.0	558	−33.5	3.6	7.9	30,764	3.0	10.2	5.0
1261	Clark County	ID	10.5	1,022	25.4	28.6	36.0	31,576	6.1	1.9	3.0

(continued)

Table 8.5 (continued)

Rank/Non-MSA county[a]	State	(1) Change in poverty rate 1989–1999	(2) Population 2000	(3) Population change in % 1990–2000	(4) % minority	(5) % education < 12 Years	(6) Median hh. income 1999 ($)	(7) Unempl. rate 2000	(8) Unempl. rate 1990	(9) Empl. growth 1995–2000
Largest increase in poverty rate										
1262 Buffalo County[b]	SD	11.8	2,032	13.4	83.3	36.1	12,692	21.7	20.4	4.7
1263 King County	TX	13.3	356	0.6	3.9	21.9	35,625	0.0	2.0	10.9
1264 Echols County	GA	14.0	3,754	37.8	22.7	39.5	25,851	3.7	4.1	61.8
Small nonadjacent to MSA[c]										
Largest decrease in poverty rate										
1 McPherson County	NE	−16.9	533	−2.4	2.3	11.4	25,750	0.0	0.0	−3.7
2 Guadalupe County[b]	NM	−16.8	4,680	11.2	45.6	31.7	24,783	7.7	6.4	−0.5
3 Billings County	ND	−16.8	888	−24.8	0.3	22.2	32,667	2.8	4.8	−8.2
4 Issaquena County[b]	MS	−16.1	2,274	16.1	63.9	41.2	19,936	13.5	10.0	23.5
5 Mason County	TX	−14.6	3,738	8.4	8.5	21.9	30,921	1.6	1.8	5.2
6 Dickens County	TX	−13.9	2,762	6.9	22.0	29.4	25,898	5.1	8.1	9.1
7 Towner County	ND	−12.6	2,876	−26.1	2.8	18.1	32,740	2.3	3.3	−5.6
8 Cottle County	TX	−11.4	1,904	−18.0	16.9	33.9	25,446	5.8	5.9	8.3
9 Kent County	TX	−11.3	859	−17.6	5.7	21.9	30,433	3.8	3.6	7.1
10 Quitman County[b]	GA	−11.1	2,598	15.0	47.1	42.2	25,875	5.8	11.5	20.4
Largest increase in poverty rate										
234 Forest County	PA	4.7	4,946	2.9	4.4	20.6	27,581	7.1	7.1	13.6
235 Butte County	ID	4.7	2,899	−0.7	7.1	17.4	30,473	5.8	2.7	5.4
236 Rock County	NE	6.4	1,756	−15.0	2.2	12.6	25,795	2.3	1.1	−4.7

237	Wheeler County	NE	6.6	886	-7.0	1.8	9.2	26,771	3.2	0.5	11.6
238	Clark County	KS	7.1	2,390	-1.2	3.9	12.6	33,857	2.6	0.5	16.0
239	San Juan County	CO	8.0	558	-33.5	3.6	7.9	30,764	3.0	10.2	5.0
240	Clark County	ID	10.5	1,022	25.4	28.6	36.0	31,576	6.1	1.9	3.0
241	Buffalo County[b]	SD	11.8	2,032	13.4	83.3	36.1	12,692	21.7	20.4	4.7
242	King County	TX	13.3	356	0.6	3.9	21.9	35,625	0.0	2.0	10.9
243	Echols County	GA	14.0	3,754	37.8	22.7	39.5	25,851	3.7	4.1	61.8

NOTE: Poverty rates and median household income are measured for 1989 and 1999 and the other variables for the period stated in the column headings. Alaska and Hawaii are not included. Percent minority is 100 minus the percentage of persons that consider white/Caucasian to be their single racial group.

[a] Nonmetropolitan area definitions follow those in place for the 2000 census as defined by the Bureau of Economic Analysis. See Chapters 2 and 6.

[b] Indicates a persistent-poverty county, which is defined as having a 20 percent or higher poverty rate in 1959, 1969, 1979, 1989, and 1999.

[c] For consistency, small nonadjacent nonmetropolitan counties are defined as having a population of less than 5,000 in 2000. Note that the 243 small non-adjacent counties are a subset of the 1,264 nonadjacent counties.

SOURCE: U.S. Census Bureau (2006e) and Bureau of Economic Analysis REIS data for employment growth (BEA 2002).

rates and five of the ten largest declines in nonadjacent counties occurred in persistent-poverty counties. Furthermore, some of the largest declines occurred in counties that had been persistent-poverty counties but had dropped below the 20 percent high-poverty threshold in 1999. For both adjacent and nonadjacent counties, the largest declines tended to occur in counties with high shares of African Americans or Hispanics in Texas or in nearby states in the Deep South. A couple of special cases are the two counties bordering Appalachia that experienced large poverty rate declines and two nonadjacent counties in the Great Plains. However, it is discouraging that none of the largest declines occurred on Native American reservations.

In the adjacent group, there are some unexpected differences between the declining and increasing poverty rate categories. Foremost of these is that the largest declines occurred in relatively less populated counties that experienced about a 7.5 percent population increase on average during the 1990s. In contrast, the largest increases in poverty rates occurred in counties where the population increased by an average of 12.5 percent, illustrating that migration was not evening out regional poverty differentials. Likewise, adjacent counties with the largest declines tend to have higher minority shares, larger shares of high-school noncompletion, and lower median household income. This pattern also extends to the two nonadjacent categories. It is heartening that poverty rates took their sharpest drops in what appear to be significantly disadvantaged counties.

In adjacent rural counties, relatively strong economies appear to be driving the largest poverty rate declines. Their unemployment rates declined by about 3 percentage points between 1990 and 2000, on average, while the unemployment rates of adjacent rural counties with the largest poverty rate increases rose. However, despite a relatively large population growth advantage for counties with the largest poverty rate increases, they only experienced about a 10 percent average increase in 1995–2000 employment growth, which is approximately the same as counties with the largest poverty rate declines. Thus, the newly created jobs in the adjacent counties with the largest poverty rate declines appear to have been filled more from the ranks of the nonemployed. It is also striking that the employment growth gap was only about 1 percentage point, on average, between the best and worst performers in terms of poverty rate changes. Hence, even the worst-performing counties tended to have job growth, suggesting other structural causes of poverty.

Among rural counties that are not adjacent to a metro area, the average poverty rate fell about 16 percentage points for the 10 counties with the largest poverty rate decreases, and it rose an average of 9 points for the 10 with the largest increases. Both groups tend to have small populations, which exceed 10,000 in only two of the 20 possible cases. Surprisingly, nonadjacent counties with the largest poverty rate declines from 1995 to 2000 typically had slower employment growth (7.8 vs. 9.4 percent) even as they had faster average population growth. The only feature that seemingly favored the nonadjacent counties with the greatest poverty rate declines is that their unemployment rate fell about 1.4 points between 1990 and 2000, as opposed to counties with the largest poverty rate increases, whose unemployment rate increased slightly. The patterns illustrate the complex nature of characterizing local poverty rate trends.

For the least-populated nonadjacent rural counties, those with the largest decreases in poverty rates tended to have declining population over the decade, while the counties with the largest increases tended to have slight gains in population, which is consistent with labor supply–driven changes in poverty. It appears disadvantaged persons disproportionately left the counties with falling poverty rates because of a lack of job opportunities; this lack is reflected by the low employment growth in most of these counties. In sum, the distinctions between those who had sharp increases in poverty rates and those who had sharp reductions are even less clear among small, nonadjacent rural counties. Thus, we need regression analysis to help sort out the underlying causes of nonmetropolitan poverty.

RURAL REGRESSION FINDINGS

To examine whether the determinants of nonmetropolitan poverty rates differ from the metropolitan averages from Chapter 7, we estimate the regression models described in Chapter 6 using the 2,204 nonmetropolitan counties. Key descriptive statistics are reported in Table 8.6, and Table 8.7 reproduces a regression table from Chapter 7. The base

Table 8.6 Nonmetropolitan County Labor Market Summary Statistics, 1990 and 2000

Group	1989–1990			1999–2000		
	(1) Total	(2) Adjacent to MSA[a]	(3) Nonadjacent to MSA	(4) Total	(5) Adjacent to MSA	(6) Nonadjacent to MSA
Population	22,416 (20,746)	28,437 (23,893)	17,648 (16,373)	24,682 (23,332)	31,836 (27,030)	19,018 (18,020)
% 1988–90 or 1998–2000 empl. growth	2.9 (5.4)	3.2 (5.2)	2.7 (5.5)	2.1 (4.1)	2.5 (4.0)	1.8 (4.2)
% 1985–90 or 1995–2000 empl. growth	6.0 (11.4)	7.6 (11.0)	4.8 (11.4)	7.5 (9.3)	8.7 (9.8)	6.5 (8.7)
1988–90 or 1998–2000 structural change	0.037 (0.020)	0.037 (0.020)	0.038 (0.021)	0.030 (0.017)	0.030 (0.016)	0.030 (0.018)
1985–90 or 1995–2000 structural change	0.070 (0.033)	0.069 (0.034)	0.071 (0.033)	0.061 (0.030)	0.061 (0.029)	0.061 (0.030)
% male employment/population	64.2 (8.0)	64.3 (7.3)	64.1 (8.4)	61.8 (8.9)	61.9 (8.8)	61.7 (9.0)
% female employment/population	46.6 (6.9)	47.0 (6.5)	46.3 (7.1)	50.3 (6.7)	50.6 (6.4)	50.1 (6.9)
% civilian male unemployment rate	6.8 (3.6)	6.8 (2.9)	6.9 (4.1)	6.0 (3.1)	5.8 (2.6)	6.1 (3.5)
% civilian female unemployment rate	7.0 (3.4)	7.2 (3.0)	6.9 (3.7)	5.9 (2.9)	5.9 (2.6)	5.9 (3.1)
% 1985–90/1995–2000 commuting zone employment growth[b]	8.0 (8.8)	9.9 (7.7)	6.4 (9.2)	8.2 (5.8)	9.4 (5.6)	7.2 (5.8)
% of workers employed in county of residence	74.7 (15.0)	68.6 (14.7)	79.5 (13.5)	69.0 (16.1)	62.4 (15.1)	74.1 (15.0)

% workers with 20–45 minute commute	24.9	28.0	22.5	27.6	30.6	25.3
	(8.5)	(7.4)	(8.5)	(8.4)	(7.3)	(8.4)
% workers with 45–90 minute commute	10.2	13.0	8.0	13.6	16.9	11.1
	(6.2)	(6.7)	(4.8)	(7.1)	(7.3)	(5.7)
N	2204	974	1230	2204	974	1230

NOTE: Unweighted descriptive statistics. Standard deviations are in parentheses. A metropolitan county is defined using 2000 Bureau of Economic Analysis REIS county definitions.

[a] "Adjacent to MSA" is defined by the U.S. Department of Agriculture as a nonmetropolitan county adjacent to a metropolitan area, using 1993 definitions.

[b] For nonmetropolitan counties, the broader labor market employment growth was defined using 1990 commuting zone definitions from the USDA's Economic Research Service (2003a).

SOURCE: U.S. Census Bureau (2006e).

1989 and 1999 nonmetropolitan poverty rate models are reported in columns (3) and (7), and most of the discussion centers on the 1999 results. Columns (4) and (8) contain the nonmetropolitan models, which include variables accounting for conditions in neighboring counties. To facilitate comparison between MSA and nonmetro counties, columns (1) to (2) and (5) to (6) report the corresponding estimates from the specifications that use the 824 MSA counties.

Turning to the results in Table 8.7, the coefficient on the lagged nonmetropolitan county poverty rate is of smaller magnitude than it is for metropolitan counties, indicating slightly less persistence for rural poverty rates in terms of responsiveness to exogenous shocks. The degree of persistence in nonmetropolitan counties declined during the 1990s. Thus the results indicate that rural counties typically adjust more quickly to changes in socioeconomic conditions.

As noted in Chapter 7, rural counties are generally more influenced by labor market conditions than are MSA counties. First, industrial structural change has a stronger impact on nonmetropolitan poverty rates. Their thinner labor markets make it harder for displaced workers who are less skilled to find suitable reemployment. The descriptive statistics from Table A.1 show that a one standard deviation change in the 1995–2000 industry restructuring measure is associated with a 0.14 percent increase in the poverty rate for the typical rural county when evaluated at the mean nonmetro county population of 24,682. When the rural county population is less than 5,000, the structural change effect approximately doubles. Hence, if a small rural county was struggling with a loss of employment in, say, the natural resource sector, the poverty rate would increase not only because job growth declined but also because labor market frictions induced by the industry restructuring would slow reemployment for some workers. Regarding the industry structure, a greater agricultural share is most associated with higher rural poverty rates (not shown).

Greater job growth has a much larger poverty-reducing impact on nonmetro county poverty rates than on MSA counties. To ensure comparability with Chapters 6 and 7, we continue to use the overall one standard deviation change in the variables from Table A.1. Using the results reported in column (7) of Table 8.7, we see that a 10.1 percent (one standard deviation) change in 1995–2000 employment growth reduces the typical nonmetropolitan county poverty rate by about 0.2 percentage points, unlike the insignificant impact it has on MSA poverty rates. As was described above, we expected a larger rural impact because of dampened migration and commuting responses.

Employment growth also indirectly reduces the poverty rate by lowering the unemployment rate and increasing the employment-population ratio. Thus, following our methods in Chapters 6 and 7, we estimated the quasireduced-form model that omits the unemployment-rate and employment-rate variables to more fully capture the direct and indirect effects of job growth (not shown). In this case, a 10.1-point increase in five-year employment growth reduces the poverty rate by about 0.25 percentage points on average, which is a little greater than when the unemployment and employment rates were held constant.

While the effects of greater job growth are not large in terms of reducing poverty rates, job growth may be more beneficial if it is targeted. For example, as described in earlier chapters, if nonmetro employment growth is concentrated in sectors that are faring well nationally, we anticipate a dampened migration response. Hence, a larger number of disadvantaged original residents would take the newly created jobs. To examine this possibility, we replaced 1995–2000 job growth with the corresponding measures of industry-mix and competitiveness employment growth; in results not shown, industry-mix job growth had more than a fourfold greater impact than generic job growth.[8] Thus, by targeting economic development efforts toward sectors that are doing well nationally, successful policies for job creation can mitigate rural poverty—more so than in urban areas. Indeed, the benefits are likely larger when the targeting is further narrowed to employing the disadvantaged and to focusing on distressed rural communities.

Because rural areas have transportation and child care constraints, which interact with each other, we expect female labor market participation to take on an even larger role in nonmetropolitan counties. Moreover, low rural wages likely mean that female employment is more vital in raising married-couple households above the poverty threshold. Thus, it is not surprising that a higher 2000 female employment rate had more than twice the effect in reducing poverty rates in rural areas than in metropolitan areas. In fact, using the results in column (7), a one standard deviation 6.9-point increase in the female employment-population ratio would reduce the typical nonmetropolitan county poverty

Table 8.7 MSA and Nonmetropolitan Poverty Rate Regression Results, 1989 and 1999

	1989				1999			
	(1) MSA base	(2) MSA broad labor mkt.	(3) Nonmetro base	(4) Nonmetro broad lab.	(5) MSA base	(6) MSA broad labor mkt.	(7) Nonmetro base	(8) Nonmetro broad lab.
Lagged poverty rate	0.49 (14.97)	0.49 (14.67)	0.47 (24.25)	0.42 (19.14)	0.43 (13.01)	0.44 (13.28)	0.38 (23.65)	0.35 (19.89)
Weighted surrounding-city poverty		−0.003 (0.15)		0.11 (5.39)		−0.01 (0.88)		0.08 (4.75)
Single-county MSAs								
Big-MSA central county	−0.13 (0.62)	0.13 (0.47)			−0.11 (0.67)	0.16 (0.67)		
Big-MSA suburban county	−0.10 (0.46)	0.15 (0.51)			−0.54 (2.85)	−0.27 (1.13)		
Small-MSA central county	0.14 (0.89)	0.36 (1.61)			0.10 (0.82)	0.31 (1.61)		
Small-MSA suburban county	−0.02 (0.12)	0.17 (0.65)			−0.19 (1.20)	0.06 (0.29)		
1985–90/1995–2000 empl. growth	−0.006 (0.76)	−0.003 (0.40)	−0.020 (3.37)	−0.016 (2.53)	−0.007 (1.35)	−0.005 (0.91)	−0.017 (3.05)	−0.017 (2.83)
1988–90/1995–2000 structural change	1.16 (0.31)	0.65 (0.17)	12.31 (2.54)	11.46 (2.44)	1.11 (0.53)	0.49 (0.23)	10.58 (3.49)	10.65 (3.68)
Pop. × structural change	−2.5e−5 (2.09)	−2.3e−5 (1.95)	−4.8e−4 (2.80)	−4.3e−4 (2.56)	−2.6e−6 (0.48)	−9.6e−7 (0.17)	−2.4e−4 (2.66)	−2.2e−4 (2.60)
% male employment/population	−0.06 (2.16)	−0.06 (2.12)	−0.09 (5.19)	−0.09 (5.34)	−0.03 (2.08)	−0.03 (1.91)	−0.03 (1.88)	−0.02 (1.19)

% female employment/population	-0.14 (5.00)	-0.14 (5.02)	-0.16 (8.27)	-0.16 (7.90)	-0.08 (3.12)	-0.08 (3.08)	-0.21 (11.50)	-0.20 (10.73)
% civilian male unemployment rate	0.32 (4.91)	0.30 (4.74)	0.15 (4.27)	0.16 (4.40)	0.23 (3.81)	0.23 (3.78)	0.14 (5.19)	0.15 (5.32)
% civilian female unemployment rate	0.02 (0.33)	0.02 (0.35)	0.07 (1.86)	0.07 (1.85)	-0.02 (0.30)	-0.02 (0.40)	-0.05 (1.36)	-0.04 (1.31)
1985–90/1995–2000 MSA empl. growth (# MSA counties ≥ 2)		-0.017 (1.41)				-0.019 (1.50)		
1985–90/1995–2000 commuting zone empl. growth				-0.02 (1.87)				-0.005 (0.55)
% of workers employed in county of residence	-0.004 (0.53)	-0.004 (0.53)		-0.003 (0.54)		0.004 (0.87)		0.01 (2.36)
% high school graduate (age ≥ 25 yrs.)	-0.10 (3.82)	-0.10 (3.79)	-0.17 (9.13)	-0.16 (8.80)	-0.15 (5.58)	-0.15 (5.54)	-0.14 (7.79)	-0.14 (7.57)
% some college, no degree (age ≥ 25 yrs.)	-0.23 (7.12)	-0.24 (7.09)	-0.19 (6.56)	-0.18 (6.43)	-0.20 (6.62)	-0.21 (6.52)	-0.11 (4.42)	-0.11 (4.57)
% associate college degree (age ≥ 25 yrs.)	-0.05 (0.68)	-0.04 (0.67)	-0.19 (4.37)	-0.18 (4.33)	-0.15 (3.18)	-0.16 (3.33)	-0.19 (4.89)	-0.21 (5.17)
% bachelor's degree or more (age ≥ 25yrs.)	0.06 (2.07)	0.06 (2.03)	-0.004 (0.16)	0.003 (0.13)	-0.10 (4.24)	-0.11 (4.29)	-0.02 (0.96)	-0.03 (1.69)
% of households female-headed with children	0.59 (7.61)	0.59 (7.41)	0.77 (13.43)	0.75 (13.26)	0.43 (6.55)	0.43 (6.59)	0.62 (10.50)	0.61 (10.69)
% of households male-headed with children	0.18 (0.72)	0.18 (0.74)	0.54 (4.40)	0.57 (4.75)	-0.14 (1.02)	-0.13 (0.97)	0.28 (3.03)	0.30 (3.30)
% population African American	-0.03 (1.74)	-0.03 (1.68)	-0.04 (4.21)	-0.04 (4.54)	-0.01 (1.59)	-0.01 (1.51)	-0.03 (3.50)	-0.03 (3.46)

(continued)

Table 8.7 (continued)

	1989				1999			
	(1) MSA base	(2) MSA broad labor mkt.	(3) Nonmetro base	(4) Nonmetro broad lab.	(5) MSA base	(6) MSA broad labor mkt.	(7) Nonmetro base	(8) Nonmetro broad lab.
% population other race	0.02	0.02	0.02	0.03	−0.04	−0.04	−0.009	−4.6e − 5
	(0.82)	(0.71)	(1.78)	(2.36)	(2.48)	(2.45)	(0.75)	(0.00)
% population Hispanic	0.02	0.02	0.01	0.009	0.002	0.003	−0.02	−0.02
	(1.96)	(2.09)	(1.27)	(0.96)	(0.26)	(0.31)	(1.98)	(2.52)
R^2	0.96	0.96	0.93	0.93	0.96	0.96	0.93	0.93
N	824	824	2204	2204	824	824	2204	2204

NOTE: The specifications follow those in columns (1), (3), (4), and (6) of Table 7.1, with some of the results suppressed for brevity. Absolute values of robust t-statistics are in parentheses. Blank means the variable was not included in the regression model. A metropolitan county is defined using 2000 Bureau of Economic Analysis REIS county definitions. See the notes to Table 7.1 for more details on variable definitions.

SOURCE: U.S. Census Bureau (2006e).

rate by a rather large 1.4 percentage points, indicating the importance of facilitating job opportunities for women in reducing rural poverty.

Male unemployment has a modestly smaller role in rural areas than in metropolitan areas. Along with the insignificant male employment rate coefficient, these results suggest that the economic well being of men—either directly, or indirectly through factors such as the marriage market—plays a relatively small role in affecting nonmetropolitan poverty.

As is consistent with arguments that transportation and child care constraints present more challenging hurdles in rural areas, both the share of households headed by single mothers and the share headed by single fathers have a much stronger adverse effect on nonmetro poverty rates. Low rural wages are probably another reason for this large rural poverty rate effect. Nonmetro county poverty rates are negatively related to the percentage of the population that is African American or Hispanic (significant at the 0.05 level) after accounting for other socioeconomic characteristics. The non–African American minority share is also negatively related to poverty rates, but the result is statistically insignificant.

The models shown in columns (4) and (8) of Table 8.7 capture the broader neighboring-county effects by including the average surrounding-county poverty rate, the five-year commuting-zone employment growth, and the percent of workers employed in their county of residence. Illustrating how labor market access and information about nearby counties is important, a greater share of workers employed in their county of residence was positively related to poverty rates in the 1999 model.[9] Likewise, the average surrounding-county poverty rate is positively related to nonmetropolitan poverty rates but is insignificant in the metropolitan models. As is consistent with Figures 2.8–2.10, these findings further support the notion of poverty clustering in rural counties, where there are spillovers across neighboring counties in residential location decisions and labor market conditions.

RURAL POVERTY AND PROXIMITY TO METRO AREAS

Being near a metropolitan area can provide significant advantages to a rural county. The close proximity may enhance the delivery of government services for the disadvantaged, and there may be more accessible child care. Close proximity also helps provide additional amenities that can help attract a professional workforce that in turn creates other employment opportunities. The larger labor market scale also greatly mitigates the problems a person may face in finding suitable labor market matches. Perhaps more importantly, closer proximity greatly increases the accessibility of jobs for the disadvantaged. Compared to nonadjacent counties, adjacent counties had faster employment growth and greater commuting-zone job growth (Table 8.6). Thus it is not surprising that a greater share of workers in counties that are adjacent to metro areas commuted longer distances and to other counties. With improved access, the average person poverty rate in adjacent nonmetropolitan counties was 2 to 3 percentage points below the average nonadjacent-county person poverty rate (see Table 2.3).

Because many adjacent nonmetropolitan counties are at least partly in the exurban fringe, their characteristics likely fall somewhere between those of metropolitan and nonadjacent rural counties. Table 8.8 reports the results of various nonmetropolitan regressions that split the sample into counties that are and are not adjacent to metropolitan areas. Columns (1) and (2) contain the 1989 adjacent-to-metropolitan models, columns (3) and (4) contain the 1989 nonadjacent models, and columns (5) through (8) report the corresponding models for 1999.

Focusing on the 1999 adjacent and nonadjacent results in columns (5) and (7), we see that there are subtle differences in key results. For example, at least in less populated counties, industry restructuring has a stronger positive impact on nonadjacent poverty rates, most likely because these labor markets are thinner. Moreover, five-year employment growth has a slightly stronger poverty-reducing impact in nonadjacent counties. The larger impact is expected because nonadjacent counties would likely attract fewer urban migrants and commuters than adjacent nonmetro counties, leaving more new job opportunities for the disadvantaged.

The greater isolation of nonadjacent counties should make them better suited for place-based policies aimed at generating employment because of the larger poverty-reducing response. To assess possible gains from targeting growth, the 1995–2000 industry-mix and competitiveness-employment growth variables were considered (not shown). For adjacent counties, the industry-mix results were insignificant, suggesting a more modest role for targeting growth. Nevertheless, for nonadjacent nonmetropolitan counties, greater industry-mix employment growth has a marked poverty-reducing impact.[10] In this case, a 10.1 percentage-point increase in industry-mix employment reduces poverty rates by 1.3 points, indicating that targeted job growth can be an effective tool in more isolated nonmetropolitan counties. Further targeting of hiring towards the disadvantaged in conjunction with policies that enhance labor force participation of women and single parents will likely produce even larger effects.

Supporting the belief that transportation and child care pose greater obstacles to employment in more isolated rural counties is the finding that the female employment rate has a slightly stronger poverty-reducing effect in nonadjacent counties. Likewise, the share of single-parent households with children has a more deleterious poverty impact in nonadjacent counties. These results are consistent with the notion that improving job opportunities, especially for women, and enhancing child care and transportation can have a stronger impact in nonadjacent counties. Also, if rural areas that are isolated are associated with even lower male wages than rural areas in general, then raising female labor force participation may be even more important for avoiding poverty for married families.

The importance of agriculture and other resource-extractive industries for many isolated rural counties appears to have increased poverty because these sectors are associated with more seasonal employment and more volatile business cycles. The typical nonadjacent county poverty rate increases a statistically significant 0.25 percentage points when the farm employment share rises by 1 percent with a corresponding decrease in the public administration share (not shown in Table 8.8). In metro-adjacent rural counties, poverty rates rise by only 0.15 points after a similar increase in agricultural employment (not shown). Moreover, a 1 percent increase in the goods employment share and a corresponding decrease in public administration is associated with a

256

Table 8.8 Adjacent and Nonadjacent Nonmetropolitan County Poverty Rate Regression Results, 1989 and 1999

	1989				1999			
	(1) Base adjacent	(2) Broad adjacent	(3) Base nonadj.	(4) Broad nonadj.	(5) Base adjacent	(6) Broad adjacent	(7) Base nonadj.	(8) Broad nonadj.
Lagged poverty rate	0.45 (15.96)	0.42 (12.28)	0.46 (17.47)	0.42 (14.24)	0.39 (16.03)	0.37 (13.58)	0.36 (17.95)	0.34 (15.11)
Weighted surrounding-city poverty		0.08 (2.41)		0.12 (4.48)		0.07 (2.65)		0.08 (3.71)
1985–90/1995–2000 empl. growth	−0.016 (1.95)	−0.015 (1.75)	−0.019 (2.31)	−0.018 (1.90)	−0.015 (2.07)	−0.017 (2.18)	−0.020 (2.27)	−0.020 (2.03)
1985–90/1995–2000 structural change	6.28 (0.94)	6.19 (0.93)	16.31 (2.55)	15.48 (2.45)	6.89 (1.99)	7.12 (2.03)	12.52 (2.75)	12.70 (2.92)
Population × structural change	−2.2e−4 (1.06)	−2.1e−4 (1.00)	−7.6e−4 (2.49)	−7.0e−4 (2.31)	−8.9e−5 (1.00)	−1.0e−4 (1.18)	−4.1e−4 (2.23)	−4.0e−4 (2.18)
% male employment/population	−0.08 (3.87)	−0.08 (3.82)	−0.10 (3.58)	−0.10 (3.74)	−0.03 (1.41)	−0.02 (1.08)	−0.03 (1.43)	−0.02 (1.10)
% female employment/population	−0.18 (6.37)	−0.17 (5.99)	−0.15 (5.48)	−0.14 (5.31)	−0.18 (6.96)	−0.17 (6.52)	−0.23 (8.85)	−0.21 (8.35)
% civilian male unemployment rate	0.20 (3.80)	0.20 (3.88)	0.13 (2.58)	0.13 (2.66)	0.16 (3.87)	0.16 (3.91)	0.13 (3.63)	0.13 (3.72)
% civilian female unemployment rate	0.09 (1.92)	0.09 (2.00)	0.06 (1.10)	0.05 (1.03)	−0.02 (0.34)	−0.01 (0.17)	−0.06 (1.49)	−0.06 (1.47)
1985–90/1995–2000 MSA empl. growth (# MSA counties ≥ 2)								
1985–90/1995–2000 commuting zone empl. growth		−0.004 (0.26)		−0.018 (1.45)		0.005 (0.37)		−0.009 (0.60)

% of workers employed in county of residence		−1.9e−3 (0.22)		−1.5e−4 (0.02)		3.2e−3 (0.42)		1.4e−2 (2.10)
Population	−1.8e−6 (0.28)	−8.2e−7 (0.13)	1.7e−7 (0.02)	−1.6e−6 (0.16)	3.6e−6 (0.77)	5.1e−6 (1.09)	1.7e−5 (1.96)	1.5e−5 (1.70)
% high school graduate (age ≥ 25 yrs.)	−0.15 (6.21)	−0.15 (5.94)	−0.17 (6.75)	−0.16 (6.50)	−0.15 (4.98)	−0.14 (4.82)	−0.13 (5.44)	−0.13 (5.38)
% some college, no degree (age ≥ 25 yrs.)	−0.17 (3.98)	−0.17 (3.88)	−0.20 (5.12)	−0.19 (4.86)	−0.08 (2.25)	−0.08 (2.25)	−0.12 (3.84)	−0.13 (3.92)
% associate college degree (age ≥ 25 yrs.)	−0.20 (3.34)	−0.20 (3.41)	−0.19 (3.15)	−0.17 (2.95)	−0.27 (4.90)	−0.29 (5.16)	−0.15 (2.91)	−0.16 (3.08)
% bachelor's degree or more (age ≥ 25 yrs.)	−0.02 (0.46)	−0.01 (0.29)	−0.006 (0.17)	0.004 (0.09)	−0.02 (0.89)	−0.03 (0.95)	−0.03 (0.97)	−0.04 (1.41)
% of households female-headed with children	0.75 (8.79)	0.74 (8.58)	0.72 (9.30)	0.71 (9.26)	0.52 (6.56)	0.52 (6.51)	0.63 (7.81)	0.62 (7.97)
% of households male-headed with children	0.53 (3.04)	0.54 (3.11)	0.50 (3.06)	0.54 (3.37)	0.21 (1.54)	0.25 (1.80)	0.32 (2.59)	0.31 (2.64)
% of population African American	−0.04 (2.99)	−0.04 (3.12)	−0.03 (2.12)	−0.04 (2.50)	−0.02 (2.04)	−0.02 (2.06)	−0.02 (1.60)	−0.02 (1.71)
% of population other race	−0.01 (0.41)	−0.003 (0.12)	0.04 (2.04)	0.04 (2.46)	−0.05 (2.78)	−0.04 (2.19)	0.01 (0.89)	0.02 (1.46)
% of population Hispanic	0.016 (0.92)	0.013 (0.76)	0.020 (1.76)	0.016 (1.40)	−0.003 (0.28)	−0.007 (0.60)	−0.013 (1.08)	−0.018 (1.55)
R^2	0.94	0.94	0.93	0.93	0.94	0.94	0.93	0.93
N	974	974	1230	1230	974	974	1230	1230

NOTE: The specifications follow those in columns (1), (3), (4), and (6) of Table 6.1, with some of the results suppressed for brevity. Absolute values of robust t-statistics are in parentheses. Blank means the variable was not included in the regression model. A nonmetropolitan county is defined using 2000 Bureau of Economic Analysis REIS county definitions. See Appendix A for more details on variable definitions. See Chapter 2 for the definition of "adjacent/nonadjacent to a metropolitan area."

SOURCE: U.S. Census Bureau (2006e).

statistically significant 0.08-percentage-point increase in the typical nonadjacent county poverty rate, vs. an imperceptible change in the adjacent county poverty rate. Hence, the act of diversifying isolated rural economies appears to have important antipoverty benefits.

Surrounding-county spillovers are examined in the 1999 adjacent and nonadjacent models in columns (6) and (8). Both rural county types are about equally affected by surrounding-county poverty rates. Yet adjacent county poverty rates are not statistically associated with commuting-zone employment growth or the percentage of workers employed in their county of residence. Nonadjacent county poverty rates are positively related to the share of workers employed in their county of residence. This finding indicates that employment accessibility in broader labor markets is one factor that can ameliorate poverty in nonadjacent counties.

Recent immigration can adversely affect rural poverty if the new arrivals compete against low-skilled natives. This possibility was considered by reestimating the models in columns (5) and (7) after adding the percentage of the population that had immigrated between the periods of 1990–1995 and 1995–2000 (not shown). The 1995–2000 foreign immigrant share had a positive and significant impact on poverty rates, whereas the early 1990s immigrant share was insignificant. For both adjacent and nonadjacent counties, a 1-percentage-point increase in the recent immigrant share is associated with a 0.4-point increase in the poverty rate. The poverty rate may increase because of higher poverty rates among immigrants and because low-income rural natives may bear some costs resulting from labor market competition with the new immigrants.[11]

To summarize the findings, poverty rates in nonmetropolitan counties that are not adjacent to metropolitan areas are more responsive to labor market conditions than their adjacent counterparts, especially for women. Likewise, other factors, such as greater adverse impacts from structural change and larger farm and goods employment shares, suggest a need to diversify the employment opportunities in nonadjacent rural counties.

CASE STUDY: SCOTTS BLUFF COUNTY, NEBRASKA

Scotts Bluff County is in the panhandle of Nebraska, located on the western border with Wyoming. It is two counties north of Interstate 80 and derives its name from a nearby plateau that marks the beginning of the geologic transition between the Great Plains and the Rockies (Curtis 2003). Scotts Bluff County contains six communities, the two largest being the cities of Scottsbluff and Gering, the county seat (ePodunk 2006). According to the latest census, 36,951 people resided in the county in 2000, including 14,732 in Scottsbluff and 7,751 in Gering (U.S. Census Bureau 2006c). Median household income equaled $32,016, 82 percent of the state average (U.S. Census Bureau 2006d).

As is consistent with the national reversal of the 1980s population decline in nonmetropolitan areas, Scotts Bluff County's population increased 2.6 percent in the 1990s, though its 2000 population was still 3.6 percent below that of 1980 (U.S. Census Bureau 2006c,e). Population growth in the 1990s was due to foreign immigration and to natural increase through propagation. Population growth in all Nebraska nonmetro areas equaled 2.3 percent in the 1990s, while metro areas experienced 13.9 percent growth (ERS 2006). With one exception, Nebraska counties adjacent to Scotts Bluff lost population in the 1990s. Box Butte, Sioux, and Banner counties lost 7.4, 4.8, and 3.9 percent of their populations, while Morrill County eked out a 0.3 percent population gain. Just across the border in Wyoming, Goshen County posted population growth of 1.3 percent.

Scotts Bluff County's population increase masks significant net out-migration from the county over the decade. Intercensal estimates suggest that the county saw a net loss of 1,275 people to other states and to other Nebraska counties in the 1990s, while the 2000 census suggests a net loss, both in-state and out-of-state, of 1,625 for 1995–2000 alone (U.S. Census Bureau 2002c). Of this net migration of 1,625 people, a net of 802—almost half—migrated to other counties in Nebraska (U.S. Census Bureau 2003). Despite overall net out-migration in the 1990s, Scotts Bluff experienced a net gain of 60 people from the four Nebraska counties that border it and 147 people from Goshen County, Wyoming. Also somewhat potentially offsetting the net out-migration between Scotts Bluff and other counties was an increase of 640 foreign-born residents in the 1990s (U.S. Census Bureau 2005c). In fact, 17.2 percent of the population in Scotts Bluff is listed as being of Hispanic or Latino origin in the 2000 census, compared to 5.5 percent for the state; 13.7 percent of the population speaks a language other than English at home (U.S. Census Bureau 2004d). Partly related to its recent immigration, Scotts Bluff's share of the adult population possessing a college degree was 17.3 percent in 2000, compared to 23.7 percent for the state. The corresponding figures for high school completion were 79.6 and 86.6 (U.S. Census Bureau 2004h).

The person poverty rate in Scotts Bluff County declined from 15.5 percent in 1989 to 14.5 percent in 1999, but its child poverty rate barely inched down, from 22.2 to 22.0 percent (U.S. Census Bureau 2004i). The Hispanic poverty rate was 30.1 percent in 1999, approximately the same as in 1989, while the Hispanic child poverty rate increased from 37.9 to 41.2 percent. These high shares put upward pressure on the overall person poverty rate, particularly as the county gained Hispanic population. Person poverty rates also decreased in the bordering Nebraska counties: 16.4 to 15.4 in Sioux, 21.8 to 13.6 in Banner, 14.8 to 14.7 in Morrill, and 11.7 to 10.7 in Box Butte. By comparison, the least populated rural areas in the nation had the largest reduction in poverty in the 1990s, declining from 17.9 to 14.9 percent (Jolliffe 2003).

Scotts Bluff County serves as a regional center for agriculture, manufacturing, medical services, information technology, finance, retail, education, tourism, and recreation (Twin Cities Development Association 2003). Prominent manufacturers include beef and sugar-beet processors, which are associated with having high shares of recent immigrants (Bodvarsson and Van den Berg 2006). Serving as a retail center, Scotts Bluff's Walmart Super Center employs 450 people. A notable tourist attraction is the Scotts Bluff National Monument, at which the Oregon Trail Museum displays pioneer and natural history exhibits (Western Nebraska Tourism Coalition 2006). The Economic Research Service of the USDA rates Scotts Bluff County as a 4 on a scale of 7 for amenity attractiveness, which it reports as being positively associated with rural U.S. population growth (McGranahan 1999).

Labor force participation remained roughly unchanged at 64 percent, while unemployment fell from 5.8 to 5.1 percent between the 1990 and 2000 censuses (U.S. Census Bureau 2004i). As an example of the connectedness between nonmetro counties, the 2000 census reported that 1,622 people commuted into Scotts Bluff County and 847 of its residents commuted out, producing a net of 775 in-commuters (U.S. Census Bureau 2004e). The vast majority of the in- and out-commuting was with the four neighboring Nebraska counties and Goshen County, Wyoming.

An evaluation of Nebraska's welfare reform initiative, Employment First, implemented statewide during July 1997, reveals a number of differences in program success between rural and urban counties (Ponza, Meckstroth, and Faerber 2002). The study consisted of a sample of January 2000 TANF recipients, for which the communities of Columbus, Gering, and Scottsbluff comprised the study's rural areas. Among its findings was that rural Nebraska recipients reported more personal obstacles to working, yet were more likely to work and less likely to be dependent on welfare. This may be evidence of greater peer pressure, preservation of middle class values, and better social support systems. But rural recipients also were less likely to find jobs that paid well or offered health benefits, and were more likely to experience job turnover and nonstandard work shifts. This occurred despite the emphasis of Nebraska's welfare reform on matching recipient interests and needs with economic opportunities, as opposed to simply placing them immediately into employment. The report recommended expanded offerings of education, job training, and career counseling to former rural recipients.

Scotts Bluff County's population remained virtually unchanged from April 1, 2000, to July 1, 2003, while Sioux County experienced slight growth and Banner, Box Butte, Goshen, and Morrill counties registered significant losses (U.S. Census Bureau 2006f). After reaching a low of 4.0 percent in 2001, Scotts Bluff's unemployment rate rose in both 2002 and 2003, reaching its highest level (5.0 percent) since its 1990s peak of 4.8 percent in 1996 (BLS 2006a). Job losses in 2003 were broad-based, occurring in agriculture, construction, manufacturing, and services (BLS 2004). Thus, it is not surprising that, following broader U.S. trends, the faltering Scotts Bluff economy led to the poverty rate increasing by 1.2 percentage points over the 2000–2002 period (U.S. Census Bureau 2005d).

POLICY IMPLICATIONS FOR FIGHTING RURAL POVERTY

The discussion in Chapter 7 noted that most economists have reservations about the effectiveness of place-based strategies as a tool for local economic development. In particular, such policies are often viewed as expensive, wasteful, prone to help those who are less in need than others, and apt to slow market adjustments that would eliminate adverse shocks or conditions. However, we contend that targeted policies may be effective in reducing poverty if tailored to localities where job accessibility appears to be the largest hindrance.

We argued in Chapter 7 that targeted tax breaks and infrastructure enhancements could be effective in central counties of metro areas. The findings in this chapter suggest an even stronger potential role for such place-based strategies in reducing rural poverty—especially in more isolated rural communities—assuming the strategies are cost-effective. Providing greater job growth and improved opportunities for women has much larger effects in nonadjacent counties than in others, while stimulating sectors that are growing faster than the national average appears especially effective at reducing their poverty rates. Additional benefits from such policies include diversifying to get away from reliance on the farm and goods sectors, which reinforces the poverty rate reductions and better sets the stage for sustainable economic development.

There have been numerous efforts to aid rural economies through such seemingly helpful means as farm supports or policies aimed at encouraging mining and lumbering. Yet these policies are narrowly focused on a declining share of the rural population and are not broad enough to support a general revitalization. These sectors simply no longer employ the large numbers they once did. The federal government has spent countless billions of dollars supporting agribusiness in the Great Plains region without stemming the population outflow. Though it is not clear how expensive it would be to boost local rural job growth rates compared to the expense of boosting local urban growth rates, it is not hard to imagine that broader-based rural development policies would be more effective than the current narrow industry-based rural policy—especially in industries that are declining nationally.

To achieve long-term economic vitality, rural communities often need an influx of modern infrastructure, including roads, water, sewage, and educational facilities. The digital divide suggests that many rural communities lag in their information and telecommunications infrastructure. Related government programs such as those administered by the U.S. Department of Housing and Urban Development have an urban bias, and federal and state governments often do not provide sufficient revenue sharing for rural communities to build or maintain infrastructure. Yet in many cases it seems more cost-effective to retain rural population where most of the necessary infrastructure is already in place, rather than build an entirely new infrastructure as this population relocates to urban areas in large numbers. It also reduces sprawl.

The potential effectiveness of place-based rural policies is further enhanced by dampened in-migration and commuting responses in smaller or more isolated economies, which leaves more jobs for the intended disadvantaged recipients (Renkow 2003). The fact that impoverished families and households tend to move to areas with already-high poverty rates reinforces the need to stimulate job growth in these locations (Nord 1998). Finally, the tendency for rural poverty to be clustered in larger regions means that there are fewer employment opportunities within driving distance.

The new-jobs tax credits and wage subsidies that will be described in Chapter 9 give one grounds to believe that targeting the most distressed, isolated rural areas will have favorable returns. In fact, there is evidence that poverty rates in the highest-poverty rural counties are more than twice as favorably affected by employment growth as in the remaining counties, illustrating the potential effects of targeting distressed counties.[12] However, in this targeting process, it should be noted that there are rural communities that do not have a critical mass of economic activity to sustain their current population. Putting scarce government resources into these communities would be wasteful and the funds would be better spent elsewhere, particularly in nearby regional centers. Likewise, there are many rural counties, especially on the Great Plains, that have experienced large, irreversible population losses for the past few decades. Such counties are undergoing an adjustment in which their disadvantaged people, along with the rest of their population, are naturally relocating to greener pastures. In these counties, it would be better to wait until the population stabilizes, as the resources would likely be of better use elsewhere.

The regression analysis suggested that rural county poverty rates, especially in more isolated counties, are mitigated by improved employment prospects for women and by fewer single-parent households. Hence, policies that facilitate improved access to child care would seem especially beneficial in rural America, particularly the farther away one gets from metropolitan centers. Likewise, given the low population density and the clustering of poverty in rural areas, transportation enhancements would be beneficial.

The greater importance of the informal economy in rural America also suggests that traditional human-capital training needs to be broadened. For example, improving basic business skills and increasing entrepreneurship might help take informal enterprises into the mainstream economy as well as help provide an alternative or a bridge for the underemployed. Programs aimed at developing business plans, marketing, identifying niche domestic and foreign markets, and providing and brokering financing may have larger payoffs than merely teaching basic skills. Indeed, such programs may directly confront the problem of outside investors being reluctant to invest in more distant rural areas with uncertain economic prospects. Trends in globalization and outsourcing accentuate the need for greater entrepreneurship to ensure that the engine of growth is more homegrown and stable. Nevertheless, this does not rule out the need for upgrading of skills in rural areas, because those areas tend to have lower average educational attainment. Hence, customized training could also be used to facilitate the attraction of new business startups.

It should be noted that, except in regions that have been undergoing persistent population losses, it is not clear whether relocation assistance policies will be effective in rural America. Unlike their metropolitan counterparts, disadvantaged rural households would often have to relocate much farther away and in larger centers than they are used to. Such moves are likely more expensive, both in terms of pecuniary costs and in the nonpecuniary, emotional costs of leaving behind friends and family, who serve as support systems. In some rural counties dominated by African Americans, Hispanics, or Native Americans, the costs of families leaving their informal networks may be prohibitive (Spilimberg and Ubeda 2004). It would likely take too many resources, which are scarce to begin with, to successfully encourage relocation of disadvantaged rural families.

SUMMARY

This chapter follows up on Chapter 7 by assessing the degree to which the underlying causes of poverty differ for nonmetropolitan counties as opposed to other types of counties. Lower population densities are expected to produce different poverty rate outcomes, both because rural labor markets differ from others and because there are likely fewer, or less-accessible, government services in rural markets. Good-quality child care also is lacking in many rural communities, which further strains single and married parents' ability to fully participate in labor market activities.

Descriptive analysis indicates a strong persistence to rural poverty. In all cases, the highest poverty rate counties were persistent-poverty counties that had 20 percent or higher poverty in 1959, 1969, 1979, 1989, and 1999. Compared to nonmetropolitan counties with the lowest poverty rates, the highest poverty rate counties tend to have greater shares of minorities and high-school noncompletion, lower median household income, and higher unemployment rates. The good news is that rural counties that experienced the greatest declines in poverty rates tended to have these same characteristics, suggesting that the most disadvantaged rural counties can improve under the right conditions. Yet one nagging problem with this premise is the persistence of extremely high poverty that is found on many Native American reservations.

Nonmetropolitan county poverty rates tended to respond more to employment growth, especially in the more isolated nonadjacent counties. In fact, job growth, when concentrated in sectors that are growing rapidly nationally, tends to markedly reduce poverty rates in nonadjacent counties, suggesting potential gains from place-based strategies. Increasing female employment also has larger poverty-reducing effects in nonmetro counties, especially in the more isolated ones. Finally, having a greater share of single-parent households increases poverty more in rural America than in metropolitan areas. Together, these results suggest that efforts to improve work supports for women can have a greater impact in nonmetro counties than elsewhere.

Given the larger role of key economic and demographic factors in nonmetropolitan counties, we argue that targeted, place-based economic-development and work-support policies can be more effective in rural America than in large urban centers. In fact, these policies are likely to be most effective in counties that are nonadjacent to metropolitan areas. Hence, we believe the type of employment zone–targeted tax credits and wage subsidies described in the final chapter should be used as a tool in reducing rural poverty. Nevertheless, we caution that some rural counties are simply so isolated or in such a downward spiral that expending additional resources on them would be fruitless.

We also recommend a large expansion in support for child care in rural communities, especially for centers that provide hours of service that can facilitate the various types of shift work that entry-level disadvantaged workers often use as stepping stones. Moreover, we support some forms of added training to augment the relatively low levels of rural human capital. But rural areas would likely also benefit from broader programs aimed at increasing entrepreneurship. Such programs would allow for more of the value added in production to be captured as area income.

Critics of place-based economic development policies have offered a host of concerns, described in Chapter 7. In terms of rural America, it is likely these critics would argue that much effort and many resources have already been expended, with seemingly few results in helping to stem population outflows. While it is true that rural America has received hundreds of billions of dollars in agriculture and related resource subsidies, it is unclear whether those subsidies have promoted economic vitality, let alone whether they have trickled down to lower income groups. Indeed, one could ask whether they have harmed the rural economy by helping to maintain an undiversified economic structure that is under persistent stress. Instead, if these billions were redirected to promoting industries with better long-run prospects as well as to improving the infrastructure and human capital of rural America, we believe there would be significant gains for the health of the overall rural economy and for those places' disadvantaged residents.[13]

The premise that most of rural America is in a downward spiral and cannot be saved is misguided. In the 1990s, nonmetropolitan population increased by 10.3 percent, which represents an increase from the 1980s. Net-migration—likely the best indicator of quality of life—was positive for nonmetropolitan counties during the 1990s.[14] Even in nonadjacent nonmetropolitan counties, population growth averaged 7.8 percent during the decade (Table 8.6). In the rural West, more people made a lifestyle choice to migrate to isolated and sparsely settled counties with fewer natural amenities (Cromartie and Wardwell 1999). Thus, reports that rural America is dead are premature. To help the disadvantaged and general population in rural counties, it is not necessarily more funds that are required, but a reallocation of resources away from policies targeted at specific industries. Of course, such policy changes would take considerable political will, and vested interests will surely fight such changes. Nevertheless, improving the plight of the rural poor and the larger rural population demands a new approach.

Notes

The two epigraphs to this chapter come from Egan (2003) and Atkinson (2004).

1. Table A.1 reports that the standard deviation of poverty rates in nonmetropolitan counties is about 2 percentage points higher than in metropolitan counties.
2. Figure A.1 goes into more detail.
3. Blank (2005), Mosely and Miller (2004), and Weber and Jensen (2004) summarize the place-based differences in rural areas and some of the research on rural poverty rate differentials.
4. In 2001, average noncore rural earnings were 62 percent of metropolitan average earnings, while the corresponding share in micropolitan areas was 69 percent (ERS 2003d).
5. For more details on the metropolitan/nonmetropolitan poverty gap, see ERS (2004a).
6. Following the convention of earlier chapters, we define the metropolitan/nonmetropolitan counties as they were defined in the 2000 census.
7. Note that the 243 isolated nonadjacent counties are a subset of the 1,264 nonadjacent counties.
8. The respective coefficients for industry-mix and competitiveness-employment growth were 0.079 ($t = 1.83$) and 0.015 ($t = 2.60$), compared to 0.017 for generic employment growth. Note that the industry-mix employment growth variable is likely measured with more error in nonmetro counties, which would bias its coefficient to zero. Greater nonmetropolitan measurement error arises because the county industry employment figure that is used to derive the industry-mix measure had to be interpolated when there was missing data in the original Bureau of

Economic Analysis employment series. Because of nondisclosure requirements, missing data was more prevalent in nonmetro counties, requiring more interpolation. Likely reflecting the effects of measurement error, the null hypothesis that the industry-mix and competitiveness-employment growth coefficients are equal can only be rejected at the 15.2 percent level.

9. Comparing column (8) to column (4), we find that from 1989 to 1999 a reversal occurs in the statistical significance of commuting-zone job growth and percent employed in county of residence, though the underlying implications are similar.

10. The adjacent-to-metropolitan-area industry-mix and competitiveness-employment growth coefficients were −0.042 ($t = 0.75$) and −0.015 ($t = 1.93$), in which the null hypothesis that the two coefficients were equal could not be rejected at any reasonable level of significance ($p = 0.63$). To be sure, measurement error may have biased these industry-mix and competitiveness results to zero. The corresponding coefficients for counties not adjacent to metro areas were −0.13 ($t = 1.95$) and −0.016 ($t = 1.67$), in which the null hypothesis that the two coefficients are equal could be rejected at the 0.10 level.

11. In neither the adjacent nor the nonadjacent case are the farm employment share and Hispanic population share results strongly affected when the immigration shares are added to the model. Likewise, following the patterns of Chapters 6 and 7, the recent foreign immigrant share had a statistically insignificant impact on 1989 poverty rates.

12. To consider this, we divided the nonmetropolitan sample into the 527 counties that had poverty rates greater than 20 percent in both 1979 and 1989 and the 1,677 counties that did not. The 1995–2000 employment growth coefficient was −0.049 ($t = 3.49$) in the high poverty sample and −0.022 ($t = 3.59$) in the remaining rural counties. In order to focus on the total effects of employment growth, the specification did not include the employment rate, unemployment rate, or mobility variables.

13. Atkinson (2004) presents an approach that could form a framework for redirecting current federal resources and subsidies toward reinvigorating rural America.

14. These figures use the 1990 definitions of metropolitan counties. For more details on rural population change, see ERS (2004b).

9

How to Win the Local Poverty War

Summary and Policy Recommendations

Forty years of movement of people and jobs away from the city have taken a toll on Philadelphia's revenue base; abandoned properties, deteriorating infrastructure, and increasing poverty and social distress have exacerbated the need for government intervention.
— Manpower Research Development Corporation, *Welfare Reform in Philadelphia*, 2003

The rural Great Plains has been losing people for 70 years, a slow demographic collapse. Without even the level of farmers and merchants that used to give these areas their pulse, many counties are also losing their very reason to exist.
— Timothy Egan, "Amid Dying Towns of Rural Plains, One Makes a Stand," *New York Times*, December 1, 2003

Just as effective causal stories focus on the simultaneous role of multiple and interactive causal factors, so effective policy solutions require attention to multiple strategies.
— Rebecca Blank, "Poverty, Policy, and Place," *International Regional Science Review*, October 2005

SYNOPSIS

After weakening in the 1980s, the link between economic growth and poverty reduction tightened again during the record expansion of the 1990s, particularly near the end of the decade. Yet strong economic performance also coincided with several public policy initiatives, including efforts to reform state and federal welfare programs. Regression and case study analysis of state-level data in Chapters 4 and 5,

269

however, reveal little evidence to support welfare reform as reducing overall poverty; instead it appears the economy was primarily responsible for poverty reduction.

In particular, the state- and national-level findings indicate that a given degree of employment growth reduces poverty more when the national economy is strong. The findings also suggest that economic development efforts targeted at industries that nationally are growing rapidly reduce poverty more than broad-based attempts to accelerate local growth. These two factors lead to better poverty outcomes because local commuting and migration flows are dampened in response to the acceleration of regional employment growth, producing greater benefits for disadvantaged current residents. Better labor market outcomes for females are more important for reducing poverty than better outcomes for males. This is true even after accounting for the influence of job growth on female labor market outcomes, which implies that other factors such as access to good-quality child care are important for females in obtaining work.

Despite the reduction in the overall poverty rate at the national level, persistent geographic pockets of poverty remain. Persistent pockets of poverty include areas in central Appalachia, the Mississippi Delta, the historic Cotton Belt in the Southeast, areas along the Rio Grande and the Mexican border, and Native American reservations in the West and the Great Plains. These pockets of extreme poverty reflect a general pattern of persistence in which areas that had high (or low) poverty in the middle of the twentieth century often have high (or low) poverty in the early twenty-first century. In general, poverty remains higher in nonmetropolitan, or rural, counties, particularly those more isolated from metropolitan areas. Higher-than-average poverty also exists in large metropolitan areas (i.e., those with a population exceeding one million). Within metropolitan areas, higher poverty occurs in central cities, whereas poverty generally is appreciably lower in the more economically vibrant outer suburbs.

While strong natural, historical, and cultural forces likely underlie many of the poverty differences across areas, county-level regression and case study analysis in Chapters 6–8 indicate that economic factors also substantially influence place-based poverty. Yet because of likely greater cross-county migration and commuting, the link between county-level employment growth and poverty is weaker than the growth-poverty link at the state and national levels. This cautions against implementing generic job creation policies on a small geographic scale. Broader geographical spillovers of economic growth on poverty across regions suggest that there should be fewer economic development efforts, but that those efforts should be centered on larger regions encompassing more people.

Nevertheless, as is consistent with state-level findings, we find that employment growth attributable to a county having a composition of nationally fast-growing industries reduced its poverty rate more than broad-based employment growth derived from all (or most) industries in the county growing faster than their respective national counterparts. We hypothesize that because the nationally fast-growing sectors are doing well everywhere, there is less inducement for employed workers already tied to these sectors through education or training to commute or migrate into the county from other regions.

Poverty in central cities, particularly among African Americans, appears to be affected by the trend of relocating jobs from inner core areas to newer suburbs, which creates a spatial mismatch between jobs and people. Spatial mismatch occurs when inner-city residents do not completely adjust to net job losses through relocation or increased commuting. Case studies suggest that this is most likely to occur in large, slower-growth, mature cities. Metropolitan poverty is particularly affected by male unemployment, even after controlling for the general influence of job growth, which suggests that additional causes beyond merely a lack of jobs are linked to male unemployment.

We find a number of differences in the relationship between poverty and the economy in nonmetropolitan counties, particularly for isolated rural areas. Compared to metro counties, rural poverty rates are more dependent on employment growth, presumably because of lower migration and commuting propensities. In what is also likely related to lower migration and commuting tendencies, targeting growth towards industries that are doing well nationally has especially strong effects on rural poverty. Increasing female employment likewise has larger poverty-reducing effects in nonmetro counties. A greater share of single-parent households increases poverty more in nonmetro areas than in metro areas, which we note as being potentially attributable to low rural wages and the greater need for two incomes for families to rise above poverty. Nonmetropolitan counties are also more affected by shifts in industry structure. This is likely related to nonmetro counties' greater dependence on a few industries and to their inhabitants' greater reluctance to relocate. Finally, poverty also appears to be more spatially clustered in nonmetro areas, with the level of poverty in each county contingent on the economic vitality of its neighbors.

POLICY RECOMMENDATIONS

Given the spatial dimensions of poverty, we cannot imagine an effective poverty-reduction program that does not aggressively address the place-based barriers that underlie the severe pockets of poverty. While helping individuals to be self-reliant is laudable, recognition needs to be given to the many root causes of poverty that exist in local communities. Besides a host of deficiencies in a community's capacity to offer services, such as inadequate transportation and child care, many areas simply do not have sufficient job opportunities for less-skilled individuals. Clearly, healthy doses of personal values and individual responsibility cannot be expected to fully overcome problems that originate at the community level. Thus, policy initiatives need to be tailored to place, recognizing each region's particular circumstances.

Our analysis points to a number of policies that could potentially reduce localized poverty. Both place-based and person-based policies are needed, and policy design should reflect their interplay. As evidenced in the quotation by Rebecca Blank at the beginning of the chapter, the complexity of place-based poverty requires simultaneous implementation of multiple strategies—implementation of an incomplete set of policies will likely prove fruitless. Finally, regional policies also must be optimally designed within the context of the national economic and policymaking environment. Policies consistent with our findings, including both those currently used in practice and new ones that we propose, follow below.

Macroeconomic Policies

Because a rising tide has once again been found to lift all boats, poverty reduction should become an explicit goal of macroeconomic policymaking. In particular, our analysis of the 1990s experience suggests that poverty reduction is more likely to occur when economic growth is sustained. Local poverty-reducing impacts of growth accumulate over time. Sustained national growth pushes unemployment rates and labor force participation rates to points where those with the least education and job skills have time to move out of poverty. Prolonged economic growth helps ensure that disadvantaged workers gain sufficient experience, confidence, and other soft and hard skills to remain employed on a consistent basis. Likewise, sustained national growth helps ensure that prosperity becomes geographically widespread, as booming areas eventually bump up against supply-side constraints, causing demand to shift to lagging regions. An example of how macroeconomic policymaking could incorporate poverty concerns would be for the Federal Reserve district banks to provide information on the antipoverty benefits of continued growth in their regions, which could be weighed against general inflation risks.

Earned Income Tax Credit (EITC)

The federal EITC has been lauded for greatly increasing labor force participation (if not hours of work) and reducing welfare roles (Hotz and Scholz 2001; Grogger 2003). Given its success, the EITC should be simplified and made more generous at the federal level and expanded at the state and local level. For example, in 2004 there were 18 states with their own versions of the EITC. Beyond states, targeted EITCs should be used in distressed substate regions. Examples of local EITCs are found in Montgomery County, Maryland, and in one used in the city of Denver during 2002.[1] Given that an EITC tax credit is directly based on income, it more directly helps those most in need. The EITC is an attractive alternative to state and local minimum wage and living wage laws, which, besides deterring employment growth, are much less focused on needy households and thus can go to workers who are in families well above the poverty threshold (Turner and Barnow 2003).

Along with job-creation strategies such as targeted tax breaks, wage subsidies, or public employment, an EITC targeted at a distressed area would provide disadvantaged workers with a supply-side carrot to encourage employment. It should be prescribed for a limited period, such as two years, to induce disadvantaged workers to gain enough experience and human capital to ensure long-lasting employment. Further, it should be limited to people who have resided in the targeted area for some set time period (say, one year) to deter people from relocating to be eligible for the credit. Such a spatially focused supply-side inducement may be the needed impetus to ensure that geographically targeted employment growth programs are successful. Moreover, along with wage subsidies targeted to residents of distressed zones, an EITC that is focused on the zone's disadvantaged residents would also provide an inducement for them to seek suitable employment outside of the zone.

Metropolitan and Urban Economic Development Policies

Because there is an apparent lack of jobs in the core of most large metropolitan areas, we believe that an effective metropolitan (urban) antipoverty strategy should encompass spatially targeted enterprise zone policies that chiefly benefit the residents of the zone. Some characteristics of these policies are as follows:

- They would be primarily targeted at central counties, especially those with greater African American population shares.

- Targeting efforts should emphasize industries that are growing faster than the national average, because such growth induces smaller in-migration flows (and likely smaller commuter flows). That is, if the industry is faring well everywhere, then growth in one location will likely attract fewer workers from elsewhere because they are already likely to be employed. Efforts should also consider targeting sectors that employ less-skilled workers at higher wages—i.e., in industries known to have positive pay differentials even after accounting for occupational structure (Andersson, Holzer, and Lane 2002, 2003; Foster-Bey and Rawlings 2002).

- The incentives and wage subsidies should be almost entirely targeted at new hires who reside within the enterprise zone. Exceptions—hires from outside the enterprise zone—must only be made for disadvantaged persons: for example, TANF recipients or unemployed workers from low-income households (Peters and Fisher 2002). The breaks should not simply go toward the firms locating in these areas because, more often than not, the newly created jobs will end up going to people who reside outside of the targeted zone.

- The incentive mechanism should be consistent with recent New Jobs Tax Credit (NJTC) and targeted wage subsidy (TWS) proposals (Bartik 2001; Schweke 2004).[2] One distinction is that we believe they should be further targeted to residents of the zone. Specifically, an NJTC would provide about a 30-percent tax credit on wages up to about $15,000 when a firm hires additional employees beyond some benchmark. Subsidies would only take effect when employment rises above 102 percent of the previous year's employment. That means subsidies are for new jobs, not existing jobs. For residents who are certified by a workforce board, the TWS would subsidize wage and benefits up to an average rate of about $8.50 an hour for 26 weeks. The TWS program would be structured to allow a community workforce board to pick potential employers who have a track record of retaining disadvantaged workers. A central benefit is that both programs target less-skilled workers, not capital.

- As is consistent with the incentive programs, there is further need for community-based placement agencies and the so-called first-source programs (Andersson, Holzer, and Lane 2003; Schweke 2004; Shelton et al. 2002). These nonprofit groups first screen and train disadvantaged workers and then place them in good employment matches. Such organizations likely have better community networks and may be more credible with businesses than a government agency. There remains a need for government programs, in which efforts to improve current programs such as the one-stop career centers are good steps.

Nonmetropolitan Economic Development Policies

The lack of well-paying jobs in many rural areas suggests the need for the same kind of enterprise zone policies there that we advocate for central-city counties. Chapter 8 describes how targeting place-based economic-development and work-support policies can be more effective in rural America than in large urban centers. These policies are likely to be most effective in counties that are farthest away from metropolitan areas.

Enterprise zones for rural areas have been part of federal and state rural development efforts. For example, in 1996 Nebraska implemented an Enterprise Zone Act in which economic distress was defined as population loss in excess of 10 percent between the two most recent censuses, and an unemployment rate twice the state average or a poverty rate in excess of 20 percent (Nebraska State Statutes 1996). Businesses are eligible to receive income and sales tax credits for new employees hired at a qualifying wage, and for investment expenditures above a certain threshold. The program's eligibility requirements for metropolitan areas differ from those of rural areas (Nebraska Department of Revenue 2006).

At the federal level, stemming from legislation in 1993, numerous empowerment zones and enterprise communities were created in rural areas in 24 states, with most concentrated in Appalachia, in areas across the South with high black poverty, and in Hispanic communities across the Southwest (Reid 1999). High poverty rates are the primary requirement for designation as either an empowerment zone or an enterprise community, and most of the areas have poverty rates in the 25–35 percent range. The primary difference between an empowerment zone and an enterprise community is that, in the former, business tax credits and other tax incentives are available.

Empowerment zones and enterprise communities should consider the following recommendations, which are specific to nonmetropolitan areas:

- Nonmetropolitan areas that serve, or can serve, as regional centers for economic activity should be identified and targeted. The poverty benefits of a growing economic center will spill over into less-developed neighbors. Regional centers also serve as a commuting magnet that benefits residents far away. Empirical results in Chapter 8 show the importance of these regional spillovers in reducing rural poverty. However, expending resources on communities that do not possess a critical mass of businesses will be wasteful, as residents of these small communities will simply purchase goods and services from larger centers. In fact, Stabler and Olfert (2002) find that financial injections into small rural communities typically end up benefiting higher-order cities more than the intended community.

- Regional economic development cooperatives or corporations should be designed for commuting zones. The advantages of organizations that encompass a broader geographic scope than just an individual city or county include pooling of resources and greater internalization of the larger regional benefits. And regional efforts would likely be better monitored for their progress than state or federal efforts and adjusted accordingly.

- For urban areas in nonmetro counties, targeting industries that are faring well nationally helps reduce migration and increases the benefits to existing local residents.

- As recommended for metro areas, tax credits should be provided for newly created jobs for workers who reside in the zone. For example, under the Nebraska Enterprise Zone Act, higher tax credits were awarded for residents hired from the zone (Rogers 1998).

- Rural counties that are simply too isolated, or are in such a downward spiral that expending additional resources on them would not produce tangible results, should be identified and made ineligible. In particular, peripheral regions that are part of larger commuting zones for regional economic centers should not be targeted for job growth. Rather, efforts should be directed at individuals in these areas to assist them in obtaining suitable employment, through either commuting or relocating.

- Empowerment zones also may need to provide infrastructure and customized training. Unlike capital tax subsidies, customized training programs can provide lasting benefits to zone residents even if targeted firms close. North Carolina has been praised for its strong emphasis on the customized training provided by community and technical colleges (Bartik 2001), which is a feature of recent Bush administration proposals (White House 2004).

- Credits and subsidies should be given to encourage entrepreneurship that takes advantage of nonmetropolitan informal economies. Such entrepreneurial activities may allow for more value added in production to be retained as area income. Thus, the credits can be based on contribution to regional income, but this needs to be closely monitored to ensure sufficient income is trickling down to the lower part of the income distribution. A trend in encouraging entrepreneurship is microlending, which began internationally in the 1980s.[3] Microlending is now finding its way into rural empowerment zones and enterprise communities. It provides individuals who possess human capital but lack financial capital with funding to start small businesses. From international applications, communities have learned to use peer groups in making approval decisions, rather than basing such decisions purely on the amount of collateral the loan applicant can offer. This type of approach works best in rural areas, where inhabitants' greater familiarity with one another facilitates the use of of peer groups. Thus, microlending would have its greatest impact where skills are most underutilized or business is most undercapitalized (Wallace 1999).

- Empowerment zones should facilitate and broker funding for broadband infrastructure and other investments needed to support firms dependent upon digital technology. In more remote areas, such investment should focus on wireless and satellite technology. Some states should consider creating a twenty-first century counterpart to the Rural Electrification Administration, which brought electric service to remote regions in the mid-twentieth century.

- Empowerment zones should also financially support research to develop promising products and services most suited for production in rural areas, such as wind power (Atkinson 2004).

- Zones should decentralize the location of government facilities, moving them away from high-cost urban areas to lower-cost rural areas, and particularly to rural areas located near regional economic centers (Atkinson 2004; Blank 2005).

- Another challenge that distressed communities and cities often face is a declining tax base and a deteriorating or crumbling infrastructure. These disadvantages can lead to municipalities imposing a heavier tax burden, which would further deter firms from locating in these communities. Hence, an additional way to aid distressed areas is through state and federal sources sharing more of their revenue (Bartik 2004). Addressing infrastructure needs has been a principal part of the federal government's strategic plans for rural empowerment zones and enterprise communities (Reid 1999).

- Particularly in disadvantaged urban and rural communities, there is often a lack of community capacity to provide services, such as transportation and child care. This capacity is the necessary glue that holds communities together, making long-term economic growth possible. A certain level of community stability is necessary to reduce the inherent risk before private investment will begin to take hold. Thus, our final strategy relates to the need for community capacity-building, enhanced community organizations, and greater social capital, all of which help enforce social stability, appropriate individual behavior, and property rights (Blank 2005). Not only should efforts focus on building governance structures, they also should ensure that the resulting institutions are transparent and accountable to the entire population. Proper governance ensures that the needs of the entire community are met, rather than simply those of local elites. Administrators of state and federal economic development and antipoverty programs could foster and monitor progress in this area.

Metropolitan Person-Based Policies

Although we believe place-based proposals are needed, they are not intended to replace necessary person-based policies. Below, we summarize some of our preferred approaches for metropolitan areas.

- Enhanced transportation incentives to facilitate reverse commuting to job-rich suburbs are worthwhile. Good examples of current efforts include funds to repair automobiles and improvement of public transport or shuttle services. In fact, there is sufficient evidence to support additional pilot projects for providing disadvantaged households with a serviceable automobile (Waller and Hughes 1999; Raphael and Rice 2002).[4]

- We believe encouraging disadvantaged households to relocate to areas that have a greater availability of jobs has some promise. Chicago's Gautreaux program of the 1970s is often cited as a program that produced long-term payoffs (Rosenbaum and DeLuca 2000). Following up on that program's success, the U.S.

Department of Housing and Urban Development implemented the Moving to Opportunity (MTO) program in the mid-1990s to help households in high-poverty neighborhoods relocate to more prosperous neighborhoods (Shroder 2001). Early evidence shows that, with sufficient counseling and assistance in finding housing, it may be possible to improve a disadvantaged household's economic and social well-being through relocation.[5] Yet we are concerned that, even under the best of circumstances, disadvantaged households would be reluctant to relocate. Already there are great incentives to leave poor neighborhoods without any assistance, but such wide-scale migration has not occurred. One likely reason is that, by moving, a household would leave behind friends, family, and contacts that often provide needed support, including child care. Another is that the poor may not be able to move to lower poverty areas because of the lack of affordable housing. Also, minorities may face discrimination from potential landlords and other obstacles in their new setting. In sum, programs such as MTO are likely only a small piece of the puzzle.

- There is an ongoing need to provide skills upgrading and training to all disadvantaged groups. However, human capital programs have a long history, and, given their cost and marginal effectiveness (Carneiro and Heckman 2003), we think that these programs are not sufficient without complementary increases in employment opportunities. Moreover, a useful supplement is counseling in job-search skills, in employment information, and in workplace expectations, as well as ongoing mentoring to encourage retention. Community nonprofit organizations should be more intensively utilized in delivering these programs.

- Disadvantaged residents need more information regarding job opportunities, and they need counseling to improve job-search skills and to retain jobs. In terms of channeling scarce resources to where they will do the most good, Chapter 7's findings indicate that these programs will likely have greater impacts in central-city counties.

- We found that greater minority population shares are not a determining factor behind higher poverty rates. Rather, we found that other factors that may be related to race, including the lack of access to good jobs and a larger share of single mothers, underlie higher minority poverty. Yet to improve access to jobs, especially for African Americans, more effective Affirmative Action programs in housing may offer gains.

- Some possible reforms for helping dislocated or unemployed workers include improving the federally supported one-stop career centers, which Congress created in 1998 to provide more flexible training assistance and job-hunting tips such as resume preparation (Wessel 2003). The Bush administration proposed reforming the 1998 Workforce Investment Act by reducing overhead and red tape and by providing more attention to actual skills that are being demanded by employers (White House 2004). The administration also wants to create more individual flexibility through $3,000 Innovation Training Accounts—personal accounts that would give workers the choice of using this funding at community colleges, community organizations, businesses, or private-training providers. A similar initiative is the $4,000 New Economy Work Scholarship proposal by the Progressive Policy Institute. Finally, others have proposed that unemployed workers receive bonuses when they find work, while still others have proposed that unemployment benefits decline over time to provide an increasing incentive to quickly find work (Wessel 2003; White House 2004). For example, in 2004 the Bush administration proposed a $50 million pilot project to provide $3,000 personal reemployment accounts for unemployed workers, to be used for child care, transportation, training, and job-search assistance. An individual could keep the balance of the account once he or she obtained work. Of course, in these latter proposals, policymakers need to weigh the tradeoff of the potential benefits of encouraging unemployed workers to take employment versus the costs incurred if unsuccessful job seekers and their families fall below the poverty threshold.

Rural Person-Based Policies

While many of the person-based policies suggested for metropolitan areas also apply to nonmetropolitan areas, different emphases may be required to address needs specific to these areas. Particular emphasis should be given to the following activities:

- Child care subsidies appear to have particularly large payoffs for increasing female labor force participation (Blau and Tekin 2003), which we found to be strongly linked to reducing poverty in nonmetropolitan areas. Moreover, in nonmetropolitan areas workers rely more on family day care than on child care centers (Gordon and Chase-Lansdale 2001). This may limit the geographic scope of the search for employment. Additional assistance, either in the form of direct cash payments to families or in the form of subsidies and tax credits, may increase the number of child care centers, allowing parents to expand their search and find better jobs. Rural areas particularly need child care centers that provide the hours of service that can accommodate the various types of shift work that entry-level disadvantaged rural residents often find themselves in. One way to marry place-based policy with person-based policy is to leverage rural schools to provide additional before- and after-school day care programs. Such programs could further utilize the school district's resources in terms of its transportation capacity, by allocating buses to help disadvantaged parents.

- Even though rural residents are more likely to own cars because their area has no public transportation, some may not be able to afford a car, which can limit their employment options. Programs that have been mentioned for metropolitan areas for assisting individuals in obtaining reliable automobile transport may be even more effective in nonmetropolitan areas.

- The low pay that is characteristic of rural areas suggests that career counseling could be more important there than in urban areas for obtaining employment with higher wages. Because government and nonprofit counseling services are probably widely scattered, added effort is required to make them better known and more accessible to rural residents.

- More training to augment the relatively low levels of rural human capital is needed. Firms requiring a higher level of skills are unlikely to locate in rural areas lacking human capital. Of course, to induce rural residents to improve their human capital, a simultaneous strategy of attracting higher-skilled firms would need to be in place. The human-capital programs would then need to focus on the needs of the firms being targeted.

Welfare Reform Policies

Welfare reform should place more emphasis on reducing poverty than on reducing caseloads. Programs should de-emphasize placing recipients immediately into any form of employment regardless of the poverty consequences, and emphasize instead moving welfare recipients permanently above the poverty line. As evidenced in many states, this may be more expensive in the short run, but over the longer run both welfare caseloads and poverty would likely be reduced. Nonetheless, the programs would still need to contain strong work incentives such as earnings disregards, sanctions for noncompliance with program directives, and time limits on benefits for those assessed as being able to obtain gainful employment. The financial support required to reduce poverty likely includes the following actions, some of which overlap with needed supports for the working poor in general.

- Attempt to train recipients and best match their skills and abilities with the job placement, such as in the state of Washington.

- Continue career counseling after the initial job placement until the recipient obtains employment with adequate wages and health benefits.

- Provide sufficient subsidies for child care expenditures.

- Financially assist current and recent recipients with transportation needs. For example, such assistance could be in the form of cash rebates or low-interest loans for purchase of automobiles.

- Provide housing subsidies until the family is at a sufficient level above poverty, and focus on subsidizing housing in areas with stronger job growth.

- Subsidize health care until recipients obtain employer-provided health benefits.

- Match the most disadvantaged, such as those suffering from mental illness, substance abuse, or spousal abuse, to appropriate social service agencies, since some individuals may be able to become self-sufficient with assistance.

CONCLUSION

We began this book by noting that society has much to gain from alleviating poverty, and that the benefits extend well beyond the direct beneficiaries. We describe how helping children in poor families can produce strong intergenerational benefits. In Chapter 6, we find that children appear to gain more from a strong local economy than do other age groups. Another theme that we put forth is that the likelihood that a given family or household experiences poverty is greatly affected by where they reside. Poverty is simply not uniformly distributed across the nation. It can be rather high in central cities and in more-isolated rural communities, and it usually is low in exurban areas and in the better-off suburbs. Even within these categories, there is tremendous diversity. Not only is poverty unevenly distributed across our communities, its incidence is very persistent. The high-poverty areas of the mid-twentieth century were generally the high-poverty areas at the beginning of the twenty-first century.

The complex set of circumstances that underlies the spatial distribution of poverty necessitates multiple, concurrent antipoverty policies tailored to place. Augmenting individual skills or other personal deficiencies alone will be inadequate when the root causes are at the community level. Antipoverty policies need to be focused and coordinated; they need to be mutually reinforcing and not working against each other. One solution at the federal level would be to consolidate economic development programs (Atkinson 2004), while at the same time giving policymakers enough freedom to avoid having to conform to one-size-fits-all solutions. Federal efforts could then be better coordinated with state and local efforts as the various levels pooled expertise, resources, and funds.

Economic development initiatives need to be informed more by research related to broader societal objectives than are the current programs, which tend to be infused with politics and power brokering. Rural America is probably the most prominent example of this—a geography where misguided industry-level subsidies are too often passed off as broader economic development. These programs have not stabilized the rural economy and may have even undermined it. Simple reallocation of resources could pay significant dividends; industry-level subsidies should only be used as part of a broader strategy to reinvigorate local economies. Only by focusing policy on broader societal interests such as poverty reduction can we get the best use out of the billions of dollars that make their way through the labyrinth of government economic-development and industry-support programs. Nevertheless, because the potential gains that would result from better focusing our efforts are so large, we are guardedly optimistic that the public will eventually demand that the necessary changes be made.

Notes

The epigraphs at the opening of this chapter come from Michalopoulos et al. (2003), Egan (2003), and Blank (2005).

1. The Montgomery County's EITC matched the Maryland EITC, which was 15 percent of the federal credit in 2001. Details of the EITC can be found on the Montgomery County Web site, http://www.montgomerycountymd.gov/mc/ news/press/00-33.html (Montgomery County 2000). Denver's 2002 EITC gave a maximum credit of $788 for low-income families with children. The program was funded through the federal allocation of TANF funds. More details of the Denver EITC program can be found on the City of Denver's Web site, http:// www.denvergov.org/newsarticle.asp?id=3647 (Denver 2002).
2. The NJTC is based on a similar federal program from the late 1970s, and the TWS program mimics a similar Minnesota program of the 1980s (Bartik 2001).
3. Microlending typically involves the provision of small loans made to micro-enterprises by noncommercial organizations such as government agencies or nonprofits. These normally employ a few people at most and have limited or no access to commercial credit.
4. Even so, we believe that transportation initiatives alone will have a limited impact on poverty. Especially in areas with heavy congestion, it will be challenging to induce disadvantaged individuals to add hours of commuting time for a low-wage job when they are already struggling with child care and other issues of survival.
5. Katz, Kling, and Liebman (2001) find evidence that the MTO program improved outcomes such as health and safety for the relocated households, but they did not find statistically significant evidence that MTO improved short-run earnings and employment or reduced welfare receipt. Kling, Ludwig, and Katz (2004) find evidence that MTO has led to less crime among girls of the households that move, but they find more mixed effects on the criminal activity of boys belonging to such households.

Appendix A

Derivation of the County Poverty Rate Empirical Model

The underlying partial-adjustment model used in the empirical analysis assumes that in year t, county i possesses an equilibrium poverty rate, POV_{it}^*, that is a function of the county's socioeconomic characteristics X_{it}. By equilibrium, we mean that there are forces that push the poverty rate back to POV_{it}^*. This process is shown in Equation (A.1):

(A.1) $\text{POV}_{it}^* = \beta X_{it}$,

where β maps the relationship between the factors in X_{it} and the equilibrium poverty rate POV_{it}^*. Dropping the subscript i for convenience, the actual poverty rate in year t (POV_t) only partially adjusts from the previous period some fraction α ($0 \leq \alpha \leq 1$) towards the equilibrium rate:

(A.2) $\text{POV}_t - \text{POV}_{t-1} = \alpha(\text{POV}_t^* - \text{POV}_{t-1})$.

Equation (A.2) simply states that the change in poverty rate is some partial fraction of the deviation of the past poverty rate from the county's equilibrium poverty rate.

If we combine Equations (A.1) and (A.2), the actual poverty rate in year t can be written as

(A.3) $\text{POV}_t = (1 - \alpha)\text{POV}_{t-1} + \alpha\beta X_t$.

The short-run poverty response to a change in one of the X variables is $\alpha\beta$, which is the coefficient for the explanatory variable in a regression of the poverty rate in year t on the lagged poverty rate and the X variables.[1] By definition, in long-run equilibrium, POV_t equals POV_{t-1}. Hence, the long-run equilibrium response to a change in the explanatory variable is $\alpha\beta/\alpha$, in which α is simply derived from the regression coefficient on the lagged poverty rate variable. Because α is less than one, the long-run response of a particular variable is greater than the short-run response, illustrating the sluggish adjustment process. A larger regression coefficient on POV_{t-1} implies either a smaller α or a slower adjustment to the equilibrium poverty rate.

An alternative approach would be to follow Levernier et al. (2000) and assume an equilibrium process. This is represented in Equation (A.3) by simply omitting the lagged poverty rate term and assuming that the current poverty rate is solely a function of the other explanatory variables. That is, the current poverty rate equals the equilibrium poverty rate, implying that the adjustment is rapid. An equilibrium process can be tested in Equation (A.3) by examining the statistical significance of the lagged poverty rate term. In our results, we generally find that the lagged poverty rate is highly statistically significant, meaning that a disequilibrium process is supported by the data. In fact, the labor market results vary greatly, depending upon whether equilibrium or disequilibrium adjustment is assumed.

Following from Equation (A.3), Box 6.1 on page 134 provides an overview of the actual empirical specification. The explanatory variables used in the model shown in Box 6.1 include the five dummy variables in the CTY_TYPE vector for

1) whether a county contains the central city of a large MSA,

2) whether the county is a suburb in a large MSA,

3) whether a county contains the central city of a small MSA,

4) whether the county is a suburb in a small MSA, and

5) whether the county is a single-county MSA.

So that the equation can be statistically estimated, the nonmetropolitan county indicator is omitted. Hence, the MSA county-type regression coefficients are measured relative to the typical nonmetropolitan county. Following from the discussion of the descriptive statistics in Chapter 2, a 2000 MSA population of 1,000,000 is used as the division between large and small MSAs.

All else being equal, poverty should be higher in central-city counties relative to suburban counties if mismatches in job skills and neighborhood effects exist. These mismatches especially apply if transportation constraints limit the ability of central-city county residents to commute to suburbs where there is greater job creation. For similar reasons, poverty is expected to be higher in nonmetropolitan counties than in suburban counties. How poverty rates differ between nonmetro counties and central-city counties is affected by the relative strengths of their specific types of labor market mismatches and neighborhood effects.

We caution that many central-city counties also include a large suburban population, which acts to make various MSA county groupings appear more homogenous. Yet the descriptive statistics discussed in Chapter 2 clearly show that suburban and central-city counties (combined with single-county MSAs) significantly differ in terms of economic and demographic characteristics. In particular, the central-city counties often include older inner-ring suburbs that

Box A.1 The 2003 Definition of Metropolitan and Micropolitan Areas

Metro and nonmetro areas are defined by the Office of Management and Budget (OMB). In 2003, OMB defined metro areas as comprising two types of counties: 1) central counties with one or more urbanized areas, and 2) outlying counties that are economically tied to the core counties, as measured by workers commuting. Metropolitan areas are centered on urbanized areas of at least 50,000 people. Outlying counties are included if 25 percent of workers living in the county commute to the central counties, or if 25 percent of the employment in the county consists of workers coming out from the central counties—the so-called reverse commuting pattern. Nonmetro counties are outside the boundaries of metro areas and are further subdivided into two types. The first is micropolitan areas, centered on urban clusters of 10,000–50,000 people. As in metro areas, outlying counties are included in a micropolitan area if the percentage of workers commuting to the central county is 25 percent or higher, or, vice versa, if 25 percent of the employment in the outlying county is made up of commuters from the central county. All remaining nonmetropolitan counties form the second type of nonmetro counties, called noncore counties.

SOURCE: ERS (2003b,c); U.S. Census Bureau (2004g).

are under stress, whose lagging performance in recent decades indicates a convergence with the central city (Hudnut 2003; Jargowsky 2003; Katz 2003). By contrast, the suburban-county classification almost always includes the newer, faster-growing (sprawling) suburbs on the fringe of the metropolitan area (Lucy and Phillips 2001). Hence, the suburban demarcation in this study tends to reflect the fastest growing parts of metropolitan areas.

County and metropolitan-area population are also included in the CTY_TYPE vector. To capture separate population scale and density effects related to productivity and job accessibility, we include the entire MSA population for metropolitan counties and a separate variable measuring the interaction of the nonmetropolitan county indicator with county population. The interaction variable will capture any differing population-scale effects for nonmetropolitan areas.

Economic factors (ECON) include several county-level measures of labor market strength. It is an empirical issue whether job growth affects poverty immediately or whether it is a cumulative process over several years. Thus, using Bureau of Economic Analysis (BEA) REIS data, employment growth over two-, five-, and ten-year periods was separately considered (i.e., for 1988–90 and 1998–2000, 1985–90 and 1995–2000, and 1980–90 and 1990–2000).[2] A negative sign for the employment growth coefficient would support the hypothesis that stronger labor markets reduce poverty. As discussed in Chapter 6, the five-year measure of job growth performs best, suggesting a lag between initial job growth and poverty rate declines.

The male and female unemployment rates are included as additional labor market measures. Similarly, the county's employment-population ratios by gender are also included in ECON. Given the inclusion of job growth, the employment rate coefficients should reflect effects beyond labor demand. We also conduct simulations to capture the fact that greater job growth not only has direct effects on poverty but also has indirect effects through changing the unemployment and employment-population rates.

Also included in ECON is recent industrial structural change (ISC). Similar to the measure used for states in Chapter 4, the ISC is simply a dissimilarity index measured as the sum of the absolute changes in the 11 BEA one-digit industry employment shares between two periods, divided by two.[3] For example, the 1995–2000 ISC measures what share of the workforce would have to shift one-digit sectors such that the two periods would have the same sectoral composition. Theory does not provide guidance as to the length of time it may take structural change to affect poverty. Thus, for both 1989 and 1999, we experimented with both the two-year and five-year measures of structural change (i.e., 1988–90 and 1998–2000, and 1985–90 and 1995–2000). In general, the two-year (1988–90) measure appeared to be superior in the 1989 poverty rate model, and the five-year (1995–2000) measure appeared to work best in 1999.[4]

A positive ISC coefficient would suggest adjustment costs in the reallocation of labor across sectors that worsen economic outcomes at the lower end of the skill distribution through increased unemployment, withdrawal from the labor force, and lower wage rates. However, restructuring is likely to have a smaller impact when there is a greater diversity of job opportunities in a labor market, because nonemployed or laid-off workers can find jobs that more readily match their skills and experience. Thus, an interaction of the ISC measure with the county's population is also added to the model, in which the improved job-matching hypothesis suggests a negative coefficient.

Labor market and other characteristics in surrounding counties may spill over and affect a county's poverty rate. First, job growth in nearby counties may create employment opportunities for a county's low-skilled residents, or, alternatively, slower job growth in neighboring counties may increase the supply of low-skilled individuals crossing into the county for employment. Thus, for some models we include the MSA five-year employment growth for metropolitan counties,[5] and for nonmetropolitan counties we include the five-year job growth rate for the county's commuting zone.[6]

Second, the percentage of workers employed in the county of residence is included as a proxy for nearby employment accessibility. After controlling for county employment growth, we expect that poverty rates should be positively associated with this measure, as it signals a lack of accessible job opportunities in nearby counties and may relate to housing discrimination and transportation. Similar accessibility measures have been utilized in spatial mismatch studies (Kain 1992; Madden 1996). Finally, to capture neighborhood spillovers, near-by migration patterns, and the supply of low-skilled workers in neighboring counties, the ten-year lagged average poverty rate of the immediate surrounding counties is included in a sensitivity analysis.

One-digit industry shares of employed county residents are included in ECON to capture the influence of industry composition on county poverty. Because the omitted category is public administration, these coefficients measure an indus-try's effect relative to public administration. Each industry-share regression co-efficient is interpreted as the response of increasing that industry's employment share by 1 percent (or 0.01) while reducing the public administration share by 1 percent (0.01).

Demographic variables (DEMOG) include five educational attainment cat-egories ranging from high school graduate to bachelor's degree. Each variable is measured as the percentage of the population greater than 24 years old with the attainment defined by that category. The percentage that are high school dropouts is the omitted group, so the education coefficients are measured rela-tive to the effects of an equivalent offsetting change in the high school non-completion share. Poverty is expected to be lower in counties with greater educational attainment. Yet we expect educational attainment to have a declin-ing marginal effect in reducing poverty. That is, at low educational attainment levels, increases in education can lift many households from below poverty status into the middle class. However, a greater share of college graduates pri-marily moves middle class families further above poverty, and there may be anomalies in college towns in which measured poverty rates will be higher even as there are high shares of recent college graduates.

Two other key demographic factors in the model are the percentage of households that are female-headed with children and the percentage that are male-headed with children. Such families are the primary recipients of wel-fare, which has a positive effect on income but negative effects through labor market disincentives. Hence, given major policy changes, any difference in the single-parent-share coefficients between the decades should partially relate to changes in incentives due to welfare reform. For one thing, if welfare reform increased labor market participation among single parents, then the size of the female- and male-head coefficients would be smaller in 1999, as these groups would appear more like the general population.

Five age-share categories are included to capture differing effects due to age. The coefficients are measured relative to the omitted prime age (25–59) category, meaning the age coefficients are measured relative to an offsetting change in the 25–59 category. In particular, the question of whether greater concentrations of children and seniors are associated with differing poverty rates is of policy importance. However, we expect that greater concentrations of young adults aged 18–24 will be positively related to poverty rates, as that group likely possesses less work experience and is generally less attached to the labor market because of higher college enrollment.

Two racial categories are included to assess the differing effects for minorities: 1) percentage of the population that is African American, and 2) percentage of the population that is minority but not African American.[7] Likewise, the percentage of the population that belongs to the Hispanic ethnic group is added to the model. Note that because Hispanic is an ethnic group, its members are also included in one of the racial groups. The interpretation of the Hispanic coefficient is more complex because Hispanics are more likely to be recent immigrants, although we also consider some models that account for immigration.

Besides commuting to more distant jobs, another way for at-risk households to avoid poverty is to migrate to areas with more favorable economic conditions. Residential mobility is associated with economic growth in general as migrants move to areas with superior labor market conditions. With job growth and other labor market indicators included in the model, migration rates should mostly reflect the mobility preferences of the population. Thus, the model includes the following three factors: the percentage of the population that 1) lived in the same house five years before the census, 2) lived in a different house but the same county five years before the census, or 3) lived in a different house but the same MSA five years before the census (MSA counties only). If these variables serve as a proxy for lower geographical mobility in the population, they should be positively related to the poverty rate.

SIMULATING THE INDIRECT EFFECTS OF JOB GROWTH

The total effect of job growth on reducing poverty rates may be understated to some degree when including unemployment and employment rates because these rates are implicitly held constant. In Table A.1, we consider this possibility with four simulations of how job growth indirectly affects poverty through these other measures. The first scenario assumes that five-year job growth does not have any indirect effects on employment-population rates or

Table A.1 Direct and Indirect Changes Due to Investment in Employment Growth (%)

	1989		1999	
	Short run	Long run	Short run	Long run
No change in the employment/population and unemployment rates				
Employment growth	−0.20	−0.37	−0.14	−0.23
Indirect effects:				
Employment/population	—	—	—	—
Unemployment rate	—	—	—	—
Total	−0.20	−0.37	−0.14	−0.23
One-fifth of the new jobs taken by original residents				
Employment growth	−0.20	−0.37	−0.14	−0.23
Indirect effects:				
Employment/population	−0.31	−0.58	−0.23	−0.38
Unemployment rate	—	—	—	—
Total	−0.51	−0.95	−0.37	−0.61
Quasireduced form omit: unemployment and employment/population rates				
Employment growth	−0.35	−0.88	−0.20	−0.40
Total	−0.35	−0.88	−0.20	−0.40
Direct estimate from employment/population and unemployment rate models[a]				
Employment growth	−0.20	−0.37	−0.14	−0.23
Indirect effects:				
Male employment/population	insig. ≈ 0	insig. ≈ 0	0.01	0.02
Female employment/population	−0.09	−0.17	insig. ≈ 0	insig. ≈ 0
Male unemployment rate	−0.04	−0.07	insig. ≈ 0	insig. ≈ 0
Female unemployment rate	−0.02	−0.04	insig. ≈ 0	insig. ≈ 0
Total	−0.35	−0.65	−0.13	−0.21

NOTE: Table shows the changes in poverty rates after a one standard deviation change in 1985–1990 and 1995–2000 employment growth. A one standard deviation change = 12.2 and 10.1 percent, respectively.

[a] The employment rate and unemployment rate responses are derived as follows. First, using the results in Table A.3, the change in the respective employment-population and unemployment rates were calculated after a one standard deviation change in five-year employment growth. Then, using Table 6.1, the respective changes in poverty rates were calculated using the estimated change in the employment-population and unemployment rates. When either the employment-growth coefficient in Table A.3 or the corresponding employment-population or unemployment rate coefficient in Table 6.1 was insignificant at the 0.10 level, the result was not reported and was estimated to be zero.

SOURCE: Authors' calculations.

on unemployment rates, which is the assumption we use in most cases. This scenario is consistent with Blanchard and Katz's (1992) finding that migration responds sufficiently quickly that, after about five years, all newly created jobs are taken by new residents, implying that the employment-population ratio and the unemployment rate are approximately unchanged. Because Blanchard and Katz considered states rather than local labor markets, they did not measure commuters from outside the county who also take many of the newly created jobs, making the authors' result even more plausible at the county level. Hence, most of the results presented in Chapters 6 through 9 are consistent with Blanchard and Katz's assumption for the long run, in that they assume no indirect effects. The first group of values in Table A.1 shows only the direct poverty rate reduction that is due to greater job growth, since there is no change in the employment/population and unemployment rates.

Blanchard and Katz's (1992) long-run conclusions have been questioned for a variety of reasons. Representative of this alternative literature are Bartik (1991, 1993b) and Partridge and Rickman (2006), who find that in-migrants take about 30–50 percent of newly created jobs in the first year. That figure rises to about 80 percent after about five years.[8] These migration responses suggest that, at least in the short run, the remaining new jobs are taken either by unemployed original residents or by nonemployed original residents who were not previously part of the labor force. This research suggests that after about five years most of the original-resident response is through attracting additional people into the labor force, in the end producing little net change in the long-run unemployment rate.[9] Thus, each locality appears to have its own equilibrium unemployment rate to which the local labor market returns after an economic shock (Bartik 1993b; Blanchard and Katz 1992; Partridge and Rickman 1997b,c).

A rough approximation of the indirect effects of five-year employment growth, then, can be derived by assuming that there is no change in the male and female unemployment rate, and that about one-fifth of the newly created jobs come through changes in the male and female participation (or employment) rate (Bartik 1993b). Because a one standard deviation increase in the 1985–1990 and 1995–2000 job growth rates equals 12.2 and 10.1 percent, this implies that the corresponding employment growth attributable to changes in the employment-population ratio equals 2.4 and 2.0 percent.

Assuming that the share of men and women in the workforce remains unchanged, a 2.4 percent (not percentage point) increase in the 1989 employment-population ratio would have reduced the short-run poverty rate by an additional 0.31 percentage points and the long-run poverty rate by an additional 0.58 points.[10] Thus, the total decline in the 1989 poverty rate from the direct and indirect effects of employment growth equals 0.51 percentage points (0.20

+ 0.31) in the short run and 0.95 points (0.37 + 0.58) in the long run. For 1999, a 2 percent greater male and female employment-population ratio would have reduced the short-run poverty rate by an additional 0.23 points and the long-run rate by an additional 0.38 points. The total direct and indirect effects from a one standard deviation increase in 1995–2000 employment growth would be a 0.37-point (0.23 + 0.14) decline in the short-run poverty rate and a 0.61-point (0.23 + 0.38) reduction in the long-run rate. The responses are summarized in the second gorup of values in Table A.1, which shows the results when one-fifth of the new jobs are taken by original residents.

We see that even though original residents take only a modest 20 percent share of the newly created jobs, if we allow job growth to also affect the employment-population rate it more than doubles the poverty rate response to an acceleration of five-year job growth. This pattern suggests that while greater job growth may directly increase wages and allow disadvantaged workers to gain needed work experience, the indirect response of increasing the share of the population at work can be important.

A weakness of the approach in Panel 2 is that it arbitrarily uses estimated employment-population and unemployment rate responses that come from studies primarily based on state and MSA data, not on county data. Thus, these estimates could be inaccurate for our purposes. To address this concern, we try two other alternatives in estimating the indirect effects of employment growth. In both cases, we assume that employment growth is what drives changes in the unemployment rate and the employment-population rate; this assumption is consistent with the causality used in many VAR studies (Bartik 1991; Blanchard and Katz 1992).

The first alternative is to estimate a quasireduced form poverty rate model by removing the two unemployment rates and the two employment-population rates from the base specification in columns (1) and (4) of Table 6.1 on page 136. In this case, the unemployment rate and the employment-population ratio are no longer held constant, and the regression coefficient on employment growth can reflect the indirect impacts through changes in these variables. The model in the third part of Table A.1 shows the results of this exercise. For 1989, the total short- and long-run job growth effects on poverty increase by twofold compared to the base results in row 1. The total short- and long-run responses increase by about one-half in the 1999 model.[11]

The second alternative approach in allowing the employment-population and unemployment rates to indirectly affect poverty rates is through a series of auxiliary regressions. Specifically, for both periods, the male and female unemployment rates and the employment-population rates were regressed on the same control variables as in the reported poverty-rate models in Table A.2, with the exception that these auxiliary models omitted the ten-year lagged pov-

Table A.2 County Regression Summary Statistics, 1990 and 2000

Group	(1) Total	1989–1990 (2) MSA county	(3) Non-MSA county	(4) Total	1999–2000 (5) MSA county	(6) Non-MSA county
Total person poverty rate, 1989 or 1999	16.7 (7.8)	12.3 (5.6)	18.4 (7.9)	14.1 (6.4)	11.0 (4.8)	15.3 (6.6)
Total person poverty rate, 1979	15.8 (7.2)	11.7 (4.9)	17.3 (7.4)			
Single-county MSA[a]	0.05 (0.21)	0.17 (0.37)		0.05 (0.21)	0.17 (0.37)	
Big-MSA central county[b]	0.03 (0.17)	0.12 (0.32)		0.03 (0.17)	0.12 (0.32)	
Big-MSA suburban county[b]	0.08 (0.27)	0.29 (0.46)		0.08 (0.27)	0.29 (0.46)	
Small-MSA central county[b]	0.05 (0.22)	0.19 (0.39)		0.05 (0.22)	0.19 (0.39)	
Small-MSA suburban county[b]	0.06 (0.24)	0.23 (0.42)		0.06 (0.24)	0.23 (0.42)	
Population	81,516 (268,219)	239,597 (478,619)	22,416 (20,746)	92,252 (297,380)	272,984 (528,087)	24,682 (23,332)
MSA population		1,200,309 (1,554,358)			1,371,422 (1,745,655)	
1988–90 or 1998–2000 empl. growth	3.5 (5.3)	5.1 (4.8)	2.9 (5.4)	2.8 (4.2)	4.7 (3.7)	2.1 (4.1)
1985–90 or 1995–2000 empl. growth	8.6 (12.2)	15.4 (11.8)	6.0 (11.4)	9.2 (10.1)	13.8 (10.8)	7.5 (9.3)

1988–90 or 1998–2000 structural change^c	0.035 (0.019)	0.029 (0.015)	0.037 (0.020)	0.028 (0.016)	0.022 (0.012)	0.030 (0.017)
1985–90 or 1995–2000 structural change^c	0.067 (0.03)	0.06 (0.024)	0.070 (0.033)	0.057 (0.029)	0.048 (0.024)	0.061 (0.030)
% male employment-population	65.8 (8.0)	70.0 (6.3)	64.2 (8.0)	63.5 (8.8)	68.0 (6.6)	61.8 (8.9)
% female employment-population	48.5 (7.4)	53.4 (6.6)	46.6 (6.9)	51.7 (6.9)	55.4 (6.1)	50.3 (6.7)
% civilian male unemployment rate	6.6 (3.3)	5.9 (2.1)	6.8 (3.6)	5.7 (2.9)	5.2 (2.0)	6.0 (3.1)
% civilian female unemployment rate	6.8 (3.1)	6.1 (2.2)	7.0 (3.4)	5.8 (2.7)	5.3 (2.1)	5.9 (2.9)
% residential employment in agriculture-forestry-fisheries	8.4 (8.2)	2.9 (2.5)	10.5 (8.6)	5.9 (6.4)	1.5 (1.7)	7.5 (6.7)
% residential employment in goods	27.3 (10.2)	26.5 (8.0)	27.6 (10.9)	24.9 (8.7)	23.3 (7.3)	25.5 (9.2)
% residential employment in transportation/public utilities	6.5 (2.1)	7.1 (2.1)	6.3 (2.0)	5.5 (1.8)	5.3 (1.8)	5.5 (1.8)
% residential employment in trade	20.7 (3.6)	22.7 (2.8)	19.9 (3.6)			
% residential employment in trade and entertainment				21.6 (4.0)	23.2 (3.2)	21.0 (4.2)
% residential employment in information				1.9 (1.0)	2.6 (1.2)	1.6 (0.8)
% residential employment in finance, insurance, and real estate	4.4 (1.8)	5.9 (2.1)	3.8 (1.2)	4.6 (1.9)	6.2 (2.2)	4.0 (1.2)

(continued)

Table A.2 (continued)

Group	(1) Total	1989–1990		(4) Total	1999–2000	
		(2) MSA county	(3) Non-MSA county		(5) MSA county	(6) Non-MSA county
% residential employment in services	27.9 (5.4)	29.9 (5.4)	27.1 (5.2)	30.3 (5.0)	32.8 (4.9)	29.4 (4.8)
% residential employment in public administration	4.8 (2.8)	4.9 (3.1)	4.7 (2.7)	5.3 (2.9)	5.1 (3.0)	5.4 (2.9)
1985–90/1995–2000 commuting zone empl. growth[d]			8.0 (8.8)			8.2 (5.8)
1985–90/1995–2000 MSA employment growth (# MSA counties ≥ 2)[e]		12.9 (7.0)			11.6 (5.8)	
% of workers employed in county of residence	72.3 (17.1)	65.9 (20.5)	74.7 (15.0)	67.4 (17.6)	63.2 (20.5)	69.0 (16.1)
% workers with 20–45 minute commute	27.9 (9.7)	35.8 (8.1)	24.9 (8.5)	30.3 (9.3)	37.4 (7.7)	27.6 (8.4)
% workers with 45–90 minute commute	10.6 (6.6)	11.6 (7.4)	10.2 (6.2)	13.8 (7.3)	14.2 (8.0)	13.6 (7.1)
% education < high school graduate (age ≥ 25 yrs.)	30.5 (10.3)	25.1 (8.2)	32.5 (10.3)	22.7 (8.7)	18.6 (6.7)	24.2 (8.9)
% high school graduate (age ≥ 25 yrs.)	34.4 (6.1)	32.5 (6.2)	35.1 (5.9)	34.8 (6.5)	31.5 (7.0)	36.0 (5.9)
% some college, no degree (age ≥ 25 yrs.)	16.4 (4.5)	18.4 (4.1)	15.6 (4.4)	20.4 (4.3)	21.4 (3.7)	20.0 (4.5)
% associate college degree (age ≥ 25 yrs.)	5.3 (2.1)	6.0 (1.7)	5.1 (2.2)	5.7 (2.0)	6.4 (1.6)	5.5 (2.0)

% bachelor's degree or more (age ≥ 25 yrs.)	13.4 (6.5)	18.1 (7.9)	11.7 (4.8)	16.4 (7.7)	22.1 (9.2)	14.3 (5.7)
% households female-headed with children	5.4 (2.3)	5.9 (1.8)	5.2 (2.4)	6.1 (2.3)	6.6 (1.9)	5.9 (2.5)
% households male-headed with children	1.4 (0.5)	1.3 (0.4)	1.4 (0.6)	2.1 (0.6)	2.1 (0.5)	2.1 (0.7)
% population white[f]	87.6 (15.2)	86.2 (12.8)	88.1 (16.0)	84.9 (15.8)	82.5 (14.2)	85.7 (16.3)
% population African American[f]	8.6 (14.3)	9.8 (11.8)	8.2 (15.1)	8.8 (14.5)	10.1 (12.3)	8.2 (15.2)
% population other race[f]	3.8 (7.4)	4.0 (5.6)	3.8 (8.0)	6.4 (8.6)	7.4 (7.6)	6.0 (9.0)
% population Hispanic[f]	4.4 (11.0)	4.7 (9.7)	4.2 (11.4)	6.1 (12.0)	7.0 (11.2)	5.8 (12.3)
% population children <7 yrs. old	10.1 (1.4)	10.3 (1.3)	10.0 (1.5)	9.0 (1.4)	9.5 (1.2)	8.8 (1.5)
% population children 7–17 yrs. old	16.8 (2.3)	15.9 (2.1)	17.1 (2.3)	16.5 (2.0)	16.2 (1.8)	16.6 (2.1)
% population adults 18–24 yrs. old	9.2 (3.4)	10.6 (3.3)	8.7 (3.3)	8.9 (3.3)	9.6 (3.3)	8.6 (3.3)
% population adults 25–59 yrs. old	44.3 (3.6)	46.9 (3.2)	43.3 (3.2)	46.3 (3.5)	48.5 (3.0)	45.5 (3.4)
% population adults 60–64 yrs. old	4.7 (1.0)	4.2 (0.9)	4.9 (1.0)	4.5 (1.0)	3.9 (0.8)	4.7 (0.9)
% population over 65 yrs. old	15.0 (4.3)	12.1 (3.5)	16.0 (4.1)	14.8 (4.1)	12.3 (3.4)	15.8 (3.9)

(continued)

Table A.2 (continued)

Group	1989–1990			1999–2000		
	(1) Total	(2) MSA county	(3) Non-MSA county	(4) Total	(5) MSA county	(6) Non-MSA county
% lived in same house 5 yrs. before	58.6	53.7	60.5	58.9	54.7	60.5
	(8.4)	(8.2)	(7.7)	(7.3)	(7.1)	(6.8)
% lived in same county but different house 5 yrs. before	21.3	22.8	20.8	20.0	22.2	19.2
	(4.5)	(5.1)	(4.2)	(4.7)	(5.2)	(4.2)
% lived in same MSA but different house 5 yrs. before if current resident of MSA	7.7	28.4		7.7	28.3	
	(12.8)	(4.3)		(12.8)	(4.3)	
N	3028	824	2204	3028	824	2204

NOTE: Unweighted descriptive statistics. A metropolitan county is defined using 2000 Bureau of Economic Analysis REIS county definitions. Standard deviations are in parentheses. A blank means the variable was not included in the regression model.

a Single-county MSA/PMSA with the exception of Los Angeles and San Diego, which are included as central-county MSAs.

b "Central county" includes the county (or counties) of the named central city (or cities) in the MSA definition in a multiple-county MSA. Suburban counties do not include any of the central city (or cities). A large MSA had a 2000 population of greater than one million.

c The structural change index is the share of the county's employment that would have to change sectors in each year so that there would be an equivalent industry structure in the two years. It is a similarity index defined as one-half the sum of the absolute value of the difference in one-digit industry employment shares between the two years.

d For nonmetropolitan counties, the broader labor market employment growth was defined using 1990 commuting zone definitions from the U.S. Department of Agriculture (http://www.ers.usda.gov/Briefing/Rurality/lmacz/).

e For multiple-county MSAs, the broader labor market employment growth was defined using the entire metropolitan area.

f "Hispanics" is an ethnic category, and Hispanics are included in the white, African American, and other race groups. Individuals who classified themselves as belonging to two or more racial categories in the 2000 census are classified in the "other race" group. Because of the two-or-more racial category in the 2000 census, the 1990 and 2000 figures are not comparable.

SOURCE: U.S. Census Bureau (2006e) and 1969–2000 U.S. Bureau of Economic Analysis REIS data (BEA 2002).

erty rate and the three measures of five-year household mobility (so as to not hold migration constant).[12] Because we are trying to examine how five-year job growth rates directly and indirectly affect poverty, we do not consider job growth measured over shorter periods. Yet, as described below, more-immediate employment growth does have a larger effect because potential migrants would not have had time to fully respond.

In a surprising outcome, Table A.3 shows that five-year employment growth reduced the male employment-population rate in both 1990 and 2000, although this relationship was only significant in the 2000 model. Actually, the negative response even runs counter to any potential endogeneity concerns. Consistent with expectations, the female-employment population ratios are lifted by greater five-year job growth, but this effect was only significant in the 1990 model. To be sure, even in the case of female employment-population rates, a 1-point increase in five-year job growth only increased the 1990 employment-population rate by about 0.04 points. While it was expected that migrants and commuters would eventually fill most of any newly created jobs, the negative response for men was still unexpected.[13] One possible reason for the unexpected male result is that a shock to labor supply created significant competition for less-skilled men. For example, jobs that many less-skilled men vied for were disproportionately taken by less-skilled women, many of them pushed into the labor market by welfare reform. This type of behavior is consistent with the large national increase in the labor force participation of female heads of households. Yet this possibility should be a focus of further research.

Table A.3 shows that a 1-percentage-point increase in the 1985–1990 employment growth rate reduced the 1990 male and female unemployment rate by about 0.02 points. However, a 1-point increase in 1995–2000 job growth had an insignificant impact on 2000 male unemployment rates, and it would only have reduced the average 2000 female unemployment rate by 0.01 points. As before, there is evidence that current employment growth has a much larger influence in reducing unemployment rates.[14] Hence, while short-term job growth does reduce unemployment rates, after about five years equilibrium forces push the typical county's unemployment rate back to its original level.

Using the auxiliary male/female employment-population and unemployment rate models, estimated changes in the employment-population and unemployment rates were derived after a corresponding one standard deviation change in 1985–1990 or 1995–2000 employment growth. Then, using the coefficients from the poverty rate models in Table 6.1, the estimated changes in the employment-population and unemployment rates were used to derive the indirect changes in the poverty rate due to job growth.[15] These indirect responses are reported in Panel 4 of Table A.1. Generally, these indirect responses are considerably smaller than the estimates in Panels 2 and 3. In fact, the indirect responses

Table A.3 Employment-Population and Unemployment Rate Auxiliary Models

	(1) Male empl./pop.	(2) Female empl./pop.	(3) Male unempl. rate	(4) Female unempl. rate
1990 models				
1985–90 empl. growth	−0.012	0.045*	−0.019*	−0.023*
	(1.29)	(4.99)*	(4.18)*	(5.18)*
1988–90 structural change	−14.290*	−14.949*	8.465*	6.088*
	(2.64)*	(2.91)*	(3.40)*	(2.50)*
Pop. × structural change	−3.7e−5	4.5e−5*	4.1e−5*	3.9e−5*
	(0.93)	(1.81)*	(2.83)*	(3.02)*
N	3028	3028	3028	3028
R^2	0.76	0.77	0.66	0.63
2000 models				
1995–2000 empl. growth	−0.032*	0.004	−0.005	−0.013*
	(2.93)*	(0.60)	(1.14)	(3.10)*
1995–2000 structural change	−4.397	−4.094	1.216	6.681*
	(1.24)	(1.59)	(0.80)	(4.45)*
Pop. × structural change	1.7e−5	1.6e−5	7.5e−6	2.2e−6
	(0.80)	(1.59)	(0.86)	(0.34)
N	3028	3028	3028	3028
R^2	0.80	0.81	0.63	0.65

NOTE: Table shows the auxiliary regression model using the dependent variable reported in the column heading. The specification is the same as in Table 6.1 except that the lagged poverty rate, employment-population rates, unemployment rates, and five-year residential mobility variables are omitted. Absolute values of robust t-statistics are in parentheses. * = significant at the 0.10 level.

SOURCE: Authors' calculations, U.S. Census Bureau (2006e), and 1969–2000 U.S. Bureau of Economic Analysis REIS data (BEA 2002).

in the 1999 model are approximately zero, and the indirect responses in the 1989 model a little larger.

Averaging the total direct and indirect responses across Panels 2-4 of Table A.1 suggests that a one standard deviation increase in job growth decreased short-run poverty rates by about 0.4 percentage points in 1989 and by about 0.8 points in the long run. This result means that about half of the 1985–1990 employment growth response was indirect, through reducing unemployment rates and increasing employment-population rates (especially the latter). However, the average total short-run response to the 1999 poverty rate after a one standard deviation increase in 1995–2000 employment growth is about one-quarter of a point, and the long-run response is only about four-tenths of a point.

The relatively modest direct and indirect poverty response to local job growth suggests that in-migrants, commuters, or nonemployed members of families above the poverty threshold eventually take many of the new jobs. Thus, if not targeted, local job growth policies such as enterprise zones will only have a modest impact on poverty rates. These results support Bartik's (2001) conclusion that the benefits of generic local economic growth are quite dispersed throughout the income distribution, not concentrated on lower income groups. These findings reaffirm the need to concentrate economic development policies on disadvantaged residents to ensure that growth trickles down.

THE ROLE OF COMMUNITY DEMOGRAPHIC ATTRIBUTES

Not surprisingly, the regression results in Table 6.1 reveal that the demographic characteristics of the population strongly relate to the community's average poverty rate. Medium levels of education are particularly influential in reducing poverty rates. The education results suggest that, relative to the high-school dropout share, a one-point increase in the share of the population having a high school degree, or some college, but not an associate degree, reduced the short-run poverty rate by 0.12–0.18 percentage points in 1999 (and by correspondingly larger long-run impacts). Clearly, these results point to the importance of reducing high-school dropout rates and encouraging some postsecondary education. Such educational attainment appears to increase the chances of obtaining stable employment with sufficiently high wages to ensure that a worker and his or her family can remain above the poverty line. In implementing such a policy, while "first chance" programs designed to increase high-school completion may be expensive, they are likely to be more successful than "second chance" programs like GED programs and training programs (Carneiro and Heckman 2003).

The bachelor's degree effects are surprisingly small in both decades. It may be that this small response reflects a university-town effect in which the college graduate share also relates to a large number of low-income students. A college degree also may simply boost the income of those already in the middle class and have a marginal impact, if any, on poverty rates. Thus, policy aimed at enhancing support for individuals to attain their four-year college degree should be based on other reasons than reducing poverty.

Female headship is one of the strongest predictors of community poverty rates. A one standard deviation increase in the female-head share with children is associated with a 1.40-percentage-point short-run increase in the poverty rate in 1999 and with a slightly larger effect in 1989.[16] Bear in mind that these responses are derived after holding labor market conditions constant. By contrast, the response to a one standard deviation increase in the male-head share with children is only about one-tenth the size of the female headship response.

Both the male and the female headship response point to the simple fact that single-parent families have fewer financial resources. Yet the significantly larger female response indicates that there are significant constraints faced by female-headed households in fully participating in the labor market. Thus, the results are suggestive of a need to facilitate ways to help single parents find employment and earn higher salaries. In particular, there is a need for better and more accessible child care, though other assistance, such as enhanced counseling for job retention and programs for skills augmentation is also needed for the least-educated group of single mothers (Moffitt 2002). The particularly large positive influence played by female headship could also indicate employer discrimination toward single mothers—perhaps related to fears that these women will miss work for child-related reasons.

The magnitude of the single-parent coefficients is somewhat smaller in the 1999 model. One possible reason is that employers may have been more willing to work around constraints faced by single parents because of the severe labor shortages of the late 1990s.[17] Another potential reason is that the 1996 federal welfare reform pushed many low-skilled single parents into the labor market, meaning these demographic groups behaved more like other low-skilled groups. Yet these results are good news in that if there were significant welfare reform labor-supply spillovers on other low-skilled workers, then the single-parent coefficients would not have greatly changed (i.e., there merely would have been a redistribution of who was in poverty, from single parents to other low-skilled workers).

The national data show that average poverty rates are much higher for racial and ethnic minorities. The findings in Table 6.1 suggest that it is not necessarily race that matters. For example, in both 1989 and 1999, the percentage of the population that is African American was negatively associated with poverty rates (at the 0.10 level). Also, compared to 1989, both the other-race share and the Hispanic share measures became more associated with less poverty in 1999. To be sure, because of classification changes in the 2000 census, the race results are not directly comparable. Yet they suggest that, at least in 1999, after accounting for socioeconomic characteristics, concentrations of racial and ethnic minorities did not produce higher county poverty rates.

The race and ethnicity results suggest that the causes of higher minority poverty rates are not so much due to direct factors as they are to concentrations of minority groups being more likely to be found in locales with weak labor markets or where the population has lower labor market skills. Nevertheless, the results are not consistent with overt labor market discrimination and thus support the finding by Holzer et al. (2003) that employer hiring discrimination based on race apparently declined during the 1990s. These results do not rule out other types of discrimination, such as in the housing market, in education, or in certain firms avoiding locating in areas with greater minority concentrations. Yet even in the case of where firms choose to locate, there is evidence that the spatial mismatch between jobs and residence of minority groups declined in the 1990s, especially in the case of African Americans—though there remains significant isolation from nearby employment (Raphael and Stoll 2002; Dworak-Fisher 2004).

One factor that could be influencing the estimated racial and Hispanic responses is the presence of recent foreign immigrants. In other analysis, greater concentrations of foreign immigrants had strong adverse effects on local poverty rates in 1999.[18] In fact, concentrations of recent immigrants appear to have had a much more adverse effect on local poverty than concentrations of minorities did.

It is not immediately clear why the five-year recent-immigrant share had such an adverse effect on 1999 poverty rates. For example, an insignificant effect would imply that, after accounting for other factors, either there is no direct immigrant effect, or there is offsetting native out-migration such that there was little net change in low-skilled labor supply (Borjas et al. 1996). Perhaps the late 1990s cohort had fewer labor market skills and more language difficulties than earlier cohorts, or perhaps welfare reform changes reduced transfer payments to recent immigrants. Yet there is some evidence that recent foreign immigrants were increasingly competing with native low-skilled workers for jobs that would lift poor households out of poverty. Specifically, in counties with higher recent immigrant shares, five-year job growth had a smaller influence on reducing 1999 poverty rates.[19] Welfare reform's labor market emphasis may be one cause of this pattern, because the lowest-skilled natives would be more likely to compete against immigrants, and their lack of financial resources would limit any offsetting migration response to the increase in labor market competition.[20]

Turning to the age composition of the population, the strong positive association between the 18-to-24 young-adult population share and poverty rates is expected. Yet, compared to 1989, when both were insignificant, it was a little surprising that the 60–64 share coefficient was positive and significant in 1999 while the 65-and-older coefficient was negative and significant. Regarding the 60–64 age group, the tremendous restructuring in the latter 1980s and the first half of the 1990s not only greatly increased worker anxiety, but it disproportionately hit middle-aged and older workers in terms of fewer reemployment opportunities and reduced reemployment earnings (Evans and Behr 1997; Farber 1997; Kletzer 1998; Mandel 1996). The problem is particularly acute for many in the 60–64 age cohort because they are not prepared to retire yet are in the least-likely cohort to be reemployed.

The household mobility results support the contention that greater mobility (after controlling for labor market conditions) is one way to alleviate poverty. For example, using Table 6.1, we see that a one standard deviation increase in the share of the population that lived in the same house five years before, and in the share of the population that changed houses but remained in the same county, together increased the 1999 short-run poverty rate by 0.63 percentage points. In other analysis, because job growth may affect residential mobility, and because mobility may be endogenously related to poverty, we experimented with the base 1999 model in column (4) of Table 6.1 by omitting these residential mobility measures (not shown). Generally, the results are similar, though the five-year employment growth coefficient was about one-half greater in this model and the male employment rate coefficient was only about one-third the size and no longer significant ($t = -0.97$). Nonetheless, we prefer to control for residential mobility because of its important implications for poverty clustering and neighborhood effects.

Welfare reform led to a host of diversion programs to encourage possible enrollees to stay in the labor market (Blank 2002). The household-mobility/migration results suggest that a potentially effective diversion would be to subsidize moving costs to counties with either stronger labor markets, better job accessibility, or a history of lower poverty rates (i.e., less persistence and better neighborhood effects). Although relocation support policies are easy to discuss in the abstract, successful relocation requires disadvantaged households to obtain a host of supports beyond merely information regarding opportunities in their new labor market (Allard 2004). These additional supports include child care, as poor households often rely on relatives for these arrangements, along with other anchors that are often provided by relatives, long-time friends, and institutions such as religious organizations (Spilimbergo and Ubeda 2004). In addition, there are other obstacles: as white flight to the suburbs demonstrates, suburban residents may resist these relocation initiatives.

Notes

1. For those who prefer examining the change in poverty rates, Equation (A.3) can be interpreted in that fashion by simply subtracting POV_{t-1} from both sides: $\text{POV}_t - \text{POV}_{t-1} = -\alpha\text{POV}_{t-1} + \alpha\beta X_t$.

2. BEA employment data is based on the number of jobs in the county, meaning that it measures labor conditions among the county's employers. Note that because the data includes 1990 or 2000, there is a one-year lead in the employment growth measures. This formulation follows Levernier et al. (2000) and reflects the notion that local labor markets are both forward- and backward-looking in that migration flows are much more strongly affected by shocks that are expected to be permanent (Topel 1986).

3. The ISC terms are constructed using the 11 industries in the BEA 2000 REIS (Regional Economic Information System) data. In their derivation, for many counties, employment was not reported for all industries in a given year because of disclosure restriction. In these cases, industry employment was interpolated and extrapolated, while ensuring that the sum of employment in the 11 industries equaled total county employment.

4. As in the case of employment growth, structural change is measured one year into the future to capture the likely possibility that labor market participants have some foresight as to future structural changes in the local labor market.

5. The MSA employment growth rate is only included if the MSA contains at least two counties, because the county's job growth would equal the MSA job growth in single-county MSAs.

6. The commuting zones are from the USDA's Economic Research Service definitions for 1990 (ERS 2003a).

7. The 2000 census created a new category, in which the respondent could indicate that he or she is a member of two or more racial categories. This multirace group is included in the non–African American category for 2000. However, this change means that the 1989 and 1999 race results are not directly comparable.

8. Blanchard and Katz (1992) find a much larger long-run response by migrants to employment growth. One reason these long-run findings have been questioned is that measurement error could bias the response (Rowthorn and Glyn 2003). Likewise, Blanchard and Katz's assumption of stationarity for the VAR model somewhat forces the long-run outcome. Others have questioned their choice of specification, including their particular lag structure (Bartik 1993b; Partridge and Rickman 2006).

9. The employment in a region E can be represented as

$E = E/LF \times LF/\text{POP} \times \text{POP}$,

where LF is the labor force and POP is the noninstitutionalized population. E/LF equals 1 minus the unemployment rate (UR) when measured in ratio form, and LF/POP is the labor-force participation rate. After taking logs, totally differentiating, and multiplying by 100, we derive the following for small changes:

(A.4) $\%\Delta E = \%\Delta(1 - UR) + \%\Delta LF/POP + \%\Delta POP$.

After noting that LF equals E+UNEP (number unemployed) and assuming that the unemployment rate is approximately unchanged in the long run, Equation (A.4) can be rewritten to observe that the employment growth rate will equal the labor force growth rate:

(A.5) $\%\Delta E = \%\Delta(1 - UR) + \%\Delta E/POP + \%\Delta POP$.

10. From Equation (A.5) in Note 9, we see that if the unemployment rate is unchanged, then the first term on the right hand side approximately equals 0. If the percentage change in 1985–1990 and 1995–2000 employment growth equals 12.0 and 10.0 percent, and one-fifth of these changes come through the employment-population ratio, then the employment-population ratio respectively changes by 2.4 and 2.0 percent in 1990 and 2000. Thus, using Table A.2, a 2.4-percentage-point increase in the 1990 average female and male employment-population ratios corresponds to increases of 1.16 and 1.58 percentage points (i.e., 0.024 × 48.5 and 0.024 × 65.8). The corresponding 2000 changes in the female and male employment-population rates after a 2 percent increase are 1.03 and 1.27 percentage points. For 1989, using the results in column (1) of Table 6.1, the short-run change in the poverty rate after a 1.16 and a 1.58 point increase in the female and the male employment-population ratio approximately equals 0.31 percentage points. After dividing through by 0.53 (1 − 0.47 using the lagged poverty rate coefficient), the long-run indirect reduction in the poverty rate approximately equals 0.58. For 2000, using the results from column (4), the short-run change in the poverty rate after a 1.03 and a 1.27 point increase in the female and the male employment-population ratio approximately equals 0.23 percentage points. After dividing by 0.61 (1 − 0.39 using the lagged poverty rate coefficient), the long-run indirect reduction in the poverty rate approximately equals 0.38.

11. Including the state fixed effects may capture some growth effects common to the entire state. In another model that omitted state fixed effects, unemployment rate, and employment-population ratio, the 1989 five-year employment growth effect was about triple the size of the reported effect in column (1) of Table 6.1 ($\beta = 0.048$, $t = 8.79$). But it was only a little over half again as large as the reported 1999 effect in column (4) ($\beta = 0.023$, $t = 4.11$). Thus, this upper-bound estimate suggests that faster job growth had relatively strong long-run effects in reducing poverty in 1989 but smaller effects in 1999.

12. These auxiliary regressions also did not control for the other employment-population or unemployment rates.

13. To examine the possibility that employment growth has greater short-run ef-

fects before commuters or migrants can fully respond, the two-year 1998–2000 employment growth rate was added to the auxiliary employment-population rate models. It was positive and significant at about the 15 percent level in the case of men, while it had a statistically significant large positive short-run effect for women (not shown). Hence, short-term employment growth appears to have a much larger influence on employment-population rates.

14. This was examined by including 1998–2000 job growth in the 2000 male and fe-male unemployment models. In regard to the two-year job growth variable, there was a large negative response that was statistically significant (not shown).

15. In the cases in Table 6.1 where the unemployment rate or the employment-popu-lation rate had an insignificant influence (at the 0.10 level) or when five-year job growth had an insignificant impact on the employment-population or the unem-ployment rate in Table A.3 (at the 0.10 level), the indirect influence on poverty was assumed to be zero.

16. The corresponding 1989 and 1999 long-run responses from a one standard devia-tion increase in the female headship share are 3.17 and 2.30 percentage points.

17. To examine whether there was a smaller single-parent effect in areas with strong labor markets, the male head with children and the female head with children shares were placed in interaction with the male and female employment-popula-tion ratio. When these interactions were added to the 1989 and 1999 models, the male interaction was insignificant, but the female interaction was negative and significant, with a modestly stronger effect in the 1989 model. Similar results were also obtained when these single-parent shares were interacted with the five-year employment growth. These results suggest that when the labor market is sufficiently tight, employers increasingly begin to hire less-skilled female heads with children.

18. Specifically, we estimated other regressions that included the percentage of the population that immigrated between 1990–1994 and 1995–2000 (not shown). The 1995–2000 immigrant share was positive and significant ($t = 4.65$) in the 1999 model (the 1990–94 immigrant share was insignificant). A one standard de-viation, 1.3-percentage-point increase in recent immigrants was associated with a more-than-0.5-point increase in short-run poverty rates. In addition, the race and Hispanic coefficients all became more inversely related to poverty rates and significant at the 0.05 level. Conversely, the corresponding immigrant shares were statistically insignificant in the 1989 model.

19. Namely, when an interaction of the 1995–2000 foreign immigrant share with the 1995–2000 job growth variable was added to the 1999 model, it was positive and significant at the 0.07 level ($t = 1.86$).

20. The possibility of an offsetting domestic resident labor-supply response was as-sessed by regressing the percent change in domestic population on the percentage of the population that are foreign immigrants who arrived in the previous decade, and other controls described below. The results suggest that for every 1 percent of the population that immigrated in the previous decade, domestic population fell by 0.80 percentage points in 1990 but by only 0.58 points in 2000. Thus there is some evidence that the offsetting low-skilled native supply response declined,

which would be consistent with greater competition among natives and recent immigrants for jobs that require fewer skills. The other controls were state fixed effects, the MSA county-type indicators, the previous decade's population (1980 or 1990), and, to proxy for deaths and births, the population shares for ages 6 years and under, 7 to 17 years, and 65 and over. The percentage change in domestic population was defined as the actual percentage of population change during the previous decade minus the percentage of the population that had immigrated during the previous decade.

References

Administration for Children and Families (ACF). 2000. *ACF News/Statistics: Change in TANF Caseloads Since Enactment of New Welfare Law.* Washington, DC: ACF, U.S. Department of Health and Human Services (DHHS). http://www.acf.dhhs.gov/news/stats/aug-dec.htm (accessed April 6, 2006).

———. 2002a. *Percent Change in AFDC/TANF Families and Recipients, August 1996–September 2001.* Washington, DC: ACF, DHHS. http://www.acf.dhhs.gov/news/stats/afdc.htm (accessed March 21, 2006).

———. 2002b. *ACF News: TANF: Total Number of Recipients, Fiscal Year 2002.* Washington, DC: ACF, DHHS. http://www.acf.dhhs.gov/news/stats/2002tanfrecipients.htm (accessed November 1, 2005).

———. 2004. *Temporary Assistance for Needy Families: Total Number of Families and Recipients, July–September 2003.* Washington, DC: ACF, DHHS. http://www.acf.dhhs.gov/news/press/2004/TANF_TOTFAM_4th2003.htm (accessed November 1, 2005).

Alabama Department of Economic and Community Affairs (ADECA). 2006. *Alabama Plant Closings/Layoffs (beginning July 14, 1998).* Montgomery, AL: ADECA. http://adeca.alabama.gov/default.aspx (accessed March 31, 2006).

Albrecht, Don E., Carol Mulford Albrecht, and Stan L. Albrecht. 2000. "Poverty in Nonmetropolitan America: Impacts of Industrial, Employment, and Family Structure Variables." *Rural Sociology* 65(1): 87–103.

Alesina, Alberto, and Dani Rodrik. 1994. "Distributive Politics and Economic Growth." *Quarterly Journal of Economics* 109(2): 465–490.

Allard, Scott W. 2004. "The New Geography of Welfare Policy in the U.S." Paper presented at the 43rd Annual Meeting of the Southern Regional Science Association, held in New Orleans, March 13.

Allard, Scott W., Richard M. Tolman, and Daniel Rosen. 2003. "Proximity to Service Providers and Service Utilization among Welfare Recipients: The Interaction of Place and Race." *Journal of Policy Analysis and Management* 22(4):599–613.

Andersson, Fredrik, Harry J. Holzer, and Julia I. Lane. 2002. "The Interactions of Workers and Firms in the Low-Wage Labor Market." Urban Institute Discussion Paper. http://www.urban.org/url.cfm?ID=410608 (accessed November 2, 2005).

———. 2003. *Worker Advancement in the Low-Wage Labor Market: The Importance of "Good Jobs."* Brookings Institution, Center on Urban and Metropolitan Policy. Survey Series. Washington, DC: Brookings Institution. http://

www.brookings.edu/es/urban/publications/200310_Holzer.pdf (accessed November 2, 2005).

Archer, Bill. 1998. "Welfare Reform's Unprecedented Success." *Washington Post*, August 10, A:17. http://www.washingtonpost.com/wp-srv/politics/special/welfare/stories/op081098.htm (accessed March 27, 2006).

Associated Press (AP). 1999. "State's Welfare Rolls Dwindling, But Is It Permanent?" August 16.

————. 2000. "State Launching Welfare Initiatives to Address Job Needs." June 23.

————. 2001. "Child-Care Subsidies Cost State More than Welfare, Repeating from Previous Cycle." May 8.

————. 2003. "Welfare Rolls Stay Flat Despite Lukewarm Economy." January 3.

————. 2004. "Census: 15.1 Percent of Alabama Residents Live in Poverty." August 26.

Atkinson, Robert D. 2004. *Reversing Rural America's Economic Decline: The Case for a National Balanced Growth Strategy*. Policy Report, February. Washington, DC: Progressive Policy Institute. http://www.ppionline.org/documents/rural_economy_0204.pdf (accessed November 4, 2005).

Barkley, David L., Mark S. Henry, and Shuming Bao. 1996. "Identifying 'Spread' versus 'Backwash' Effects in Regional Economic Areas: A Density Functions Approach." *Land Economics* 72(3): 336–357.

Bartik, Timothy J. 1991. *Who Benefits from State and Local Economic Development Policies?* Kalamazoo, MI: W.E. Upjohn Institute for Employment Research.

————. 1993a. *Economic Development and Black Economic Success*. Upjohn Institute Technical Report No. 93-001. Kalamazoo, MI: W.E. Upjohn Institute for Employment Research.

————. 1993b. "Who Benefits from Local Job Growth, Migrants or the Original Residents?" *Regional Studies* 27(4): 297–311.

————. 1994. "The Effects of Metropolitan Job Growth on the Size Distribution of Family Income." *Journal of Regional Science* 34(4): 483–502.

————. 1996. "The Distributional Effects of Local Labor Demand and Industrial Mix: Estimates Using Individual Panel Data." *Journal of Urban Economics* 40(2): 150–178.

————. 2000. "Displacement and Wage Effects of Welfare Reform." In *Finding Jobs: Work and Welfare Reform*, David Card and Rebecca M. Blank, eds. New York: Russell Sage Foundation, pp. 72–122.

————. 2001. *Jobs for the Poor: Can Labor Demand Policies Help?* New York: Russell Sage Foundation.

————. 2002a. "Instrumental Variable Estimates of the Labor Market Spillover Effects of Welfare Reform." Upjohn Institute Staff Working Paper No. 02–078. Kalamazoo, MI: W.E. Upjohn Institute for Employment Research. http://www.upjohninstitute.org/publications/wp/02-78.pdf (accessed July 25, 2006).

———. 2002b. "Spillover Effects of Welfare Reforms in State Labor Markets." *Journal of Regional Science* 42(4): 667–701.

———. 2004. "Incentive Solutions." Upjohn Institute Staff Working Paper No. 04-99, presented at the University of Minnesota Humphrey Institute of Public Affairs conference "Reining in the Competition for Capital," Minneapolis, MN, February 27. http://www.hhh.umn.edu/projects/prie/c4c_papers.htm (accessed December 5, 2005).

Bartik, Timothy J., and Randall W. Eberts. 1999. "Examining the Effect of Industry Trends and Structure on Welfare Caseloads." In *Economic Conditions and Welfare Reform*, Sheldon H. Danziger, ed. Kalamazoo, MI: W.E. Upjohn Institute for Employment Research, pp. 119–157.

Beale, Calvin L. 2004. "Anatomy of Nonmetro High-Poverty Areas: Common in Plight, Distinctive in Nature." *Amber Waves* 2(1): 21–27. http://www.ers.usda.gov/AmberWaves/February04/Features/Anatomy.htm (accessed December 5, 2005).

Becker, Gary. 1962. "Investment in Human Capital: A Theoretical Analysis." *The Journal of Political Economy* 70 (5, Part 2): 9–49.

Beeson, Patricia E., and David N. DeJong. 2002. "Divergence." *Contributions to Macroeconomics* 2(1): 1–36.

Beeson, Patricia E., and Randall W. Eberts. 1989. "Identifying Productivity and Amenity Effects in Interurban Wage Differentials." *Review of Economics and Statistics* 71(3): 443–452.

Bennett, Neil G., Hsien-Hen Lu, and Younghwan Song. 2002. "Welfare Reform and Changes in the Economic Well-Being of Children." NBER Working Paper 9399. Cambridge, MA: National Bureau of Economic Research. http://ideas.repec.org/p/nbr/uberwo/9399.html (accessed December 6, 2005).

Bera, Anil K., and Mann J. Yoon. 1993. "Specification Testing with Locally Misspecified Alternatives." *Econometric Theory* 9(4): 649–658.

Berube, Alan, and William H. Frey. 2002. *A Decade of Mixed Blessings: Urban and Suburban Poverty in Census 2000.* Census 2000 Survey Series. Washington, DC: Brookings Institution, Center on Urban and Metropolitan Policy. http://www.brookings.edu/dybdocroot/es/urban/publications/berubefreypoverty.pdf (accessed December 6, 2005).

Birmingham News. 2003. "Not All Kids: State Scales Back Children's Health Insurance Plan." Editorial, November 26.

Bishaw, Alemayehu, and John Iceland. 2003. *Poverty 1999: Census 2000 Brief.* Washington, DC: U.S. Census Bureau. http://www.census.gov/prod/

2003pubs/c2kbr-19.pdf (accessed November 7 , 2005).

Bitler, Marianne P., Jonah B. Gelbach, and Hilary W. Hoynes. 2003. "Some Evidence on Race, Welfare Reform, and Household Income." *American Economic Review* 93(2): 293–298.

Black, Dan A., and Seth G. Sanders. 2004. *Labor Market Performance, Poverty, and Income Inequality in Appalachia*. Demographic and Socioeconomic Change in Appalachia Series. Washington, DC: Population Reference Bureau and Appalachian Regional Commission. http://www.prb.ong/pdf04/LaborMarketPoverty/pdf (accessed December 15, 2005).

Blanchard, Olivier Jean, and Lawrence F. Katz. 1992. "Regional Evolutions." *Brookings Papers on Economic Activity* 1992(1): 1–75.

Blank, Rebecca M. 1993. "Why Were Poverty Rates So High in the 1980s?" In *Poverty and Prosperity in the USA in the Late Twentieth Century*, Dimitri B. Papadimitriou and Edward N. Wolff, eds. New York: St. Martin's Press, pp. 19–55.

———. 2000. "Fighting Poverty: Lessons from Recent U.S. History." Distinguished Lecture on Economics in Government. *Journal of Economic Perspectives* 14(2): 3–19. http://www.ssc.wisc.edu/~andreoni/Econ441/blank.pdf (accessed December 15, 2005).

———. 2002. "Evaluating Welfare Reform in the United States." *Journal of Economic Literature* 40(4): 1105–1166.

———. 2005. "Poverty, Policy, and Place: How Poverty and Policies to Alleviate Poverty Are Shaped by Local Characteristics." *International Regional Science Review* 28(4): 441–464. http://irx.sagepub.com/cgi/reprint/28/4/441 (accessed July 24, 2006).

Blank, Rebecca M., and Alan S. Blinder. 1986. "Macroeconomics, Income Distribution, and Poverty." In *Fighting Poverty: What Works and What Doesn't*, Sheldon H. Danziger and Daniel H. Weinberg, eds. Cambridge, MA: Harvard University Press, pp.180–208.

Blank, Rebecca M., and David Card. 1993. "Poverty, Income Distribution, and Growth: Are They Still Connected?" *Brookings Papers on Economic Activity* 1993(2): 285–339.

Blank, Rebecca M., and Lucie Schmidt. 2001. "Work, Wages, and Welfare." In *The New World of Welfare*, Rebecca M. Blank and Ron Haskins, eds. Washington, DC: Brookings Institution, pp. 70–102.

Blau, David, and Erdal Tekin. 2003. "The Determinants and Consequences of Child Care Subsidies for Single Mothers." NBER Working Paper No. 9665. Cambridge, MA: National Bureau of Economic Research.

Blomquist, Glenn C., Mark C. Berger, and John P. Hoehn. 1988. "New Estimates of Quality of Life in Urban Areas." *American Economic Review* 78(1): 89–107.

Bluestone, Barry. 1990. "Comment" on Blackburn, Bloom, and Freeman, "Why Has the Economic Position of Less-Skilled Male Workers Deteriorated in the United States?" In *A Future of Lousy Jobs? The Changing Structure of U.S. Wages*, Gary Burtless, ed. Washington, DC: Brookings Institution, pp. 68–76.

Bodvarsson, Orn B., and Hendrik Van den Berg. 2006. "How Does Immigration Affect Labor Demand? Model and Test." In *The Economics of Immigration and Social Diversity*, Solomon W. Polachek, Carmel Chiswick, and Hillel Rapoport, eds. Vol. 24, Research in Labor Economics series. Amsterdam: Elsevier, pp. 135–166.

Borjas, George J. 1996. *Labor Economics*. New York: McGraw-Hill.

———. 2003. "The Labor Demand Curve *Is* Downward Sloping: Reexamining the Impact of Immigration on the Labor Market." *Quarterly Journal of Economics* 118(4): 1335–1376.

Borjas, George J., Richard B. Freeman, and Lawrence F. Katz. 1996. "Searching for the Effect of Immigration on the Labor Market." *American Economic Review* 86(2): 246–251.

Bound, John, and Harry J. Holzer. 2000. "Demand Shifts, Population Adjustments, and Labor Market Outcomes during the 1980s." *Journal of Labor Economics* 18(1): 20–54.

Brauner, Sarah, and Pamela J. Loprest. 1999. *Where Are They Now? What States' Studies of People Who Left Welfare Tell Us*. No. A-32 in the series New Federalism: Issues and Options for States. Washington, DC: Urban Institute. http://www.urban.org/url.cfm?ID=309065 (accessed April 20, 2006).

Brookings Institution. 2003a. *Philadelphia in Focus: A Profile from Census 2000*. Living Cities: The National Community Development Initiative. Washington, DC: Brookings Institution. http://www.brookings.org/es/urban/livingcities/philadelphia.htm (accessed March 31, 2006).

———. 2003b. *Phoenix in Focus: A Profile from Census 2000*. Living Cities: The National Community Development Initiative. Washington, DC: Brookings Institution. http://www.brookings.org/es/urban/livingcities/phoenix.htm (accessed March 31, 2006).

Brown, David L., and Mildred E. Warner. 1991. "Persistent Low-Income Nonmetropolitan Areas in the United States: Some Conceptual Challenges for Development Policy." *Policy Studies Journal* 19(2): 22–41.

Brown, Dennis M., and Eileen S. Stommes. 2004. "Rural Governments Face Public Transportation Challenges and Opportunities." *Amber Waves* 2(1): 11. http://www.ers.usda.gov/amberwaves/February04/Findings/RuralGovernments.htm (accessed April 20, 2006).

Brueckner, Jan K., and Richard W. Martin. 1997. "Spatial Mismatch: An Equilibrium Analysis." *Regional Science and Urban Economics* 27(6): 693–714.

Brueckner, Jan K., and Yves Zenou. 2003. "Space and Unemployment: The Labor-Market Effects of Spatial Mismatch." *Journal of Labor Economics* 21(1): 242–266.

Bureau of Economic Analysis (BEA). 2002. *Regional Economic Information System, 1969–2000.* CD-ROM. Washington, DC: BEA, U.S. Department of Commerce.

———. 2006. *Regional Economic Accounts, Table SA25—Employment by Industry.* Washington, DC: BEA, U.S. Department of Commerce. http://www.bea.gov/bea/regional/spi/default.cfm (accessed March 31, 2006).

Bureau of Labor Statistics (BLS). 2002. *Table 1. Average Annual Wages for 2001 and 2002 for All Covered Workers (1) by Metropolitan Area.* Washington, DC: BLS, USDOL. http://www.bls.gov/cew/msa2002.txt (accessed March 31, 2006).

———. 2004. *BLS Release of 2004 First Quarter Preliminary Data from the Quarterly Census of Employment and Wages.* Washington, DC: BLS, USDOL. http://www.bls.gov/cew/cewsnote2.htm (accessed April 3, 2006).

———. 2005. *Geographic Profile of Employment and Unemployment.* Washington, DC: BLS, USDOL. http://www.bls.gov/gps/home.htm (accessed March 28, 2006).

———. 2006a. *Local Area Unemployment Statistics.* Washington, DC: BLS, USDOL. http://www.bls.gov/lau (accessed March 27, 2006).

———. 2006b. *Consumer Price Indexes.* Washington, DC: BLS, USDOL. http://www.bls.gov/cpi/home.htm (accessed March 31, 2006).

———. 2006c. *Bureau of Labor Statistics Data.* Washington, DC: BLS, USDOL. http://www.bls.gov/data (accessed March 24, 2006).

———. 2006d. *Labor Force Statistics from the Current Population Survey.* Washington, DC: BLS, USDOL. http://data.bls.gov/PDQ/outside.jsp?survey=ln (accessed April 4, 2006).

———. 2006e. *Most Requested Statistics: Consumer Price Index.* Washington, DC: BLS, USDOL. http://data.bls.gov/cgi-bin/surveymost?cu (accessed April 4, 2006).

Cancian, Maria, Sheldon Danziger, and Peter Gottschalk. 1993. "Working Wives and Family Income Inequality Among Married Couples." In *Uneven Tides, Rising Inequality in America*, Sheldon H. Danziger and Peter Gottschalk, eds. New York: Russell Sage Foundation, pp. 195–222.

Card, David. 2001. "Immigrant Inflows, Native Outflows, and the Local Labor Market Impacts of Higher Immigration." *Journal of Labor Economics* 19 (January): 22–64.

Carneiro, Pedro M., and James J. Heckman. 2003. "Human Capital Policy."

IZA Discussion Paper No. 821. Bonn, Germany: Institute for the Study of Labor.

Carrington, William J., and Asad Zaman. 1994. "Interindustry Variation in the Costs of Job Displacement." *Journal of Labor Economics* 12(2): 243–275.

Case, Anne, Angela Fertig, and Christina Paxson. 2003. "From Cradle to Grave? The Lasting Impact of Childhood Health and Circumstance." NBER Working Paper 9788. Cambridge, MA: National Bureau of Economic Research.

Center on Budget and Policy Priorities (CBPP). 2000. *Research Evidence Suggests that Housing Subsidies Can Help Long-Term Welfare Recipients Find and Retain Jobs*. Washington, DC: CBPP. http://www.cbpp.org/6-27-00hous.htm (accessed March 14, 2006).

Chandler, Kim. 2003. "State Thins Subsidized Day-Care Rolls; Waiting List Tops 16,000 Poor Children." *Birmingham News*, October 27, A:1.

Chapman, Jeff, and Jared Bernstein. 2003. "Immigration and Poverty: How Are They Linked?" *Monthly Labor Review* 126(4): 10–15.

Children's Defense Fund. 2003a. *Renewing TANF and Child Care: Making the Right Choices for Minnesota Children and Families*. Washington, DC: Children's Defense Fund. http://www.childrensdefense.org/familyincome/welfare/tanf_fact_sheets_2003/MN_TANF_Fact_Sheet_2003.pdf (accessed March 20, 2006).

———. 2003b. *Renewing TANF and Child Care: Making the Right Choices for Alabama's Children and Families*. Washington, DC: Children's Defense Fund. http://www.childrensdefense.org/familyincome/welfare/tanf_fact_sheets_2003/AL_TANF_Fact_Sheet_2003.pdf (accessed March 20, 2006).

———. 2003c. Renewing TANF and Child Care: Making the Right Choices for Washington's Children and Families. Washington, DC: Children's Defense Fund. http://www.childrensdefense.org/familyincome/welfare/tanf_fact_sheets_2003/WA_TANF_Fact_Sheet_2003.pdf (accessed May 22, 2006).

Clark, Todd E. 1998. "Employment Fluctuations in U.S. Regions and Industries: The Roles of National, Region-Specific, and Industry-Specific Shocks." *Journal of Labor Economics* 16(1): 202–229.

Cook, Rebecca. 2003. "Tots, Parents, Workers Protest Child Care Cuts." *Bellingham Herald*, February 18. http://www.earlychildhoodfocus.org/modules.php?name=News&file=article&sid=1417 (accessed March 28, 2006).

Corcoran, Mary, Roger Gordon, Deborah Laren, and Gary Solon. 1992. "The Association Between Men's Economic Status and Their Family and Community Origins." *Journal of Human Resources* 27(4): 575–601.

Council of Economic Advisers. 1999. *The Effects of Welfare Policy and the Economic Expansion on Welfare Caseloads: An Update*. http://clinton4.nara.gov/WH/EOP/CEA/html/welfare/techv2.html (accessed April 25, 2006).

Crandall, Mindy S., and Bruce A. Weber. 2004. "Local Social and Economic Conditions, Spatial Concentrations of Poverty and Poverty Dynamics." *American Journal of Agricultural Economics* 86(5): 1276–1281.

Cromartie, John B., and John M. Wardwell. 1999. "Migrants Settling Far and Wide in the Rural West." *Rural Development Perspectives* 14 (August): 2–8.

Crowder, Carla. 2001. "Welfare Families Hit Limit. Officials: Those Off Assistance Still Struggle." *Birmingham News*, November 23.

———. 2003. "State Families on Assistance Hit 3-Year High." *Birmingham News*, June 7.

Currie, Janet. 2000. *Early Childhood Intervention Programs: What Do We Know?* Washington, DC: Brookings Institution. http://www.brookings.edu/es/research/projects/cr/doc/currie20000401.pdf (accessed April 25, 2006).

Curtis, Wayne. 2003. "A Landscape That Whispers." *New York Times*, August 3, A:5–6. http://query.nytimes.com/gst/fullpage.html?sec=travel&res=9C04E3DB173EF930A3575BC0A9659C8B63 (accessed April 3, 2006).

Cutler, David M., and Edward L. Glaeser. 1997. "Are Ghettos Good or Bad?" *Quarterly Journal of Economics* 112(3): 827–872.

Cutler, David M., and Lawrence F. Katz. 1991. "Macroeconomic Performance and the Disadvantaged." *Brookings Papers on Economic Activity* 2(1991): 1–74.

Davis, Bob. 2002. "Southern Town's Struggles Are a Job-Market Snapshot." *Wall Street Journal Online*. Princeton, NJ: Dow Jones and Company. http://www.careerjournal.com/salaryhiring/regional/20021118-davis.html (accessed July 25, 2006).

Davis, Elizabeth E., Laura S. Connolly, and Bruce A. Weber. 2003. "Local Labor Market Conditions and the Jobless Poor: How Much Does Local Job Growth Help in Rural Areas?" *Journal of Agricultural and Resource Economics* 28(3): 503–518.

Davis, Elizabeth E., and Bruce A. Weber. 2002. "How Much Does Local Job Growth Improve Employment Outcomes of the Rural Working Poor?" *Review of Regional Studies* 32(2): 255–274.

Decatur Daily. 2003. "IP to Cut 3,000 Jobs Worldwide; Effect Unclear." *Decatur Daily*, September 11, C:5.

DeFina, Robert H. 2004. "The Impacts of Unemployment on Alternative Poverty Rates." *Review of Income and Wealth* 50(1): 69–85.

Denver, City and County of. 2002. "First-Ever City-Sponsored Earned Income Tax Credit." News archive. Denver: City and County of Denver. http://www.denvergov.org/newsarticle.asp?id=3647 (accessed April 4, 2006).

Department of Health and Human Services (DHHS). 2000. *State Implementation of Major Changes to Welfare Policies, 1992–1998. Table B: Approval and Implementation Dates of Major AFDC Waivers Policies, 1992–1996.* Washington, DC: DHHS. http://aspe.hhs.gov/hsp/Waiver-Policies99/Table _B.PDF (accessed March 31, 2006).

———. 2004. "Welfare Rolls Drop Again." News release, March 30. http:// www.hhs.gov/news/press/2004pres/20040330.html (accessed April 28, 2006).

Dworak-Fisher, Keenan. 2004. "Intra-Metropolitan Shifts in Labor Demand and the Adjustment of Local Markets." *Journal of Urban Economics* 55(3): 514–533.

Economic Research Service (ERS). 1993. *Natural Amenities Scale.* Washington, DC: ERS, U.S. Department of Agriculture (USDA). http://www.ers .usda.gov/data/NaturalAmenities/natamenf.xls (accessed May 23, 2006).

———. 2003a. *Briefing Rooms: Measuring Rurality: Commuting Zones and Labor Market Areas.* Washington, DC: ERS, USDA. http://www.ers.usda .gov/Briefing/Rurality/lmacz (accessed March 29, 2006).

———. 2003b. *Briefing Rooms: Measuring Rurality: What Is Rural?* Washington, DC: ERS, USDA. http://www.ers.usda.gov/Briefing/Rurality/ WhatisRural (accessed April 3, 2006).

———. 2003c. *Briefing Rooms: Measuring Rurality: What Is a Micropolitan Area?* Washington, DC: ERS, USDA. http://www.ers.usda.gov/Briefing/ Rurality/MicropolitanAreas (accessed April 3, 2006).

———. 2003d. *Briefing Rooms: Rural Income, Poverty, and Welfare: Non- farm Earnings.* Washington, DC: ERS, USDA. http://www.ers.usda.gov/ briefing/Incomepovertywelfare/nonfarmearnings (accessed April 3, 2006).

———. 2004a. *Briefing Rooms: Rural Income, Poverty, and Welfare: Rural Poverty.* Washington, DC: ERS, USDA. http://www.ers.usda.gov/Briefing/ IncomePovertyWelfare/ruralpoverty (accessed March 21, 2006).

———. 2004b. *Rural Population and Migration: Rural Population Change and Net Migration.* Washington, DC: ERS, USDA. http://www.ers.usda .gov/briefing/Population/popchange (accessed April 4, 2006).

———. 2006. *Data Sets. State Fact Sheets: Nebraska.* Washington, DC: ERS, USDA. http://www.ers.usda.gov/StateFacts/NE.htm (accessed April 6, 2006).

Egan, Timothy. 2003. "Amid Dying Towns of Rural Plains, One Makes a Stand." Vanishing Point: The Empty Heartland Series. *New York Times,* December 1, A:1.

Ellwood, David T., and Rebecca M. Blank. 2001. "The Clinton Legacy for America's Poor." KSG Faculty Research Working Paper Series RWP01- 028. Cambridge, MA: Harvard University, John F. Kennedy School of Government.

Ellwood, David T., and Christopher Jencks. 2004. "The Spread of Single-Parent Families in the United States since 1960." KSG Faculty Research Working Paper Series RWP04-008. Cambridge, MA: Harvard University, John F. Kennedy School of Government. http://ksgnotes1.harvard.edu/Research/wpaper.nsf/rwp/RWP04-008 (accessed April 25, 2006).

ePodunk. 2006. *Scotts Bluff County, Nebraska, County Profile*. Pittsford, NY: ePodunk. http://www.epodunk.com/cgi-bin/genInfo.php?locIndex=22436 (accessed April 3, 2006).

Evans, Alan W. 1990. "The Assumption of Equilibrium in the Analysis of Migration and Interregional Differences: A Review of Some Recent Research." *Journal of Regional Science* 30(4): 515–531.

Evans, Judith, and Peter Behr. 1997. "Tight Job Market Not Swelling Paychecks: Area Unemployment Down but Insecurity Prevents Many Workers from Demanding Big Raises." *Washington Post*, March 22, D:1.

Farber, Henry S. 1997. "The Changing Face of Job Loss in the United States, 1981–1995." *Brookings Papers on Economic Activity* 1997(Microeconomics): 55–142.

Farrell, Mary, Selen Opcin, and Michael Fishman. 2001. *How Well Have Rural and Small Metropolitan Labor Markets Absorbed Welfare Recipients?* Washington, DC: Assistant Secretary for Planning and Evaluation, DHHS. http://aspe.hhs.gov/HSP/rural-lm01 (accessed March 31, 2006).

Felsenstein, Daniel, and Joseph Persky. 1999. "When Is a Cost Really a Benefit? Local Welfare Effects and Employment Creation in the Evaluation of Economic Development Programs." *Economic Development Quarterly* 13(1): 46–54.

Figlio, David N., and James P. Ziliak. 1999. "Welfare Reform, the Business Cycle, and the Decline in AFDC Caseloads." In *Economic Conditions and Welfare Reform*, Sheldon H. Danziger, ed. Kalamazoo, MI: W.E. Upjohn Institute for Employment Research, pp. 17–48.

Findeis, Jill L., and Leif Jensen. 1998. "Employment Opportunities in Rural Areas: Implications for Poverty in a Changing Policy Environment." *American Journal of Agricultural Economics* 80(5): 1000–1007.

Fisher, Gordon M. 1997. *The Development of the Orshansky Poverty Thresholds and Their Subsequent History as the Official U.S. Poverty Measure*. Poverty Measurement Working Paper. Washington, DC: U.S. Census Bureau. http://www.census.gov/hhes/poverty/povmeas/papers/orshansky.html#C2 (accessed November 2, 2005).

Fisher, Peter. 2004. "The Fiscal Consequences of Competition for Capital." Paper presented at the Humphrey Institute of Public Affairs conference "Reining in the Competition for Capital," held in Minneapolis, MN, February 27-28. http://www.hhh.umn.edu/img/assets/6158/fisher_paper.pdf (accessed April 25, 2006).

Fletcher, Cynthia Needles, Jan L. Flora, Barbara J. Gaddis, Mary Winter, and Jacquelyn S. Litt, 2002. "Small Towns and Welfare Reform: Iowa Case Studies of Families and Communities." In *Rural Dimensions of Welfare Reform*, Bruce A. Weber, Gregory J. Duncan, and Leslie A. Whitener, eds. Kalamazoo, MI: W.E. Upjohn Institute for Employment Research, pp. 201–230.

Forbes, Kristin J. 2000. "A Reassessment of the Relationship between Inequality and Growth." *American Economic Review* 90(4): 869–887.

Foster-Bey, John, and Lynette A. Rawlings. 2002. *Can Targeting Industries Improve Earnings for Welfare Recipients Moving from Welfare to Work? Preliminary Findings*. Washington, DC: Urban Institute. http://www.urban.org/url.cfm?ID=410537 (accessed April 26, 2006).

Freeman, Donald G. 2003. "Poverty and the Macroeconomy: Estimates from U.S. Regional Data." *Contemporary Economic Policy* 21(3): 358–371.

Freeman, Richard B. 1993. "How Much Has De-Unionization Contributed to the Rise in Male Earnings Inequality?" In *Uneven Tides: Rising Inequality in America*, Sheldon H. Danziger and Peter Gottschalk, eds. New York: Russell Sage Foundation, pp. 133–164.

———. 2001. "The Rising Tide Lifts…?" In *Understanding Poverty*, Sheldon H. Danziger and Robert H. Haveman, eds. Cambridge, MA: Harvard University Press, pp. 97–126.

Freeman, Richard B., and William M. Rodgers III. 1999. "Area Economic Conditions and the Labor Market Outcomes of Young Men in the 1990s Expansion." NBER Working Paper No. 7073. Cambridge, MA: National Bureau of Economic Research.

Frey, William H. 1995. "Immigration and Internal Migration 'Flight' from U.S. Metropolitan Areas: Toward a New Demographic Balkanisation." *Urban Studies* 32(4–5): 733–757.

Gabriel, Paul E., and Susanne Schmitz. 1995. "Favorable Self-Selection and the Internal Migration of Young White Males in the United States." *Journal of Human Resources* 30(3): 460–471.

Gallin, Joshua Hojvat. 2004. "Net Migration and State Labor Market Dynamics." *Journal of Labor Economics* 22(1): 1–22.

Gennetian, Lisa, Virginia Knox, and Cynthia Miller. 2000. *Reforming Welfare and Rewarding Work: A Summary of the Final Report on the Minnesota Family Investment Program*. New York: Manpower Demonstration Research Corporation. http://www.mdrc.org/publications/27/summary.html (accessed April 26, 2006).

Gibbs, Robert M. 1994. "The Information Effects of Origin on Migrants' Job Search Behavior." *Journal of Regional Science* 34(2): 163–178.

———. 2002. "Rural Labor Markets in an Era of Welfare Reform." In *Rural*

Dimensions of Welfare Reform, Bruce A. Weber, Greg J. Duncan, and Leslie A. Whitener, eds. Kalamazoo, MI: W.E. Upjohn Institute for Employment Research, pp. 51–76.

Gladden, Tricia, and Christopher Taber. 2000. "Wage Progression among Less Skilled Workers." In *Finding Jobs: Work and Welfare Reform*, David Card and Rebecca M. Blank, eds. New York: Russell Sage Foundation, pp. 160–192.

Glaeser, Edward L. 1998. "Are Cities Dying?" *Journal of Economic Perspectives* 12(2): 139–160.

Glaeser, Edward L., Hedi D. Kallal, Jose A. Scheinkman, and Andrei Shleifer. 1992. "Growth in Cities." *Journal of Political Economy* 100(6): 1126–1152.

Glaeser, Edward L., Jed Kolko, and Albert Saiz. 2001. "Consumer City." *Journal of Economic Geography* 1(1): 27–50.

Glasmeier, Amy K., and Tracey L. Farrigan. 2003. "Poverty, Sustainability, and the Culture of Despair: Can Sustainable Development Strategies Support Poverty Alleviation in America's Most Environmentally Challenged Communities?" *Annals of the American Academy of Political and Social Science* 590(November): 131–149.

Gobillon, Laurent, Harris Selod, and Yves Zenou. 2003. "Spatial Mismatch: From the Hypothesis to the Theories." CEPR Discussion Paper No. 3740. London: Centre for Economic Policy Research.

Goetz, Stephen J. 1999. "Migration and Local Labor Markets." In *The Web Book of Regional Science*, Scott Loveridge, ed. Morgantown, WV: Regional Research Institute, West Virginia University. http://www.rri.wvu.edu/WebBook/Goetz/contents.htm (accessed April 26, 2006).

Gordon, Rachel A., and Lindsay Chase-Lansdale. 2001. "Availability of Child Care in the United States: A Description and Analysis of Data Sources." *Demography* 38(2): 299–316.

Graves, Philip E., and Thomas A. Knapp. 1988. "Mobility Behavior of the Elderly." *Journal of Urban Economics* 24(1): 1–8.

Greene, William H. 1997. *Econometric Analysis.* 3rd ed. Upper Saddle River, NJ: Prentice Hall.

Greenstone, Michael, and Enrico Moretti. 2003. "Bidding for Industrial Plants: Does Winning a 'Million Dollar Plant' Increase Welfare?" NBER Working Paper No. 9844. Cambridge, MA: National Bureau of Economic Research.

Greenwood, Michael J. 1997. "Internal Migration in Developed Countries." In *Handbook of Population and Family Economics,* Vol. 1B, Mark R. Rosenzweig and Oded Stark, eds. Amsterdam: North-Holland, pp. 647–720.

Greenwood, Michael J., Gary L. Hunt, Dan S. Rickman, and George I. Treyz. 1991. "Migration, Regional Equilibrium, and the Estimation of Compensating Differentials." *American Economic Review* 81(5): 1382–1390.

Grogger, Jeffrey. 2003. "Welfare Transitions in the 1990s: The Economy, Welfare Policy, and the EITC." NBER Working Paper No. 9472. Cambridge, MA: National Bureau of Economic Research.

Grogger, Jeffrey, and Charles Michalopoulos. 2003. "Welfare Dynamics under Time Limits." *Journal of Political Economy* 111(3): 530–554.

Gundersen, Craig, and James P. Ziliak. 2004. "Poverty and Macroeconomic Performance across Space, Race, and Family Structure." *Demography* 41(1): 61–86.

Harvey, Mark, Gene F. Summers, Kathleen Pickering, and Patricia Richards. 2002. "The Short-Term Impacts of Welfare Reform in Persistently Poor Rural Areas." In *Rural Dimensions of Welfare Reform,* Bruce A. Weber, Greg J. Duncan, and Leslie A. Whitener, eds. Kalamazoo, MI: W.E. Upjohn Institute for Employment Research, pp. 375–409.

Haskins, Ron. 2001. "Effects of Welfare Reform on Family Income and Poverty." In *The New World of Welfare,* Rebecca M. Blank and Ron Haskins, eds. Washington, DC: Brookings Institution, pp. 103–136.

———. 2003. "Welfare Reform Reauthorization Testimony." U.S. Congress. Senate. Committee on Finance. Welfare Reform: Past Successes, New Challenges, 108th Cong., 1st sess., February 20. http://www.brookings.edu/views/testimony/haskins/20030220.htm (accessed May 2, 2006).

Haveman, Robert, and Jonathan Schwabish. 2000. "Has Macroeconomic Performance Regained its Antipoverty Bite?" *Contemporary Economic Policy* 18(4): 415–427.

Henderson, J. Vernon, Ari Kuncoro, and Matthew Turner. 1995. "Industrial Development in Cities." *Journal of Political Economy* 103(5): 1067–1090.

Henry, Mark S., David L. Barkley, and Shuming Bao. 1997. "The Hinterland's Stake in Metropolitan Area Growth." *Journal of Regional Science* 37(3): 479–501.

Herbert, Bob. 1999. "The Other America." *New York Times*, April 8, A:27.

Holcomb, Pamela A., Kathryn A. Schlichter, Stefanie R. Schmidt, and Jacob Leos-Urbel. 2001. *Recent Changes in Alabama Welfare and Work, Child Care, and Child Welfare Systems.* Washington, DC: Urban Institute.

Holzer, Harry J. 1991. "The Spatial Mismatch Hypothesis: What Has the Evidence Shown?" *Urban Studies* 28(1): 105–122.

———. 1996. *What Employers Want: Job Prospects for Less Educated Workers.* New York: Russell Sage Foundation.

———. 1999. "Will Employers Hire Welfare Recipients? New Survey Evidence from Michigan." *Journal of Policy Analysis and Management* 18(3): 449–472.

Holzer, Harry J., Keith Ihlanfeldt, and David Sjoquist. 1994. "Work, Search and Travel among White and Black Youth." *Journal of Urban Economics* 35(May): 320–345.

Holzer, Harry J., and Robert J. LaLonde. 2000. "Job Change and Job Stability among Less Skilled Young Workers." In *Finding Jobs: Work and Welfare Reform,* Rebecca M. Blank and David Card, eds. New York: Russell Sage Foundation, pp. 123–159.

Holzer, Harry J., Steven Raphael, and Michael A. Stoll. 2003. "Employers in the Boom: How Did the Hiring of Unskilled Workers Change during the 1990s?" Working Paper Series. Los Angeles: Center for the Study of Urban Poverty, University of California, Los Angeles. http://www.sscnet.ucla.edu/issr/csup/uploaded_files/boom12.pdf (accessed July 24, 2006).

Holzer, Harry J., and Jess Reaser. 2000. "Black Applicants, Black Employees, and Urban Labor Market Policy." *Journal of Urban Economics* 48(3): 365–387.

Hopfensperger, Jean. 2000. "Study Assesses Who's Succeeding under Welfare Rules." *Minneapolis Star Tribune*, March 22, B:3.

———. 2005. "The Front Line of Welfare Reform: The Age of the Easy Welfare Check is Waning." *Minneapolis Star Tribune*, August 16, A:1.

Hotz, V. Joseph, and John Karl Scholz. 2001. "The Earned Income Tax Credit." NBER Working Paper No. 8078. Cambridge, MA: National Bureau of Economic Research.

House Ways and Means Committee. 2000. *Green Book: Background Material and Data on Programs within the Jurisdiction of the Committee on Ways and Means. 17th ed. Section 7: Temporary Assistance for Needy Families (TANF).* Washington, DC: House Ways and Means Committee. http://aspe.hhs.gov/2000gb/sec7.txt (accessed March 13, 2006).

Howe, Patrick. 2004. "State Plummets in Ranking of Child Care Generosity." *St. Paul Pioneer Press*, January 29.

Hoynes, Hilary W. 2000a. "Local Labor Markets and Welfare Spells: Do Demand Conditions Matter?" *Review of Economics and Statistics* 82(3): 351–368.

———. 2000b. "The Employment, Earnings, and Income of Less Skilled Workers over the Business Cycle." In *Finding Jobs: Work and Welfare Reform,* David Card and Rebecca M. Blank, eds. New York: Russell Sage Foundation, pp. 23–71.

Hudnut, William. 2003. *Half Way From Everywhere: A Portrait of America's First Tier Suburbs.* Washington, DC: Urban Land Institute.

Ihlanfeldt, Keith R. 1997. "Information on the Spatial Distribution of Job Opportunities within Metropolitan Areas." *Journal of Urban Economics* 41(2): 218–242.

Ihlanfeldt, Keith R., and David L. Sjoquist. 1998. "The Spatial Mismatch Hypothesis: A Review of Recent Studies and Their Implications for Welfare Reform." *Housing Policy Debate* 9(4): 849–892.

Ihlanfeldt, Keith R., and Madelyn V. Young. 1996. "The Spatial Distribution of Black Employment between the Central City and the Suburbs." *Economic Inquiry* 34(4): 693–707.

Ingram, Gregory K. 1998. "Patterns of Metropolitan Development: What Have We Learned?" *Urban Studies* 35(7): 1019–1035.

Internal Revenue Service (IRS). 2003. *2005 1040 Instructions: Including Instructions for Schedules A, B, C, D, E, F, I, and SE*. Washington, DC: IRS. http://www.irs.gov/pub/irs-pdf/i1040.pdf (accessed March 27, 2006).

Jalan, Jyotsna, and Martin Ravallion. 2002. "Geographic Poverty Traps? A Micro Model of Consumption Growth in Rural China." *Journal of Applied Econometrics* 17(4): 329–346.

Jargowsky, Paul A. 2003. *Stunning Progress, Hidden Problems: The Dramatic Decline of Concentrated Poverty in the 1990s*. Living Cities Census Series. Washington, DC: Brookings Institution, Center on Urban and Metropolitan Policy. http://www.brookings.edu/es/urban/publications/jargowskypoverty.pdf (accessed April 26, 2006).

Johnson, Nicholas. 2001. *A Hand Up: How State Earned Income Tax Credits Help Working Families Escape Poverty in 2001*. Summary. Washington, DC: Center on Budget and Policy Priorities. http://www.cbpp.org/10-18-01sfp.htm (accessed March 27, 2006).

Johnson, Nicholas, and Ed Lazere. 1998. *Rising Number of States Offer Earned Income Tax Credits: In the Last Two Years, Five States Have Enacted New State EITCs or Expanded Existing Credits*. Washington, DC: Center on Budget and Policy Priorities. http://www.cbpp.org/9-14-98sfp.htm (accessed March 27, 2006).

Jolliffe, Dean. 2003. "Nonmetro Poverty: Assessing the Effect of the 1990s." *Amber Waves* 1(4): 30–37. http://www.ers.usda.gov/Amberwaves/September03/Features/NonmetroPoverty.htm (accessed April 3, 2006).

Kain, John F. 1992. "The Spatial Mismatch Hypothesis: Three Decades Later." *Housing Policy Debate* 3(2): 371–460.

Kaldor, Nicholas. 1970. "The Case for Regional Policies." *Scottish Journal of Political Economy* 17(3): 337–348.

Karoly, Lynn A., Peter Greenwood, Susan S. Everingham, Jill Houbé, M. Rebecca Kilburn, C. Peter Rydell, Matthew Sanders, and James Chiesa. 1998. *Investing in Our Children: What We Know and Don't Know about the Costs and Benefits of Early Childhood Interventions*. Washington DC: RAND Corporation.

Kasinitz, Philip, and Jan Rosenberg. 1996. "Missing the Connection: Isolation and Employment on the Brooklyn Waterfront." *Social Problems* 43(2): 180–196.

Katz, Bruce. 2003. Foreword to *Half Way From Everywhere: A Portrait of America's First Tier Suburbs.* by William Hudnut. Washington, DC: Urban Land Institute.

Katz, Lawrence F., Jeffrey R. Kling, and Jeffrey B. Liebman. 2001. "Moving to Opportunity in Boston: Early Results of a Randomized Mobility Experiment." *Quarterly Journal of Economics* 116(2): 607–654.

Kilkenny, Maureen, and Sonja Kostova Huffman. 2003. "Rural/Urban Welfare Program and Labor Force Participation." *American Journal of Agricultural Economics* 85(4), 914–927.

Kirschenman, Joleen, and Kathryn M. Neckerman. 1991. "'We'd Love to Hire Them, But . . .': The Meaning of Race for Employers." In *The Urban Underclass*, Christopher Jencks and Paul E. Peterson, eds. Washington, DC: Brookings Institution, pp. 203–232.

Klawitter, Marieka M., Dawn Griffey, and Erika VanNynatten. 2002. *Work-First Study: 3000 Washington Families: Employment for 1999 and 2000 TANF Recipients.* Seattle, WA: Daniel J. Evans School of Public Affairs, University of Washington. http://www.workfirst.wa.gov/about/ EmploymentReport4_02.pdf (accessed March 20, 2006).

Kletzer, Lori G. 1998. "Job Displacement." *Journal of Economic Perspectives* 12(1): 115–136.

Kling, Jeffrey R., Jens Ludwig, and Lawrence F. Katz. 2004. "Neighborhood Effects on Crime for Female and Male Youth: Evidence from a Randomized Housing Voucher Experiment." NBER Working Paper No. 10777. Cambridge, MA: National Bureau of Economic Research.

Koralek, Robin, Nancy M. Pindus, Jeffrey Capizzano, and Roseana Bess. 2001. *Recent Changes in New Jersey Welfare and Work, Child Care, and Child Welfare Systems.* Washington, DC: Urban Institute.

Koretz, Gene. 1992. "Trickle-Down Economics May Not Help the Poor." *Business Week* 1992(February 24): 26.

Kraybill, David, and Maureen Kilkenny. 2003. "Economic Rationales For and Against Place-Based Policies." Staff General Research Paper No. 11730. Ames, IA: Iowa State University, Department of Economics. Paper presented at the American Agricultural Economics Association–Rural Sociological Society annual meeting, "Spatial Inequality: Continuity and Change in Territorial Stratification," held in Montreal, July 27–30.

Kraybill, David, and Linda Lobao. 2001. *County Government Survey: Changes and Challenges in the New Millennium.* Rural County Governance Center Research Report No. 1. Washington, DC: National Association of Counties.

Krugman, Paul. 1991. *Geography and Trade*. Cambridge, MA: MIT Press.

Kuttner, Robert. 2000. "The States Are Ending Welfare as We Know It—but Not Poverty." Economic Viewpoint. *Business Week* 3685(June 12): 36.

Larson, Donald K. 1989. "Transitions of Poverty amidst Employment Growth: Two Nonmetro Case Studies." *Growth and Change* 20(2): 19–34.

Leichenko, Robin M. 2003. "Does Place Still Matter? Accounting for Income Variation across American Indian Tribal Areas." *Economic Geography* 79(4): 365–386.

Levernier, William, Mark D. Partridge, and Dan S. Rickman. 1998. "Differences in Metropolitan and Nonmetropolitan U.S. Family Income Inequality: A Cross-Country Comparison." *Journal of Urban Economics* 44(2): 272–290.

———. 2000. "The Causes of Regional Variations in U.S. Poverty: A Cross-County Analysis." *Journal of Regional Science* 40(3): 473–498.

Lichter, Daniel T., and Leif Jensen. 2002. "Rural America in Transition: Poverty and Welfare at the Turn of the Twenty-First Century." In *Rural Dimensions of Welfare Reform*, Bruce A. Weber, Greg J. Duncan, and Leslie A. Whitener, eds. Kalamazoo, MI: W.E. Upjohn Institute for Employment Research, pp. 77–112.

Llobrera, Joseph. 2004. *Food Stamp Caseloads Are Rising*. Washington, DC: Center on Budget and Policy Priorities. http://www.cbpp.org/1-15-02fa.htm (accessed January 2, 2006).

Llobrera, Joseph, and Bob Zahradnik. 2004. *A Hand Up: How State Earned Income Tax Credits Help Working Families Escape Poverty in 2004. Summary*. Washington, DC: Center on Budget and Policy Priorities. http://www.cbpp.org/5-14-04sfp.htm (accessed March 27, 2006).

Loeb, Susanna, Bruce Fuller, Sharon Lynn Kagan, Bidemi Carroll, and Jan McCarthy. 2003. "Child Care in Poor Communities: Early Learning Effects of Type, Quality, and Stability." NBER Working Paper No. 9954. Cambridge, MA: National Bureau of Economic Research.

Loprest, Pamela. 2003. *Fewer Welfare Leavers Employed in Weak Economy*. Snapshots of America's Families III, No 5. Washington, DC: Urban Institute. http://www.urban.org/url.cfm?ID=310837 (accessed April 27, 2006).

Lucas, Robert E.B. 2001. "The Effects of Proximity and Transportation on Developing Country Population Migrations." *Journal of Economic Geography* 1(3): 323–339.

Lucy, William H., and David L. Phillips. 2001. *Suburbs and the Census: Patterns of Growth and Decline*. Survey Series. Washington, DC: Brookings Institution, Center on Urban and Metropolitan Policy. http://www.brookings.edu/es/urban/census/lucy.pdf (accessed April 27, 2006).

Madden, Janice Fanning. 1996. "Changes in the Distribution of Poverty across and within the U.S. Metropolitan Areas, 1979–89." *Urban Studies* 33(9): 1581–1600.

———. 2000. *Changes in Income Inequality within U.S. Metropolitan Areas.* Kalamazoo, MI: W.E. Upjohn Institute for Employment Research.

Mandel, Michael J. 1996. "Economic Anxiety." *Business Week* 1996(March 11): 50–56.

Manpower Demonstration Research Corporation (MDRC). 2003. "Major Study of Welfare Reform in Philadelphia Finds Employment Increased but Poverty and Hardship Remain Widespread." News release, October 17. New York: MDRC. http://www.mdrc.org/PressReleases/ucp_press_release.htm (accessed May 22, 2006).

Marston, Stephen. 1985. "Two Views of the Geographic Distribution of Unemployment." *Quarterly Journal of Economics* 10(1): 57–79.

Martin, Jonathan. 2004. "Tough Love for Welfare Families." *Seattle Times,* February 23, A:1.

Martin, Richard W. 2004. "Spatial Mismatch and the Structure of American Metropolitan Areas, 1970–2000." *Journal of Regional Science* 44(3): 467–488.

McDermott, Mark. 2001. *Assessing Washington State's WorkFirst Welfare Reform: A Failure in Promoting Upward Mobility and Steady Employment.* Seattle: Statewide Poverty Action Network.

McGranahan, David A. 1999. *Natural Amenities Drive Rural Population Change. Agricultural Economic Report No. 781.* Washington, DC: ERS, USDA. http://www.ers.usda.gov/publications/aer781/aer781.pdf (accessed April 3, 2006).

McKinnish, Terra. 2005. "Importing the Poor: Welfare Magnetism and Cross-Border Welfare Migration." *Journal of Human Resources* 40(1): 57–76.

McMillen, Daniel P. 2003. "Spatial Autocorrelation or Model Misspecification?" *International Regional Science Review* 26(2): 208–217.

———. 2004. "Employment Densities, Spatial Autocorrelation, and Subcenter in Large Metropolitan Areas." *Journal of Regional Science* 44(2): 225–243.

McMurrer, Daniel P., and Isabel V. Sawhill. 1997. "Planning for the Best of Times." Op-ed. *Washington Post,* August 18, A:19.

Meyer, Bruce D., and Dan T. Rosenbaum. 2001. "Welfare, the Earned Income Tax Credit, and the Labor Supply of Single Mothers." *Quarterly Journal of Economics* 116(3): 1063–1114.

Michalopoulos, Charles, Kathryn Edin, Barbara Fink, Mirella Landriscina, Denise F. Polit, Judy C. Polyne, Lashawn Richburg-Hayes, David Seith, and Nandita Verma. 2003. *Welfare Reform in Philadelphia: Implementation, Effects, and Experiences of Poor Families and Neighborhoods. The Project on Devolution and Urban Change: Summary Report.* New York:

Manpower Demonstration Research Corporation (MDRC). http://www
.mdrc.org/publications/352/summary.pdf (accessed April 5, 2006).

Mieszkowski, Peter, and Edwin S. Mills. 1993. "The Causes of Metropolitan Suburbanization." *Journal of Economic Perspectives* 7(3): 135–147.

Miller, Kathleen K., and Bruce A. Weber. 2004. *Persistent Poverty and Place: How Do Persistent Poverty Dynamics and Demographics Vary Across the Rural-Urban Continuum?* Measuring Rural Diversity Series 1(1). Starkville, MS: Southern Rural Development Center. http://www.rupri.org/rprc/miller_weber.pdf (accessed April 27, 2006).

Mills, Bradford F., and Gautam Hazarika. 2003. "Do Single Mothers Face Greater Constraints to Workforce Participation in Non-Metropolitan Areas?" *American Journal of Agricultural Economics* 85(1): 143–161.

Mills, Gregory, Robert Kornfeld, Diane Porcari, and Don Laliberty. 2001. *Evaluation of the Arizona EMPOWER Welfare Reform Demonstration: Final Report.* Cambridge, MA: Abt Associates.

Minnesota Department of Human Services. 2003. *2003 Maternal and Child Health State Advocacy: 2003 Legislative Wrap-Up.* St. Paul, MN: Minnesota Department of Human Services. http://www.mnhomelesscoalition.org/2003_advocacy.html (accessed June 14, 2004).

Minnesota Public Radio. 2003. "Session Ends, Spin Begins." *News and Features: Session 2003, May 30.* St. Paul, MN: Minnesota Public Radio. http://news.minnesota.publicradio.org/features/2003/05/29_mccalluml_hhs/ (accessed May 22, 2006).

Mishel, Lawrence, Jared Bernstein, and John Schmitt. 2001. *The State of Working America 2000–2001.* Washington, DC: Economic Policy Institute.

Moffit, Robert A. 1999. "The Effect of Pre-PRWORA Waivers on AFDC Caseloads and Female Earnings, Income, and Labor Force Behavior." In *Economic Conditions and Welfare Reform*, Sheldon H. Danziger, ed. Kalamazoo, MI: W.E. Upjohn Institute for Employment Research, pp. 91–118.

———. 2002. *From Welfare to Work: What the Evidence Shows.* Welfare Reform and Beyond Project Policy Brief No. 13. Washington, DC: Brookings Institution. http://www.brook.edu/es/research/projects/wrb/publications/pb/pb13.htm (accessed April 27, 2006).

Moffitt, Robert A., and LaDonna A. Pavetti. 2000. "Time Limits." In *Finding Jobs: Work and Welfare Reform*, David Card and Rebecca M. Blank, eds. New York: Russell Sage Foundation, pp. 507–535.

Montgomery County. 2000. "Duncan Joins State Official as First Local Earned Income Tax Credit Checks Mailed." Montgomery County, Maryland, Press Release. Rockville, MD: Montgomery County. http://www.montgomerycountymd.gov/mc/news/press/00-33.html (accessed April 4, 2006).

Moore, Stephen. 1997. *Ending Welfare Reform as We Know It.* Daily Commentary, January 24. Washington, DC: Cato Institute. http://www.cato.org/dailys/1-24-97.html (accessed April 27, 2006).

Morgan, David R., and Kenneth Kickham. 2001. "Children in Poverty: Do State Policies Matter?" *Social Science Quarterly* 82(3): 478–493.

Mosely, Jane M., and Kathleen K. Miller. 2004. *What the Research Says about Spatial Variations in Factors Affecting Poverty.* Rural Poverty Research Institute (RUPRI) Brief 2004-1. Columbia, MO: RUPRI.

Murphy, Kevin M., and Robert Topel. 1997. "Unemployment and Nonemployment." *American Economic Review* 87(2): 295–300.

National Center for Children in Poverty (NCCP). 2004. *50-State Data Wizards.* New York: NCCP. http://nccp.org/wizard/wizard.cgi (accessed April 25, 2006).

National Conference of State Legislatures (NCSL). 2005. *Welfare Caseload Watch.* Denver: NCSL. http://www.ncsl.org/statefed/welfare/caseloadwatch.htm (accessed January 2, 2006).

Nebraska Department of Revenue. 2006. *Nebraska Tax Incentives.* Lincoln, NE: Nebraska Department of Revenue. http://www.revenue.ne.gov/incentiv (accessed April 4, 2006).

Nebraska State Statutes. 1996. *Enterprise Zone Act.* Lincoln, NE: Nebraska Legislature. http://assist.neded.org/ezone.html (accessed April 4, 2006).

New Jersey Department of Human Services. 2004. *A New Beginning: The Future of Child Welfare in New Jersey.* Trenton, NJ: New Jersey Department of Human Services. http://www.state.nj.us/humanservices/cwrp/June%209%20Final%20version.pdf (accessed March 28, 2006).

———. 2006a. *Welfare Services.* Trenton, NJ: New Jersey Department of Human Services. http://www.state.nj.us/humanservices/workfirstnj.html (accessed March 14, 2006).

———. 2006b. *Supportive Assistance to Individuals and Families (SAIF).* Work First New Jersey. Trenton, NJ: New Jersey Department of Human Services. http://www.state.nj.us/humanservices/dfd/SAIF%20english%20only.pdf (accessed March 20, 2006).

New York Times. 1996. "The Welfare Bill." August 1, A:24.

———. 1998. "Black and Hispanic Poverty Falls, Reducing Overall Rate for Nation." September 25, A:1.

Nord, Mark. 1998. "Poor People on the Move: County-to-County Migration and the Spatial Concentration of Poverty." *Journal of Regional Science* 38(2): 329–351.

———. 2000. "Does It Cost Less to Live in Rural Areas? Evidence from New Data on Food Security and Hunger." *Rural Sociology* 65(1): 104–125.

Office of the Legislative Auditor. 2000. *Welfare Reform.* Program Evaluation Report. St. Paul, MN: Office of the Legislative Auditor, State of Minnesota.

http://www.auditor.leg.state.mn.us/ped/2000/pe0003.htm (accessed June 2, 2006).

Okun, Arthur M. 1975. *Equality and Efficiency: The Big Tradeoff.* Washington, DC: Brookings Institution.

O'Neill, June E., and M. Anne Hill. 2001. *Gaining Ground? Measuring the Impact of Welfare Reform on Welfare and Work.* Civic Report No. 17, Center for Civic Innovation. New York: Manhattan Institute for Policy Research.

O'Regan, Katherine M., and John M. Quigley. 1991. "Labor Market Access and Labor Market Outcomes for Urban Youth." *Regional Science and Urban Economics* 21(2): 277–293.

Orrenius, Pia M., and Madeline Zavodny. 2003. "Does Immigration Affect Wages? A Look at Occupation-Level Evidence." Federal Reserve Bank of Atlanta Working Paper 2003-2. Atlanta: Federal Reserve Bank of Atlanta.

Page, Marianne E., and Gary Solon. 2003. "Correlations between Brothers and Neighboring Boys in Their Adult Earnings: The Importance of Being Urban." *Journal of Labor Economics* 21(4): 831–856.

Partridge, Mark D. 1997. "Is Inequality Harmful for Growth? Comment." *American Economic Review* 87(5): 1019–1032.

———. 2001. "Exploring the Canadian-U.S. Unemployment and Nonemployment Rate Gaps: Are There Lessons for Both Countries?" *Journal of Regional Science* 41(4): 701–734.

———. 2003. "Part-Time Workers and Economic Expansion: Comparing the 1980s and 1990s with U.S. State Data." *Papers in Regional Science* 82(1): 51–74.

———. 2005. "Does Income Distribution Affect U.S. State Economic Growth?" *Journal of Regional Science* 45(2): 363–394.

Partridge, Mark D., and Dan S. Rickman. 1995. "Differences in State Unemployment Rates: The Role of Labor and Product Market Structural Shifts." *Southern Economic Journal* 62(1): 89–106.

———. 1997a. "Has the Wage Curve Nullified the Harris-Todaro Model? Further U.S. Evidence." *Economics Letters* 54(3): 277–282.

———. 1997b. "The Dispersion of U.S. State Unemployment Rates: The Role of Market and Nonmarket Equilibrium Factors." *Regional Studies* 31(6): 593–606.

———. 1997c. "State Unemployment Differentials in the 1990s: Equilibrium Factors vs. Differential Employment Growth." *Growth and Change* 28(3): 360–379.

———. 1999a. "A Note on the Benefits to Current Residents of State Employment Growth: Is There an Industry Mix Effect on Migration?" *Journal of Regional Science* 39(1): 167–181.

———. 1999b. "Which Comes First, Jobs or People? An Analysis of the Recent Stylized Facts." *Economics Letters* 64(1): 117–123.

———. 2002. "Did the New Economy Vanquish the Regional Business Cycle?" *Contemporary Economic Policy* 20(4): 456–469.

———. 2003a. "Do We Know Economic Development When We See It?" *Review of Regional Studies* 33(1):17–39.

———. 2003b. "The Waxing and Waning of Regional Economies: The Chicken-Egg Question of Jobs vs. People." *Journal of Urban Economics* 53(1): 76–97.

———. 2006. "Fluctuations in Aggregate U.S. Migration Flows and Regional Labor Market Flexibility." *Southern Economic Journal* 72(4): 958–980.

Pear, Robert. 2003. "Welfare Spending Shows Huge Shift." *New York Times*, October 13, late edition, A:1.

Perry, Marc J., and Paul J. Mackun. 2001. *Population Change and Distribution, 1990 to 2000. Census 2000 Brief, C2KBR/01-2.* Washington, DC: U.S. Census Bureau. http://www.census.gov/prod/2001pubs/c2kbr01-2.pdf (accessed March 31, 2006).

Persson, Torsten, and Guido Tabellini. 1994. "Is Inequality Harmful for Growth?" *American Economic Review* 84(3): 600–621.

Peters, Alan H., and Peter S. Fisher. 2002. *State Enterprise Programs: Have They Worked?* Kalamazoo, MI: W.E. Upjohn Institute for Employment Research.

———. 2004. "The Failures of Economic Development Incentives." *Journal of the American Planning Association* 70(1): 27–37.

Pickering, Kathleen. 2004. "Welfare Policy on American Indian Reservations: Two Approaches, Two Outcomes among the Lakota of South Dakota." *Perspectives on Poverty, Policy, and Place* 1(4): 5–6.

Pissarides, Christopher. 1991. "Macroeconomic Adjustment and Poverty in Selected Industrial Countries." *The World Bank Economic Review* 5(2): 207–229.

Ponza, Michael, Alicia Meckstroth, and Jennifer Faerber. 2002. *Employment Experiences and Challenges among Urban and Rural Clients in Nebraska. Final Report.* Princeton, NJ: Mathematica Policy Research Inc. http://www.mathematica-mpr.com/publications/PDFs/employexp.pdf (accessed April 3, 2006).

Powers, Elizabeth T. 1995. "Inflation, Unemployment, and Poverty Revisited." *Federal Reserve Bank of Cleveland Economic Review* 31(3): 2–13.

Primus, Wendell. 2001. "Comment" on "Effects of Welfare Reform on Family Income and Poverty," by Ron Haskins. In *The New World of Welfare*, Rebecca M. Blank and Ron Haskins, eds. Washington, DC: Brookings Institution, pp. 130–136.

Quayle, Dan. 1992. "The Vice President Speaks." Commonwealth Club of California speech. http://www.commonwealthclub.org/archive/20thcentury/92-05quayle-speech.html (accessed April 27, 2006).

Raphael, Steven. 1998. "The Spatial Mismatch Hypothesis and Black Youth Joblessness: Evidence from the San Francisco Bay Area." *Journal of Urban Economics* 43(1): 79–111.

Raphael, Steven, and Lorien Rice. 2002. "Car Ownership, Employment, and Earnings." *Journal of Urban Economics* 52(1): 109–130.

Raphael, Steven, and Michael A. Stoll. 2002. *Modest Progress: The Narrowing Spatial Mismatch Between Blacks and Jobs in the 1990s.* Living Cities Census Series. Washington, DC: Brookings Institution, Center on Urban and Metropolitan Policy.

Raphael, Steven, Michael A. Stoll, and Harry J. Holzer. 2000. "Are Suburban Firms More Likely to Discriminate against African Americans?" *Journal of Urban Economics* 48(3): 485–508.

Raphael, Steven, and Rudolf Winter-Ember. 2001. "Identifying the Effect of Unemployment on Crime." *Journal of Law and Economics* 44(1): 259–283.

Ravallion, Martin, and Quentin T. Wodon. 1999. "Poor Areas, or Only Poor People?" *Journal of Regional Science* 39(4): 689–711.

Rawls, John. 1971. *A Theory of Justice.* Cambridge, MA: Harvard University Press.

Reid, J. Norman. 1999. "Community Empowerment: A New Approach for Rural Development." *Rural Development Perspectives* 14(1): 9–13.

Renkow, Mitch. 2003. "Employment Growth, Worker Mobility, and Rural Economic Development." *American Journal of Agricultural Economics* 85(2): 503–513.

Renkow, Mitch, and Dale M. Hoover. 2000. "Commuting, Migration, and Rural-Urban Population Dynamics." *Journal of Regional Science* 40(2): 261–288.

Roback, Jennifer. 1982. "Wages, Rents, and the Quality of Life." *Journal of Political Economy* 90(6): 1257–1278.

Rogers, Cami A. 1998. "State Guidelines: The Jobs Creation Tax Credit." *Journal of Property Tax Management* 9(4): 43–67.

Rogers, Cynthia L. 1997. "Job Search and Unemployment Duration: Implications for the Spatial Mismatch Hypothesis." *Journal of Urban Economics* 42: 109–132.

Romer, Christina D., and David H. Romer. 1999. "Monetary Policy and the Well-Being of the Poor." *Federal Reserve Bank of Kansas City Economic Review* 84(1): 21–49.

Rosario, Ruben. 2003. "Sweeping Welfare Changes Proposed." *St. Paul Pioneer Press*, January 31.

Rosenbaum, James E., and Stefanie DeLuca. 2000. *Is Housing Mobility the Key to Welfare Reform? Lessons from Chicago's Gautreaux Program.* Survey Series. Washington, DC: Brookings Institution, Center on Urban and Metropolitan Policy. http://www.brookings.edu/es/urban/rosenbaum.pdf (accessed July 24, 2006).

Rowthorn, Robert, and Andrew Glyn. 2003. "Convergence and Stability in U.S. Regional Employment." Oxford University Economics Series Working Paper 092. Oxford: Oxford University Department of Economics.

Rural Sociological Society Task Force on Persistent Rural Poverty (RSS). 1993. *Persistent Poverty in Rural America.* Boulder, CO: Westview Press.

Saiz, Albert. 2003. "The Impact of Immigration on American Cities: An Introduction to the Issues." *Federal Reserve Bank of Philadelphia Business Review* 2003(4): 14–23.

Sawicki, David S., and Mitch Moody. 1997. "The Effects of Intermetropolitan Migration on the Labor Force Participation of Disadvantaged Black Men in Atlanta." *Economic Development Quarterly* 11(1): 45–66.

Schoeni, Robert F., and Rebecca M. Blank. 2000. "What Has Welfare Reform Accomplished? Impacts on Welfare Participation, Employment, Income, Poverty, and Family Structure." NBER Working Paper No. 7627. Cambridge, MA: National Bureau of Economic Research.

Schwartz, Aba. 1976. "Migration, Age, and Education." *Journal of Political Economy* 84(4): 701–720.

Schweke, William. 2004. "'You Want Employment? We Will Give You Employment!' Do Better Job Creation Subsidies Hold Real Promise for Business Incentive Reformers?" Paper presented at the Humphrey Institute of Public Affairs conference "Reining in the Competition for Capital," held in Minneapolis, February 27–28. http://www.hhh.umn.edu/img/assets/6158/schweke_paper.pdf (accessed April 28 2006).

Scott, Janny. 2005. "Life at the Top in America Isn't Just Better, It's Longer." *New York Times*, May 16, A:1.

Sethi, Rajiv, and Rohini Somanathan. 2004. "Inequality and Segregation." *Journal of Political Economy* 112(6): 1296–1321.

Shelton, Ellen, Greg Owen, Amy Bush Stevens, Justine Nelson-Christinedaughter, Corinna Roy, and June Heineman. 2002. "Whose Job Is It? Employers' Views on Welfare Reform." In *Rural Dimensions of Welfare Reform*, Bruce A. Weber, Greg J. Duncan, and Leslie A. Whitener, eds. Kalamazoo, MI: W.E. Upjohn Institute for Employment Research, pp. 345–374.

Shroder, Mark. 2001. "Moving to Opportunity: An Experiment in Social and

Geographic Mobility." *Cityscape: A Journal of Policy Development and Research* 5(2): 57–68.

Sjoquist, David L. 2001. "Spatial Mismatch and Social Acceptability." *Journal of Urban Economics* 50(3): 474–490.

Slesnick, Daniel T. 1993. "Gaining Ground: Poverty in the Postwar United States." *Journal of Political Economy* 101(1): 1–38.

Smith, James P., and Finis Welch. 1986. *Closing the Gap: Forty Years of Economic Progress for Blacks*. RAND Report R-3330-DOL. Santa Monica, CA: RAND Corporation.

Smith, Tony E., and Yves Zenou. 2003. "Spatial Mismatch, Search Effort and Urban Spatial Structure." *Journal of Urban Economics* 54(1): 129–156.

Spilimbergo, Antonio, and Luis Ubeda. 2004. "Family Attachment and the Decision to Move by Race." *Journal of Urban Economics* 55(3): 478–497.

Stabler, Jack C., and M. Rose Olfert. 2002. *Saskatchewan's Communities in the 21st Century: From Places to Regions*. Canadian Plains Report No. 11. Regina, SK: Canadian Plains Research Center.

Stevens, Ann Huff. 1999. "Climbing Out of Poverty, Falling Back In: Measuring the Persistence of Poverty over Multiple Spells." *Journal of Human Resources* 34(3): 557–588.

Stevens, Val. 2003. "WorkFirst Changes Help More People." Opinion. *Seattle Post-Intelligencer*, October 28, B:7.

Stoll, Michael A. 1999. "Spatial Job Search, Spatial Mismatch, and the Employment and Wages of Racial and Ethnic Groups in Los Angeles." *Journal of Urban Economics* 46(1): 129–155.

Stoll, Michael A., Harry J. Holzer, and Keith R. Ihlanfeldt. 2000. "Within Cities and Suburbs: Racial Residential Concentration and the Spatial Distribution of Employment Opportunities across Sub-Metropolitan Areas." *Journal of Policy Analysis and Management* 19(2): 207–231.

Stoll, Michael A., and Steven Raphael. 2000. "Racial Differences in Spatial Job Search Patterns: Exploring the Causes and Consequences." *Economic Geography* 76(3): 201–223.

Thompson, Terri S., Kathleen Snyder, Karin Malm, and Carolyn T. O'Brien. 2001. *Recent Changes in Washington Welfare and Work, Child Care, and Child Welfare Systems*. Assessing the New Federalism, State Update No. 6. Washington, DC: Urban Institute.

Tobin, James, 1994. "Poverty in Relation to Macroeconomic Trends, Cycles, and Policies." In *Confronting Poverty: Prescriptions for Change*, Sheldon H. Danziger, Gary D. Sandefur, and Daniel H. Weinberg, eds. Cambridge, MA: Harvard University Press, pp. 147–167.

Topel, Robert H. 1986. "Local Labor Markets." *Journal of Political Economy* 94(3): S111–143.

————. 1994. "Regional Labor Markets and the Determinants of Wage Inequality." *American Economic Review* 84(2): 17–22.

Tout, Kathryn, Karin Martinson, Robin Koralek, and Jennifer Ehrle. 2001.
*Recent Changes in Minnesota Welfare and Work, Child Care, and Child
Welfare Systems.* Assessing the New Federalism, State Update No. 3. Wash-
ington, DC: Urban Institute.

Turner, Margery Austin. 1992. "Discrimination in Urban Housing Markets:
Lessons from Fair Housing Audits." *Housing Policy Debate* 3(2): 185–
216.

Turner, Mark D., and Burt S. Barnow. 2003. *Living Wage and Earned Income
Tax Credit: A Comparative Analysis.* Washington, DC: Employment Policies Institute. http://www.epionline.org/studies/turner_01-2003.pdf (accessed April 28, 2006).

Turner, Susan C. 1997. "Barriers to a Better Break: Employer Discrimination
and Spatial Mismatch in Metropolitan Detroit." *Journal of Urban Affairs*
19(2): 123–141.

Twin Cities Development Association. 2003. *Business Profile.* Scottsbluff,
NE: Twin Cities Development Association. http://www.tcdne.org/business
.htm (accessed April 3, 2006).

U.S. Census Bureau. 2001. *Profile of the Foreign-Born Population in the
United States: 2000.* Current Population Reports: Special Studies. Series
P23-206. Washington, DC: U.S. Census Bureau. http://www.census.gov/
prod/2002pubs/p23-206.pdf (accessed April 28, 2006).

————. 2002a. *Census Historical Poverty Tables: CPH-L-162. Persons by
Poverty Status in 1969, 1979, and 1989, by State.* Washington, DC: U.S.
Census Bureau. http://www.census.gov/hhes/poverty/census/cphl162.html
(accessed March 24, 2006).

————. 2002b. *Table D-1. Places—Area and Population.* In *County and
City Data Book: 2000.* Washington, DC: U.S. Census Bureau. http://www
.census.gov/prod/2002pubs/00ccdb/cc00_tabD1.pdf (accessed November
8, 2005).

————. 2002c. *Table CO-99-4: County Population Estimates for July 1, 1999,
and Demographic Components of Population Change: April 1, 1990, to
July 1, 1999.* Washington, DC: U.S. Census Bureau. http://www.census
.gov/popest/archives/1990s/co-99-04/99C4_31.txt (accessed April 6, 2006).

————. 2003. *County-to-County Migration Flow Files.* Washington, DC:
U.S. Census Bureau. http://www.census.gov/population/www/cen2000/
ctytoctyflow.html (accessed April 3, 2006).

————. 2004a. *Historical Poverty Tables: Table 2. Poverty Status of People by
Family Relationship, Race, and Hispanic Origin: 1959 to 2003.* Washing-

ton, DC: U.S. Census Bureau. http://www.census.gov/hhes/poverty/histpov/
hstpov2.html (accessed March 24, 2006).

———. 2004b. *Historical Poverty Tables: Table 4. Poverty Status of Families,
by Type of Family, Presence of Related Children, Race, and Hispanic Origin: 1959 to 2003*. Washington, DC: U.S. Census Bureau. http://www.census
.gov/hhes/poverty/histpov/hstpov4.html (accessed November 1, 2005).

———. 2004c. *Historical Poverty Tables: Table 3. Poverty Status of People,
by Age, Race, and Hispanic Origin: 1959 to 2003*. Washington, DC: U.S.
Census Bureau. http://www.census.gov/hhes/poverty/histpov/hstpov3.html
(accessed November 7, 2005).

———. 2004d. *Historical Poverty Tables: Table 21. Number of Poor and
Poverty Rate, by State: 1980 to 2003*. Washington, DC: U.S. Census Bu-
reau. http://www.census.gov/hhes/poverty/histpov/hstpov21.html (accessed
March 27, 2006).

———. 2004e. *MCD/County-to-MCD/County Worker Flow Files*. Washington, DC: U.S. Census Bureau. http://www.census.gov/population/www/
cen2000/mcdworkerflow.html (accessed April 3, 2006).

———. 2004f. *Census 2000 Urban and Rural Classification*. Washington,
DC: U.S. Census Bureau. http://www.census.gov/geo/www/ua/ua_2k.html
(accessed April 4, 2006).

———. 2004g. *About Metropolitan and Micropolitan Statistical Areas*. Washington, DC: U.S. Census Bureau. http://www.census.gov/population/www/
estimates/aboutmetro.html (accessed May 14, 2004).

———. 2004h. *Poverty: How the Census Bureau Measures Poverty*. Washington, DC: U.S. Census Bureau. http://www.census.gov/hhes/poverty/povdef
.html (accessed November 2, 2005).

———. 2004i. "Welfare Rolls Drop Again." News release, March 30. http://
www.hhs.gov/news/press/2004pres/20040330.html (accessed May 1, 2006).

———. 2005a. *Table 6. Estimates of Average Annual Rates of the Components
of Population Change for Counties of Washington: April 1, 2000, to July
1, 2004*. Washington, DC: U.S. Census Bureau. http://www.census.gov/
popest/counties/tables/CO-EST2004-06-53.xls (accessed March 28, 2006).

———. 2005b. *Small Area Income and Poverty Estimates: Model-Based Estimates for States, Counties and School Districts*. Washington, DC: U.S.
Census Bureau. http://www.census.gov/hhes/www/saipe (accessed March
30, 2006).

———. 2005c. *Summary File 3: 2000 Census of Population and Housing.
Technical Documentation*. Washington, DC: U.S. Census Bureau. http://
www.census.gov/prod/cen2000/doc/sf3.pdf (accessed April 6, 2006).

———. 2005d. *Small Area Income and Poverty Estimates: Estimates for Ne-*

braska Counties, 2003. Washington, DC: U.S. Census Bureau http://www
.census.gov/cgi-bin/saipe/saipe.cgi (accessed April 6, 2006).

————. 2005e. *Poverty Thresholds: Poverty Thresholds by Size of Family and Number of Children.* Washington, DC: U.S. Census Bureau, Current Population Survey. http://www.census.gov/hhes/poverty/threshld.html (accessed March 21, 2006).

————. 2005f. *Uncle Sam's Reference Shelf: USA Counties 1998.* CD-ROM. Washington, DC: U.S. Census Bureau. http://www.census.gov/statab/www/county.html (accessed March 21, 2006).

————. 2006a. *Income.* Washington, DC: U.S. Census Bureau. http://www
.census.gov/hhes/www/income/reports.html (accessed March 27, 2006).

————. 2006b. *American FactFinder: Select Geography.* Washington, DC: U.S. Census Bureau. http://factfinder.census.gov/servlet/DTGeoSearchBy ListServlet?ds_name=DEC_2000_SF3_U&_lang=en&_ts=162138345856 (accessed April 4, 2006).

————. 2006c. *American FactFinder: FactFinder.* Washington, DC: U.S. Census Bureau. http://factfinder.census.gov/home/saff/main.html?_lang=en (accessed April 6, 2006).

————. 2006d. *State and County QuickFacts.* Washington, DC: U.S. Census Bureau. http://quickfacts.census.gov/qfd/states/31000.html (accessed April 6, 2006).

————. 2006e. *American FactFinder: Data Sets.* Washington, DC: U.S. Census Bureau. http://factfinder.census.gov/servlet/DatasetMainPageServlet? _program=DEC&_tabld=DEC2&_submenuld=datasets_1&_lang=en& _ts=162398086989 (accessed April 7, 2006).

————. 2006f. *Population Estimates, Counties.* Washington, DC: U.S. Census Bureau. http://www.census.gov/popest/counties/tables/CO-EST2005-01-31 .xls (accessed April 6, 2006).

————. 2006g. *Data Access Tools.* Washington, DC: U.S. Census Bureau. http://www.census.gov/main/www/access.html (accessed May 23, 2006).

U.S. Department of Justice. 2005. *Crime and Victims Statistics.* Washington, DC: U.S. Department of Justice, Bureau of Justice Statistics. http://www
.ojp.usdoj.gov/bjs.cvict.htm (accessed March 20, 2006).

U.S. Department of Labor (USDOL). 2005. *Bureau of Labor Statistics Data.* Washington, DC: U.S. Department of Labor, Bureau of Labor Statistics.

Viscusi, W. Kip. 1986. "Market Incentives for Criminal Behavior." In *The Black Youth Employment Crisis*, Richard B. Freeman and Harry J. Holzer, eds. National Bureau of Economic Research project report. Chicago: University of Chicago Press, pp. 301–346.

Waldfogel, Jane, and Susan E. Mayer. 2000. "Gender Differences in the Low-Wage Labor Market." In *Finding Jobs: Work and Welfare Reform*, David

Card and Rebecca M. Blank, eds. Russell Sage Foundation: New York, pp. 193–232.

Wallace, Geoffrey, and Rebecca M. Blank, 1999. "What Goes Up Must Come Down?" In *Economic Conditions and Welfare Reform*, Sheldon H. Danziger, ed. Kalamazoo, MI: W.E. Upjohn Institute for Employment Research, pp. 49–90.

Wallace, George. 1999. "Business Assistance: Microlending is Latest Trend in Business Assistance." *Rural Conditions and Trends* 10(1): 18–23.

Waller, Margy, and Alan Berube. 2002. *Timing Out: Long-Term Welfare Caseloads in Large Cities and Counties*. Survey Series. Washington, DC: Brookings Institution, Center on Urban and Metropolitan Policy.

Waller, Margy, and Mark Alan Hughes. 1999. *Working Far From Home: Transportation and Welfare Reform in the Ten Big States*. Progressive Policy Institute (PPI) policy report. Washington, DC: PPI. http://www.ppionline.org/documents/far_from_home.pdf (accessed May 1, 2006).

Washington State Institute for Public Policy. 1999. *Welfare and Employment Outcomes of the WorkFirst Program*. Olympia, WA: Washington State Institute for Public Policy. http://www.wsipp.wa.gov/rptfiles/tanfafdc.pdf (accessed March 20, 2006).

Washington WorkFirst. 2003. *Support Services Staff Memo, July 1, 2003*. Olympia, WA: Washington WorkFirst. http://www.workfirst.wa.gov/statestaff/supsvsmemo1703.htm (accessed March 29, 2006).

———. 2006. *A Job, a Better Job, a Better Life*. Olympia, WA: Washington WorkFirst. http://www.workfirst.wa.gov (accessed March 20, 2006).

Wasmer, Etienne, and Yves Zenou. 2002. "Does City Structure Affect Job Search and Welfare?" *Journal of Urban Economics* 51(3): 515–541.

Weber, Bruce A., Greg J. Duncan, and Leslie A. Whitener. 2001. "Welfare Reform in Rural America: What Have We Learned?" *American Journal of Agricultural Economics* 83(5): 1282–1292.

Weber, Bruce A., and Leif Jensen. 2004. "Poverty and Place: A Critical Review of Rural Poverty Literature." RPRC Working Paper 04-03. Columbia, MO: Rural Poverty Research Center. http://rupri.org/rprc/wp0403.pdf (accessed May 1, 2006).

Weinberg, Bruce A. 2004. "Testing the Spatial Mismatch Hypothesis Using Inter-City Variations in Industrial Composition." *Journal of Urban Economics* 34(5): 505–532.

Weinberg, Bruce A., Patricia B. Reagan, and Jeffrey J. Yankow. 2004. "Do Neighborhoods Affect Hours Worked? Evidence from Longitudinal Data." *Journal of Labor Economics* 22(4): 891–924.

Weinstein, Deborah, and Helen Blank. 2003. *Welfare Reform: Building on Success: Reauthorization of Temporary Assistance for Needy Families and*

Child Care and Development Block Grant. Washington, DC: Children's Defense Fund Action Council.

Wessel, David. 2003. "Finding the Cure for Joblessness Remains a Riddle." *Wall Street Journal,* October 13, A:1.

Western Nebraska Tourism Coalition (WNTC). 2006. *Natural History: Scotts Bluff National Monument.* Ogallala, NE: WNTC. http://www.westnebraska .com/Area_Attractions/Scotts_Bluff/SBMonu.htm (accessed April 3, 2006).

White House. 2004. "Fact Sheet: Better Training for Better Jobs." News release, April 5. http://www.whitehouse.gov/news/releases/2004/04/print/ 20040405-7.html (accessed May 1, 2006).

Whitener, Leslie A., Bruce A. Weber, and Greg J. Duncan. 2002. "Introduction: As the Dust Settles: Welfare Reform and Rural America." In *Rural Dimensions of Welfare Reform,* Bruce A. Weber, Greg J. Duncan, and Leslie A. Whitener, eds. Kalamazoo, MI: Upjohn Institute, pp. 1–22.

Wilson, William Julius. 1987. *The Truly Disadvantaged: The Inner City, the Underclass, and Public Policy.* Chicago: University of Chicago Press.

Wingfield, Kyle. 2004. "Auto Gains Not Making Up for Other Industries' Losses." Associated Press, April 17.

Wood, Robert G., Anu Rangarajan, and John Deke. 2003. *WFNJ Clients Under Welfare Reform: How Is an Early Group Faring Over Time?* Work First New Jersey evaluation. Princeton, NJ: Mathematica Policy Research.

Yankow, Jeffrey J. 2003. "Migration, Job Change, and Wage Growth: A New Perspective on the Pecuniary Return to Geographic Mobility." *Journal of Regional Science* 43(3): 483–516.

Zax, Jeffrey S., and John F. Kain. 1996. "Moving to the Suburbs: Do Relocating Companies Leave Their Black Employees Behind?" *Journal of Labor Economics* 14 (3): 472–504.

Zenou, Yves. 2002. "How Do Firms Redline Workers?" *Journal of Urban Economics* 52(3): 391–408.

Zenou, Yves, and Nicolas Boccard. 2000. "Racial Discrimination and Redlining in Cities." *Journal of Urban Economics* 48(2): 260–285.

Ziliak, James P., David N. Figlio, Elizabeth E. Davis, and Laura S. Connolly. 2000. "Accounting for the Decline in AFDC Caseloads: Welfare Reform or the Economy?" *Journal of Human Resources* 35(3): 570–586.

Ziliak, James P., Craig Gundersen, and David N. Figlio. 2003. "Food Stamp Caseloads over the Business Cycle." *Southern Economic Journal* 69(4): 903–919.

The Authors

Mark D. Partridge is the C. William Swank Chair of Rural-Urban Policy at Ohio State University and a professor in the Department of Agricultural, Environmental, and Development Economics. Prior to that, he was the Canada Research Chair in the New Rural Economy at the University of Saskatchewan. His scholarly publications have appeared in journals such as the *American Economic Review*, the *Journal of Regional Science*, the *Journal of Public Economics*, the *Journal of Urban Economics*, and the *Review of Economics and Statistics*. His current research interests include understanding regional labor markets as well as investigating the rural-urban interface and exurban growth and change. He has served as president of the Southern Regional Science Association and is on the editorial boards of the *Journal of Regional Science* and the *Review of Regional Studies*. He has also testified before the United States Congress on issues related to immigration policy. Partridge received his PhD in economics from the University of Illinois.

Dan S. Rickman is professor of economics and holder of the OG&E Chair in Regional Economic Analysis at Oklahoma State University. His publications have appeared in scholarly journals such as the *American Economic Review*, the *Review of Economics and Statistics*, the *Journal of Urban Economics*, and the *Journal of Regional Science*. He has been listed among the intellectual leaders in the field of regional science by studies of regional science publication patterns. His research interests include regional labor markets, regional economic forecasting and modeling, and regional economic growth. He also has worked closely with state and local governments on issues related to economic development. Among his professional activities, he is coeditor of the *Review of Regional Studies* and he serves on the editorial board of the *Journal of Regional Science*. Rickman received his PhD in economics from the University of Wyoming.

Index

The italic letters *b, f, n,* and *t* following a page number indicate that the subject information of the heading is within a box, figure, note, or table, respectively, on that page.

About the Institute

The W.E. Upjohn Institute for Employment Research is a nonprofit research organization devoted to finding and promoting solutions to employment-related problems at the national, state, and local levels. It is an activity of the W.E. Upjohn Unemployment Trustee Corporation, which was established in 1932 to administer a fund set aside by Dr. W.E. Upjohn, founder of The Upjohn Company, to seek ways to counteract the loss of employment income during economic downturns.

The Institute is funded largely by income from the W.E. Upjohn Unemployment Trust, supplemented by outside grants, contracts, and sales of publications. Activities of the Institute comprise the following elements: 1) a research program conducted by a resident staff of professional social scientists; 2) a competitive grant program, which expands and complements the internal research program by providing financial support to researchers outside the Institute; 3) a publications program, which provides the major vehicle for disseminating the research of staff and grantees, as well as other selected works in the field; and 4) an Employment Management Services division, which manages most of the publicly funded employment and training programs in the local area.

The broad objectives of the Institute's research, grant, and publication programs are to 1) promote scholarship and experimentation on issues of public and private employment and unemployment policy, and 2) make knowledge and scholarship relevant and useful to policymakers in their pursuit of solutions to employment and unemployment problems.

Current areas of concentration for these programs include causes, consequences, and measures to alleviate unemployment; social insurance and income maintenance programs; compensation; workforce quality; work arrangements; family labor issues; labor-management relations; and regional economic development and local labor markets.